The Cambridge History

of

English Literature

Edited by

A. W. Ward, Litt.D., F.B.A.

Master of Peterhouse

and

A. R. Waller, M.A.

Peterhouse

Volume I

From the Beginnings to the Cycles of
Romance

New York: The Macmillan Company
Cambridge, England: at the University Press
1933

PRINTED IN THE UNITED STATES OF AMERICA
BY THE FERRIS PRINTING COMPANY

PREFACE

IN the preliminary statement of the aims and objects of this *History*, communicated to those who were invited to become contributors to it, the editors emphasised the following purposes of their undertaking.

(*a*) A connected account was to be given of the successive movements of English literature, both main and subsidiary; and this was intended to imply an adequate treatment of secondary writers, instead of their being overshadowed by a few great names.

(*b*) Note was to be taken of the influence of foreign literatures upon English and (though in a less degree) of that of English upon foreign literatures.

(*c*) Each chapter of the work was to be furnished with a sufficient bibliography.

Very few words seem needed here, in addition to the above by way of preface to the first volume of the *History;* this volume and its successors must show how far editors and contributors have been able to carry out in practice the principles by which they have been guided. It may, however, be expedient, while directing attention to a few details in the general plan of the work, to dwell rather more fully on one or two of the ideas which will be kept in view throughout its course.

In an enquiry embracing the history of motives, causes, and ends, it is often far less important to dwell on "leading" personalities and on the main tendencies of literary production, than to consider subsidiary movements and writers below the highest rank, and to trace, in apparently arid periods, processes which were often carried on, as it were, underground, or seemed to be such as could safely be ignored. It cannot be too often urged that there are few, if any, isolated phenomena; the voices may be voices crying in the wilderness, but they belong to those who prepare the way. While, therefore, anxious that not less than justice shall be dealt out to the works of better-known writers, the editors have tried so to plan these volumes that something more than the mere justice with which works designed on a smaller scale have had to content themselves may be given to less known writers and to so-called fugitive literature.

In the interest both of the general reader and of the student, it has been decided to insert footnotes below the text, where references seem required. These have been kept as brief as possible, in order that they may not distract attention. Further notes are, in special cases, added in the appendix and bibliographies at the end of the volume. The names of a few writers not dealt with in the text will be found in the bibliographies; but these names have not, it is hoped, been forgotten in the index. And the birth and death dates of most of the English writers mentioned in the text will be found in the index, rather than in the body of the work.

An occasional attempt has been made to give the student some assistance by means of critical hints in the bibliographies, and to point out where he may best obtain fuller information of a more special nature than can possibly be given within the limits of a general history. To attempt an exhaustive treatment of any one writer, however eminent or however insignificant, to supply analyses of well-known books which are, or should be, on the same shelves as those which may hold these volumes, or to devote much space to the repetition of biographical facts—all this has seemed to lie outside the scope of the present work.

While it is desired to preserve a certain unity in the contents of each volume—an easier task, probably, in the case of those dealing with later than of those treating of earlier times—yet the editors have no belief in "hard and fast" limits as encompassing any epoch, and their wish is that this *History* should unfold itself, unfettered by any preconceived notions of artificial eras or controlling dates. They venture, therefore, to remind their critics, to whom they confidently look for an indication of mistakes, that some of the subjects which may seem to have been omitted may prove to have been deliberately reserved for later treatment. To force an account of literary, educational, or scientific movements into chronological shackles, and make it keep step year by year with the progress of external events, or to present it as an orderly development when its edges are, in truth, woefully ragged, is not always either possible or desirable. From time to time, buried treasure comes to light; things seemingly of a day suddenly reveal the strength that is in them and become things for all time; and the way then lies open for a profitable retrospect. Thus, the editors have thought it simpler to defer an enquiry into the first glimmerings of the English drama and an account of the miracle plays until towards the close of the second volume, and to deal, on broad lines, with the progress of the English language, as the vehicle of English literature, with changes in English prosody and with the work of universities and scholarship, towards the end of successive periods, rather than piecemeal at successive stages of each.

With regard to future volumes—since the history of a nation's literature cannot be divorced from some consideration of its political, religious, and social life, including its manners as well as its phases of sentiment and fashion, its trivial thoughts no less than its serious moments—the editors have thought it well to make some provision for treating certain subjects more or less closely allied to literature pure or proper. Such are the literature of science and philosophy; and that of politics and economics; parliamentary eloquence; the work of schools and universities and libraries; scholarship; the pamphlet literature of religious and political controversy; the newspaper and the magazine; the labours of the press and the services of booksellers; homely books dealing with precept and manners and social life; domestic letters and street songs; accounts of travel and records of sport—the whole range of letters, in its widest acceptation, from the "Cambridge Platonists" to the "fraternity of vagabonds." And, since the literatures of the British Colonies and of the United States are, in the main, the literature of the mother-country, produced under other skies, it is intended to give, in their proper place, some account of these literatures also.

Though the editors are jointly responsible for the work as a whole—both text and bibliographies—it is obvious that an undertaking of this nature could no more be accomplished by one or two men than the *Cambridge Modern History* could have been written by a few hands. It could only be begun, and can only be carried to completion by the continued co-operation of many scholars, who, whether British or American, hold their common heritage as a thing of worth, and by the ungrudging assistance of continental scholars, whose labours in the field of our national literature entitle them to the gratitude of Englishmen. This twofold assistance the editors have been fortunate enough to secure for the volumes already in immediate preparation. In addition to chapters written by English scholars, from without Cambridge as well as from within, the readers of the *Cambridge History of English Literature* will have the benefit of contributions from specialists of other countries; and it is the sincere hope of the editors that they may enjoy the same generous support until their task is done.

It remains to thank those who, apart from the actual contributors, have aided the editors in the work of the earlier volumes now in hand. And, first, they would desire to remember with gratitude the labours of their predecessors: Thomas Warton, whose *History of English Poetry* may be, and, in many respects, has been, superseded, but is never likely to be forgotten or cast aside; Thomas Wright, whose industry and enthusiasm in the cause of medieval letters and archaeology allows us to forget his failings; George Lillie Craik, whose modest efforts kindled in many men still living their first affection for English letters; Henry Morley, who devoted a laborious and zealous life to the noble end of making English writers widely accessible to students and who died before he could complete the last and most important piece of work he set himself to do; Bernard ten Brink, whose history of English literature to the death of Surrey must long remain unsurpassed on its own ground—"Great things"; as he himself said of Surrey's tragic end, "he might still have accomplished, but what he did accomplish has not been lost to posterity." Hippolyte Taine, the master of analysis and the first to show the full significance of the study of a nation's literature for the study of its general history; Hermann Hettner, in whose *History of English Literature from* 1660 *to* 1770, and the companion accounts of French and German literature in the eighteenth century, the comparative method is luminously applied; Georg Brandes, whose *Main Currents in the Literature of the Nineteenth Century* reveals an extraordinary quickness of intellectual insight and a not less uncommon breadth of moral sympathy; Henry Duff Traill, whose brilliant gifts are held in affectionate remembrance by those who have come under their spell, and whose symposium, *Social England*, should be in the hands of all who desire to possess "a record of the progress of the people"; L. Petit de Julleville, whose *Histoire de la Langue et de la Littérature française* has been of special value and assistance in the planning of the present work; Grein, Kölbing, Mätzner, Wülker, Zupitza and many other eminent Teutonic scholars who have made, and are making, the paths smoother for their contemporaries and for their successors. The brilliant *Histoire Littéraire du Peuple Anglais* of M. J. J. Jusserand has been constantly in the hands of the editors of this work, and the *Encyclopaedia Britannica* and the *Dictionary of National Biography* have, as a matter of course, been laid under contribution, together with the extremely useful Chambers's *Cyclopaedia of English Literature*, a work which, used with delight in its old form, many years ago, by the writers of this preface, has, in its revised garb, proved of considerable use. The invaluable *Beiträge zur Geschichte der deutschen Sprache und Literatur*, with which is associated the names of H. Paul, W. Braune, and E. Sievers, has been repeatedly referred to, and always with advantage, while the bibliographies will show what use has been made of *Anglia, Englische Studien, Romania*, the publications of American Universities and of Modern Language associations. In this last connection may be mentioned the *Modern Language Review*, recently reconstituted under the editorship of Prof. J. G. Robertson. For advice on certain points in the present volume, or for assistance in other ways, the editors' thanks are also due to Dr. F. J. Furnivall, whose labours, together with those of the band of fellow-workers in the Early English Text Society, have done much to remove the reproach that Englishmen were not alive to the beauties of their own literature; to Professor W. W. Skeat, Miss Steele Smith, Prof. G. L. Kittredge and to Prof. Alois Brandl, with other eminent members of the *Deutsche Shakespeare Gesellschaft;* and to the writings of Dr. Stopford A. Brooke, Professor

Albert S. Cook, Prof. T. R. Lounsbury and Prof. W. H. Schofield. Other debts, too numerous to set forth in detail, it has only been possible to acknowledge by the insertion of names and titles of works in the bibliographies; but our thanks will, we trust, be read "between the lines" by all our fellow-workers.

A. W. W.
A. R. W.

Peterhouse, Cambridge
2 August, 1907

CONTENTS

CHAPTER I

THE BEGINNINGS

By A. R. WALLER, M.A., Peterhouse.

PAGE

Characteristics of the earliest Poetry. The Gleemen. Theodore and
Hadrian. National Strife 1

CHAPTER II

RUNES AND MANUSCRIPTS

By A. C. PAUES, Ph.D. Upsala, Newnham College.

The National Germanic Alphabet. Runes in Scandinavian and Old
English Literature. The Ruthwell Cross. The Franks Casket.
The Roman Alphabet. The Irish School of Writing. Tablets,
parchment, vellum, paper, pens, ink, and binding. Scribes and
scriptoria 7

CHAPTER III

EARLY NATIONAL POETRY

By H. MUNRO CHADWICK, M.A., Fellow of Clare College.

Early National Poems the work of Minstrels. Teutonic Epic Poetry.
Beowulf: Scandinavian Traditions; Personality of the Hero; Origin
and Antiquity of the Poem; the Religious Element. *Finnsburh.*
The Waldhere Fragments. *Widsith. Deor. The Wanderer.*
The Seafarer. The Wife's Complaint. The Husband's Message.
The Ruin. Religious Poetry of Heathen Times . . . 21

CHAPTER IV

OLD ENGLISH CHRISTIAN POETRY

By M. BENTINCK SMITH, M.A.,
Headmistress of St. Leonard's School, St. Andrews.

Celtic Christianity. Changes wrought by the New Spirit. Caedmon's
Hymn. Genesis, Exodus, Daniel. Crist and Satan. Cynewulf.
His Personality. *Crist, Juliana, The Fates of the Apostles,
Elene. Andreas. The Dream of the Rood. Guthlac, The
Phoenix, Physiologus, Riddles.* Minor Christian Poems. *The
Riming Poem, Proverbs, The Runic Poem, Salomon and Saturn.*
The Schools of Caedmon and Cynewulf 45

CHAPTER V

LATIN WRITINGS IN ENGLAND TO THE TIME OF ALFRED

By Montague Rhodes James, Litt.D.

Provost of King's College.

PAGE

Gildas and *The History of the Britons*. "Hisperic" Latin. Nennius and *Historia Brittonum*. The Roman Mission to Kent and its results. Aldhelm and his School. Bede's *Ecclesiastical History*. Bede's *Letter to Egbert of York*. Alcuin. Lives of Saints. Visions. Minor writings 72

CHAPTER VI

ALFRED AND THE OLD ENGLISH PROSE OF HIS REIGN

By P. G. Thomas, M.A., Professor of English Language and Literature at Bedford College, University of London.

Asser's *Life of Alfred*. The *Handbook* and *Pastoral Care*. Translations of Orosius and Bede. Codes of Law. *De Consolatione Philosophiae*. The metres in Alfred's *Boethius*. Augustine's *Soliloquies*. The *Chronicle*. Gregory's *Dialogues*. Works attributed to Alfred. His Literary Achievement 97

CHAPTER VII

FROM ALFRED TO THE CONQUEST

By John S. Westlake, M.A., Trinity College.

The *Chronicle*. The Monastic Reform. *Blickling Homilies*. The Works of Aelfric. Wulfstan. Byrhtferth. *Lindisfarne, Rushworth*, and *West Saxon Glosses*. Legends of the Holy Rood. Legends of the East. Quasi-scientific works. The Ballads and Poems in *The Chronicle*. *Judith*. *The Battle of Maldon* or *Byrhtnoth's Death*. *Menologium*. *Be Domes Daege* 119

CHAPTER VIII

THE NORMAN CONQUEST

By A. R. Waller.

Dunstan. The Coming Change. The Wisdom of the East. Lanfranc. Anselm. Norman Gifts 165

Contents

CHAPTER IX

LATIN CHRONICLERS FROM THE ELEVENTH TO THE THIRTEENTH CENTURIES

By W. Lewis Jones, M.A., Professor of English Language and Literature at the University College of North Wales.

PAGE

England and Normandy. Characteristics of the Chroniclers. The Northumbrian School of English Medieval History. Simeon of Durham. Florence of Worcester. Eadmer and Ordericus Vitalis. William of Malmesbury. *Gesta Stephani. Henry of Huntingdon.* Geoffrey of Monmouth. William of Newburgh. Benedict of Peterborough. Richard Fitz-Neale. Roger of Hoveden. Ralph of Diceto. Richard of Devizes. Jocelin of Brakelond. Giraldus Cambrensis. Walter Map. Matthew Paris. Minor Chroniclers . 173

CHAPTER X

ENGLISH SCHOLARS OF PARIS AND FRANCISCANS OF OXFORD

Latin Literature of England from John of Salisbury to Richard of Bury

By J. E. Sandys, Litt.D., Fellow of St. John's College and Public Orator of the University of Cambridge.

The University of Paris. English Scholars of Paris. John of Salisbury. Peter of Blois. Walter Map. Other Writers of Latin. Gervase. Nigel Wireker. Jean de Hauteville. Alain de Lille. Geoffrey de Vinsauf. Alexander Neckam. Joannes de Garlandia. Giraldus Cambrensis. Michael Scot. Franciscans and Dominicans. Franciscans of Oxford. Alexander of Hales. Robert Grosseteste and the Franciscans. Adam Marsh. Roger Bacon. Duns Scotus. William of Ockham. Walter Burleigh. Scholars of Oxford. John Baconthorpe. Thomas Bradwardine. Richard of Bury . . 203

CHAPTER XI

EARLY TRANSITION ENGLISH

By J. W. H. Atkins, M.A., Professor of English Language and Literature at the University College of Wales, Aberystwyth, Fellow of St. John's College.

The Proverbs of Alfred. Poema Morale. Literary Revolt of the 13th Century. *Ormulum.* Hortatory Verse and Prose. *Genesis and Exodus. The Bestiary. An Bispel. Sawles Warde. Hali Meidenhad. Lives of the Saints. Ancren Riwle.* The Virgin Cult and Erotic Mysticism. *The Luve Ron.* Layamon's *Brut. The Owl and Nightingale* 241

CHAPTER XII

THE ARTHURIAN LEGEND

By W. Lewis Jones, M.A., Professor of English Language and
Literature at the University College of North Wales,
Bangor, formerly Scholar of Queens' College.

PAGE

Early Welsh Tradition. Nennius and Gildas. Early Welsh Poetry.
Kulhwch and Olwen. The *Mabinogion*. Geoffrey of Monmouth.
Caradoc of Llancarvan. The French Romances. Wace. Laya-
mon. Subsidiary Legends. Merlin. Gawain. Lancelot and
Guinevere. The Holy Grail. Tristram and Iseult. Celtic Liter-
ature 270

CHAPTER XIII

METRICAL ROMANCES, 1200-1500

I

By W. P. Ker, M.A., Fellow of All Souls College, Oxford,
Professor of English Literature, University College, London.

French Influences. Benoit de Ste. More and Chrétien de Troyes.
Translators' difficulties. History of the English Romances. Mat-
ter and Form. The "matter of France," "of Britain," and "of
Rome." Sources and Subjects. Forms of Verse. Traditional
Plots. Breton Lays. Fairy Tales. *Sir Gawayne* and *Sir Tris-
trem*. *The Tale of Gamelyn* and *The Tale of Beryn*. Relation of
Romances to Ballads 308

CHAPTER XIV

METRICAL ROMANCES, 1200-1500

II

By J. W. H. Atkins.

The Carolingian Element. English Romances: *Havelok, Horn, Guy
of Warwick, Beves of Hamtoun*. The literature of Antiquity:
Troy, King Alisaunder, Richard Cœur de Lion. Oriental Fable:
Flores and Blancheflour, The Seven Sages of Rome. Celtic Romances.
The Gawain Cycle. *Ipomedon, Amis and Amiloun, Sir Cleges, Sir
Isumbras, The Squire of Low Degree*. *William of Palerne*, etc.
Anonymity of the work embodied in the Romances. Qualities
and Defects 335

CHAPTER XV

" PEARL," " CLEANNESS," " PATIENCE," AND " SIR GAWAYNE "

By I. GOLLANCZ, Litt.D., Christ's College, Professor of English
Language and Literature, King's College, London, Secretary of the British Academy.

PAGE

Sources and Metre of *Pearl. Cleanness* and *Patience. Sir Gawayne
and the Grene Knight.* Sources of *Sir Gawayne.* The Question
of Authorship. Hypothetical Biography of the Poet. Ralph
Strode. Huchoun of the Awle Ryale. *Erkenwald*, etc . . 357

CHAPTER XVI

LATER TRANSITION ENGLISH

I

LEGENDARIES AND CHRONICLERS

By CLARA L. THOMSON.

Robert of Gloucester. Thomas Bek. *The South English Legendary.*
Northern Homilies and Legends. *The Northern Psalter. Cursor
Mundi.* Robert Mannyng of Brunne's *Handlyng Synne.* Char-
acteristics of Mannyng's style. Mannyng's Debt to Wadington.
Mannyng's *Chronicle. The Medytacyuns.* William of Shoreham.
The Ayenbite of Inwyt. Adam Davy. Laurence Minot . . 374

CHAPTER XVII

LATER TRANSITION ENGLISH

II

SECULAR LYRICS; TALES; SOCIAL SATIRE [1]

By A. R. WALLER.

Middle English Lyrics. *The Proverbs of Hendyng. The Deeds of
Hereward. The Land of Cokaygne. Dame Siriz. The Vox and
the Wolf. The Turnament of Totenham. The Tale of Gamelyn.
Gesta Romanorum.* John de Bromyarde. *The Childhood of
Jesus.* Political verses. Songs of the Soil. John Ball. The
Black Death 402

[1] Further chapters on Fugitive Social Literature of the 14th and 15th
centuries will be found in Vol. II.

CHAPTER XVIII

THE PROSODY OF OLD AND MIDDLE ENGLISH

By GEORGE SAINTSBURY, M.A., Merton College, Oxford, Professor of Rhetoric and English Literature in the University of Edinburgh.

PAGE

Old English Verse. The Transition. Foreign Influence. The Alliterative Revival   416

CHAPTER XIX

CHANGES IN THE LANGUAGE TO THE DAYS OF CHAUCER

By HENRY BRADLEY, M.A., (Oxon.).

Continuity of the English Language. "English" and "Saxon." Periods of English. Changes in Grammar. Old English Grammar. Changes in Declension. Conjugation in Middle English. Influence of the Norman Conquest. Pronunciation and Spelling. Middle English Spelling. Development of Sounds. Changes in Vocabulary. Words adopted from French. Scandinavian Words in English. Loss of Native Words. The Poetical Vocabulary. English Dialects in the Fourteenth Century   424

CHAPTER XX

THE ANGLO-FRENCH LAW LANGUAGE

By the late F. W. MAITLAND, LL.D., Downing Professor of the Laws of England.
(By permission of the Council of the Selden Society.)

Retention of French in the Courts. The Making of Legal Terms   .   455

Appendix to Chapter VII. By J. S. Westlake   461

The Cambridge History of
English Literature

CHAPTER I

The Beginnings

BY the time the English settlements in Britain had assumed permanent form, little seems to have been left from the prior Roman occupation to influence the language and literature of the invaders. Their thought and speech, no less than their manners and customs, were of direct Teutonic origin, though these were afterwards, in some slight degree, modified by Celtic ideas, derived from the receding tribes, and, later, and in a greater measure, by the Christian and Latin elements that resulted from the mission of St. Augustine. Danish inroads and Norman-French invasions added fresh qualities to the national character and to its modes of expression; but, in the main, English literature, as we know it, arose from the spirit inherent in the viking makers of England before they finally settled in this island.

Of the origins of Old English poetry we know nothing; what remains to us is chiefly the reflection of earlier days. The fragments that we possess are not those of a literature in the making, but of a school which had passed through its age of transition from ruder elements. The days of apprenticeship were over; the Englishman of the days of *Beowulf* and *Widsith*, *The Ruin* and *The Seafarer*, knew what he wished to say, and said it, without exhibiting any apparent trace of groping after things dimly seen or apprehended. And from those days to our own, in spite of periods of decadence, of apparent death, of great superficial change, the chief constituents of English literature— a reflective spirit, attachment to nature, a certain carelessness of "art," love of home and country and an ever present consciousness that there are things worse than death—these have, in the main, continued unaltered. "Death is better," says Wiglaf, in *Beowulf*, "for every knight than ignominious life,"

and, though Claudio feels death to be "a fearful thing," the
sentiment is only uttered to enable Shakespeare to respond
through the lips of Isabella, "And shamed life a hateful."

It is, for instance, significant of much in the later history of
the English people and of their literature, that the earliest
poems in Old English have to do with journeyings in a distant
land and with the life of the sea. Our forefathers had inhabited maritime regions before they came to this island; the terror
and the majesty and the loneliness of the sea had already cast
their natural spells on "far-travelled" "seafarers" when English literature, as we know it, opens. The passionate joy of the
struggle between man and the forces of nature, between seamen
and the storms of the sea, finds its expression in the relation of
the struggle between Beowulf and the sea monster Grendel,
and of the deeds of Beowulf and his hard-fighting comrades.
Though *die Nordsee ist eine Mordsee*, love of the sea and of sea
things and a sense of the power of the sea are evident in every
page of *Beowulf*. The note is struck in the very opening of the
poem, wherein the passing of the Danish king Scyld Scefing, in
a golden-bannered ship, is told in lines that recall those in which
a later poet related the passing of an English king, whose barge
was seen to

> pass on and on, and go
> From less to less and vanish into light.

The life of those whose task it was to wander along "the
ocean-paths" across "the ice-cold" northern sea, where feet
were "fettered by the frost," is described in *The Seafarer* as a
northern fisher of to-day might describe it, could he "unlock
the word-hoard"; English and northern also is the spirit of the
lines in the same poem wherein is described the spell cast by
the sea on its lovers:

> For the harp he has no heart, nor for having of the rings,
> Nor in woman is his weal; in the world he's no delight,
> Nor in anything whatever save the tossing o'er the waves!
> O for ever he has longing who is urged towards the sea.[1]

These "wanderers" are of the same blood as the sea kings
and pirates of the old sagas, and their love of nature is love of
her wilder and more melancholy aspects. The rough woodland
and the stormy sky, "the scream of the gannet" and "the

[1] Stopford Brooke's version.

moan of the sea-mew" find their mirror and echo in Old English literature long before the more placid aspects of nature are noted, for it is not to be forgotten that, as Jusserand says, the sea of our forefathers was not a Mediterranean lake.[1] The more placid aspects have their turn later, when the conquerors of the shore had penetrated inland and taken to more pastoral habits; when, also, the leaven of Christianity had worked.

The first English men of letters of whom we have record—smiths of song, as the poet-priests are called in *The Ynglinga Saga*—were the gleemen of minstrels who played on the harp and chanted heroic songs while the ale-mug or mead-cup was passed round, and who received much reward in their calling. The teller of the tale in *Widsith* is a typical minstrel of this kind, concerned with the exercise of his art. The scop[2] composed his verses and "published" them himself; most probably he was a great plagiarist, a forerunner of later musicians whose "adoption" of the labours of their predecessors is pardoned for the sake of the improvements made on the original material. The music of skirling bagpipes and of the regimental bands of later times is in the direct line of succession from the chanting of tribal lays by bards as warriors rushed to the fight; the "chanties" of modern sailors stand in the place of the songs of sea-rovers as they revelled in the wars of the elements, or rested inactive on the lonely seas. And the gift of song was by no means confined to professionals. Often the chieftain himself took up the harp and sang, perhaps a little boastfully, of great deeds. At the other end of the scale, we hear of the man whose duty it was to take a turn at the stable-work of a monastery being sad at heart when the harp was passed round and he had no music to give; and the plough-lad, when he had drawn his first furrow, revealed both his capacity for song and his nature-worship, with faint, if any, traces of Christianity, in lines perhaps among the oldest our language has to show:

> Hal wes thu, folde, fira modor,
> beo thu growende on godes faethme;
> fodre gefylled firum to nytte.

---

[1] *La mer des Anglo-Saxons n'est pas une Méditerranée lavant de ses flots bleus les murs de marbre des villas: c'est la mer du Nord, aux lames grises, bordée de plages stériles et de falaises de craie.*—*Histoire Littéraire du Peuple Anglais,* I, 60.

[2] A minstrel of high degree, usually attached to a court.

Hale be thou Earth, Mother of men!
Fruitful be thou in the arms of the god.
Be filled with thy fruit for the fare-need of man[1]!

Of the history of these early poems, as much as is known, or as can fairly be set forth, is given in the following pages. *Beowulf*—romance, history and epic—is the oldest poem on a great scale, and in the grand manner, that exists in any Teutonic language. It is full of incident and good fights, simple in aim and clear in execution; its characters bear comparison with those of the *Odyssey* and, like them, linger in the memory; its style is dignified and heroic. The invasion and conquest of "England" by the English brought heathendom into a Christian communion, and *Beowulf* is the literary expression of the temper, the thoughts and the customs of these invaders. Its historical worth, apart, altogether, from its great literary value, can scarcely be over-estimated. The Christian elements in it are, probably, alterations of later minstrels; in the main, it presents an ideal of pagan virtues: strength, manliness, acquiescence in the decrees of fate—"what is to be must be"—yet recognition of the fact that "the must-be often helps an undoomed man when he is brave," a sentiment that finds echo in later days and in other languages besides our own.

In *The Complaint of Deor*, and in its companion elegies, we are probably nearer to original poems than in the case of narrative verse, built up of lays and added to year after year by different hands; and we can ask for little better at the hands of Old English poets. *Deor* shows us the same spirit of courage in adversity seen in *Beowulf;* and its philosophical refrain (besides shadowing forth the later adoption of rime by reason of a refrain's recurring sound) is that of a man unbowed by fate. In form as well as in utterance, the verses are those of a poet who has little to learn in the art of translating personal feeling into fitting words.

It is a real, an unaffected, an entirely human though non-Christian, accent that we hear in the impassioned fragment called *The Ruin*. The Wyrd that every man must dree has whirled all material things away and has left but a wreck behind. And in *The Wanderer* also we see the baleful forces of nature and fate at work as they appeared to pagan eyes:

[1] Stopford Brooke's version.

See the storms are lashing on the stony ramparts;
Sweeping down, the snow-drift shuts up fast the earth—
Terror of the winter when it cometh wan!
Darkens then the dusk of night, driving from the nor'rard
Heavy drift of hail for the harm of heroes.

All is full of trouble, all this realm of earth!
Doom of weirds is changing all the world below the skies;
Here our foe is fleeting, here the friend is fleeting,
Fleeting here is man, fleeting is the woman,
All the earth's foundation is an idle thing become.[1]

The lighter note of love, of which we have a faint echo in *The Husband's Message*, is rare in Old English poetry. The times in which these poems were written were full of war and national struggle; not until long after the settlers had made their permanent home in the new land does the poet turn to the quieter aspects of nature or celebrate less strenuous deeds.

We can only use comparative terms, however, in speaking of the peaceful years. Apart from the civil struggles of the English in their new home, only two hundred years elapsed after St. Augustine's conversion of Kent before the Danes began to arrive and, in the centuries that followed, the language of lamentation and woe that Gildas had used in connection with the struggle between Briton and Saxon was echoed in the writings of Alcuin when Lindisfarne was burned, in the homilies of Wulfstan and in the pages of the *Chronicle*. Yet in the years that had passed England had risen to literary pre-eminence in Europe. She took kindly to the Latin and Greek culture brought her in the seventh century by the Asian Theodore and the African Hadrian, scholars learned in worldly, as well as in divine, lore, who "made this island, once the nurse of tyrants, the constant home of philosophy."[2] The love of letters had been fostered in the north by English scholars; by Bede's teacher, Benedict Biscop, foremost of all, who founded the monasteries of Jarrow and Wearmouth, enriched them with books collected by himself and, in his last days, prayed his pupils to have a care over his library. Bede's disciple was Egbert of York, the founder of its school and the decorator of its churches, and Alcuin obtained his education in the cloister school of his native city.

[1] Stopford Brooke's version.   [2] William of Malmesbury, I, 12.

The seven liberal arts of the *trivium* (grammar, logic, rhet oric) and the *quadrivium* (astronomy, arithmetic, geometry music) were so ably taught and so admirably assimilated in the monastic schools that, when Alcuin forsook York for the palace-school of Charles the Great, he appealed for leave to send French lads to bring back "flowers of Britain" to Tours, from the "garden of Paradise" in York, a "garden" described by him in often quoted lines.[1]

There came an end to all this when "the Danish terror" made a waste from the Humber to the Tyne. Northumbria had aided Rome and Charles the Great in the service of letters while the rest of Europe, save Ireland, had little to show, and now men were too busy fighting for home and freedom to think of letters. It was not until the days of Alfred that the tide began again to turn from continental to English shores, becoming a flood-tide when the second invasion of Northmen added a Norman strain to English blood.

The literature of the beginnings in England, therefore, appears to be the literature of its successive conquerors: English ousting Briton, Christian suppressing Pagan, Norman overruling English. For a time, the works of Englishmen have to be sought in Latin; for certain periods of civil struggle, of defeat, of serfdom, they cannot be found at all. But the literary spirit revives, having assimilated the foreign elements and conquered the conquerors. The "natural magic" of the Celtic mind, the Christian spirit which brought Greece and Rome in its train and "the matter of France" have all three become part of the Englishman's intellectual heritage.

[1] *Poema de Pontificibus et Sanctis Ecclesiae Eboracensis.*

CHAPTER II

Runes and Manuscripts

WHEN the English still lived in their continental homes they shared with the neighbouring kindred tribes an alphabet which may well be described as the national Germanic alphabet, since there is evidence that it was used throughout the Germanic territory, both in the outposts of Scandinavia and in the countries watered by the Rhine and the Danube. The origin of this early script is obscure; some writers hold that it was borrowed from the Latin alphabet, whereas others think that it was of Greek origin. From its wide use amongst the Germanic tribes, we must, perforce, conclude that it was of considerable antiquity, at all events older than the earliest Scandinavian inscriptions, which, in all probability, go back as far as the third century of our era. That it was used in the fourth century is proved since, at that time, Ulfilas, bishop of the West Goths, had borrowed from it the signs of *u* and *o* for his newly-constructed alphabet. Moreover, there can be no doubt that the Goths must have brought the knowledge of it from their early homes in the north before the great wave of the Hunnish invasion swept them away from kith and kindred, finally setting them down on the shores of the Danube and the Black Sea.

The name of these early Germanic characters seems also to have been the same amongst all the tribes. Its Old English form, *rún*, differs little from the corresponding early German or Scandinavian forms, and the meaning of the word (mystery, secret, secret counsel) seems also widely spread. This word lived on through Middle English times, and a derivative *rúnian* appears in Shakespeare as *roun* or *round* (a form still retained in the expression " to *round* in one's ear "). The separate letters were known as *rúnstafas* and the interpretation of them as *rǽdan*, which in modern English still lives on in the expression "to read a riddle."

The runes were, in all probability, originally carved in wood, and sometimes filled in with red paint to make them more distinct. The technical term for this cutting or engraving is, in Old English, *wrítan*, which, in its transferred meaning of "to write," has survived to the present day. The wood was fashioned into tablets or staves, as we learn from the well-known lines of Venantius Fortunatus, a writer of the sixth century who refers[1] to the barbaric rune as being painted on tablets of ashwood or smooth sticks. Such a tablet was originally called *bóc* (a tablet of beechwood), and may be regarded as the ancestor, in a double sense, of the modern word "book." Other materials used were metal, principally in the form of weapons, coins, rings and other ornaments, household and other implements; drinking-horns were often adorned with runic inscriptions, and runes have also been found on smaller objects of horn and bone. Moreover, in England and Scandinavia there occur runic inscriptions on stone monuments, and there are also some which have been hewn out of rocks. Parchment seems to have been introduced at a late period, and, of the few manuscripts remaining entirely written in runes, none go back further than the thirteenth century.

There is considerable uncertainty as to the earliest purpose of the runes, whether they were originally used as real characters of writing, or, as the name suggests, as mystical signs, bearers of potent magic. But, since the power and force of the spoken word easily pass into the symbol for which it stands, it is not improbable that the latter meaning is secondary, the spell becoming, so to speak, materialised in the graven letter, and, even in this form, retaining all its original power for good or evil. For the earliest Germanic literature abounds in proofs of the magic nature of runes; from the *Edda* poems down to the latest folk-songs of the present day there is continuous evidence of their mystic influence over mankind. Runes could raise the dead from their graves; they could preserve life or take it, they could heal the sick or bring on lingering disease; they could call forth the soft rain or the violent hailstorm; they could break

---

[1] Carm. VII, 18, 19.

chains and shackles or bind more closely than bonds or fetters;
they could make the warrior invincible and cause his sword to
inflict none but mortal wounds; they could produce frenzy and
madness or defend from the deceit of a false friend. Their origin was, moreover, believed to be divine, since Odin is represented in the *Edda* as sacrificing himself in order to learn their
use and hidden wisdom. Odin was also the greatest "rune-
master" of the ancient Germanic world, and Saxo relates[1]
how the god sometimes stooped to use them for purposes of
personal revenge. A cold-hearted maiden who rejected his
suit he touched with a piece of bark, whereon spells were written. This made her mad; but according to Saxo, it was "a
gentle revenge to take for all the insults he had received."
Saxo also relates[2] a gruesome tale how, by means of spells
engraved on wood, and placed under the tongue of a dead man,
he was forced to utter strains terrible to hear, and to reveal the
no less terrible secrets of the future. In the Icelandic Sagas,
references to the supernatural power of the runes are equally
explicit. In the Saga of Egill Skallagrímsson, who lived in the
tenth century, it is told how a maiden's illness had been increased because the would-be healer, through ignorance, cut
the wrong runes, and thus endangered her life. Egill destroys
the spell by cutting off the runes and buring the shavings in the
fire; he then slips under the maiden's pillow the staff whereon
he had cut the true healing runes. Immediately the maiden
recovers.

Side by side with the early magic use of runes there is also
clear evidence that, at an earlier period, they served as a means
of communication, secret or otherwise. Saxo relates, in this
respect,[3] how Amlethus (Hamlet) travelled to England accompanied by two retainers, to whom was entrusted a secret letter
graven on wood, which, as Saxo remarks, was a kind of writing-
material frequently used in olden times. In the *Egilssaga*
mentioned above, Egill Skallagrmísson's daughter Thorgerðr
is reported to have engraved on the *rúnakefli* or "runic staff"
the beautiful poem *Sunatorrek*, in which her aged father laments
the death of his son, the last of his race.

These few instances, taken from amongst a great number,
prove that runes played an important part in the thoughts and

[1] Ed. Holder, p. 79.　　[2] Ed. Holder, p. 22.　　[3] Ed. Holder, p. 92.

lives of the various Germanic tribes. The greater number of runic inscriptions which have come down to our times, and by far the most important, are those engraved on stone monuments. Some of these merely bear the name of a fallen warrior, while others commemorate his exploits, his death, or his life as a whole. These inscriptions on stones and rocks occur only in England and Scandinavia, from which fact we may, perhaps, infer that this use of runes was a comparatively late development. Some of the very earliest extant inscriptions may be regarded as English, since they are found either within Angeln, the ancient home of the nation—for instance, those of Torsbjaerg,—or not far from that district.

From what has been said, it is clear that the English, on their arrival in this island, must have been conversant with their national alphabet, and the various uses thereof. It may be worth while to examine somewhat more closely its original form and the changes which it underwent after the migration In its early Germanic form the runic alphabet consisted of twenty-four signs, usually arranged in three sets of eight which, from their respective initial letters, bore in Old Norse the names of Freyr, Hagall and Týr. The alphabet itself is generally known as the *fuþark* from the first six of its letters. Each rune had a name of its own, and a well-defined place in the alphabet. The order is specifically Germanic, and can be ascertained from old alphabets found on a gold coin at Vadstena in Sweden, and on a silver-gilt clasp dug up at Charnay in Burgundy. After the migration and subsequent isolation of the English, it became necessary, in course of time, to modify the early alphabet and to make it more conformable with the changing sounds of the language. Four new signs were added, and some of the older ones modified in order to represent the altered value of the sounds. Thus there arose a specifically Old English alphabet, of which not less than three specimens have been preserved. One of these is on a small sword found in the Thames and now in the British Museum; another is contained in the Salzburg manuscript 140 of the tenth century, now at Vienna; the third occurs in an Old English runic song. The last two, moreover, present the names of the runes in their Old English form. Apart from the standard English type found in the above-mentioned three alphabets, a local Norwegian vari-

ety, of a far simpler character, was current in the Isle of Man,
as appears from certain Norse inscriptions there, dating from
the latter half of the eleventh century.

It is, however, difficult to determine in what manner and to
what extent runes were used by the English settlers, for here
the evidence is by no means as abundant and explicit as in the
far north.   Christianity was introduced into England at an
early period, centuries before it was brought to distant Scandinavia, and the new religion laboured, and laboured successfully,
to eradicate all traces of practices and beliefs that smacked of
the devil, with which potentate the heathen gods soon came to be
identified.   Nevertheless, we have some evidence, which, despite
its scantiness, speaks eloquently of the tenacity of old beliefs,
and the slow lingering of superstition.   Bede furnishes us with
a striking proof that the English, at a comparatively late date,
believed in the magic properties of runes.   In his *Historia
Ecclesiastica* (iv, 22) he relates the fate of a nobleman called
Imma, who was made a prisoner in the battle between Ecgfrith,
king of Northumbria, and Aethelred, king of Mercia, A.D.
679, and whose fetters fell off whenever his brother, who thought
him dead, celebrated mass for the release of his soul.   His
captor, however, who knew nothing about the prayers, won-
dered greatly, and inquired whether the prisoner had on him
litterae solutoriae, that is, letters which had the power of loosening bonds.[1]   Again, in *Beowulf* (l. 591), a person who broached
a theme of contention is said to "unbind the runes of war."
In the poem called *Daniel* (l. 741), the mysterious and terrible
writing on the wall of Belshazzar's palace is described as a rune.
In the *Dialogue of Salomon and Saturn*[2] there is a curious trav-
esty of an old heathen spell.   In treating of the powers and
virtues of the Pater Noster, the poet gradually inserts all the
runes that serve to make up the prayer, each, however, being
accompanied by the corresponding Latin capital letter.   Thereupon he advises every man to sing the Pater Noster before drawing his sword against a hostile band of men, and also to put the
fiends to flight by means of God's word; otherwise they will
stay his hand when he has to defend his life, and bewitch his
weapon by cutting on it fatal letters and death signs.   We

---

[1] The Old English version renders this by *alysendlecan rúne*, "loosening
runes."

[2] Ed. Kemble, pp. 14 and 99.

could scarcely wish for a better illustration of the way in which Christianity combated the old beliefs, substituting the Pater Noster for the ancient heathen war-spell, reading a new meaning into the old rites and shifting to fiends and devils the power of making runes of victory or of death, a power formerly in the hands of pagan gods.

When used as ordinary writing characters, without any taint of magic, runes appear to have met with more tolerant treatment. The earliest inscriptions extant in this country consist mainly of proper names, in most cases those of the owners of the engraved article. The Thames sword, for instance, bears, in addition to the runic alphabet, the name of its owner, Beagnoþ. Again, Beowulf is represented as finding in Grendel's cave a sword of ancient workmanship, with rune-staves on the hilt, giving the name of the warrior for whom the sword had first been made. Similarly, an eighth century ring bears, partly in runic, partly in Roman, characters, the legend "Æþred owns me, Eanred engraved me." There are also references in Old English literature to the use of runes as a means of communication. We are reminded of the *rúna-kefli* of the Icelandic sagas on reading the little poem called *The Husband's Message* (see p. 42), where a staff, inscribed with runes, is supposed to convey to a wife the message of her lord, bidding her cross the sea in search of the distant country where he had found gold and land. But still more important are those inscriptions which have actually survived and which are mainly found on stone monuments. They are confined almost exclusively to the north, and the greater number of them belong to the seventh and eighth centuries, for absolutely no inscriptions have survived from the first one hundred and fifty years subsequent to the English invasion. These inscriptions are almost all due to Christian influence. Chief among these monuments, so far as English literature is concerned, are the Ruthwell Cross in Dumfriesshire, possibly dating back to the eighth century,[1] on which are inscribed extracts from *The Dream of the Rood*, and the Bewcastle Column in Cumberland, probably erected to the memory of Alchfrith, son of the Northumbrian king Oswy (642–670).

Runic inscriptions have, moreover, been discovered on coins

[1] But see A. S. Cook, *The Dream of the Rood*, Oxford, 1905, pp. ix ff.

and various other objects, the most important being the beautiful Clermont or Franks casket. The top and three of the sides
are now in the British Museum, the fourth side is in the Museo
Nazionale at Florence. The casket is made of whalebone, and
the scenes carved on it represent an episode from the Weland-
saga, the adoration of the Magi, Romulus and Remus nursed
by the she-wolf and, lastly, a fight between Titus and the Jews.
The carving on the Florence fragment is still unexplained.
The legends engraved around these episodes are intended to
represent the capture of the whale and to elucidate the carving.
On linguistic grounds it has been thought probable that the
casket was made in Northumbria at the beginning of the eighth
century.[1]

In several Old English MSS. runes are found in isolated
cases, for instance in *Beowulf*, and in the *Durham Ritual*. In
the riddles of the *Exeter Book* the occasional introduction of
runes sometimes helps to solve the mystery of the enigma, and
sometimes increases the obscurity of the passage. Occasionally
a poet or scribe will record his name by means of a runic acrostic introduced into the text. Thus, the poems *Crist, Juliana,
Elene* and the Vercelli fragment bear the runic signature of
their author, Cynewulf.

Runes went out of use during the ninth and tenth centuries.
Their place had, however, been usurped long before that period
by the Roman alphabet, which the English received from the
early Irish missionaries. The advent of Christianity and the
beginnings of English literature are intimately connected, for
the missionary and the Roman alphabet travelled together,
and it was owing to the Christian scribe that the songs and
sagas, the laws and customs, the faith and the proverbial wisdom of our forefathers, were first recorded and preserved. It is,
indeed, difficult to realise that, before the conversion of the
English to Christianity, during the sixth and seventh centuries,
the whole, or, at all events, by far the greater part, of the intellectual wealth of the nation was to be sought on the lips of the
people, or in the retentive memory of the individual, and was
handed down from generation to generation by means of song
and recitation. Caesar relates[2] how this was the case in Gaul,
where the accumulated wisdom of the Druids, their religion

---

[1] Napier, *English Misc.*, p. 380.   [2] *De Bello Gallico*, VI, 14.

and their laws, were transmitted by oral tradition alone, since
they were forbidden to put any of their lore into writing,
although, for other purposes, the Greek alphabet was used.
What wonder if the young Gauls who served their apprenticeship to the Druids had, as Caesar says, to learn "a great
number of verses," and often to stay as long as twenty
years before they had exhausted their instructors' store of
learning.

Before entering, however, on the history of the Irish alphabet in England, it may be of interest to note that an even earlier
attempt had been made to introduce Roman characters among
the English. This was due to the efforts of Augustine and
his missionaries, who established a school of handwriting in the
south of England, with Canterbury as a probable centre. A
Psalter of about A.D. 700, now in the Cottonian collection of the
British Museum, and a few early copies of charters constitute,
however, the only evidence of its existence that survives.
From these we learn that the type of alphabet taught was the
Roman rustic capital though of a somewhat modified local
character. This paucity of records makes it seem likely that
the school of the Roman missionaries had but a brief period of
existence, and wholly failed to influence the native hand.

Not so, however, with the Irish school of writing in the
north.

The Irish alphabet was founded on the Roman half-uncial
hand, manuscripts of this type having been brought over to
Ireland by missionaries, perhaps during the fifth century.
Owing to the isolated position of the island and the consequent
absence of extraneous influence, a strongly characteristic national hand developed, which ran its uninterrupted course
down to the late Middle Ages. This hand was at first round in
character and of great clearness, beauty and precision; but, at
an early period, a modified, pointed variety of a minuscule
type developed out of it, used for quicker and less ornamental
writing.

In the seventh century Northumbria was Christianised by
Irish missionaries, who founded monasteries and religious settlements throughout the north. What, then, more natural
than that these zealous preachers of the Word should teach their
disciples not only the Word itself, but also how to write it

down in characters pleasing to the Almighty, and not in rude and uncouth signs which conveyed all the power and magic of the heathen gods? Thus it came to pass that the English of the north learnt the exquisite penmanship of the Irish, and proved themselves such apt pupils that they soon equalled their former masters. In fact, the earliest specimens of the Northumbrian hand can scarcely be distinguished from their Irish models.

In course of time, moreover, the English threw off the conventions and restraints which fettered the Irish hand and developed a truly national hand, which spread throughout England, and which, in grace of outline and correctness of stroke, even surpassed its prototype.

As might have been expected, the English adopted both the round and pointed varieties of their Irish teachers. One of the earliest and most beautiful examples of the former is *The Book of Durham* or *The Lindisfarne Gospels*,[1] written about A.D. 700 by Eadfrith, bishop of Lindisfarne. And, as a specimen of the latter, may be mentioned a fine copy of Bede's *Ecclesiastical History* in the University Library of Cambridge, written not long after 730, which possesses an additional interest as preserving one of the earliest pieces of poetry in the English language, *The Hymn of Caedmon*, in the original Northumbrian dialect. The pointed hand branched off into a number of local varieties and was extensively used down to the tenth century, when it became influenced by the French or Carolingian minuscule. Towards the end of the century all Latin MSS. were, as a matter of fact, written in foreign characters, whereas the English hand came to be exclusively used for writing in the vernacular. For instance, a Latin charter would have the body of the text in the French minuscule, but the English descriptions or boundaries of the property to be conveyed would be written in the native hand.

After the Conquest, the native hand gradually disappeared, the only traces of it left being the adoption by the foreign alphabets of the symbols ᵖ, ᴣ, þ (ð) to express the peculiarly English sounds for which they stood. The rune ᵖ, however, fell into disuse about the beginning of the fourteenth century, its place having been taken by *uu* (*vv*) or *w;* while ð (th) occurs

---

[1] Brit. Mus. Cotton Nero, D. 4.

occasionally as late as the end of the same century. Of far superior vitality were þ and ȝ, the former bearing a charmed life throughout Middle English times, though, in the fifteenth century and later, þ often appeared in the degenerated form of *y*, while ȝ was retained in order to represent spirant sounds, afterwards denoted by *y* or *gh*.

During the late twelfth, thirteenth and fourteenth centuries the history of English handwriting was practically that of the various Latin hands of the French school. The fifteenth century finally witnessed the dissolution of the medieval book-hand of the minuscule type, the many varieties of it being apparent in the types used by the early printers. The legal or charter-hand, introduced with the Conquest, was, however, not superseded by the printing-presses, but ran an undisturbed though ever varying course down to the seventeenth century, when its place was taken by the modern current hand, fashioned on Italian models. A late variety still lingers on, however, in the so-called chancery-hand seen in the engraved writing of enrolments and patents.

Turning to the materials used for writing in medieval England, we gain at once a connecting link with the runic alphabet, since the wooden tablet, the *bóc*, again appears, though in a somewhat different fashion. A thin coating of wax was now spread over the surface, and the writing was scratched on it with a pointed instrument of metal or bone which, in Old English, was known as *graef*, and in the later centuries by the French term *poyntel*. The use of these tablets was widely, spread in the Middle Ages; they served for the school-boy's exercises and for bills and memoranda of every description, for short letters and rough copies—for anything that was afterwards to be copied out, more carefully, on vellum. In German illuminated MSS. poets are represented as writing their songs and poems on waxen tablets, and, as early as the sixth century, *The Rule of St. Benet* makes provision for the distribution of tablets and styles to monks. There is, also, evidence of the use of these tablets by Irish monks, who, it may be supposed, would introduce them to their English pupils. And, consequently, we find that Aldhelm, who died in 709, writes a riddle of which the answer is "tablet"—a fact which presupposes a knowledge of the existence of tablets among his contemporaries. Again, in Ethelwold's *Benedictionale* of the tenth century, Zacharias (*Luke*, i, 3) is represented as writing on a waxen tablet.[1]

In the twelfth century we learn concerning Anselm, archbishop of Canterbury (†1109), that he was in the habit of making the first sketch of his works on waxen tablets; and, in *The Canterbury Tales*, Chaucer relates how the summoner's "fellow" had "a pair of tables all of ivory, and a poyntel ypolished fetisly."

Far more important, practical and durable as writing material, however, was parchment or vellum, the use of which prevailed throughout the Middle Ages. The Old English name for this was *bóc-fel*, literally "book-skin," replaced in Middle English by the French terms *parchment* and *velin* (vellum). These terms, originally, were not interchangeable, *vellum* being, as its name indicates, prepared from calf-skins, parchment from sheep-skins.[2]

At first, the evidence goes to show that monasteries had to prepare their own parchment, either by the help of the monks themselves or of laymen engaged for the purpose. Later, however, the parchment-makers took their place as ordinary craftsmen, and supplied religious and other houses with the necessary material. Thus we find that, in the year 1300, Ely bought five dozen parchments and as many vellums, and, about half a century later, no less than seventy and thirty dozen respectively in order to supply the want of writing material for a few years only. Vellum was, at times, magnificently coloured, the text being, in such cases, inscribed in letters of gold or silver. The most famous example is the *Codex argenteus* at Upsala. Archbishop Wilfrid of York (664–709) is said to have possessed the four Gospels written on purple vellum in letters of purest gold, a fact which his biographer records as little short of the marvellous. In the British Museum there remains to this day an Old English MS. of the Gospels the first leaves of which are written in golden letters on purple vellum.[3]

Apart from these *éditions de luxe*, which naturally must

---

[1] *Archaeol.* xxiv, pl. 27.

[2] From *Hamlet*, v, 1, it appears, however, as if Shakespeare was unaware of this difference: "Is not parchment made of sheep-skins?"—"Ay, my lord, and of calf-skins too."

[3] Royal, 1, E. 6.

have been of enormous cost, ordinary working parchment was a very expensive writing material, and it is small wonder if, on that account, it gradually had to give way before a new and less costly material.   It appears that, from times immemorial, the manufacture of paper from linen rags and hemp was known to the Chinese, who, apparently, taught their art to the Arabs, since paper was exported by that nation at an early date.   In the twelfth century paper was known in Spain and Italy, and thence it spread slowly northwards, though it did not come into more general use until the fourteenth century.   In the fifteenth century paper manuscripts were very frequent in England, as can be assumed from the great number still remaining in public and private libraries.

For writing, both on parchment and on paper, the quill was used, known in Old English times as *feðer*, in Middle English by the French term *penne*.   The existence of the quill as an implement of writing is proved by one of the oldest Irish MSS., where St. John the Evangelist is represented holding a quill in his hand.   Again, Aldhelm has a riddle on *penna*, in the same way as he had one on the *tablet*.   Other necessary implements for writing and preparing a MS. were a lead for ruling margins and lines, a ruler, a pair of compasses, scissors, a puncher, an awl, a scraping-knife and, last but not least, ink, which was usually kept in a horn, either held in the hand by the scribe, or placed in a specially provided hole in his desk.   In Old English times it was known, from its colour, as *blaec*, but, after the Conquest, the French term *enque*, our modern English *ink*, was adopted.   The terms *horne* and *ink-horne* are both found in old glossaries.

When the body of the text was finally ready, the sheets were passed to the corrector, who filled the office of the modern proof-reader, and from him to the rubricator, who inserted, in more or less elaborate designs, and in striking colours, the rubrics and initials for which space had been left by the scribe. The pieces of parchment were then passed to the binder, who, as a rule, placed four on each other and then folded them, the result being a quire of eight leaves or sixteen pages.   The binding was generally strong and solid in character: leather was used for the back and wooden boards for the sides, which were usually covered with parchment of leather or velvet.   Thus was established the form and fashion of the book as we know it, whether written or printed.

Besides the book-form, parchment was also made up into rolls, which were especially used for chronological writings and deeds of various kinds.[1]

The men who wrote both roll and book, and to whose patience and devotion we owe so much of our knowledge of the times gone by, were, at first, the monks themselves; it being held that copying, especially of devotional books, was a work pleasing to God and one of the best possible ways in which men, separated from the world, could labour.

Gradually, however, there grew up a professional class of scribes, whose services could be hired for money, and who can be proved to have been employed at an early period in the monasteries of England and abroad. Nuns were also well versed in writing. Moreover, where schools were attached to monasteries the *alumni* were early pressed into service, at all events to copy out books needed for their own instruction.

The cloister was the centre of life in the monastery, and in the cloister was the workshop of the patient scribe. It is hard to realise that the fair and seemly handwriting of these manuscripts was executed by fingers which, on winter days, when the wind howled through the cloisters, must have been numbed by the icy cold. It is true that, occasionally, little *carrells* or studies in the recesses of the windows were screened off from the main walk of the cloister, and sometimes a small room or cell would be partitioned off for the use of a single scribe. This room would then be called the *scriptorium*, but it is unlikely that any save the oldest or most learned of the community were afforded this luxury. In these *scriptoria* of various kinds the earliest annals and chronicles in the English language were penned, in the beautiful and painstaking forms in which we know them.

There is no evidence for the existence of buildings specially set apart for libraries until the later Middle Ages. Books were stored in presses, placed either in the church or in convenient places within the monastic buildings. These presses were then added to as need arose, or, perhaps, a small room was set apart for the better preserving of the precious volumes. Books were

[1] Cf. the term "Master of the Rolls."

frequently lost through the widespread system of lending both to private persons and to communities, and, though bonds were solemnly entered into for their safe return, neither anathema nor heavy pledges seemed sufficient to ensure the return of the volumes.

But all losses through lending, or fire, or pillage, were as nothing compared with the utter ruin and destruction that overtook the literature of England, as represented by the written remains of its past, when the monasteries were dissolved. By what remains we can estimate what we have lost, and lost irrevocably; but the full significance of this event for English literary culture will be discussed in a later chapter.

CHAPTER III

Early National Poetry

T HE poetry of the Old English period is generally grouped in two main divisions, national and Christian. To the former are assigned those poems of which the subjects are drawn from English, or rather Teutonic, tradition and history or from the customs and conditions of English life; to the latter those which deal with Biblical matter, ecclesiastical traditions and religious subjects of definitely Christian origin. The line of demarcation is not, of course, absolutely fixed. Most of the national poems in their present form contain Christian elements, while English influence often makes itself felt in the presentation of Biblical or ecclesiastical subjects. But, on the whole, the division is a satisfactory one, in spite of the fact that there are a certain number of poems as to the classification of which some doubt may be entertained.

We are concerned here only with the earlier national poems. With one or two possible exceptions they are anonymous, and we have no means of assigning to them with certainty even an approximate date. There can be little doubt, however, that they all belong to times anterior to the unification of England under King Alfred (A.D. 886). The later national poetry does not begin until the reign of Aethelstan.

With regard to the general characteristics of these poems one or two preliminary remarks will not be out of place. First, there is some reason for believing that, for the most part, they are the work of minstrels rather than of literary men. In two cases, *Widsith* and *Deor*, we have definite statements to this effect, and from Bede's account of Caedmon we may probably infer that the early Christian poems had a similar origin. Indeed, it is by no means clear that any of the poems were written

down very early.   Scarcely any of the MSS. date from before
the tenth century and, though they are doubtless copies, they
do not betray traces of very archaic orthography.   Again, it is
probable that the authors were as a rule attached to the courts
of kings or, at all events, to the retinues of persons in high position.   For this statement also we have no positive evidence
except in the cases of *Widsith* and *Deor;* but it is favoured by
the tone of the poems.   Some knowledge of music and recitation seems, indeed, to have prevailed among all classes.   Just
as in *Beowulf* not only Hrothgar's bard but even the king
himself is said to have taken part among others in the recitation
of stories of old time, so Bede, in the passage mentioned
above, relates how the harp was passed around at a gathering of villagers, each one of whom was expected to produce
a song.   But the poems which survived, especially epic poems,
are likely to have been the work of professional minstrels, and
such persons would naturally be attracted to courts by the
richer rewards—both in gold and land—which they received
for their services.   It is not only in Old English poems that
professional minstrels are mentioned.   From Cassiodorus (*Varia-
rum*, II, 40 f.) we learn that Clovis begged Theodric, king of the
Ostrogoths, to send him a skilled harpist.   Again, Priscus, in
the account of his visit to Attila,[1] describes how, at the evening
feast, two men, whom probably we may regard as professional
minstrels, came forward and sang of the king's victories and
martial deeds.   Some of the warriors, he says, had their fighting spirit roused by the melody, while others, advanced in age,
burst into tears, lamenting the loss of their strength—a passage
which bears rather a striking resemblance to Beowulf's account
of the feast in Hrothgar's hall.

It is customary to classify the early national poems in two
groups, epic and elegiac.   The former, if we may judge from
Beowulf, ran to very considerable length, while all the extant
specimens of the latter are quite short.   There are, however,
one or two poems which can hardly be brought under either of
these heads, and it is probably due to accident that most of the
shorter poems which have come down to us are of an elegiac
character.

---

[1] K. Müller, *Fragmenta Historicorum Graecorum*, IV, p. 92.

The history of our national epic poetry is rendered obscure by the fact that there is little elsewhere with which it may be compared. We need not doubt that it is descended ultimately from the songs in which the ancients were wont to celebrate deeds of famous men, such as Arminius[1]; but, regarding the form of these songs, we are unfortunately without information. The early national epic poetry of Germany is represented only by a fragment of 67 lines, while the national poetry of the north, rich as it is, contains nothing which can properly be called epic. It cannot, therefore, be determined with certainty, whether the epos was known to the English before the invasion or whether it arose in this country, or, again, whether it was introduced from abroad in later times. Yet the fact is worth noting that all the poems of which we have any remains deal with stories relating to continental or Scandinavian lands. Indeed, in the whole of our early national poetry, there is no reference to persons who are known to have lived in Britain. Kögel put forward the view that epic poetry originated among the Goths, and that its appearance in the north-west of Europe is to be traced to the harpist who was sent to Clovis by Theodric, king of the Ostrogoths. Yet the traditions preserved in our poems speak of professional minstrels before the time of Clovis. The explanation of the incident referred to may be merely that minstrelsy had attained greater perfection among the Goths than elsewhere. Unfortunately Gothic poetry has wholly perished.

Although definite evidence is wanting, it is commonly held that the old Teutonic poetry was entirely strophic. Such is the case with all the extant Old Norse poems, and there is no reason for thinking that any other form of poetry was known in the north. Moreover, in two of the earliest Old English poems, *Widsith* and *Deor*, the strophes may be restored practically without alteration of the text. An attempt has even been made to reconstruct *Beowulf* in strophic form; but this can only be carried out by dealing with the text in a somewhat arbitrary manner. In *Beowulf*, as indeed in most Old English poems, new sentences and even new subjects begin very frequently in the middle of the verse. The effect of this is, of course, to produce a continuous metrical narrative, which is essentially foreign to the strophic type of poetry. Further, it is not to be overlooked

[1] Cf. Tacitus, *Ann.* II, 88.

that all the strophic poems which we possess are quite short. Even *Atlamál*, the longest narrative poem in the *Edda*, scarcely reaches one eighth of the length of *Beowulf*. According to another theory epics were derived from strophic lays, though never actually composed in strophic form themselves. This theory is, of course, by no means open to such serious objections. It may be noted that, in some of the earliest Old Norse poems, *e.g. Helgakviða Hundingsbana* II. and *Helgakviða Hiörvarðssonar* the strophes contain only speeches, while the connecting narrative is given quite briefly, in prose. Such pieces might very well serve as the bases of epic poems. The greater length of the latter may, then, be accounted for by the substitution of detailed descriptions for the short prose passages, by the introduction of episodes drawn from other sources and perhaps also by the combination of two or more lays in one poem. In any such process, however, the original materials must have been largely transformed.

By far the most important product of the national epos is *Beowulf*, a poem of 3183 lines, which has been preserved practically complete in a MS. of the tenth century, now in the British Museum. It will be convenient at the outset to give a brief summary of its contents.

The poem opens with a short account of the victorious Danish king Scyld Scefing, whose obsequies are described in some detail. His body was carried on board a ship, piled up with arms and treasures. The ship passed out to sea, and none knew what became of it (ll. 1–52). The reigns of Scyld's son and grandson, Beowulf and Healfdene, are quickly passed over, and we are next brought to Hrothgar, the son of Healfdene. He builds a splendid hall, called Heorot, in which to entertain his numerous retinue (ll. 53–100). His happiness is, however, destroyed by Grendel, a monster sprung from Cain, who attacks the hall by night and devours as many as thirty knights at a time. No one can withstand him, and, in spite of sacrificial offerings, the hall has to remain empty (ll. 101–193). When Grendel's ravages have lasted twelve years, Beowulf, a nephew of Hygelac, king of the Geatas, and a man of enormous strength, determines to go to Hrothgar's assistance. He embarks with fourteen companions and, on reaching the Danish coast, is directed by the watchman to Hrothgar's abode (ll. 194–319). The king, on being informed of his arrival, relates how he had known and befriended Ecgtheow, Beowulf's father. Beowulf states the object of his coming, and the visitors are invited to feast (ll. 320 –497). During the banquet Beowulf is taunted by Hunferth (Unferth), the king's "orator," with having failed in a swimming contest against a certain Breca. He replies, giving a different version of the story, according to which he was successful (ll. 498–606). Then the queen (Wealhtheow) fills Beowulf's cup, and he announces his determination to conquer or die. As night draws on, the king and his retinue leave the hall to the visitors (ll. 607–665). They go to sleep, and Beowulf puts off his armour, declaring that he will not use his sword. Grendel bursts into the hall and devours one of the knights. Beowulf, however, seizes him by the arm, which he tears off after a desperate struggle, and the monster takes to flight, mortally wounded (ll. 665–833). Beowulf displays the arm, and the Danes come to express their admiration of his achievement. They tell stories of heroes of the past, of Sigemund and his nephew Fitela and of the Danish prince Heremod.[1] Then Hrothgar himself arrives, congratulates Beowulf on his victory and rewards him with rich gifts (ll. 834–1062). During the feast which follows, the king's minstrel recites the story of Hnaef and Finn (ll. 1063–1159), to which we shall have to return later. The queen comes forward and, after addressing Hrothgar together with his nephew and colleague Hrothwulf, thanks Beowulf and presents him with a valuable necklace (ll. 1160–1232). This necklace, it is stated (ll. 1202–1214), was afterwards worn by Hygelac and fell into the hands of the Franks at his death. Hrothgar and Beowulf now retire, but a number of knights settle down to sleep in the hall. During the night Grendel's mother appears and carries off Aeschere, the king's chief councillor (ll. 1233–1306). Beowulf is summoned and the king, overwhelmed with grief, tells him what has happened and describes the place where the monsters were believed to dwell. Beowulf promises to exact vengeance (ll. 1306–1399). They set out for the place, a pool overshadowed with trees, but apparently connected with the sea. Beowulf plunges

---

[1] For these persons cf. the Old Norse poem *Hyndlulióð*, strophe 2, *Völsunga Saga* cap. 7–10, etc.

into the water and reaches a cave,where he has a desperate encounter with the monster. Eventually he succeeds in killing her
with a sword which he finds in the cave. He then comes upon
the corpse of Grendel and cuts off its head. With this he returns
to his companions, who had given him up for lost (ll. 1397–1631).
The head is brought in triumph to the palace, and Beowulf
describes his adventure. The king praises his exploit and contrasts his spirit with that of the unfortunate prince Heremod.
From this he passes to a moralising discourse on the evils of
pride (1632–1784). On the following day Beowulf bids farewell to the king. They part affectionately, and the king
rewards him with further gifts. Beowulf and his companions
embark and return to their own land (1785–1921). The
virtues of Hygd, the young wife of Hygelac, are praised, and
she is contrasted with Thrytho, the wife of Offa, who, in her
youth, had displayed a murderous disposition (ll. 1922–1962).
Beowulf greets Hygelac and gives him an account of his adventures. Part of his speech, however, is taken up with a subject
which, except for a casual reference in ll. 83–85, has not been
mentioned before, namely, the relations between Hrothgar
and his son-in-law Ingeld, prince of the Heathobeardan.
Ingeld's father, Froda, had been slain by the Danes and he was
constantly incited by an old warrior to take vengeance on the
son of the slayer. Then Beowulf hands over to Hygelac and
Hygd the presents which Hrothgar and Wealhtheow had given
him, and Hygelac in turn rewards him with a sword and with a
large share in the kingdom (ll. 1963–2199).

A long period is now supposed to elapse. Hygelac has
fallen, and his son Heardred has been slain by the Swedes.
Then Beowulf has succeeded to the throne and reigned gloriously for fifty years (ll. 2200–2210). In his old age the land
of the Geatas is ravaged and his own home destroyed by a fire-
spitting dragon which, after brooding for three hundred years
over the treasure of men long since dead, has had its lair robbed
by a runaway slave. Beowulf, greatly angered, resolves to
attack it (ll. 2210–2349). Now comes a digression referring to
Beowulf's past exploits, in the course of which we learn that he
had escaped by swimming when Hygelac lost his life in the land
of the Frisians. On his return Hygd offered him the throne,
but he refused it in favour of the young Heardred. The latter,

however, was soon slain by the Swedish king Onela, because he
had granted asylum to his nephews, Eanmund and Eadgils, the
sons of Ohthere. Vengeance was obtained by Beowulf later,
when he supported Eadgils in a campaign which led to the king's
death (ll. 2349–2396). Beowulf now approaches the dragon's
lair. He reflects on the past history of his family. Haethcyn,
king of the Geatas, had accidentally killed his brother Here-
beald, and their father, Hrethel, died of grief in consequence.
His death was followed by war with the Swedes, in which first
Haethcyn and then the Swedish king Ongentheow (Onela's
father) were slain. When Hygelac, the third brother, perished
among the Frisians, Daeghrefn, a warrior of the Hugas, was
crushed to death by the hero himself (ll. 2397–2509). Beowulf
orders his men to wait outside while he enters the dragon's
barrow alone. He is attacked by the dragon, and his sword
will not bite. Wiglaf, one of his companions, now comes to the
rescue; but the rest, in spite of his exhortations, flee into a
wood. As the dragon darts forward again Beowulf strikes it
on the head; but his sword breaks, and the dragon seizes him
by the neck. Wiglaf succeeds in wounding it, and Beowulf,
thus getting a moment's respite, finishes it off with his knife
(ll. 2510–2709). But the hero is mortally wounded. At his
request Wiglaf brings the treasure out of the lair. Beowulf
gives him directions with regard to his funeral, presents him
with his armour and necklace and then dies (ll. 2709–2842.)
The cowardly knights now return and are bitterly upbraided
by Wiglaf (ll. 2842—2891). A messenger brings the news to
the warriors who have been waiting behind. He goes on to
prophesy that, now their heroic king has fallen, the Geatas
must expect hostility on all sides. With the Franks there has
been no peace since Hygelac's unfortunate expedition against
the Frisians and Hetware, while the Swedes cannot forget
Ongentheow's disaster, which is now described at length. The
warriors approach the barrow and inspect the treasure which
has been found (ll. 2891—3075). Wiglaf repeats Beowulf's
instructions, the dragon is thrown into the sea and the king's
body burnt on a great pyre. Then a huge barrow is constructed
over the remains of the pyre, and all the treasure taken
from the dragon's lair is placed in it. The poem ends with
an account of the mourning and the proclamation of the

king's virtues by twelve warriors who ride round the barrow.

Many of the persons and events mentioned in *Beowulf* are known to us also from various Scandinavian records, especially Saxo's *Danish History, Hrólfs Saga Kraka, Ynglinga Saga* (with the poem *Ynglingatal*) and the fragments of the lost *Skiöldunga Saga*. Scyld, the ancestor of the Scyldungas (the Danish royal family), clearly corresponds to Skiöldr, the ancestor of the Skiöldungar, though the story told of him in *Beowulf* does not occur in Scandinavian literature. Healfdene and his sons Hrothgar and Halga are certainly identical with the Danish king Hafdan and his sons Hróarr (Roe) and Helgi; and there can be no doubt that Hrothwulf, Hrothgar's nephew and colleague, is the famous Hrólfr Kraki, the son of Helgi. Hrothgar's elder brother Heorogar is unknown, but his son Heoroweard may be identical with Hiörvarðr, the brother-in-law of Hrólfr. It has been plausibly suggested also that Hrethric, the son of Hrothgar, may be the same person as Hroereker (Roricus), who is generally represented as the son or successor of Ingialdr. The name of the Heathobeardan is unknown in the north, unless, possibly, a reminiscence of it is preserved in Saxo's Hothbroddus, the name of the king who slew Roe. Their princes Froda and Ingeld, however, clearly correspond to Fróð (Frotho IV) and his son Ingialdr, who are represented as kings of the Danes. Even the story of the old warrior who incites Ingeld to revenge is given also by Saxo; indeed, the speaker (Starcatherus) is one of the most prominent figures in his history. Again, the Swedish prince Eadgils, the son of Ohthere, is certainly identical with the famous king of the Svear, Aðils, the son of Óttarr, and his conflict with Onela corresponds to the battle on lake Vener between Aðils and Áli. The latter is described as a Norwegian; but this is, in all probability, a mistake arising from his surname *hinn Upplenzki*, which was thought to refer to the Norwegian Upplönd instead of the Swedish district of the same name. The other members of the Swedish royal family, Ongentheow and Eanmund, are unknown in Scandinavian literature. The same remark applies, probably, to the whole of the royal family of the Geatas, except, perhaps, the hero himself. On the other hand, most of the persons mentioned in the minor episodes or incidentally—Sigemund and Fitela,

Heremod, Eormenric, Hama, Offa—are more or less well known from various Scandinavian authorities, some also from continental sources.

With the exception of *Ynglingatal*, which dates probably from the ninth century, all the Scandinavian works mentioned above are quite late and, doubtless, based on tradition. Hence they give us no means of fixing the dates of the kings whose doings they record—unless one can argue from the fact that Harold the Fairhaired, who appears to have been born in 850, claimed to be descended in the eleventh generation from Aðils. Indeed, we have unfortunately no contemporary authorities for Swedish and Danish history before the ninth century. Several early Frankish writings, however, refer to a raid which was made upon the territories of the Chattuarii on the lower Rhine about the year 520. The raiders were defeated by Theodberht, the son of Theodric I, and their king, who is called Chohilaicus (Chlochilaicus) or Huiglaucus, was killed. This incident is, without doubt, to be identified with the disastrous expedition of Hygelac against the Franks, Hetware (Chattuarii) and Frisians, to which *Beowulf* contains several references. We need not hesitate, then, to conclude that most of the historical events mentioned in *Beowulf* are to be dated within about the first three decades of the sixth century.

In Gregory of Tours' *Historia Francorum* (III, 3) and in the *Gesta Regum Francorum* (cap. 19) the king of the raiders is described as *rex Danorum;* in the *Liber Monstrorum*,[1] however, as *rex Getarum*. As Getarum can hardly be anything but a corruption of *Beowulf's* Geatas the latter description is doubtless correct. The Geatas are, in all probability, to be identified with the Gautar of Old Norse literature, *i.e.* the people of Götaland in the south of Sweden. It may be mentioned that Procopius, a contemporary of Theodberht, in his description (*Goth.* II, 15) of "Thule," *i.e.* Scandinavia, speaks of the Götar (Gautoi) as a very numerous nation.

The hero himself still remains to be discussed. On the whole, though the identification is rejected by many scholars, there seems to be good reason for believing that he was the same person as Böðvarr Biarki, the chief of Hrólfr Kraki's knights. In *Hrólfs Saga Kraka*, Biarki is represented as coming

[1] Berger de Xivrey, *Traditions Tératologiques*, p. 12.

to Leire, the Danish royal residence, from Götaland, where his brother was king.   Shortly after his arrival he killed an animal demon (a bear according to Saxo), which was in the habit of attacking the king's farmyard at Yule.   Again, according to *Skaldskaparmál*, cap. 44 (from *Skiöldunga Saga*), he took part with Aðils in the battle against Áli.   In all these points his history resembles that of Beowulf.   It appears from *Hrólfs Saga Kraka* that Biarki had the faculty of changing into a bear. And Beowulf's method of fighting, especially in his conflict with Daeghrefn, may point to a similar story.   On the other hand, the latter part of Biarki's career is quite different from that of Beowulf.   He stayed with Hrólfr to the end and shared the death of that king.   But the latter part of Beowulf's life can hardly be regarded as historical.   Indeed, his own exploits throughout are largely of a miraculous character.

There is another Scandinavian story, however, which has a very curious bearing on the earlier adventures of Beowulf. This is a passage in *Grettis Saga* (cap. 64 ff.), in which the hero is represented as destroying two demons, male and female. The scene is laid in Iceland; yet so close are the resemblances between the two stories, in the character of the demons, in the description of the places they inhabit and in the methods by which the hero deals with them, as well as in a number of minor details, that it is impossible to ascribe them to accident.   Now Grettir seems to be a historical person who died about the year 1031.   The presumption is, then, that an older story has be-become attached to his name.   But there is nothing in the account that gives any colour to the idea that it is actually derived from the Old English poem.   More probably the origin of both stories alike is to be sought in a folk-tale, and, just as the adventures were attributed in Iceland to the historical Grettir, so in England, and, possibly, also in Denmark, at an earlier date they were associated with a historical prince of the Götar. From the occurrence of the local names *Beowanham* and *Grendles mere* in a Wiltshire charter [1] some scholars have inferred that the story was originally told of a certain Beowa, whom they have identified with Beaw or Beo, the son of Scyld (Sceldwea) in the West Saxon genealogy.   But since this person is, in all probability, identical with the first (Danish) Beowulf of the

[1] Kemble, *Cod. Dipl.* 353.

poem, and since the name Beowa may very well be a shortened form of Beowulf, while the other names are obscure, the inference seems to be of somewhat doubtful value. On the whole there is, perhaps, more to be said for the view that the asssociation of Beowulf with the folk-tale arose out of some real adventure with an animal. This, however, must remain largely a matter of speculation. The fight with the dragon is, of course, common motive in folk-tales. An attempt has been made to show that Beowulf's adventure has a specially close affinity with a story told by Saxo of the Danish king Frotho I. But the resemblance between the two stories is not very striking.

With regard to the origin and antiquity of the poem it is impossible to arrive at any definite conclusions with certainty. From investigations which have been made into its linguistic and metrical characteristics the majority of scholars hold that it was originally composed in a northern or midland dialect —though it has been preserved only in West Saxon form—and that it is at least as old as any other considerable piece of Old English poetry which we possess. The question of antiquity, however, is complicated by the doubt which is commonly felt as to the unity of the poem. Moreover, it cannot be denied that this feeling of doubt is, at least to some extent, justified. In its present form the poem must date from Christian times as it contains a considerable number of passages of distinctly Christian character. On the other hand, the relationships of the various Danish and Swedish kings can hardly have been remembered otherwise than in a more or less stereotyped form of words for more than a generation after their lifetime. Hence we are bound to conclude that the formation of the poem, or, at all events, that of the materials from which it was made up, must have occupied at least the greater part of a century.

It is generally thought that several originally separate lays have been combined in the poem, and, though no proof is obtainable, the theory in itself is not unlikely. These lays are usually supposed to have been four in number and to have dealt with the following subjects: (i) Beowulf's fight with Grendel, (ii) the fight with Grendel's mother, (iii) Beowulf's return, (iv) the fight with the dragon. In view of the story in *Grettis Saga* I am very much inclined to doubt whether it is justifiable to separate the first two incidents. The fight with the dragon, however, is certainly quite distinct, and the part of the poem dealing with Beowulf's reception by Hygelac may also have originally formed the subject of a separate lay. Some scholars have gone much further than this in their analysis of the poem. According to one view nearly half of it is the work of interpolators; according to another the present text is a composite one made up from two parallel versions. It is much to be doubted, however, whether any really substantial result has been obtained from these investigations into the "inner history" of the poem. The references to religion seem to afford the only safe criterion for distinguishing between earlier and later elements. Thus, it is worth noting that in ll. 175 ff. the Danes are represented as offering heathen sacrifices, a passage which is wholly inconsistent with the sentiments afterwards attributed to Hrothgar. But at what stage in the history of the poem was the Christian element introduced?

Certainly this element seems to be too deeply interwoven in the text for us to suppose that it is due to additions made by scribes at a time when the poem had come to be written down. Indeed there is little evidence for any additions or changes of this kind. We must ascribe it, then, either to the original poet or poets or to minstrels by whom the poem was recited in later times. The extent to which the Christian element is present varies somewhat in different parts of the poem. In the last portion (ll. 2200–3183) the number of lines affected by it amounts to less than four per cent., while in the section dealing with Beowulf's return (ll. 1904—2199) it is negligible. In the earlier portions, on the other hand, the percentage rises to between nine and ten, but this is partly due to four long passages. One fact worth observing is that the Christian element is about equally distributed between the speeches and the narrative. We have noticed above that, according to a theory which has much in its favour, epics are derived from "mixed" pieces, in which speeches were given in verse and narrative in prose. If Christian influence had made itself felt at this stage, we should surely have expected to find it more prominent in the narrative than in the speeches, for the latter would, presumably, be far less liable to change.

There is one curious feature in the poem which has scarcely received sufficient attention, namely the fact that, while the poet's reflections and even the sentiments attributed to the various speakers are largely, though not entirely, Christian, the customs and ceremonies described are, almost without exception, heathen. This fact seems to point, not to a Christian work with heathen reminiscences, but to a heathen work which has undergone revision by Christian minstrels. In particular, I cannot believe that any Christian poet either could or would have composed the account of Beowulf's funeral. It is true that we have no references to heathen gods, and hardly any to actual heathen worship. But such references would necessarily be suppressed or altered when the courts became Christian. Indeed, there is a fairly clear case of alteration in ll. 175 ff., to which I have already alluded. It may, perhaps, be urged that, if the work had been subjected to such a thorough revision, descriptions of heathen ceremonies would not have been allowed to stand. But the explanation may be that the ceremonies in question had passed out of use before the change of religion. In the case of cremation, which is the prevalent form of funeral rite found in the poem, we have good reason for believing this to be true. Hence, such passages could not excite the same repugnance among the clergy as they would have done in countries where the ceremonies were still practised.

I am disposed, then, to think that large portions at least of the poem existed in epic form before the change of faith and that the appearance of the Christian element is due to revision. The Christianity of *Beowulf* is of a singularly indefinite and undoctrinal type, which contrasts somewhat strongly with what is found in later Old English poetry. In explanation of this fact it has been suggested that the poem was composed or revised under the influence of the missionaries from Iona. But is there really any reason for thinking that the teaching of the Irish missionaries would tend in that direction? A more obvious explanation would be that the minstrels who introduce the Christian element had but a vague knowledge of the new faith. Except in ll. 1743 ff., where there seems to be a reference to *Ephesians*, vi, 16, the only passages of the Bible made use of are those relating to the Creation, the story of Cain and Abel and the Deluge. In the first case (ll. 90 ff.) one can hardly help suspecting a reference to Caedmon's hymn, and the others also may just as well have been derived from Christian poems or songs as from the Bible itself. In any case, however, the fact noted favours the conclusion that the revision took place at an earlier date.

Apart from *Beowulf*, the only remains of national epic poetry which have come down to us are a short but fine fragment (50 lines) of *Finnsburh* and two still shorter fragments (32 and 31 lines respectively) of *Waldhere*. Regarding the former our information is sadly defective. The MS. is lost and the text, as given by Hickes, is extremely corrupt. The story, however, though obscure to us, must have been extremely popular in early times. It is the subject of a long episode in *Beowulf* (see above, p. 25), and three of the chief characters are mentioned in *Widsith*. Familiarity with it is shown also by a mistake in the genealogy in the *Historia Brittonum*, § 31.

The fragment opens with the speech of a young prince rousing his followers to defend the hall in which they are sleeping, apparently within Finn's fortress. They rush to the doors, the chief men being Hengest (perhaps the prince), Sigeferth, Eaha, Ordlaf and Guthlaf. A short altercation follows between Sigeferth and Garulf, who is apparently one of the attacking force. The battle goes on for five days, and many of the assailants, including Garulf, fall. The defenders, however, maintain their position without loss, and we are told that never was a better recompense yielded by sixty knights to their lord than Hnaef now received from his followers. Then a wounded warrior, who is not named, brings the news to his king—at which point the fragment breaks off.

The episode in *Beowulf* furnishes us with considerably more information than the fragment itself. Hnaef, a vassal of the Danish king Healfdene, has fallen at the hands of the Frisians, whom apparently he had gone to visit—whether as friend or foe is not clear. His men, however, maintain a stout defence, and so great are the losses of the Frisians that their king, Finn, has to make terms with them. An agreement is then arrived at between their leader Hengest and the king. They are to enter Finn's service and to be treated by him as generously as the Frisians themselves; and no taunt is to be raised against them on the ground that they have made terms with the man who slew their lord. A great funeral pyre is constructed for the bodies of the slain, and Hildeburh, apparently the wife of Finn and sister of Hnaef, bewails the loss of both her brother and her son. Hengest and his companions stay wth Finn throughout the winter, though sorely tempted to exact vengeance. Eventually, Guthlaf and Oslaf (Ordlaf?) attack and slay Finn with many of his men. The queen is carried away to Denmark with much treasure.

There are no certain references to this story in Scandinavian or German literature, though Ordlaf and Guthlaf are probably to be identified with two Danish princes mentioned in Arngrim Jónsson's epitome of *Skiöldunga Saga*, cap. 4. The tragic events with which the story deals must clearly be referred to the time of those great movements in the regions of the North Sea, between the fourth and sixth centuries, to which Latin writers occasionally allude. The fact that Hnaef is called a vassal of Healfdene, Hrothgar's father, points to about the middle of the fifth century. It is by no means impossible, therefore, that the Hengest of this story is identical with the Hengest who founded the kingdom of Kent.

The MS. fragments of *Waldhere* (*Waldere*) are preserved in the Royal Library at Copenhagen. For this story, fortunately, information is available from a number of continental sources. It is the subject of a Latin epic poem (*Waltharius*) by Ekkehard of St. Gall, dating from the first half of the tenth century; of a Bavarian poem dating from the first half of the thirteenth century, of which only small fragments are preserved; and of two episodes in the Norwegian *Vilkina Saga* (§§ 128 f., 241-4; cf. 331), which is of Low German origin. Incidental references to it occur in several Middle High German poems, and there is also a Polish version of the story, the earliest form of which is in *Chronicon Boguphali Episcopi*, dating from the thirteenth or fourteenth century. It will be convenient here to give a brief summary of Ekkehard's story, as this is the earliest of the continental authorities and appears to have the closest resemblance to our fragments.

Alphere, king of Aquitaine, had a son named Waltharius, and Heriricus, king of Burgundy, an only daughter named Hiltgund, who was betrothed to Waltharius. While they were yet children, however, Attila, king of the Huns, invaded Gaul, and the kings, seeing no hope in resistance, gave up their children to him as hostages, together with much treasure. Under like compulsion treasure was obtained also from Gibicho, king of the Franks, who sent as hostage a youth of noble birth named Hagano. In Attila's service, Waltharius and Hagano won great renown as warriors, but the latter eventually made his escape. When Waltharius grew up he became Attila's chief general; yet he remembered his old engagement with Hiltgund. On his return from a victorious campaign he made a great feast for the king and his court, and when all were sunk in drunken sleep, he and Hiltgund fled laden with much gold. On their way home they had to cross the Rhine near Worms. There the king of the Franks, Guntharius, the son of Gibicho, heard from the ferryman of the gold they were carrying and determined to secure it. Accompanied by Hagano and eleven other picked warriors, he overtook them as they rested in a cave in the Vosges. Waltharius offered him a large share of the gold in order to obtain peace; but the king demanded the whole together with Hiltgund and the horse. Stimulated by the promise of great rewards, the eleven warriors now attacked Waltharius one after another, but he slew them all. Hagano had tried to dissuade Guntharius from the attack; but now, since his nephew was among the slain, he formed a plan with the king for surprising Waltharius. On the following day they both fell upon him after he had quitted his stronghold, and, in the struggle that ensued, all three were maimed. Waltharius, however, was able to proceed on his way with Hiltgund, and the story ends happily with their marriage.

Both our fragments refer to the time immediately before the final encounter. The first is taken up with a speech, apparently by the lady, in which Waldhere is exhorted to acquit himself in the coming fight in a manner worthy of his former deeds. Guthhere has unjustly begun hostilities and refused the offer of a sword and treasure. Now he will have to go away empty-handed, if he does not lose his life. Between the two fragments probably not very much has been lost. The second is occupied by an altercation between Guthhere and Waldhere, in which the former praises his sword and the latter his coat of mail. Waldhere states that the king had tried

to get Hagena to attack him first.   Victory, however, comes to
the faithful from above.   Both the fragments contain Christian
allusions.

It has been suggested that the Old English poem was a
translation from an early German one; but the evidence adduced
is far from satisfactory.   The speeches given in the fragments
have nothing corresponding to them in Ekkehard's text, and
there is a noteworthy difference in the portraiture of the
heroine's character.   Probably, nothing more than the tradition was derived from abroad, and at a very early date, if we
may judge from the form of the names.

In the fragments, Guthhere is represented as king of the
Burgundians.   Since there can be no doubt that he is the Bur-
gundian king Gundicarius (Gundaharius) who was defeated
and slain by the Huns about the year 437, we must conclude
that Ekkehard's nomenclature was affected by the political
geography of his own day, when Worms was a Frankish town.
The other chief characters are known only from German and
Scandinavian tradition.   But the story may very well be
founded on fact, as it is likely enough that Attila did take hostages from the princes of eastern Gaul.   In the Bavarian fragments the hero belongs not to Aquitaine but to Langres.   Now,
the country round Langres and Chalon-sur-Saône (Hiltgund's
home in the Latin poem), although the latter was included in the
Burgundy of the tenth century, must once have been settled by
Franks from the Netherlands; for we find here, in later times,
districts called *pagus Hamauorum* and *pagus Hattuariorum*.
This settlement, as Zeuss pointed out long ago, probably took
place in the reign of Constantius Chlorus.   Hence, there may
have been Frankish princes at Chalon and Langres in the time
of Attila.

The rest of the poems which we have to treat in this chapter
are preserved in the *Exeter Book*.   It will be convenient to take
Widsith first; for, though not an epic itself, it contains much
matter in common with poems of that type.   Indeed, so many
princes and peoples are mentioned in the course of the poem
that its importance for the history of the migration period can
hardly be overestimated.

In the introduction (ll. 1–9) it is stated that the poet belonged to the Myrgingas, a people or rather dynasty whose territories, apparently, were conterminous with those of the Angli (cf. ll. 41 ff.), and that, in company with a princess named Ealhhild, he visited the court of the Gothic king Eormenric. Then, in ll. 10 ff., he begins to enumerate the princes with whom he was acquainted. This list contains the names of many kings famous in history and tradition, together with those of the peoples which they governed, the formula employed being "A. ruled over B." Among them we find Gifica (Gibicho), Breca, Finn, Hnaef, Saeferth (Sigeferth?) and Ongentheow, who have been mentioned above, as well as Attila, Eormenric, Theodric (king of the Franks) and others, some of whom are not known from other sources. In ll. 35–44 there is a reference to the single combat of Offa, king of Angel, a story which is given by Saxo (pp. 113 ff.), Svend Aagesen and the *Vitæ Duorum Offarum*. In ll. 45–49 we hear of the long and faithful partnership of Hrothgar and Hrothwulf and of their victory over Ingeld, an incident to which *Beowulf* (ll. 83 ff.) has only a vague allusion. Then, in ll. 50 ff. the poet again speaks of his journeys and gives a list of the nations he had visited. This list is twice interrupted (ll. 65–67, 70–74) by references to the generosity with which he had been treated by Guthhere, king of the Burgundians, and by Aelfwine (Alboin) in Italy.[1] In ll. 76–78 there is another interruption referring to the power of Casere, *i.e.* the Greek Emperor. Then, in ll. 88 ff., the poet tells of the gifts he had received from Eormenric, from his lord Eadgils, prince of the Myrgingas, and from Ealhhild, and also of his own skill as a minstrel. At l. 109, he begins an enumeration of the Gothic heroes he had visited, most of whom are known to us from Jordanes, *Völsunga Saga* (probably also *Hervarar Saga*), *Vilkina Saga* and German traditions. In ll. 119 ff. he speaks of the ceaseless warfare round the forest of the Vistula, when the Goths had to defend their country against the Huns. The list closes with a reference to the martial deeds of Wudga and Hama, who are mentioned also in *Waldhere* and *Beowulf* as well as in *Vilkina Saga*, the former also in many other continental authorities. The epilogue consists of a short reflection on the life of wandering minstrels and on the advantages gained by princes in treating them generously.

[1] Cf. Paulus Diaconus, *Hist. Lang.*, I, 27.

Apart from the introduction and epilogue, which may originally have been in prose, this poem appears to have been composed in strophic form. Its date cannot be determined with certainty. There is nothing, however, to prevent us from assigning it to the seventh century or even an earlier date; for, though a Christian element is present (ll. 15, 82–87, 131–134), it is very slight and may be removed without affecting the structure of the poem. Alboin, who died about 572, is probably, the latest person mentioned. Now Ealhhild's father bears the same name (Eadwine) as Alboin's father, *i.e.* Audoin, king of the Langobardi, a fact which has led many scholars to believe that Ealhhild was Alboin's sister, and, consequently, that the poet lived towards the close of the sixth century. This hypothesis, however, involves, practically, the reconstruction of the whole poem; for the poet repeatedly speaks of his visits to Eormenric who, as we know from Ammianus Marcellinus (xxxi, 3. 1.), died about two centuries before Alboin, and clearly implies that Ealhhild was his contemporary, whereas he only once alludes to Alboin, in a passage covering five lines. The identity of the two names is, therefore, probably a mere coincidence. As a matter of fact, the heroes commemorated in the poem lived at wide intervals from one another, though Eormenric and persons apparently contemporary with him figure more prominently than the rest. With greater probability one might suppose that traditions existed of a famous minstrel who lived at the court of a prince named Eadgils, and that on the basis of these traditions later minstrels built up lists of the chief national heroes known to them. Against this suggestion, however, stands the fact that the minstrel's name is really unknown, for *Widsith* is an obviously fictitious name (meaning "far-travelled") and must be explained by the statement in ll. 2 f. as to the extent of the poet's journeys. On the other hand, any hypothesis which would represent the minstrel as a fictitious character is open to the objection that, in that case, he would hardly have been associated with so obscure a person as Eadgils, prince of the Myrgingas, a family not mentioned except in this poem. On the whole, then, the hypothesis that the kernel of the poem is really the work of an unknown fourth-century minstrel, who did visit the court of Eormenric, seems to involve fewer difficulties than any other. In that case, of course, such passages as ll. 82 ff. must be regarded as merely the last stage in a process of accretion which had been going on for some three centuries.

The elegy of *Deor* is a much shorter poem than *Widsith* (42 lines in all) and in its general tone presents a striking contrast to it. While *Widsith* tells of the glory of famous heroes and, incidentally, of the minstrel's own success, *Deor* is taken up with stories of misfortune, which are brought forward in illustration of the poet's troubles. The strophic form is preserved throughout and, except in the last fifteen lines, which seem to have been somewhat remodelled, each strophe ends with a refrain (a phenomenon for which it would be difficult to find a parallel in Old English poetry): "That (trouble) was got over (or brought to an end); so can this be."

Originally, perhaps, every strophe referred to a different story of trouble. Thus, strophe 1 deals with the misfortunes suffered by Weland at the hands of Nithhad and strophe 2 with the wrongs done by Weland to Beaduhild. For both these we may refer to the Old Norse poem *Völundarkviða*. In strophe 3 we hear of the passionate love of Geat, presumably the mythical person from whom the English kings traced their descent. Strophe 4 speaks of the thirty years' exile of a certain Theodric, probably the same Theodric who, in *Waldhere*, is associated with Widia (Wudga). In German tradition, from the *Hildebrandslied* onwards, as well as by most modern writers, he is identified with Theodric, king of the Ostrogoths (Dietrich von Bern). Strophe 5 deals with the cruelty of Eormenric and the suffering of his people. What follows is not so clear, and ll. 31–34 are the work of a Christian. The closing lines, however, are very remarkable. The poet states that he had been the bard of the Heodeningas, and that he had been displaced from his office by a skilful minstrel called Heorrenda. Now, the name Heodeningas must mean either the descendants of Heoden or, like the Old Norse Hiaðningar, Heoden (Heðinn) himself and his people. The story of Heðinn's flight with Hildr, the daughter of Högni, was well known in the north[1] and, apparently, also in England, if we may judge from *Widsith*, l. 21. Again, Heorrenda is identical with Hiarrandi, the name of Heðinn's father

[1] Cf. *Skaldskaparmál*, cap. 50, *Sörla Tháttr*, cap. 5 ff., Saxo, pp. 158 ff.

in the Norse accounts; in the Austrian poem *Kudrun*, however, which seems to contain the same story in a corrupt form, Horant is a near relative of Hetel (Heðinn) and also a famous minstrel. Hagena (Högni), according to *Widsith*, was king of the Holmryge, a people probably in eastern Pomerania, and Heoden also may have belonged to the same region. When these persons lived we do not know; but such evidence as we have points to a period anterior to the sixth century. There is nothing in the story to justify the supposition that they are of mythical origin.

Here again, as in the case of *Widsith*, it is possible that a poem has been built round the memory of a famous minstrel, —one who met with misfortune in later life. Yet we have no knowledge of such a person from other sources, while the statement given in the poem itself as to its origin is quite definite. If this statement is true, the poem must, of course, be very ancient. But there seems to be no valid reason for disputing its antiquity; for the four lines which show Christian influence may very well be a later addition, while the supposed identity of the exiled Theodric with Theodric the Ostrogoth must be regarded as a somewhat doubtful hypothesis at the best.

The rest of the shorter poems contain no proper names. Their subjects seem to be drawn rather from typical characters and situations than from the experiences of historical or legendary persons. They are of quite uncertain date, though, doubtless, much later than the two poems we have just discussed. They betray little or no trace of strophic form.

The Wanderer is a rather long elegy (115 lines), depicting the sufferings of a man who has lost his lord. Alone and friendless, he travels over the sea, seeking a home where he can find protection. In sleep, visions of his former happiness come back to him. When he awakes his heart sinks at the sight of the grey waves and the falling snow. Then he passes on to reflect on the vicissitudes of human life and on the ruined castles which may be seen in all directions, testifying to the destruction that has overtaken their owners. The poem throws an interesting light on the close nature of the relationship subsisting in early times between lord and man. It has been suggested that Cynewulf was the author; but this view is now generally abandoned.   Indeed, the Christian element is slight and may be due to later additions.

The Seafarer is a poem of about the same length as *The Wanderer* and resembles it in several passages rather closely.   The sequence of thought, however, is much less clear.   The poet begins by reflecting on the miseries which he has endured when travelling by sea in winter—miseries of which the landsman in his comfortable castle knows nothing.   Yet in ll. 33 ff. he says that he has an irresistible impulse to try the seaman's life.   He who feels this desire cannot be deterred by any of the pleasures of home, however fortunately circumstanced he may be.   From l. 64 onwards he begins a comparison between the transitory nature of earthly pleasures and the eternal rewards of religion, concluding with an exhortation to his hearers to fix their hopes on heaven.

In order to explain the apparent contradictions of the poem some scholars have proposed to take it as a dialogue between an old seaman and a young man who wishes to try the seaman's life; but there is a good deal of disagreement as to the distribution of the lines.   The second half of the poem, with its religious reflections, is believed by many to be a later addition.   If that be not the case, it is at least questionable whether we are justified in classing *The Seafarer* among national poems.

The Wife's Complaint is another poem which presents serious difficulties owing to obscurity in the train of thought.   Indeed, in at least one passage the obscurity is so great that one can hardly believe the text as it stands to be correct.   The speaker is a woman who bewails the ever increasing troubles with which she is beset.   First her husband departed from her over the sea.   Then, apparently at the instigation of his relatives, she is imprisoned in an old dwelling dug out of the earth under an oak, where she sits in solitude bewailing her troubles the whole day long.   She has no friends at hand, and all the vows of lasting love which she and her husband had exchanged in time past have come to nothing.

The Husband's Message, so far as it can be read, is a much simpler poem; but, unfortunately, a number of letters have been lost in ll. 2–6 and 32–40 owing to a large rent in the MS. The poem is in the form of a speech addressed, apparently by means of a staff inscribed with runic letters, to a woman of royal rank. The speech is a message from the woman's husband (or possibly lover), who has had to leave his country in consequence of a vendetta. It is to the effect that he has succeeded in gaining for himself a position of wealth and dignity in another land. He now wishes to assure her that his devotion is unchanged, to remind her of the vows they had made in times past and to ask her to sail southwards to join him as soon as spring comes.

This is the gist of the poem as it appears in almost all editions. It has recently been pointed out, however, that the seventeen lines which immediately precede it in the MS. and which have generally been regarded as a riddle—unconnected with the poem itself—seem really to form the beginning of the speech. In these lines the object speaking states that once it grew by the seashore, but that a knife and human skill have fitted it to give utterance to a message which requires to be delivered privately.

Again, more than one scholar has remarked that the poem looks very much like a sequel to *The Wife's Complaint*. Others have denied the connection between the two poems on the ground that in *The Wife's Complaint*, l. 15, the lady's imprisonment is attributed to the husband himself. But it should be observed that this passage is scarcely intelligible in its present form and, further, that it seems to conflict with what is said elsewhere in the poem. On the whole the balance of probability seems to me to be in favour of the connection.

The Ruin follows *The Husband's Message* in the *Exeter Book* and suffers from the same rent. It differs somewhat in character from the rest of these poems in that the misfortunes which it tells of are those not of a person but of a place. First the poet describes an ancient building, or rather group of buildings, deserted, roofless and tottering. Then he goes on to reflect that these buildings were once richly adorned, full of proud warriors and gay with feasting—until the day came when their defenders were annihilated. As it is clearly stated that the buildings were of stone, and stress is laid on the marvellous skill shown in their construction, there can be little doubt that the subject is drawn from one of the Roman cities or castles in Britain. The reference to many banqueting halls in l. 24 seems to point to a place of considerable size; and, from the mention of hot baths in ll. 39 ff., several scholars have inferred that Bath is intended. But, unfortunately, so much of the text is lost that the description cannot clearly be made out.

A brief reference should be added, in conclusion, to the few traces that remain of the religious poetry of heathen times. The higher forms of such poetry, such as the hymns used in royal sanctuaries or at great popular festivals, have entirely perished. The songs which have been preserved seem to be in the nature of incantations for securing the fertility of the fields or for warding off witchcraft, and even these are largely transformed through Christian influence. Some of them occur in descriptions of the magical ceremonies at which they were sung. We may notice especially the verses used for the blessing of the plough when the first furrow is drawn. They are addressed to "Erce, the mother of the earth," and are in the form of a prayer that the Almighty will grant her rich fields full of barley and wheat. Then the earth is greeted as "mother of mankind." Other verses, less affected by Christian ideas, speak of the shafts shot by female beings (witches or valkyries) which ride through the air, and of the means by which these shafts can be averted or expelled. Another set of verses, in which the god Woden is mentioned, describes the magic properties of nine herbs. It is probable that all these songs, together with the descriptions of the ceremonies accompanying them, were written down at a comparatively late period, when the heathen practices which survived among the peasantry—apart from the more harmful species of magic—were no longer regarded as dangerous.

CHAPTER IV

Old English Christian Poetry

O NLY two names emerge from the anonymity which
shrouds the bulk of Old English Christian poetry,
namely, those of Caedmon and Cynewulf; and in the
past, practically all the religious poetry we possess has been attributed to one or other of these two poets. But, as we shall
see, the majority of the poems to be considered here should
rather be regarded as the work of singers whose names have
perished, as folk-song, as manifestations of the spirit of the
people—in the same sense in which the tale of Beowulf's adventures embodied the aspirations of all valiant thegns, or the epic of
Waldhere summarised the popular ideals of love and honour.
The subject of the Christian epic is indeed, for the most part,
apparently, foreign and even at times Oriental: the heroes of
the Old and New Testaments, the saints as they live in the
legends of the church, furnish the theme. The method of treatment hardly differs, however, from that followed in non-Christian poetry; the metrical form with rare exceptions is the alliterative line constructed on the same principles as in *Beowulf;*
Wyrd has become the spirit of providence, Christ and His
apostles have become English kings or chiefs followed, as in
feudal duty bound, by hosts of clansmen; the homage paid to
the Divine Son is the allegiance due to the scion of an Anglian
king, comparable to that paid by Beowulf to his liege lord
Hygelac, or to that displayed by Byrhtnoth on the banks of the
Panta; the ideals of early English Christianity do not differ
essentially from those of English paganism. And yet there is a
difference.

The Christianity of England in the seventh and eighth centuries, and the Latin influences brought in its wake, which
inspired the poetry under discussion, was a fusion, a commin-

gling, of two different strains.   Accustomed as we are to date
the introduction of Christianity into England from the mission
of St. Augustine, we are apt to forget that, prior to the landing
of the Roman missionary on the shores of Kent, Celtic missionaries from the islands of the west had impressed upon the
northern kingdoms, the earliest home of literary culture in
these islands, a form of Christianity differing in many respects
from the more theological type preached and practised by
St. Augustine and his followers.   Oswald, the martyr king of
Northumbria, had been followed from Iona, where, in his youth,
he had found sanctuary, by Aidan, the apostle of the north, to
whose missionary enterprise was due the conversion of the
rude north Anglian tribes.   The monastery at Streoneshalh, or
Whitby, for ever famous as the home of Caedmon, was ruled
by the abbess Hild in accordance with Celtic, not Roman, usage;
and though, at the synod of Whitby in 664, the unity of the
church in England was assured by the submission of the northern church to Roman rule, yet the influence of Celtic Christianity may be traced in some of the features that most characteristically distinguish Christian from non-Christian poetry.   It
would for instance, be hard to deny that the depth of personal
feeling expressed in a poem like *The Dream of the Rood*, the joy
in colour attested by the vivid painting of blossom and leaf
in *The Phoenix* and the melancholy sense of kinship between
the sorrow of the human heart and the moaning of the grey
cold waves that make *The Seafarer* a human wail, are elements
contributed to English poetry by the Celts.   St. Columba
had built his monastery on the surf-beaten shores of the Atlan-
tic, where man's dependence on nature was an ever-present
reality.   The Celtic monastery was the home of a brotherhood
of priests, and the abbot was the father of a family as well as its
ecclesiastical superior.   The Christian virtues of humility and
meekness, in which the emissaries of the British church found
Augustine so deficient, were valued in Iona above orthodoxy
and correctness of religious observance; and the simplicity of
ecclesiastical organisation characteristic of Celtic Christianity,
differing from the comparatively elaborate nature of Roman
organisation and ritual, produced a simple form of Christianity,
readily understood by the unlettered people of the north.   It is
the personal relation of the soul to God the Father, the human-

ity of Christ, the brotherhood of man, the fellowship of saints, that the Celtic missionaries seem to have preached to their converts; and these doctrines inspired the choicest passages of Old English religious poetry, passages worthy of comparison with some of the best work of a later, more self-conscious and introspective age.

This subjectivity is a new feature in English literature; for most non-Christian English poetry is sternly epic. *Beowulf* is a tale of brave deeds nobly done, with but few reflections concerning them. At rare intervals, scattered here and there throughout the poem, we meet with some touch of sentiment, a foreboding of evil to come, a few words on the inexorable character of fate, an exhortation to do great deeds so that in Walhalla the chosen warrior may fare the better, occasionally a half-Christian reference to an all-ruling Father (probably the addition of a later and Christian hand); but, as a rule, no introspection checks the even flow of narrative: *arma virumque cano*. When Christianity became the source of poetic inspiration, we find the purely epic character of a poem modified by the introduction of a lyric element. The hero no longer aspires to win gold from an earthly king; his prize is a heavenly crown, to be won, it may even be, in spiritual conflict; the glories of life on earth are transitory; earthly valour cannot atone for the stains of sin upon the soul; the beauty of nature, in her fairest aspects, cannot compare with the radiance of a better land; the terror that lurks waiting for the evil-doer upon earth fades away at the contemplation of that day of wrath and mourning when the Judge of all the earth shall deal to every man according to his deeds. The early Christian poet does not sing of earthly love; we have no erotic poetry in pre-Conquest England; but the sentiment that gives life to the poetry of Dante and Milton is not absent from the best of our early poet's attempts at religious self-expression.

Beyond the fact that his name seems to imply that he was of Celtic descent, we have no knowledge of the historical Caedmon other than that to be derived from the often-quoted passage in Bede:

In the monastery of this abbess [*i.e.* the abbess Hild at Streoneshalh] there was a certain brother specially distinguished and honoured by divine grace, for he was wont to make songs such

as tended to religion and piety.   Whatsoever he had learned from
scholars concerning the Scriptures he forthwith decked out in poetic language with the greatest sweetness and fervour. . . .   Many
others, also, in England, imitated him in the composition of religious
songs.   He had not, indeed, been taught of men, or through men,
to practise the art of song, but he had received divine aid, and his
power of song was the gift of God.   Wherefore he could never
compose any idle or false song, but only those which pertained to
religion and which his pious tongue might fitly sing.   The man
had lived in the world till the time that he was of advanced age,
and had never learnt any poetry.   And as he was often at a feast
when it was arranged, to promote mirth, that they should all in turn
sing to the harp, whenever he saw the harp come near him he
arose out of shame from the feast and went home to his house.
Having done so on one occasion, he left the house of entertainment,
and went out to the stables, the charge of the horses having been
committed to him for that night.   When, in due time, he stretched
his limbs on the bed there and fell asleep, there stood by him in a
dream a man who saluted him and greeted him, calling on him by
name,   "Caedmon, sing me something."   Then he answered and
said,   "I cannot sing anything, and therefore I came out from
this entertainment and retired here, as I know not how to sing."
Again he who spoke to him said,   "Yet you could sing."   Then said
Caedmon,   "What shall I sing?"   He said,   "Sing to me the beginning of all things."   On receiving this answer, Caedmon at once
began to sing, in praise of God the Creator, verses and words which
he had never heard, the order of which is as follows [*quorum iste est
sensus*];   "Now let us praise the guardian of the heavenly kingdom,
the power of the Creator and the counsel of His mind, the works
of the Father of glory: how He, the eternal Lord, originated every
marvel.   He, the holy Creator, first created the heaven as a
roof for the children of the earth, then the eternal Lord, guardian
of the human race, the almighty Ruler, afterwards fashioned the
world as a soil for men."   Then he arose from his sleep, and he had
firmly in his memory all that he sang while asleep.   And to these
words he soon added many others, in the same style of song,
worthy of God.   Book iv, ch. 24.   (Trans. Miller.)

Bede goes on to narrate how, the matter having been made
known to the abbess, she caused the best scholars to test the
new poet's powers, and how, when it was proved that a divine
gift had, indeed, been bestowed upon the neat-herd, she urged
him to abandon his worldly calling and become a monk.
Which thing he did, and, progressing in his new vocation,

all that he could learn by listening he pondered in his heart and, ruminating like some clean beast, he turned it into the sweetest of songs. His song and his music were so delightful to hear, that even his teachers wrote down the words from his lips and learnt them. He sang first of the earth's creation and the beginning of man and all the story of Genesis, which is the first book of Moses, and afterwards about the departure of the people of Israel from the land of Egypt and their entry into the land of promise; and about many other narratives in the books of the canon of Scripture; and about Christ's incarnation and His passion and His ascension into heaven; and about the coming of the Holy Ghost, and the teaching of the apostles; and again about the day of judgment to come, and about the terror of hell torment, and about the kingdom of heaven, he composed many a song. And he also composed many others about the divine blessings and judgments.

While making due allowance for a possible desire on Bede's part to extol the fame of an earlier contemporary—Bede himself died in 735—we should remember that Bede is one of the most careful and trustworthy of historians, and that he lived not far from the scene of Caedmon's life; it would, therefore, appear that we have not sufficient reason for rejecting as untrue the enumeration of Caedmon's literary achievements as given in the above passage.

The hymn as first published in its Northumbrian form[1] by Wanley in his *Catalogus historico-criticus* (1705), p 287, as *canticum illud Saxonicum Caedmonis a Baeda memoratum;* and from that day to this it has been regarded by the majority of scholars as the genuine work of Caedmon.

Bede gives a Latin version of the lines, which corresponds very closely to the original, but which he introduces thus. *Caedmon coepit cantare. . . versus quorum iste est sensus;* and, in conclusion, he reiterates: *Hic est sensus, non autem ordo ipse verborum,* as if he had given a merely approximate rendering of his original. Much discussion has hinged upon the exact meaning to be attached to the words *sensus* and *ordo,* though Bede is evidently alluding merely to the difficulty of reproducing poetry in prose, for he continues: *neque enim possunt carmina quamvis optime composita, ex alia in aliam linguam ad verbum sine detrimento sui decoris ac dignitatis transferri.* The West Saxon version of the lines is preserved in the English translation

[1] See Cambridge Univ. MS. Lib. Kk, 5, 16, Fol. 128.

of Bede's *Ecclesiastical History*,[1] with the introductory comment: "þara endebyrdnis þis is." Now "endebyrdnis" simply
means *ordo*, and it may be safe to assume that both Bede's
Latin version and the West Saxon version are attempts at
translation from the original Northumbrian.

Bede's detailed enumeration of Caedmon's other achievements must be held responsible for the attribution to Caedmon
of a large number of religious poems of a similar character
extant only in West Saxon form, in the Bodl. MS. Junius XI, an
opinion which, in the light of modern critical scholarship, is no
longer tenable. Indeed, no one would to-day seriously maintain even that these poems are all by one author; it is more
likely, as we shall see, that more than one writer has had a hand
in each. But the fact that it is impossible to claim these particular poems for Caedmon does not militate against the probability of his having composed similar, though, perhaps, shorter
pieces, which may have been worked upon later by more scholarly hands. Religious poetry, sung to the harp as it passed
from hand to hand, must have flourished in the monastery of the
abbess Hild, and the kernel of Bede's story concerning the birth
of our earliest poet must be that the brethren and sisters on
that bleak northern shore spoke "to each other in psalms and
hymns and spiritual songs."

The most important of the religious poems at one time attributed to Caedmon are *Genesis*, *Exodus*, *Daniel*.

From the point of view of the historian of literature, *Genesis*
is the most interesting of these. It is a poetical paraphrase of
the first of the canonical books in the Old Testament, extending
to the story of the sacrifice of Isaac by Abraham. The poem
opens with the praise of the Creator in a style recalling the
lines quoted by Bede. The poet then proceeds to relate the
revolt and fall of the angels (which, according to ancient theology, necessitated the creation of man to fill the vacant place
in heaven), and then the creation of the earth, in accordance
with the opening chapters of the *Vulgate*. At this point we
have a repetition of the first *motif*, the fall of the angels; Satan,
in anger at having fallen from his high estate, avenges himself
on God by tempting man; and the rest of the narrative proceeds
in accordance with the Biblical narrative.

[1] Cf. *post*, Chapter VI.

Attention has been drawn to metrical and linguistic peculiarities distinguishing the second version (*Genesis* B) of the fall of the angels and the temptation (ll. 235–851) from the rest of the poem; but it remained for Sievers to point out that this obviously interpolated passage was borrowed from a foreign source, that the structure of the alliterative lines resembled that in vogue amongst continental Saxons, and that the vocabulary and syntax were now and again Old Saxon, not English. Relying upon the accuracy of his observation in detail, he then hazarded the bold conjecture that these lines were an Anglicised version of a portion of an Old Saxon paraphrase of the Old Testament, long lost, composed by the author of the Old Saxon paraphrase of the New Testament, commonly known as the *Heliand*. This brilliant conjecture has since been confirmed by the discovery in the Vatican library of portions of the Old Saxon original, which dates from the latter portion of the ninth century.[1] One of the Old Saxon fragments so found corresponded to a passage in the Old English *Genesis*. Caedmonian authorship is, therefore rendered impossible for the interpolation, and the scholarship of the author seems to preclude the possibility that an unlearned man was the author of the rest of the poem, though Caedmon's hymns may have been familiar to, and used by, the writer. It matters little whether we assume the interpolated passage to be the work of an Old Saxon monk resident in England, but unable to dissociate himself entirely from native habits of speech, or whether we look upon it as a somewhat imperfect translation from Old Saxon by some Old English monk whom professional duties—we need only think of Boniface—had brought into contact with the learning and literature of the continent. At any rate it is an early, and a pleasing, instance of the fruitful exchange of literary ideas between two great nations.

The relative age of the two poems is a matter still under discussion. *Genesis* B cannot have been composed earlier than the second half of the ninth century, since we know that the author of the *Heliand*, upon whose work it is based, wrote in response to a command from King Lewis the Pious; but we have hardly any data for determining whether it is earlier or later in date of composition than *Genesis* A. Its author, like the

[1] Cf. the Latin *Praefatio* prefixed to the *Heliand*.

author of the *Heliand*, apparently made use of the works of bishop Avitus of Vienne, the medieval Latin poet.

Genesis A contains not a few passages illustrative of that blending of heathen and Christian elements which is characteristic of Old English religious poetry. The description of Old Testament fights shows that the spirit of the author of the *Battle of Finnsburh* is to be found beneath the veneer of Christianity. And, on the other hand, the description of the dove, seeking rest and finding none, could only be the work of a Christian poet. The tenderness of feeling for the dumb creation and the joy in "rest after toil" which it expresses are due to Christian influences upon the imaginative powers of an Old English scop.

Genesis B contains some fine poetic passages. The character of Satan is admirably conceived, and the familiar theme of a lost paradise is set forth in dignified and dramatic language not unworthy of the height of its great argument. In the dark regions and "swart mists" of Hell, Satan and his host, swept thither by the Lord of Heaven himself, indulge in a joy that is purely heathen, in contemplating the vengeance to be taken on the race that has supplanted them in the favour of God.[1]

Exodus is a paraphrase of a portion only of the book from which it takes its name, *i.e.* the passage of the Israelites through the Red Sea and the destruction of the Egyptians. Part of the poem,[2] in which the ancestors of the Israelites are enumerated and described, is, possibly, the work of a second poet, as it is simpler in style than the body of the poem, and the theme is not entirely relevant; there is certainly a break after l. 445. The distinctive feature of the poem is the beauty and vigour with which martial scenes are depicted. Here, again, the feeling of the old epic writers, under another guise, is clearly apparent. Not even in *Judith* or *The Battle of Maldon* do we find more successful attempts in dramatic grouping; the din and clash of battle, though no actual battle is described, the war-wolf and the raven greedy for prey, the heaving of the shields, the brandishing of battle-bills, recall the martial tone of the best war-poetry

---

[1] For a discussion of the possible relation between the Satan of *Genesis* B and the Satan of *Paradise Lost*, cf. Stopford Brooke, *Early English Literature*, vol. II, pp. 101 ff., and Morley, *English Writers*, vol. II, p. 109.

[2] Ll. 362–445.

of our battle-loving ancestors. The author of *Genesis* A writes as though afraid to depart even from the wording of his original; the author of *Exodus*, possessed by the lust for word-painting, draws upon an exuberant imagination steeped in reminiscences of brave blows and doughty deeds, not even nominally Christian.

The poem entitled *Daniel* need not detain us. After a historical introduction, for which the poet is not indebted to his source, he versifies selected portions of the book of *Daniel*.[1] The poem has one new feature. The author uses his material for homiletic purposes and inculcates certain moral virtues: for instance, the duty of humility and obedience to the will of God. *Daniel* is transmitted in the Junian codex. A portion of the subject, dealing with the episode of the three children in the fiery furnace, is transmitted also in the *Exeter Book*, in a short poem of 75 lines called *Azarias*, in which are the beautiful lines descriptive of the change wrought by the appearance of the angel of the Lord:

> Then 'twas in the oven when the angel came,
> Windy cool and winsome, to the weather likest
> When is sent to earth in the summer tide,
> Dropping down of dew-rain at the dawn of day.[2]

Three Minor poems, originally thought to be one, and by Grein called *Crist and Satan*, should be mentioned here, since, by reason of their being transmitted in the codex MS. Bodl. xi, they, together with the three more important poems just discussed, have been attributed to Caedmon. The first of them deals with the subject of the *Fall of the Angels*, the second with *Christ's Harrowing of Hell* and His resurrection, together with a brief account of His ascension and coming to judgment, the third with Christ's *Temptation*. Only the first is complete. All three, probably, belong to the end of the ninth century and all have a homiletic tendency. The second has been compared with the *Crist* of Cynewulf with which it is linked by virtue of theme as well as by style. The description of the last judgment suggests the more impressive picture of that event contained in *Crist*, and the *Harrowing of Hell* recalls, and can sustain

[1] Up to chapter v., 22. [2] Stopford Brooke's version.

comparison with, examp'es of later more elaborate treatment of
the same subject. By their religious fervour, and by their
apparently ruder form, it is possible that these poems are nearer
to the original body of Caedmon's work than the poems previously discussed.

The finest of all the poems erroneously attributed to Caedmon is the fragment entitled *Judith*. As there seems to be
ground for supposing that this beautiful fragment, worthy of
the skill of a scop whose Christianity had not sufficed to quell
his martial instincts, his pride in battle and his manly prowess,
is of later date than has been thought by certain historians, it is
dealt with in a later chapter of the present volume.

Turning to Cynewulf and the poems that may be, or have
been, attributed to him, we are on somewhat safer ground.
The personality of the poet is, indeed, wrapped in an obscurity
hardly less deep than that which hides Caedmon. The only
truth at which we can arrive concerning him is that he must be
the author of four well-known poems, since he marked them
as his own by the insertion of his signature in runes. Conjecture has been busy to prove that he may have been identical
with a certain abbot of Peterborough, who lived about the
year 1000. But this hypothesis has ceased to be tenable since
we know that the West Saxon transcript of his poems, the only
form in which the accredited ones are preserved, cannot be the
original; moreover, the abbot invariably spelt his name Cin-
wulf. Equally impossible is the theory that he was Cynewulf,
bishop of Lindisfarne, who died in 781 or 783. The later lived
in troublous times, and nothing we know of his life agrees with
inferences we may reasonably draw from autobiographical
allusions in Cynewulf's poems. A theory that the author was
certainly of Northumbrian origin was, in the first instance,
based upon an erroneous interpretation of the first riddle in
a collection of Old English *Riddles* long attributed to him.
Dietrich gave the solution as Coenwulf, the supposed Northumbrian form of the name Cynewulf. But, apart from the
fact that syllabic riddles are not known in Old English literature, we must remember that, on the four occasions when the
poet spelt his own name, he used one or other of two forms, *i.e.*
Cynewulf or Cynwulf. Both these forms must go back to an
older one in which the medial *e* appeared as *i*. In Northumbria,

this medial *i* became *e*, roughly speaking, about 800; in Mercia the transition was practically accomplished by 750. This fact lends colour to the hypothesis of Wülker that Cynewulf was a Mercian, a theory which A. S. Cook has adopted in support of a conjecture of his own, namely, that the poet was a certain Cynulf, an ecclesiastic who was present, as his signature to a decree proves, at a synod held at Clovesho in 803. The synod was an important one, in so far as at it the archbishop of Canterbury was recognised as primate of the English church. Cynulf's signature, following close upon that of the bishop of Dunwich, leads A. S. Cook to the further assumption that he was a priest in the diocese of Dunwich, where he would have ample opportunity for studying those sea-effects the description of which is so characteristic of his poetry. Whether or not Cynewulf is to be identified with this ecclesiastic, there is no doubt that the assumption of Mercian origin would do away with one or two difficulties which the assumption of Northumbrian origin in the narrower sense leaves unsolved. During the latter half of the eighth century, Northumbria was, politically, too troubled to be a "kindly nurse" of letters, though, on the other hand, it might be asserted that the political unrest of Northumbria may be reflected in the melancholy nature and "autumnal grace" of Cynewulf's poetry. Again, though there is no doubt that a Mercian origin would facilitate the transcription of poems into West Saxon, yet we have West Saxon transcripts of other originally Northumbrian poems, a fact which affects the value of geographical arguments of this nature.

The most valid, albeit negative, argument against taking the term Northumbrian to mean simply non-West Saxon, hence, possibly, Mercian, is that we have no definite evidence for the existence of a Mercian school of poetry, such as the development of a poet like Cynewulf seems to postulate. His undisputed work is of too mature a character to seem to be the spontaneous product of a self-made singer, unfostered by literary society. Moreover, he excels more especially in descriptions of the sea and the sea-coast, a point in which a dweller inland might easily have been deficient. Notable in this respect are *Elene*, which we know to be his, and *Andreas*, which is very possibly his. The following lines, for instance, must surely be the work of one whose daily life had been spent in contact with the sea:

> Over the sea marges
> Hourly urged they on . . . the wave-riding horses.
> Then they let o'er Fifel's wave foaming stride along
> Steep-stemmed rushers of the sea.   Oft withstood the bulwark,
> O'er the surging of the waters, swinging strokes of waves.[1]

Further, assuming *Guthlac* B to be by Cynewulf,[2] we may note the fact that the fen-journey of the original has been transformed into a sea-voyage, and this would appear to tell against an East Anglian authorship.

The final result of much discussion seems to resolve itself into this: that Cynewulf was not a West Saxon, but, probably, a Northumbrian, though Mercian origin is not impossible; and that he wrote towards the end of the eighth century.   This latter point will find further support when we proceed to discuss the indvidual poems.

We know nothing else concerning Cynewulf with any degree of certainty.   We infer from the nature of his poetry that he was of a deeply religious nature, but it is hazardous to deduce the character of a poet from his apparently subjective work; we learn that he lived to an old age, which he felt to be a burden; that, at some time of his life, he had known the favour of princes and enjoyed the gifts of kings; he must have been the thegn or scop of some great lord, and not merely an itinerant singer or gleeman, as some critics have held.   He was a man of learning, certainly a good Latin scholar, for some of his work is based upon Latin originals.   Critics are not agreed as to the period of life in which he occupied himself with the composition of religious poetry, nor as to the chronological order of his works. Some scholars assume that, after leading until old age the life of a man of the world, and attaining some distinction as an author of secular poetry—of which, by the way, if the *Riddles* are rejected, we have no trace—he became converted by the vision described in *The Dream of the Rood*, and devoted himself ever afterwards to religious poetry, the last consummate effort of his poetic powers being *Elene*.   There are two drawbacks

---

[1] Stopford Brooke's version.   [2] See p. 64.

to this theory, the first being that we cannot base biographical deductions with any certainty upon a poem like *The Dream of the Rood*, which we have no historical grounds for claiming as Cynewulf's; the second, that it is difficult to assume that a man advanced in years could have composed so large a quantity of religious poetry as, even after the most rigid exclusion of the unlikely, we are compelled to attribute to him. Other critics hold that *The Dream of the Rood* was followed immediately by *Elene*, and that all other Cynewulfian poems were written later. If that be so, the poet's art must have undergone very rapid deterioration, for all the other poems attributed to him are inferior to *Elene* and *The Dream*.

The poems marked as Cynewulf's own by the insertion of runes are *Crist, Juliana, The Fates of the Apostles* and *Elene*. *Crist* is the first poem in the codex known as the *Exeter Book*, a manuscript preserved in the cathedral library at Exeter. The first eight pages, and, consequently, the opening portion of *Crist*, are missing. The manuscript probably dates from the eleventh century and is, apparently, written throughout by one and the same hand. *Juliana* is contained in the same book, and, of other poems attributed to Cynewulf, and certainly belonging to his school, *Guthlac, Andreas* and *The Phoenix* will be mentioned below.

Crist falls into three clearly defined parts, the first dealing with the advent of Christ on earth, the second with His ascension, the third with His second advent to judge the world. The second part contains Cynewulf's signature in runes.[1] The unity of the poem has not remained unquestioned. Scholars have brought forward linguistic and metrical arguments to prove that we are dealing not with one but with three poems; that source, theme and treatment differ so greatly as to render the assumption of a common authorship for all three incredible, and to reduce us to the necessity of denying authorship by Cynewulf to any but the second part, which is signed by him. Almost the best argument brought forward by these iconoclastic critics is the undoubted fact that Cynewulf's signature occurs, as a rule, near the conclusion of a poem, not in the middle, and that it does so occur towards the end of the second part. A further valid argument against the unity of the poem might be

[1] Ll. 797 ff.

derived from the theme of the second part. This deals with
Christ's reception in Heaven after His sojourn on earth, and
only by some stretch of imagination can the event be looked
upon as parallel to His twofold coming on earth. Yet critics
have discovered a link with the first part in a passage definitely
referring to Christ's first advent,[1] and the references to the last
judgment in the runic passage have been regarded as an antici-
pation of the third part. The question is a nice one and is not,
at present, capable of solution. If we assume the unity of the
poem, Cynewulf is, undoubtedly, the author; if we deny it, we
are confronted with the further difficulty of determining the
authorship of the first and third parts. From a literary point
of view, *Crist* is, perhaps, the most interesting of Cynewulf's
poems. It illustrates fully the influence of Latin Christianity
upon English thought. The subject is derived from Latin
homilies and hymns: part I, the advent of Christ, seems to be
largely based upon the *Roman Breviary*, part II upon the ascension sermon of Pope Gregory, part III upon an alphabetic Latin
hymn on the last judgment, quoted by Bede in *De Arte Metrica*.
In addition, the Gospel of St. Matthew and Gregory's tenth
homily have furnished suggestions. Yet the poet is no mere
versifier of Latin theology. We are confronted, for the first
time in English literature, with the product of an original
mind. The author has transmuted the material derived from
his sources into the passionate out-pourings of personal religious
feeling. The doctrines interspersed are, of course, medieval
in tone: one of the three signs by which the blessed shall realise
their possession of God's favour is the joy they will derive from
the contemplation of the sufferings of the damned. But, for
the most part, the poem is a series of choric hymns of praise,
of imaginative passages descriptive of visions not less sublime
than that of *The Dream of the Rood.*

Crist is followed immediately in the *Exeter Book* by the poem
entitled *Juliana*. This is an Old English version of the *Acta S.
Julianae virginis martyris*. The proof of Cynewulfian authorship lies, as has already been said, in the insertion of his name
in runes. The martyr is supposed to have lived about the time
of the emperor Maximian. She, of course, successfully over-

[1] Ll. 586–599.

comes all the minor temptations with which she is confronted, including an offer of marriage with a pagan, and, finally, having routed the devil in person, endures martyrdom by the sword.

Equally insignificant considered as poetry, but of the utmost importance as a link in a chain of literary evidence, are the lines known as *The Fates of the Apostles*. The title sufficiently indicates the contents. The poem is preserved in the *Vercelli Book;* a codex containing both verse and prose, and, for some unknown reason, in the possession of the chapter of Vercelli, north Italy. The first ninety-five lines, which follow immediately after the poem called *Andreas*, occupy fol. 52 b–53 b. They were considered an anonymous fragment until Napier discovered that a set of verses on fol. 54 a, which had hitherto been assumed to have no connection with the lines preceding them, were, in reality, a continuation of the lines on fol. 53 and that they contained the name of Cynewulf in runes. The authenticity of *Fata Apostolorum* was, thereby, raised above dispute; but the gain to Cynewulf's literary reputation was not great.

Yet critics, anxious to vindicate the claim of our greatest pre-Conquest poet to whatever poetry may seem worthy of him, have tried to twist the occurrence of Cynewulf's signature in *The Fates of the Apostles* into an additional plea in favour of his authorship of *Andreas*, the poem immediately preceding it in the *Vercelli Book*. This poem deals with the missionary labours of St. Andrew, and is based, probably, upon a lost Latin version of a Greek original (in Paris), the Πράξεις 'Ανδρέου καὶ Ματθαίου. St. Andrew is commanded by God to go to the assistance of St. Matthew, who is in danger of death at the hands of the Mermedonians, cannibal Ethiopians. He sets out in a boat manned by our Lord and two angels. Having landed safely, he becomes of great spiritual comfort to the captive, but is himself taken prisoner and tortured. He delivers himself and converts the Mermedonians by working a miracle. The distinguishing feature of the poem, which links it with passages in *Beowulf* and *The Seafarer*, is the skill with which its author gives expression to his passion for the sea. *Andreas* is a romance of the sea. Nowhere else are to be found such superb descriptions of the raging storm, of the successful struggle of man with the powers of the deep. It illustrates, moreover, in an unusual degree, the blending of the old spirit with the new. St. Andrew, though professedly a Christian saint, is, in reality, a viking; though crusader in name he is more truly a seafarer on adventure bent. The Christ he serves is an aetheling, the apostles are folctogan—captains of the people—and temporal victory, not merely spiritual triumph, is the goal.

Could it be proved that *The Fates of the Apostles* is merely an epilogue to the longer poem preceding it, the adventures of one of the twelve being related in greater detail than is vouchsafed to them treated collectively, we should be enabled to attribute with greater certainty than is otherwise possible the poem of *Andreas* to Cynewulf, an author of whom, on aesthetic grounds, it is not unworthy. Its authenticity would then be vouched for by the runic signature contained in the shorter poem. This hypothesis is, however, more ingenious than convincing. The poem *Andreas*, as it stands, lacks, indeed, as definite a conclusion as many other poems possess; there is, for instance, no *finit* or "amen" to denote the end, but, unfortunately for the inventors of the hypothesis, *The Fates of the Apostles* does not lack a beginning; nor are St Andrew's labours omitted from the general review of the good works done by the twelve, which might possibly have been expected had the author of *The Fates of the Apostles* also been the author of the longer history of St. Andrew. There is more ground for accepting a theory originated by Sievers with regard to the last sixteen lines of the fragment containing Cynewulf's signature, discovered by Napier. In the opinion of Sievers these sixteen lines would not only be an inordinately lengthy conclusion to so short a poem as *The Fates*, but they are superfluous in so far as they are a mere repetition of the lines which had preceded the runic passage. He would, therefore, wish to see in them the conclusion of some lost poem of Cynewulf, and only accidentally attached to *The Fates of the Apostles*. Upholders of the theory of the Cynewulfian authorship of *Andreas* might be able to claim them as the missing conclusion to that poem, and the fact of their being attached to a piece of undoubtedly Cynewulfian work might strengthen the attribution of *Andreas* to our poet. But, after fully weighing the arguments on either side, we must confess that the evidence so far forthcoming does not suffice for a satisfactory solution of the question.

Elene is, undoubtedly, Cynewulf's masterpiece. The subject is contained in the *Acta Sanctorum* of 4 May. Grimm also referred to the same subject as occurring in the *Legenda aurea* of Jacobus a Voragine. It is impossible to decide whether the legend first reached England in a Latin or in an older Greek form. The story is that of the discovery of the true cross by Helena, the mother of the emperor Constantine. The search carried to so successful a conclusion was instituted by the emperor in consequence of the famous vision, the sign of a cross in the sky bearing the inscription *In hoc signo vinces*. Much history hangs upon this tale. Its immediate importance for us is that the conversion of the emperor by this means became the starting-point for the adoration of the cross: the symbol which had hitherto been one of ignominy became one of triumph and glory. The festival of the exaltation of the cross was established in the western church in 701, in consequence of the supposed discovery in Rome of a particle of the true cross. This event is duly recorded by Bede in *De sex aetatibus saeculi*, the news having, no doubt, been brought to England by Abbot Ceolfrid, who was in Rome at the time. At any rate, if this event be considered too remote to have influenced Cynewulf's choice of a subject, we may remember that he probably lived through a part of the iconoclastic controversy which raged from 726 to 842, and which contributed perhaps more than anything else to an increased veneration of the cross. Indeed, the poetry of the cross in England has been regarded as the first-fruit of the impetus given to its worship by the condemnation of the worship of all other symbols. The two festivals of the cross, the invention on 3 May and the exaltation on 14 September, were both observed in the old English church.

Cynewulf's poem on Helena's search for the true cross is contained in fourteen cantos or "fitts." It is written in a simple, dramatic style, interspersed with imaginative and descriptive passages of great beauty. The glamour and pomp of war, the gleam of jewels, the joy of ships dancing on the waves, give life and colour to a narrative permeated by the deep and serious purpose of the author. The fifteenth fitt, superfluous from the point of view of the story, is valuable as documentary evidence bearing on the poet's personality. It contains not only his signature in runes, but is a "fragment of a great confession," unveiling to us the manner of the man to whom the cross became salvation.

"I am old," he says, "and ready to depart, having woven word-craft and pondered deeply in the darkness of the world. Once I was gay in the hall and received gifts, appled gold and treasures. Yet was I buffeted with care, fettered by sins, beset with sorrows, until the Lord of all might and power bestowed on me grace and revealed to me the mystery of the holy cross. Now know I that the joys of life are fleeting, and that the Judge of all the world is at hand to deal to every man his doom."

Two useful deductions may be made from this passage. In the first place, the poet was evidently advanced in age when he composed this poem, a point already alluded to; in the second, he ascribes his conversion to a true understanding of the cross. In other poems, notably *Crist*, Cynewulf reveals an almost equal veneration for the symbol of man's redemption.

But the poem which, above all others, betrays the spirit of tender yet passionate veneration, of awe and adoration for " the wondrous cross on which the Prince of glory died," is *The Dream of the Rood*. It is transmitted to us in a West Saxon form in the *Vercelli Book*, and portions of it are to be found carved in runes on the Ruthwell cross in Dumfriesshire.[1]   The poem is now claimed as Cynewulf's by probably the majority of English scholars, though it is possible that he worked on older material. At the same time, we have none but aesthetic evidence to go upon. A resemblance has been fancied or detected between the reference to the cross in the concluding portion of *Elene* discussed above and the subject and treatment of this

[1]In addition there is cut upon the cross an inscription which was interpreted to mean "Caedmon made me," and, upon this supposed signature, was based the attribution of *The Dream of the Rood* to Caedmon. The inscription, if decipherable at all, may have been the sculptor's autograph. In no case could it, apparently, be a reference to the poet Caedmon, for the language of the poem on the Ruthwell cross is younger than that of the MS. poem, possibly of the tenth century. The decoration of the cross, also, is thought to be too elaborate and ornate for eighth century work and can hardly be dated much earlier than the tenth century. See Chapter II *ante* and the bibliography to that chapter, especially the writings of Victor and A. S. Cook, *The Dream of the Rood*.

A somewhat similar, though very short, example of an inscription in the first person is preserved on a cross at Brussels :—

Rod is min nama : ʒeo ic ricne cyninʒ
baer byfiʒende, blode bestemed.

poem. It would be possible to overrate the value of this coincidence. References to the cross are frequent in both prose and verse. They need prove nothing beyond the undoubtedly early custom of the adoration. At the same time, the two poems have much in common: the character of the intimate self-revelation contained in each, the elegiac tone of the reflections on the transitoriness of the world and the sinfulness of man, the phraseology and syntactical structure are alike to a degree which makes the Cynewulfian authorship of both more than probable. *The Dream of the Rood* is the choicest blossom of Old English Christian poetry; religious feeling has never been more exquisitely clothed than in these one hundred and forty lines of alliterative verse. It is full of imaginative power and enters deeply into the mysteries of sin and of sorrow. We have no other instance of a dream-poem in pre-Conquest England, though Bede relates several visions. The poet dreamt a dream and in it saw the holy rood decked with gems and shining gloriously. Angels guarded it, and, at its sight, the singer was afeared, for he was stained with guilt. As he watched, the tree changed colour; anon it was adorned with treasure, anon stained with gore; and, as he watched, it spoke, and told the story of the crucifixion, the descent from the cross, the resurrection. This conception of the cross as being gifted with power of speech lends a charm to the poem. The address is followed by the poet's reflection on what he has seen: the cross shall be henceforth his confidence and help. The concluding ten lines of the poem seem superfluous and are possibly a later accretion. The theme concludes with line 146. The characteristic opening of the poem may be noted. As in *Beowulf*, *Andreas*, *Exodus* and other poems the singer arrests the attention of his hearers by the exclamation: "Hwaet!"=Lo, comparable to the "Listneth, lordings" of the later minstrels. The device must have been a common one in days when the harp was struck at festive gatherings and the scop urged his claim to a hearing by a preliminary chord.

We must pass on to other poems that have, with more or less show of reason, been attributed to Cynewulf. Of these, the longest is the life of the Mercian saint Guthlac. It falls into two parts, the first, apparently, having been composed during the lifetime of the anchorite who is the subject of the poem, the

second being based upon the Latin *Vita* by Felix of Croyland.
The main question that has been discussed has been whether
both parts are by one and the same author or not, and whether
Cynewulf can lay claim to one or both parts. If only one part
can be attributed to him it should be part II (*Guthlac* B). Since
the conclusion to this part is missing, it may, conceivably, have
contained Cynewulf's signature in runes. There is no gap in
the MS. between the conclusion of *Crist* and the beginning of
Guthlac, and Gollancz has assumed that the passage commonly
read as the conclusion of *Crist* (ll. 1666–1694) really forms the
introduction to *Guthlac*. These lines are, no doubt, superfluous as regards *Crist*, but they are yet more unsuitable considered
as an introduction to *Guthlac*, which begins, quite appropriately,
with a common epic formula "Monze sindon" (cf. the opening
of *The Phoenix*). It would be better to assume them to be a
fragment of some independent poem on the joys of the blessed.

The death of Guthlac is related in lines full of strength and
beauty. The writer has entered into the spirit of the last great
struggle with the powers of darkness and death, even as Bunyan
did when he related the passage of Christian through the Valley
of the Shadow of Death. The wondrous light that shines over
Guthlac's hut before he dies irresistibly recalls the waving
lights in the sky familiar to every northerner, and when we
read that, at the saint's entry into the heavenly mansions, the
whole land of England trembled with rapture, we feel that,
whether Cynewulf wrote the poem or not, we are in the presence
of a poet who does not lack imaginative power of a high order.

The Phoenix has been attributed to Cynewulf by a large
number of competent critics. The first portion of it is based
upon a Latin poem attributed to Lactantius, and there is some
ground for assuming Cynewulf's acquaintance with that Latin
author, since a copy of the book was contained in Alcuin's library at York, and Cynewulf may very well have been a scholar
in the school at York.[1] The second part of the poem, the allegorical application of the myth to Christ, is based on the writings
of Ambrose and Bede. The characteristic feature of the poem
is its love of colour and wealth of gorgeous descriptive epithets.
Especially noteworthy, in this respect, is the description of the
land where the phoenix dwells:

[1] Cook, *Christ*, p. lxiv.

Winsome is the wold there; there the wealds are green,
Spacious spread below the skies; there may neither snow nor rain,
Nor the furious air of frost, nor the flare of fire,
Nor the headlong squall of hail, nor the hoar-frost's fall,
Nor the burning of the sun, nor the bitter cold,
Nor the weather over-warm, nor the winter shower,
Do their wrong to any wight—but the wold abides
Ever happy, healthful there.[1]

This passage illustrates not only the feeling of English poets towards nature, but also the development that took place in consequence of the influence of Latin letters. The Northumbrian poets were not unskilled in the depiction of scenes with which they were familiar; but in *The Phoenix* we have, for the first time, a poet attempting, under literary influence, and with an obviously conscious striving after artistic effect, to paint an ideal landscape, the beauty and gentleness of summer climes, the wealth of tropical nature, the balminess of a softer air, where there shall be no more, or only a sun-lit-sea, unlike the sullen gloom of the northern waters.

The conclusion of the poem is of an unusual kind. It consists of eleven lines in a mixture of English and Latin, the first half of each line being English, the second half Latin, the Latin alliterating with the English.

Portions of an Old English *Physiologus* have also been attributed to Cynewulf. Allegorical bestiaries were a favourite form of literature from the fifth century down to the Middle Ages. They consisted of descriptions of certain beasts, birds and fishes which were considered capable of an allegorical significance. The allegorical meaning was always attached to the description, much as a moral is appended to a fable. The development of this form of literature was due to the fondness for animal symbolism characteristic of early Christian art. Only three specimens of such descriptions are extant in Old English literature. They deal with the panther, the whale and the partridge. The panther is complete, there is a gap in the description of the whale, of the partridge there is hardly sufficient to prove that the bird described was really a partridge. It is uncertain whether these pieces were merely isolated attempts at imitation of a foreign model or whether they formed part of a

[1] Stopford Brooke's version.

complete Old English *Physiologus*. Two somewhat divergent texts of a Latin *Physiologus* (B and C), belonging to the ninth century, have been discovered. The resemblance between the Latin text and the Old English is fairly striking in B where, after twenty-two other animals have been described, we have the panther, the whale and the partridge; probably both Old English and Latin versions are derived from a common source. The panther, as usual, is symbolical of Christ, and the whale, which lures seafarers to moor their "ocean-mares" to it, thinking its back an island, represents the "accuser of the brethren" and its gaping mouth is the gate of Hell.

The assumption that the first of a series of Old English *Riddles*, 95 in all, was a charade meaning Cynewulf, or Coenwulf, caused the collection to be attributed to him. These riddles are transmitted in the *Exeter Book*. They are closely connected with similar collections of Latin riddles, more especially one by Aldhelm. Aldhelm's work is based upon that of the fifth century Latin poet Symphosius, and Aldhelm was the first English writer to acclimatise the Latin riddle in England. Forty riddles by Archbishop Tatwine, which were expanded by Eusebius to the number of 100, are also extant. The author of the Old English riddles derived most of his inspiration from Aldhelm, but he also seems to have gone direct to Symphosius and to have made some slight use of the work of Eusebius and Tatwine.

The theory that the solution of the first riddle was the name Coenwulf, *i.e.* Cynewulf, was refuted by Trautmann, in 1883, and, later, by Sievers, on linguistic and other grounds.

The peculiarly English tone and character of the riddles is, in some measure, due to Aldhelm's example. For, though he wrote in Latin, his style differentiates his work from that of the Latin authors, and accounts for the popularity this form of literature acquired in England. Furthermore, the author or authors of the Old English riddles borrow themes from native folk-song and saga; in their hands inanimate objects become endowed with life and personality; the powers of nature become objects of worship such as they were in olden times; they describe the scenery of their own country, the fen, the river, and the sea, the horror of the untrodden forest, sun and moon engaged in perpetual pursuit of each other, the nightingale and the swan, the plough guided by the "grey-haired enemy of the wood," the bull breaking up the clods left unturned by the plough, the falcon, the arm-companion of aethelings—scenes, events, characters familiar in the England of that day. Riddle XLI, *De Creatura*, and Riddle IX, on the Nightingale, which are subjects taken from Aldhelm, may be compared with the Latin versions to prove how far the more imaginative English poet was from being a mere imitator, and the storm and iceberg riddles breathe the old northern and viking spirit. Riddle XXXVI is also preserved in Northumbrian in a MS. at Leyden.

The most varied solutions have, from time to time, been suggested for some of the riddles, and the meaning of many is by no means clear. The most recent attempt at a solution of the first riddle has been made by Scofieid and Gollancz. They see in this short poem an Old English monodrama in five acts, wherein a lady boasts of fidelity to her lover, but, during his absence, proves faithless and lives to endure the vengeance of her husband in the loss of her child.

We may note, in conclusion, a group of minor poems which have one characteristic feature in common, namely, the note of personal religion; they are, for the most part, lyric or didactic in character, dealing with the soul's need of redemption. Of these, the *Death Song* attributed to Bede by his pupil Cuthbert, who gives an approximate Latin rendering of it,[1] is preserved in a Northumbrian version in a MS. at St. Gall and belongs to the same period as Caedmon's *Hymn*.

One of the most interesting of the group is the *Address of the Lost Soul to the Body*, a frequent theme in later literature. It is one of the very few Old English poems preserved in two versions, one in the *Exeter*, the other in the *Vercelli Book*. In the latter codex is contained a fragment of a very rare theme, the *Address of the Saved Soul to the Body*. A poem on the day of doom is transmitted in the *Exeter Book*. It is a general admonition to lead a godly, righteous and sober life, after the fashion of many similar warnings in later literature.

A group of four short poems, of which three are preserved in the *Exeter Book*, deal with attributes common to mankind: The *Gifts of Men* (Bi monna craeftum)—based, largely, upon the 29th homily of Pope Gregory, and, hence, sometimes

[1] Epistola Cuðberti ad Cuðwinum.

attributed to Cynewulf; the *Fates of Men* (Bi manna wyrdum), which, though allied in theme to the previous poem, differs very considerably from it in treatment; the *Mind of Man* (Bi manna mode) and the *Falsehood of Man* (Bi manna lease), which may be described as poetical homilies.

The *Riming Poem* is a solitary instance of the occurrence in English poetry of the consistent use of end-rime and alliteration in one and the same poem. The theme "sorrow's crown of sorrows is remembering happier things" recalls the epilogue to *Elene*, but the resemblance is not sufficiently striking to justify the attribution of the poem to Cynewulf. The metrical form is an accurate imitation of the *Hoefuðlausn* of Egill Skallagríms-son, which was composed in Northumberland at the court of Aethelstan.

It is generally thought that gnomic or didactic poetry, which seems to have been very popular during the Old English period, had its origin in the religious exercises of heathen times. Certainly it is well represented in the mythological poems of the *Edda*, whether we take the proverb form, as in the first part of *Hávamál*, or the form of question and answer, as in *Vafþrúðn-ismál* and other poems. Old English proverbs are, however, almost entirely deprived of heathen colouring. One collection, amounting altogether to 206 lines in three sections, is preserved in the *Exeter Book*, and another, containing 66 lines, serves as a preface to one of the texts of the *Chronicle*. The proverbs in the two collections are of much the same kind, giving, in each case, the chief characteristic of the thing mentioned, *e.g.* "frost shall freeze," or "a king shall have government." Generally, however, they run into two or more lines, beginning and ending in the middle, so that the whole collection has the form of a connected poem. In this class of literature we may, perhaps, also include *A Father's Instruction*, a poem consisting of ten moral admonitions (94 lines in all) addressed by a father to his son somewhat after the nature of the *Proverbs* of Solomon. In form, it may be compared with *Sigrdrífumál* and the last part of *Hávamál*, but the matter is very largely Christian. Mention must also be made of *The Runic Poem*, which, likewise, has Scandinavian parallels. Each of the letters of the runic alphabet had its own name, which was also the word for some animal, plant or other article, *e.g.* riches, buffalo, thorn; and it is the properties of these which the poem describes, allotting three or four lines to each. The other form of didactic poetry, the dialogue, is represented in Old English in the poem known as *Salomon and Saturn*. This alliterative poem is preserved in two MSS. in the Library of Corpus Christi College, Cambridge. King Solomon, as the representative of Jewish wisdom, is represented as measuring forces with Saturn, a docile learner and mild disputant. The Old English dialogue has its counterpart in more than one literature, but, in other countries, Marcolf, who takes the place of Saturn, gets the best of the game, and saucy wit confounds the teacher.

Any attempt to estimate the development attained by Old English literature, as shown by the work of the two schools of poetry which the names of Caedmon and Cynewulf connote, must, of necessity, be somewhat superficial, in view of the fragmentary nature of much of the work passed under review. Caedmon stands for a group of singers whose work we feel to be earlier in tone and feeling, though not always in age, than that which we know to be Cynewulf's or can fairly attribute to him. Both schools of thought are Christian, not rarely even monkish; both writers, if not in equal measure, are sons of their age and palpably inheritors of a philosophy of life pagan in many respects. It is safe to say that, in both groups, there is hardly a single poem of any length and importance in which whole passages are not permeated with the spirit of the untouched *Beowulf*, in which turns of speech, ideas, points of view, do not recall an earlier, a fiercer, a more self-reliant and fatalistic age. God the All-Ruler is fate metamorphosed; the powers of evil are identical with those once called giants and elves; the Paradise and Hell of the Christian are as realistic as the Walhalla and the Niflheim of the heathen ancestor.

Yet the work of Cynewulf and his school marks an advance upon the writings of the school of Caedmon. Even the latter is, at times, subjective and personal in tone to a degree not found in pure folk-epic; but in Cynewulf the personal note is emphasised and becomes lyrical. Caedmon's hymn in praise of the Creator is a sublime statement of generally recognised facts calling for universal acknowledgment in suitably exalted terms; Cynewulf's confessions in the concluding portion of *Elene* or in *The Dream of the Rood*, or his vision of the day of judgment in

Crist, are lyrical outbursts, spontaneous utterances of a soul which has become one with its subject and to which self-revelation is a necessity. This advance shows itself frequently, also, in the descriptions of nature. For Cynewulf, "earth's crammed with heaven, and every common bush afire with God"; it is, perhaps, only in portions of *Exodus* and in passages of *Genesis* B that the Divine immanence in nature is obviously felt by the Caedmonian scop.

The greatest distinction between the one school and the other, is due, however, to the degree in which Cynewulf and his group show their power of assimilating foreign literary influences. England was ceasing to be insular as the influence of a literary tongue began to hold sway over her writers. They are scholars deliberately aiming at learning from others—they borrow freely, adapt, reproduce. Form has become of importance; at times, of supreme importance; the attempt, architecturally imperfect as it may be, to construct the trilogy we know as *Crist* is valuable as a proof of consciousness in art, and the transformation that the riddles show in the passage from their Latin sources furnishes additional evidence of the desire to adorn.

Yet, it is hard not to regret much that was lost in the acquisition of the new. The reflection of the spirit of paganism, the development of epic and lyric as we see them in the fragments that remain, begin to fade and change; at first Christianity is seen to be but thin veneer over the old heathen virtues, and the gradual assimilation of the Christian spirit was not accomplished without harm to the national poetry, or without resentment on the part of the people. "They have taken away our ancient worship, and no one knows how this new worship is to be performed," said the hostile common folk to the monks, when the latter were praying at Tynemouth for the safety of their brethren carried out to sea. "We are not going to pray for them. May God spare none of them," they jibed, when they saw that Cuthbert's prayers appeared to be ineffectual. It was many a year before the hostility to the new faith was overcome and the foreign elements blended with the native Teutonic spirit. The process of blending can be seen perfectly at work in such lines as *The Charm for Barren Land*, where pagan feeling and nominal Christianity are inextricably mixed. There, earth spells are mingled with addresses to the Mother of Heaven. But, in due season, the fusion was accomplished, and, in part, this was due to the wisdom with which the apostles of Christianity retained and disguised in Christian dress many of the festivals, observances and customs of pre-Christian days. That so much of what remains of Old English literature is of a religious nature does not seem strange, when it is remembered through whose hands it has come down to us. Only what appealed to the new creed or could be modified by it would be retained or adapted, when the Teutonic spirit became linked with, and tamed by, that of Rome.

CHAPTER V

Latin Writings in England to the Time of Alfred

IT is outside the scope of this work to survey the various scattered documents of British origin which were produced outside Britain. Moreover, the influence of most of them upon the main stream of English literature was, beyond all doubt, extremely slight. Among the writings thus excluded from consideration may be mentioned the remains of Pelagius, who seems to have been actually the earliest British author, the short tract of Fastidius, "a British bishop," on the Christian life and the two wonderful books of St. Patrick—the *Confession* and the *Letter to Coroticus*—which, in spite of their barbaric style, whereof the author was fully conscious, are among the most living and attractive monuments of ancient Christianity. Outside our province also falls the earliest piece of Latin verse produced in these islands, the *Hymn of St. Sechnall;* and also the hymns of the Bangor antiphonary, the writings of Columban and the lives and remains of the Irish missionaries abroad. All these are named here principally lest it should be supposed that they have been forgotten.

We pass to our earliest indigenous literary products; and the list of these is headed by two somewhat uncouth fragments, marked off from almost all that follow them by the fact that they are British and not English in origin. These are the book of Gildas and the *History of the Britons*.

Concerning the career of Gildas the Wise, we are told much in the lives of him by a monk of Rhuys, and by Caradoc of Lancarvan, which belong respectively to the early part of the eleventh century and to the twelfth; but almost all the data that can be regarded as trustworthy are derived from Gildas's own book and from brief notices in Irish and Welsh annals. As examined by Zimmer and Theodor Mommsen, these sources tell us that Gildas, born about the year 500 A.D., was living in the west of England and wrote the book which we possess shortly before 547; that, perhaps, he journeyed to Rome; that he spent the last years of his life in Britanny and probably died there in 570; and that not long before his death (probably also in his younger days) he visited Ireland. He is represented by various authorities as having been a pupil of St. Iltut at Lantwit Major in Wales, together with other great saints of the time.

The book of his which remains to us is thus entitled by its most recent editor, Mommsen: "Of Gildas the Wise concerning the destruction and conquest of Britain, and his lamentable castigation uttered against the kings, princes and priests thereof." The manuscripts differ widely in the names they assign to it.

The author himself in his opening words describes his work as an epistle. For ten years it has been in his mind, he says, to deliver his testimony about the wickedness and corruption of the British state and church; but he has, though with difficulty, kept silence. Now, he must prove himself worthy of the charge laid upon him as a leading teacher, and speak. But first, he will, with God's help, set forth shortly some facts about the character of the country and the fortunes of its people. Here follows that sketch of the history of Britain which, largely used by Bede and by the compilers of the *History of the Britons*, is almost our only literary authority for the period. In compiling it, Gildas says he has not used native sources, which, if they ever existed, had perished, but "narratives from beyond the sea." What this precisely means it is not easy to determine. The only historical authors whose influence can be directly traced in his text are Rufinus's version of Eusebius, Jerome's *Chronicle* and Orosius; and none of these records the local occurrences which Gildas relates. Moreover, the story, as he tells it, clearly appears to be derived from oral traditions (in some cases demonstrably incorrect) rather than copied from any older written sources. It may be that Gildas drew his knowledge from aged British monks who had settled in Ireland or Britanny: it may be that by the *relatio transmarina* he merely means the foreign historians just mentioned. Brief and rather vague as it is, the narrative may be accepted as representing truly enough the course of events.

It occupies rather more than a quarter of the whole work, and brings us down to the time, forty-four years after the British victory of Mount Badon, when the descendants of the hero of that field, Ambrosius Aurelianus, had departed from the virtues of their great ancestor, and when, in the view of our author, the moral and spiritual state of the whole British dominion had sunk to the lowest level of degradation. In the pages that follow, he attacks, successively and by name, five of the princes of the west: Constantine of Devon and Cornwall, Aurelius Caninus, whose sphere of influence is unknown, Vortipor of Pembrokeshire, Cuneglasus, king of an unnamed territory; and the "dragon of the isle," Maglocunus, who is known to have reigned over Anglesey and to have died in the year 547. Each of these is savagely reproached with his crimes—sacrilege, perjury, adultery and murder—and each is, in milder terms, entreated to return to the ways of peace.

Up to this point the epistle is of great interest, though tantalising from its lack of precise detail. It now becomes far less readable. The whole of the remainder is, practically, a *cento* of biblical quotations, gathering together the woes pronounced in Scripture against evil princes and evil priests, and the exhortations found therein for their amendment. The picture which the author draws of the principate and of the clergy is almost without relief in its blackness. He does just allow that there are a few good priests; but corruption, worldliness and vice are rampant among the majority.

That Gildas was convinced of the urgency of his message there is no room to doubt. Like Elijah at Horeb, he feels that he is left alone, a prophet of the Lord; and every word he writes comes from his heart. Yet, if we are certain of his sincerity, we are at least equally confident that his picture must be too darkly coloured. We have complained that he lacks precision: it must be added that he loves adjectives, and adjectives in the superlative degree. Doubtless Salonius and Sagittarius, the wicked bishops of Gap and Embrun, of whom Gregory of Tours has so much to say, had their counterparts in Britain; but there were also St. Iltut, St. David and many another, renowned founders of schools and teachers of the young, whose labours cannot have been wholly fruitless.

In style, Gildas is vigorous to the point of turgidity. His breathless periods are often wearisome and his epithets multitudinous. Perhaps the most pleasant sample of his writings is the paragraph in which he enumerates with an ardent and real affection the beauties of Britain. In a few instances he shows that tendency to adorn his page with rare and difficult words which seems to have had a great attraction for the Celtic mind.

It is evident that he considers himself a Roman citizen in some sense. To him, Latin is "our tongue," as opposed to English; and the impression given by this phrase is confirmed by the whole tenor of his writing. His sources of inspiration, as we have in part seen, are Roman. To those already mentioned we may add the names of Vergil and, perhaps, Juvenal and Claudian.

In summing up the impression which he leaves upon us, we may say that his eyes are fixed regretfully upon a great past; there is no hint of hope for the future. The thought that the heathen English might become a source of light to the western world is one that has never dawned upon him. In short, Gildas is a dark and sad figure. Night is falling round him; all that he has been taught to prize is gone from him or going; and, when he looks upon his land, "behold darkness and sorrow, and the light is darkened in the heavens thereof."

The literary history of the book is not very complicated. The compilers of the *History of the Britons* used it, and so did Bede, and the authors of the lives of Gildas and of other Breton saints. In the twelfth century it was a rare book in England, as William of Newburgh tells us: but Geoffrey of Monmouth had it before him in the first half of that century.

We have, besides the epistle *par excellence*, relics of other epistles of Gildas, in which his peculiar style is very recognisable, and also some penitential canons. Of these latter, we need only say that the precise extent of the material in them which can be certainly assigned to Gildas is still in dispute.

Another fragment of Gildan literature, upon whose authenticity a curious literary question depends, is the hymn called *Lorica* or *Cuirass*. This is a metrical prayer, in which the suppliant asks for divine protection against "the mortality of this

year" and against evil demons, and enumerates each limb and
organ of his body. The form which the prayer takes, though
not common, is not unique. A similar hymn in Irish is attributed to St. Patrick, and there are others of Irish origin. The
attribution of this particular *Lorica* to Gildas (Gillus, the name
in the manuscript, is pretty clearly meant for Gildas) is not
unanimous: one Lathacan, Laidcenn, or Loding (probably an
Irish prince of the seventh century) is named by several copies
—once as having brought the hymn to Ireland. Zimmer is
confident in maintaining that Gildas is the author: Mommsen
dissents from this view.

It may seem an indifferent matter whether this particular
hymn is a work of the sixth or seventh century; but the fact is
that its style and vocabulary are of considerable interest as
throwing light on the culture of its time, and they connect it
with a longer document or group of documents, the date and
provenance of which it would be very interesting to settle.

In its latter portion, where it enumerates the various parts
of the body, *Lorica* is, to a large extent, a collection of the most
obscure foreign and archaic words which the author could scrape
together. Hebrew, Greek and Latin are mingled in the most
curious way, and are so disguised and corrupted that, in many
cases, we are only able to divine their meaning by the help of
glosses. It may be allowable to quote a single line—

> gygram cephalem cum iaris et conas—

which is said to mean

> head, head with hair and eyes.

The other group of writings in which a similarly extraordinary vocabulary occurs is represented principally by the work
called *Hisperica Famina*, which we possess in more than one
text. It is arranged in a series of sections, numbering in all
somewhat over 600 lines, of a kind of assonant non-metrical
structure. Each line usually consists of two parts. The first
part contains one or two epithets, and the verb and subject are
in the second part. Each section contains a description of some
scene or object—the day's work, the sea, fire, the wind, a chapel,
an encounter with robbers. The writer is evidently a member
of something like a monastic school; and all that we can certainly say of his surroundings is that he is brought into contact

with Irish people, for they are distinctly mentioned in the text.

It is impossible to give any idea of the obscurity of *Hisperica Famina* without quoting or translating passages; and nothing short of the genius of Sir Thomas Urquhart could find equivalents for the amazing words used by the writer. This one point is evident, that the same school produced *Lorica* and *Hisperica Famina*. Was that school located in England or Ireland? If Gildas be author of *Lorica*, it follows, in all probability, that the author of *Hisperica Famina* was a man brought up, like Gildas, in a south Welsh school such as that of St. Iltut, and, subsequently, settled in Ireland, where he wrote *Hisperica Famina*. In this case we must place him in the sixth century. One piece of evidence which points in this direction can hardly be set aside. The hymn attributed to St. Columba and known as *Altus prosator* contains very marked specimens of the Hisperic Latinity. That this composition is really of Columba's age is the belief of its latest editors; and, if that be granted, there is no need to seek for further proof that *Hisperica Famina* could have been produced in the sixth century, and that, whether Irish in origin or not, its peculiarities were adopted by genuinely Irish authors.

The *Historia Brittonum* has been the centre of many controversies as to its date and origin. As set forth in Theodor Mommsen's edition, it consists of the following tracts, which together form what has been called *Volumen Britanniae*, or the *Book of Britain*: 1. A calculation of epochs of the world's history, brought down to various dates by various scribes or editors. 2. The history of the Britons down to a time immediately after the death of Vortigern. 3. A short life of St. Patrick. 4. A chapter about Arthur.[1] 5. Genealogies of Saxon kings and a calculation of epochs. 6. A list of cities of Britain. 7. A tract on the wonders of Britain.

As to the probable date of this curious *congeries* of writings, it is held that they were compiled by a Briton somewhere about the year 679, after which additions were made to them. In particular, about the year 800, a recension of the whole was made by one Nennius. He represents himself as a pupil of Elbodugus

[1] See the chapter on the early history of the Arthurian legend in the present volume.

(who is known to have been bishop of Bangor, and to have died in 809) and also, seemingly, as a pupil of one Beulan, for whose son Samuel he made his revision of the book.   He may, very possibly, be identical with the Nemnivus of whom we have some curious relics preserved in a Bodleian manuscript.

The revision of Nennius is not extant in a complete form. Our best authority for it is an Irish version made in the eleventh century by Gilla Coemgin.   Some of the Latin copies have preserved extracts from the original, among which are the preface of Nennius and some verses by him.   A principal point to be remembered in this connection is that it is scarcely correct to speak of the *History of the Britons* as being the work of Nennius.[1]

The sources employed by the original compiler or compilers of the various tracts which make up the "volume of Britain" are both native and foreign.   He or they have drawn largely upon Celtic legend, written or oral.   Other writings which have been used to a considerable extent are Gildas, Jerome's *Chronicle* and a lost life of St. Germanus of Auxerre.   Slighter traces of a knowledge of Vergil, Caesar, Isidore, and a map resembling the *Peutinger Table*, are forthcoming.

Of the authors to whom the book was known in early times it is only necessary to name two.   In all probability, Bede was acquainted with it, though he does not mention it as having been one of his sources of information.   Geoffrey of Monmouth made fairly extensive use of it.   The copy which he had evidently attributed the authorship to Gildas, as do three at least of our extant manuscripts.

It is hardly possible to speak of the *History* as possessing a distinctive style.   Where the author attempts a detailed narrative, his manner reminds us of the historical portions of the Old Testament.   The books of *Chronicles*, with their mixture of genealogy and story, afford a near and familiar parallel.

If we possessed the whole of the revision by Nennius in its Latin form, we should most likely find that he had infused into it something of the learned manner beloved of his race and age. At least, his preface and his verses indicate this.   Greek and Hebrew words occur in the verses, and one set of them is so

---

[1] The view here expressed is, in the main, that of Zimmer and Mommsen. It must be mentioned that another hypothesis regards Nennius as primarily responsible for the whole compilation.   If this be accepted, there can be no possibility of Bede's having used the book.

written that the initials of the words form an alphabet. The original author of the *History* had no such graces. His best passage is the well-known tale of Vortigern.

Within a generation after the death of Gildas the Roman mission came to Kent, and the learning of the Latins, secular as well as sacred, was brought within reach of the English. The seventh century saw them making copious use of this enormous gift, and Latin literature flourished in its new and fertile soil.

Probably the coming of archbishop Theodore and abbot Hadrian to Canterbury in the year 668 was the event which contributed more than any other to the progress of education in England. The personalities of these two men, both versed in Greek as well as in Latin learning, determined, at least at first, the quality and complexion of the literary output of the country. But theirs was not the only strong influence at work. In the first place, the fashion of resorting to Ireland for instruction was very prevalent among English students; in the second place, the intercourse between England and Rome was incessant. Especially was this the case in the monasteries of the north. To take a single famous instance: five times did Benedict Biscop, abbot of Wearmouth, journey from Britain to Rome, and, on each occasion, he returned laden with books and artistic treasures. A less familiar example may also be cited. Cuthwin, bishop of the east Angles about 750, brought with him from Rome a life of St. Paul full of pictures; and an illustrated copy of Sedulius, now at Antwerp (in the Plantin Museum), has been shown to have belonged to the same owner.

Four books which have been preserved to our times may be cited as tangible monuments of the various influences which were being exercised upon the English in the seventh century. The "Gregorian Gospels" at Corpus Christi College, Cambridge (MS. 286), written in the seventh century and illustrated with pictures which, if not painted in Italy, go back to Italian originals, represent the influence of Augustine. The Graeco-Latin copy of the *Acts of the Apostles* at Oxford (Laud. Gr. 35) may well have been brought to this country by Theodore or Hadrian. The Lindisfarne Gospels show the blend of Celtic with Anglian art, and contain indications of a Neapolitan archetype. The *Codex Amiatinus* of the Latin Bible, now at

Florence, written at Wearmouth or Jarrow and destined as a present for the Pope, shows England acknowledging her debt to Rome.

The first considerable literary figure among English writers of Latin is undoubtedly Aldhelm, who died bishop of Sherborne in 709. Much of his life was passed at Malmesbury, and the account given by William of Malmesbury, on the authority of king Alfred's *Handbook*, of Aldhelm's skill as a poet in the vernacular, and of his singing to the harp songs of his own composing by which he hoped to teach the country people, is probably the only fact associated with his name in the minds of most. Glad as we should be to possess these English poems, it is certain that Aldhelm and his contemporaries must have thought little of them in comparison with his Latin works. There may have been many in the land who could compose in English; but there were assuredly very few who were capable of producing writings such as those on which Aldhelm's reputation rests.

For our purpose one fact derived from a letter of Aldhelm himself is of extreme importance. In his youth he was for a considerable time a pupil of Hadrian of Canterbury.

A late biographer, Faricius, credits Aldhelm with a knowledge of Greek (derived from two teachers procured by king Ine from Athens), of Hebrew and of Latin, which tongue no one had employed to greater advantage since Vergil. These statements cannot be taken quite as they stand. We do not hear from any other source of the Athenian teachers, and the Greek which Aldhelm undoubtedly knew he could perfectly well have learned from Hadrian. There is, practically, nothing to show that he knew Hebrew, and we need not spend time in examining the remark about Vergil. In spite of this and similar exaggerations, the fact remains that Aldhelm's learning is really very great for his time.

The writings of his which we possess are the following:

1. A number of letters. 2. A prose treatise on the praise of virginity. 3. A versification, in hexameters, of the same treatise. 4. A prose book on the number seven and on meters, especially the hexameter, containing also a collection of one hundred riddles in verse. 5. Occasional poems, principally inscriptions for altars or the like.

Of the letters (several of which have been preserved among the correspondence of St. Boniface) two are of particular interest. The first of these, addressed to the Welsh king Geraint, complains of the irregularities of the British clergy in regard to the form of the tonsure and the observance of Easter, and of their unchristian attitude towards the English clergy, with whom they refuse to hold any intercourse. It warns the king of the dangers incurred by those who are cut of communion with the church of Peter, and begs him to use his influence in favour of union. The style and vocabulary of this letter are unusually plain and straightforward. Few words appear to be inserted simply for the sake of adorning the page. It is a sincere and business-like document.

The other offers a wide contrast. It is written to one Eahfrid on his return from Ireland, whither he had gone for purposes of study, and is intended to show that equally good teaching could be obtained in England. With this in view, Aldhelm pours out all the resources of an extremely rich and varied vocabulary upon his correspondent. In the opening lines the figure of alliteration is employed to an alarming extent: out of sixteen consecutive words fifteen begin with a *p*. Once or twice the writer breaks without rime or reason into Greek (the phrase *ad doxam onomatis kyrii* is a good example); and Latinised Greek words stud the text, together with unfamiliar Latin. Elaborate passages of metaphor, too, occur—one about bees, of which Aldhelm is specially fond—and the whole affords as concentrated a sample of the author's "learned" style as it is possible to find in a small compass. An interesting feature in the theme is a panegyric on Theodore and Hadrian, who are extolled as capable of routing and putting to shame all the scholars of Ireland.

It is evident that this letter was much admired, for it survives in a good many copies, in juxtaposition with the treatise on virginity, with which it has no connection.

The two books in prose and verse on virginity were the most popular of Aldhelm's writings. A short sketch of their contents must be given.

The prose treatise is addressed to a group of nuns, some of whom have English names, while others have adopted the names of virgin saints. They are headed by Hildelitha, who

afterwards became abbess of Barking. We have, first, a thanks-
giving for the learning and virtue of the community, a lengthy
comparison of nuns to bees and a panegyric on the state of
virginity, with a warning against the eight principal vices.
Then follows the main body of the work, consisting of a number
of examples of men and women who have excelled in chastity.
The first order of these is taken from the Old Testament (Elijah,
Elisha, Jeremiah, Daniel, the Three Children); the second
from the New (John Baptist, John Evangelist, Thomas, Paul,
Luke). From the subsequent history of the church come
Clement of Rome, Sylvester, Ambrose, Martin, Gregory Na-
zianzen, Basil, Felix. A group of hermits and monks follows:
Antony, Paul, Hilarion, John, Benedict. Then, some who
suffered for chastity as confessors (Malchus, Narcissus, Athanasius) or as martyrs (Babylas, Cosmas and Damian, Chrysanthus
and Daria, Julian and Basilissa). Last among the male examples are two more hermits, Amos and Apollonius. Next
follow the heroines: the Virgin Mary, Cecilia, Agatha, Lucy,
Justina, Eugenia, Agnes, Thecla, Eulalia, Scholastica, Christina,
Dorothea, Constantina, Eustochium, Demetrias, Agape, Irene
and Chionia, Rufina and Secunda, Anatolia and Victoria. In
most of these cases the substance of the saint's history is given,
sometimes at considerable length.

After this, a few examples are cited of persons who were in
some way notable in connection with chastity, though not all
celibate: Joseph, David, Samson, Abel, Melchizedek are brought
forward. A warning against splendour of attire occupies some
space and is followed by an apology for the style of the work,
as having been written under the pressure of many occupations.
The conclusion of the whole is a request for the prayers of the
recipients.

The poetical form of the treatise is later than the prosaic.
It begins with a very elaborate double acrostic, the initials and
finals of the lines forming one and the same hexameter verse:
the initials are to be read downward and the finals upwards. The
book is this time addressed to an abbess Maxima, whose English
name does not appear to be known. The arrangement of the
poem coincides generally, but not exactly with that of the
prose book. The preliminary praise of virginity is shorter.
Some examples (Thomas, Felix, Christina, Dorothea) are

omitted, and a couple (Gervasius and Protasius, and Jerome) added.

After the story of Anatolia and Victoria the poem diverges from prose and gives a description of the eight principal vices, modelled, not very closely, upon Prudentius's *Psychomachia*. It ends by deprecating criticism and by asking for the prayers of the reader.

The source and style of these books are the chief matters which engage our attention. With regard to the source of the prose treatise in particular, we see that Aldhelm had access to a very considerable library of Christian authors. It included (taking the citations as they occur in the text) an unidentified work in which an angel appears as speaker (not *The Shepherd of Hermas*), Isidore, Pseudo-Melito's *Passion of John*, *Acts of Thomas*, *Revelation of Paul* (in the fullest Latin text), *Recognitions of Clement*, *Acts of Sylvester*, Paulinus's *Life of Ambrose*, Sulpicius Severus, lives of Gregory and Basil, Athanasius's *Life of Antony*, *Vitae Patrum*, Gregory's *Dialogues*, Rufinus's version of Eusebius, Jerome's letter and his *Life of Malchus*, and an extensive collection of *Passions of Martyrs*. Among poets, Vergil and Prosper are prominent. In this enumeration only the obvious sources have been reckoned. A list of the books whose influence is perceptible in phrases or allusions would be of equal length.

The style recalls the intricate ornamentation of the Celtic manuscripts of the time. The thought is simple, as are the ingredients of the patterns in the manuscripts; but it is involved in exhausting periods, and wonderful words are dotted about in them like spangles. We have seen that, to some scholars in this age, learning meant chiefly the knowledge of strange words. Aldhelm is not free from this delusion. A fairly close rendering of a paragraph from the prose treatise will convey a better idea of his manner than many lines of description.

Paul, formerly Saul, the Benjamin of the prophecy, at morning devouring the prey and at evening dividing the spoil; who, by his fearsome bidding, compelled the pythoness, prophesying the vanities of deceit through the spirit of necromancy and thereby heaping up in abundance the sumptuous wealth of her lords and enriching them to satiety with the pleasant treasures of her gains to set before her impudent lips the door of dumb silence; and who, marvellous to tell, spent unhurt four times six hours in the deep bottom of the sea, and bore four times forty blows, less one, by the sharp torment of cruelty: was it not in virtue of his prerogative of intact purity that, exploring the third heaven, he beheld the souls of the citizens above with virgin glances, and sought out the hidden things of the celestial host in an experience of matters that might not be spoken; though the *Revelation* (as they call it) *of Paul* babbles of his visiting the delights of flowery paradise in a golden ship. Yet the divine law forbids the followers of the catholic faith to believe anything beyond what the ordinance of canonical truth publishes, and the decisions of orthodox Fathers in written decretals have commanded us to give up utterly and banish far from us this and other fevered fancies of spurious books, as thundering words horrifying to the ear.

Another important production of our author—important as exemplifying his secular learning, though it never attained the popularity of his other works—is the *Letter to Acircius* (king Aldfrith of Northumbria), which contains a disquisition on the number seven, a treatise on the hexameter and a collection of riddles in verse. The portion of the book which deals with metre is illustrated by very many examples from Latin poets. A large number of the classical quotations must, no doubt, be put down to the credit of the grammarian Audax, from whom much of the text is borrowed; but a very considerable proportion is, certainly, derived from Aldhelm's own reading. We may be sure, for instance, that he had access to Vergil, Ovid, Lucan, Cicero, Pliny, Sallust, Solinus. The list of Christian poets is astonishing: Juvencus, the author of the versified Latin Old Testament, who is now called Cyprianus, Sedulius, Arator, Alcimus Avitus, Prudentius, Prosper, Corippus, Venantius Fortunatus, Paulinus of Périgueux and an otherwise unknown Paulus Quaestor are all used. A little group of Spanish authorities, in particular the grammatical work of Julian of Toledo, is a curious feature. The traces of Horace, Juvenal, Persius, Seneca, Dracontius, Sidonius are slight. Orosius, Lactantius, Junilius and a number of grammarians may close our catalogue, which, it will be recognised, is a very impressive one.

The riddles which occur in the midst of this treatise are among the most attractive part of Aldhelm's work. They are modelled on those of Symphosius (a fifth century writer) but are not, like his, confined to the limits of three lines apiece.

They are, for the most part, ingenious little descriptions of simple objects: *e.g.*—to take a series at random—the locust, the nightcrow, the gnat, the spindle, the cupping-glass, the evening, the dagger, the bubble. That this form of wit-sharpening made a great appeal to the mind of our ancestors is amply evident from many passages in the Old English literature,— notably *The Dialogue of Salomon and Saturn*, and the documents related thereto; and are not the periphrases of all early Scandinavian poetry exemplifications of the same tendency? As we have seen, Aldhelm's riddles were copiously imitated by Englishmen in later centuries.[1]

We have seen something of the number of Latin authors who were known to Aldhelm. It may be added here that, in a letter to Hedda, bishop of Winchester, he describes himself, apparently, as engaged in the study of Roman law, and, certainly, as occupied with metres and with the science of astronomical calculation.

It would be interesting to be able to show that, besides knowing the Greek language (as we are sure he did), he possessed Greek books, apart from Latin versions; but it is not really possible to find much evidence to this effect. He once cites *Judith* "according to the Septuagint"; in another place he calls the *Acts of the Apostles* the *Praxapostolos;* elsewhere he gives the name of a work of St. Basil in Greek, and mentions Homer and Hesiod. Not much can be built on these small foundations. The probability is that he read Greek books when studying under Hadrian, but that in later life he possessed none of his own.

Summing up the literary work of Aldhelm, we find in him a good representative of the pupils of Theodore and Hadrian, on whom both Roman and Greek influences have been exercised; and we see in him also one for whom the grandiloquence of the Celt, the love of an out-of-the way vocabulary, of sound rather at the cost of sense, had great attraction. We cannot truly declare that the literature of the world would be much the poorer for the loss of his writings; but it is fair to say that there is in them, despite all their affectation, a great deal of freshness and vigour; that they are marked by the faults of youth rather than by those of senescence. That they were immensely popular

[1] See *ante*, Chapter IV. p. 66.

we can see from the number of existing copies of the treatise on virginity and the letter to Aldfrith. Most of these are early and are distinguished by the beauty of their script. One, now at Lambeth, has a rather well-known frontispiece representing the author and a group of nuns.

Additional evidence of the importance of Aldhelm as a literary figure is afforded by the existence of what we may call the Aldhelmian school of English Latinists. The works of these are neither many in number nor large in compass; but the distribution of the writers covers a fairly considerable space both geographically and in time. Little attention has hitherto been paid to them in this country, and, on all accounts, they deserve notice.

First among them may be reckoned a series of five interesting little poems which have been preserved (as have several of Aldhelm's letters) among the correspondence of St. Boniface. They are written in pairs of eight-syllabled lines.

The first of these has in its opening couplet an allusion to Aldhelm's[1] name, and seems to be addressed to him by a *cantor* at Malmesbury. In a very spirited fashion it describes a storm in late June, which unroofed the dormitory or some other of the buildings of a monastery where the writer was. It is not easy to see whether this place was Malmesbury abbey or a monastic house in Devonshire. The second poem is, as appears from an accompanying letter, by one Aethilwald (usually but not rightly identified with Ethelbald, king of the Mercians from 716 to 757) and describes a visit to Rome, dwelling with great particularity upon some silken fabrics which the pilgrims had brought back with them. Of the remaining three, one is a short prayer, the next an address to Aldhelm, who is called *Cassis prisca* (*i.e.*, Old helmet), most likely by Aethilwald, and the last is supposed to be Aldhelm's reply thereto. These poems are very favourable specimens of the Aldhelmian style.

Two direct imitators of Aldhelm, Tatwin and Eusebius, come next under consideration. Both were men of eminence: Tatwin died archbishop of Canterbury in 734, and Eusebius is almost certainly identical with Hwaetberct, abbot of Wearmouth and Jarrow from 716. Two collections of riddles in

---

[1] Henry Bradley has pointed out (*English Historical Review*, 1900, p. 291) that the first poem is, most likely, addressed to Helmquist, not Aldhelm; and that the fifth is by Aethilwald and addressed to one Oua.

Latin hexameters by these persons have survived. In that of Tatwin ingenuity is prominent: he makes the initials and finals of the first line of each riddle into an acrostic of hexameters. That of Eusebius is supplementary to Tatwin's; it makes up the forty riddles of the latter to one hundred, the number contained in Aldhelm's collection, which had undoubtedly served as a model to both writers. St. Boniface (d. 755) is the last note-worthy individual who can be claimed as a member of this school. He employs the short eight-syllabled lines as the vehicle of an acrostic on the words *Nithardus vive felix;* and he writes a series of enigmas on the virtues and vices, in hexa-meters, in which the acrostic is extensively employed. Some of his letters, too, are couched in the true Aldhelmian style. Several of his correspondents, moreover, and the authors of a good many letters not addressed to him which are nevertheless preserved with his own, bear the same stamp. Among them are three or four short poems in eight-syllabled metre. Espe-cially noteworthy are a letter from Lul and others to an abbess Cuneburga and an anonymous letter to an abbess and a nun.

The Aldhelmian school, with the single exception of Euse-bius (Hwaetberct), consists of men nurtured in the south and west of England. The two other great men who remain to be considered are representatives of the north. We have hinted already that the Latin culture of the northern English was more directly dependent upon Rome than was that of Canter-bury, with its eastern flavour, or that of the west, where Celtic influence may be suspected. We do not forget Aidan's work in the north; yet that had but faint effects upon literature; and the fact remains that the eccentricities and affectations of Aldhelm have no parallel in the work of Bede.

Bede is by far the greatest name which our period presents. Like the later Alcuin, he was of European reputation; but he owed that reputation to the sheer excellence of his books. Alcuin occupied a great and influential position, and used the opportunities which it gave him with the best effect. But he has left no writing which we value much for its own sake. Bede, on the other hand, made an indelible mark on the litera-ture of succeeding centuries, and our debt to him can hardly be exaggerated.

Not many lives of great men have been less eventful. It

seems probable that the longest journey he ever took was from
Jarrow to York, and that the greatest crisis of his life was the
pestilence in 686 which decimated the monks of Jarrow. He
died in 735 at Jarrow, where, practically, his whole life of sixty-
three years had been spent. The story of his last hours, as
Cuthbert (afterwards abbot of Wearmouth and Jarrow) tells
it in his famous letter to Cuthwin, is of unapproached beauty
in its kind. One of the latest utterances of the great scholar
is an index to the tone and temper of the whole man.

"It is time," he said, "if so it seem good to my Maker, that I
should be set free from the flesh, and go to Him who, when I was not,
fashioned me out of nothing. I have lived a long time, and my merciful Judge has ordained my life well for me. The time for me to be
set free is at hand, for indeed my soul much desires to behold my
King Christ in His beauty."

Over and over again has the life of Bede been sketched, and
the long and varied list of his works reviewed and discussed.
By none has this been better done than by Plummer, in connection with his admirable edition of the *History*. From this
source we borrow the chronology of Bede's writings which will
be here set forth.

To the period between 691 and 703 belong the tracts on
metre, on figures of speech in Scripture, on orthography; to 703
the small work *De Temporibus;* to 708 the letter to Plegwin on
the six ages. The metrical life of Cuthbert was written before
705. In or before 716 fall the commentaries on the *Apocalypse*,
Acts, catholic *Epistles*, *Luke*, *Samuel* and two exegetical letters
to Acca; after 716 the history of the abbots of Wearmouth and
Jarrow, and commentary on *Mark;* about 720 the prose life of
Cuthbert and commentary on *Genesis;* before 725 the book *De
Natura Rerum;* in 725 the large work *De Temporum Ratione;*
in 725–731 commentaries on *Ezra* and *Nehemiah*, and books on
the Tabernacle and the Temple; the *Ecclesiastical History of the
English Race* in 731; *Retractationes* on the *Acts* and the letter
to Egbert must be placed after this. For the following works
no date can be accurately fixed: on the Holy Places, questions
on the books of *Kings*, commentaries on *Proverbs*, *Canticles*, the
Song of Habakkuk, *Tobit*, the martyrology, homilies, hymns
and a few minor tracts.

The names of these books suggest to us, first of all, Bede's

industry and, next, his wide range of interests. Theology, no
doubt, is a dominant factor in the list, but we have, besides,
natural science, grammar and history; nor is poetry excluded.

It is not possible here to do more than briefly characterise
the mass of his works. Of the grammatical treatises and those
which relate to natural science it may be said that they are,
to a very large extent, compilations. To Pliny and Isidore, in
particular, Bede owes much in the book *De Natura Rerum*.
Similarly, his commentaries are often little more than *catenae*
of extracts from the four Latin Doctors. Probably the supplementary comment on the *Acts*, called *Retractationes*, is one of
the most interesting to us of the series, since it demonstrates
Bede's knowledge of Greek, and shows that he had before him,
when writing, the Graeco-Latin copy of the *Acts* already mentioned, which is now in the Bodleian.

The historical works are, of course, those which distinguish
Bede above all others. There are four books which come under
this head. Two of them may be very shortly dismissed. First,
the *Martyrology*. We cannot be sure how much of this, in its
present form, is Bede's, for it has been enlarged, as was natural
enough, by many hands. The popularity of it is evident from
the fact that it formed the basis of recensions by Florus of
Lyons, Rabanus of Mainz, Ado of Vienne, Notker of St. Gall
and Usuard. Next the short work *De Temporibus*, written
in 705. This consists of a few brief chapters on the divisions of
time and the calculations connected with the observance of
Easter, and ends with a very curt chronicle of the chief events
in the six ages of the world's history. In 725 Bede expanded this
little tract into a much larger book, *De Temporum Ratione*, and
the chronicle of the six ages of the world with which this concludes has been one of the most far-reaching in its influence of
all his works. It served as a model and as a source of information to numberless subsequent chroniclers. "In chronology,"
says Plummer, "Bede has the enormous merit of being the first
chronicler who gave the date from Christ's birth, in addition to
the year of the world, and thus introduced the use of the Diony-
sian era into western Europe." One of the main topics of the
book, the methods of calculating the date of Easter, is one
which interested the men of his day far more than ourselves.
A principal reason for this lies in the nearness and urgency of
the controversies which so long divided the Celtic from the

English church on this subject.   It was also one of the few which brought the mathematical side of men's intellects into play in the service of religion.

The *Ecclesiastical History of the English Race* is, as we know, Bede's greatest and best work.   If a panegyric were likely to induce our readers to turn to it for themselves, that panegyric should be attempted here.   Probably, however, a brief statement of the contents and sources of the five books will be more to the purpose.   The first book, then, beginning with a description of Britain, carries the history from the invasion of Julius Caesar to the year 603, after the arrival of Augustine. Among the sources used are Pliny, Solinus, Orosius, Eutropius, Marcellinus Comes, Gildas, probably the *Historia Brittonum*, a *Passion of St. Alban* and the *Life of St. Germanus of Auxerre* by Constantius.

The second book begins with the death of Gregory the Great, and ends in 633, when Edwin of Northumbria was killed and Paulinus retired to Rochester.

It is in this book that the wonderful scene is described in which Edwin of Northumbria takes counsel with his nobles as to the acceptance or rejection of the Gospel as preached by Paulinus; and here occurs the unforgetable simile of the sparrow flying out of the winter night into the brightly-lighted hall and out again into the dark.

In the third book we proceed as far as 664.   In this section the chief actors are Oswald, Aidan, Fursey, Cedd and Wilfred.

The fourth book, beginning with the death of Deusdedit in 664 and the subsequent arrival of his successor Theodore, with abbot Hadrian, deals with events to the year 698.   The chief figures are Chad, Wilfrid, Ethelburga, Etheldreda, Hilda, Caedmon, Cuthbert.

In the fifth and last book we have stories of St. John of Beverley, of the vision of Drythelm, and others, accounts of Adamnan, Aldhelm, Wilfrid, the letter of abbot Ceolfrid to Nechtan, king of the Picts, the end of the Paschal controversy, a statement of the condition of the country in 731, a brief annalistic summary and a list of the author's works.

In the dedication of the *History* to Ceolwulf, king of Northumbria, Bede enumerates the friends who had helped him in the collection of materials, whether by oral or written information. The chief of these were Albinus, abbot of Canterbury, Nothelm, afterwards archbishop, who, among other things, had copied documents preserved in the archives of Rome, and Daniel, bishop of Winchester. Bede used to the full, besides, his opportunities of intercourse with the clergy and monks of the north who had known the great men of whom he writes.

It is almost an impertinence, we feel, to dwell upon the great qualities which the *History* displays. That sincerity of purpose and love of truth are foremost in the author's mind we are always sure, with whatever eyes we may view some of the tales which he records. "Where he gives a story on merely hearsay evidence, he is careful to state the fact"; and it may be added that where he has access to an original and authoritative document he gives his reader the full benefit of it.

From the literary point of view the book is admirable. There is no affectation of learning, no eccentricity of vocabulary. It seems to us to be one of the great services which Bede rendered to English writers that he gave currency to a direct and simple style. This merit is, in part, due to the tradition of the northern schoool in which he was brought up; but it is to his own credit that he was not led away by the fascinations of the Latinity of Aldhelm.

The popularity of the *History* was immediate and great. Nor was it confined to England. The two actually oldest copies which we possess, both of which may have been written before Bede died, were both produced, it seems, on the continent, one (now at Namur) perhaps at St. Hubert's abbey in the Ardennes, the other (at Cambridge) in some such continental English colony as Epternach.

The two lives of St. Cuthbert and the lives of the abbots of Wearmouth and Jarrow must not be forgotten. The last-named, based to some extent upon an anonymous earlier work, has very great beauty and interest; not many pictures of monastic life are so sane, so human and, at the same time, so productive of reverence and affection in the reader.

The two lives of St. Cuthbert are less important in all ways. The metrical one is the most considerable piece of verse attempted by Bede; that in prose is a not very satisfactory expansion of an earlier life by a Lindisfarne monk.

Enough has probably been said to give a general idea of
the character of Bede's studies and acquirements. Nothing
could be gained by transcribing the lists of authors known
to him, which are accessible in the works of Plummer and of
Manitius. There is nothing to make us think that he had
access to classical or Christian authors of importance not
known to us. He quotes many Christian poets, but not quite
so many as Aldhelm, and, clearly, does not take so much interest
as his predecessor in pagan authors.

The letter to Egbert of York, perhaps the latest document
we possess from Bede's pen, deserves a special and separate
mention. It is, in brief, a pastoral epistle; and it gives (what
we could only gather indirectly from his other works) the
clearest evidence of Bede's lively interest in the religious life
of the people at large, and his wise and noble conception of
the duties of a Christian minister. His advice to Egbert is
prompted by "a real and unassuming spirit of humility and
affection," and it is thoroughly practical in its statement,
alike of the abuses which need reform, and of the means of
reforming them. The suggestions offered by Bede are those
of a man at once spiritually minded and versed in the affairs of
his time; they are, moreover, based on an intimate knowledge
of the history of the church with which he is dealing. Rarely
as he may have trodden the regions outside the walls of his
monastery, it is plain from this letter alone that Bede may
be reckoned as one of the most effective contributors, by
his advice and influence, to the spreading of Christianity in
northern England.

No enumeration of works, no accumulation of epithets
will give the picture of a man's mind. And it is the personality of Bede which we come to regard with affection, when
we have read the book into which he has infused most of his
own character. That book is the *History*, and from the study
of it few will rise without the feeling that Bede was one of the
best of men.

It cannot be maintained that the influence of Alcuin's
writings upon the literature of his country was very important.
As a product of the great school of York, he does, indeed, bear
witness to the admirable training which that school could fur-

nish. The debt which the schools of Charles the Great owed,
through Alcuin, to England must never be forgotten. This is
the central fact, so far as England is concerned, in Alcuin's
career. His written works, mostly produced on the continent,
were not of a kind to affect very markedly the development of
literature; and the condition of England during the period of
Alcuin's residence abroad was such that English scholars could
make no use of what he was able to impart. The fact is that,
very shortly before Alcuin left England for ever, the Scandinavians had begun that desolating series of raids upon this
country which ended by exterminating the learning and literature of Northumbria and paralysed intellectual effort all over
the land.

In an often quoted poem on the saints of York, Alcuin
enumerates the principal authors whose works were to be
found in the library collected there by Egbert and Albert.
Within a generation after the poem was written, that library
had ceased to exist; and so had that earlier treasury of books
at Wearmouth which Benedict Biscop commended in the last
years of his life to the special care of his monks. The end of the
eighth century and the course of the ninth saw learning gradually obliterated in England, until the efforts of Alfred revived
an interest in the things of the mind among his countrymen.

Had it not been for this catastrophe we might have found
English scholars taking part with Alcuin in the adoptionist
controversy, or contributing to the revision of the *Vulgate*
which is associated with his name. As it is, the ninth century, to the historian of our Latin literature, is almost a blank.

Alcuin, to resume, was not a great writer. The clearest
indications of his general culture and his manifold activities
may, perhaps, be gathered from his numerous poems and his
letters. These latter, with some of his grammatical works,
were the only part of his writings which attained popularity
in England. His controversial books are of less enduring
interest: it is given to few to follow with intelligent appreciation
the dispute which he waged with Felix of Urgel and Elipandus
of Toledo upon the question whether Christ, in His human
nature, was or was not to be called the "adoptive" Son of
God. The liturgical works, again—the homiliary, lectionary

and sacramentary—which made so deep a mark upon the
church-life of the continent, are works of compilation. As
to the revision of the text of the Latin Bible, clear evidence
that it was the work of Alcuin is not yet producible; but the
probability is very strong that he was at least prominent, if
not supreme, in the undertaking.

But, though the tale of Alcuin's labours is an imposing
one, it is the intellectual stimulus which he imparted, and
the long line of scholars which owed to him its existence,
that forms his true monument. He ranks with Bede as an
inspirer of men; but the vehicle by which his inspiration
was conveyed was rather the voice of the teacher than the
written words.

With Alcuin we close the list of the considerable authors
who fall within our period. But there still remain some few
writings of the eighth and ninth centuries which demand a
word of notice. These consist mainly of lives of saints,
visions, poems and devotional literature.

The anonymous lives of the abbots of Wearmouth and
Jarrow, and the life of Cuthbert by a Lindisfarne monk—both
so extensively used by Bede—have been mentioned already.
The earliest life of Gregory the Great, to which an English
origin is attributed, should not be forgotten here. It is discussed by Plummer in an appendix to the edition of Bede's
History.

More important than this, from the literary point of view,
are the lives of Wilfrid of York by Eddius Stephanus, and of
Guthlac by Felix. Both of these belong to the eighth century.
The former begins in a way which may indicate either indo
lence or modesty on the part of its author, who transcribes,
with few alterations and without acknowledgment, the preface of the anonymous life of Cuthbert. The reading of the life
will probably conduce to the most favourable interpretation
being placed upon this proceeding; for, unflinching partisan
as he is, Eddius makes us think of him kindly. Many a man
would have spoken much more bitterly of the opponents of
his hero; and, though Eddius persistently and gallantly disguises that hero's faults, we do not feel so much that he is a bad
historian as that he is a wrongly faithful friend.

Felix, the biographer of Guthlac, is far more picturesque in

style than Eddius. Unlike the latter, he has fallen under the
spell of Aldhelm. He has been fascinated, too, by the tales of
the demon hordes who haunted the lonely hermit of the fens,
and has portrayed them in language which, whether directly
or not, was reproduced in vernacular poetry not many generations later.

Closely connected with these biographies of saints are the
visions of the next world. Several of them are reported by
Bede, notably the vision of Fursey, the Irish hermit, and of
Drythelm. Two more (one of them in a fragmentary condition)
are preserved among the correspondence of Boniface. Like
the life of Guthlac these apocalypses had firm hold upon
popular imagination, and some of them appear in the homilies
of Aelfric in an English dress. They owed their origin, it
may be remarked, in a great measure to the *Dialogues* of Gregory and the apocryphal *Revelation of Paul*—which latter, as
we have seen, was known to Aldhelm. It is possible that the
far older *Revelation of Peter* may have survived in some form
accessible to the English church of the seventh and eighth
centuries. Evidence is not wanting to show that an Italian
apocalypse of the seventh century, that of St. Barontus of
Pistoja, was studied in England not long after our period.[1]

In the department of poetry the only considerable work
which remains to be mentioned is the poem of one Ethelwulf
upon the history of a monastery the identity of which is not
yet certainly established. The house in question was clearly
connected with Lindisfarne, and is thought to have been at
Crayke near York. The poem is dedicated to Egbert, who was
bishop of Lindisfarne in the first quarter of the ninth century,
and is constructed on the model of Alcuin's versified history
of the saints of the church of York. It contains among other
things an account of a vision of the next world, similar to
those mentioned in the last paragraph.

Of devotional literature, by which we mean more particularly collections of prayers and hymns for private use, there is a
fairly large quantity preserved in manuscripts which belong
to the period under consideration. The most remarkable

---

[1] See a passage towards the end of a 11th (?) century Old English MS.,
Corpus Christi College, Cambridge, 367, quoted in *The Sources of Abp. Parker's
MSS. at C.C.C.C.*, James, M. R., Cambridge Antiquarian Society, 1899, p. 62.

of these is perhaps the volume called the *Book of Cerne,* now in the University Library at Cambridge. Both Celtic and Spanish influences have been traced in many of the compositions in this and other like works. Much light may eventually be thrown by this class of literature upon the intellectual as well as the religious surroundings of the clergy and monks of the eighth and ninth centuries.

A not inconsiderable portion of the Latin writings of these same centuries consists of documents connected with church law. Books called *Penitentials* exist under the names of Theodore Bede and Egbert of York; and there are, besides, canons of church councils and the like. But these have really no claim to the name of literature and a mere mention of them must suffice.

These, then, are the chief remains of the Latin literature which was produced in England before the time of Alfred. The period of greatest activity lasted, we have seen, for about a hundred years, from A.D. 690 to 790. It is marked by the rise of two great schools, those of Canterbury and York, and by the work of one great scholar. The south of England produced works characterised by a rather perverted and fanciful erudition. It was the north which gave birth to Bede, the one writer of that age whose works are of first-rate value, and to Alcuin, whose influence was supreme in the schools of the continent.

CHAPTER VI

Alfred and the Old English Prose
of his Reign

THE reign of Alfred acquired its chief glory from the personality of the king. He had many titles to fame. His character was made up of so many diverse elements that he seemed, at one and the same time, to be military leader, lawgiver, scholar and saint, and these elements were so combined that the balance of the whole was never disturbed. In the minds of posterity Alfred lives as the type of an ideal Englishman.

In each of the departments of his activity the king's work was of permanent value. His efforts, though essentially pioneer in character, laid a solid and permanent foundation for the superstructure which was to be raised by his successors. As king, he ruled a portion only of modern England and left much to be completed by his descendants. But the centralising policy which he inaugurated and successfully realised—the policy of making Wessex the nucleus of England's expansion—alone made possible the growth of an enlarged kingdom. Alfred's ideals for Wessex reflect a large vision and much practical wisdom, and the reign is as remarkable for its educational as for its political progress. His conceptions were cosmopolitan rather than insular. He never lost sight of the importance of keeping his kingdom in organic relation with European civilisation—a lesson stamped upon his mind ever since, in his early years (856), during the pontificate of one of the greatest of the popes, Leo IV, he had visited Rome and the court of Charles the Bald. This visit made a vivid impression upon Alfred's mind. His father's marriage with the emperor's daughter Judith cemented relationships with the continent and the insularity of Britain was henceforth broken down. The importance for literature of this emergence from isolation cannot be over-estimated. Charles the Great had gathered round him at Aachen a cultured circle of scholars and writers, and had promoted a renascence of classical study, the influence of which was still powerful in the days of Charles the Bald. The illuminated MSS. of the French court of the ninth century—the St. Denis and Metz Bibles, the Psalter and book of Gospels, in particular—are conspicuous examples of artistic skill. After his accession Alfred looked to the Frankish empire for assistance in his task of reviving learning in Wessex. At his request, Grimbald, a monk of St. Bertin in Flanders, and John of Corvey came over to Britain, and were appointed abbots of Winchester and Aethelney respectively. The king diligently promoted scholarship, and himself undertook to translate into West Saxon recognised works in Latin prose. At the same time he increased the number of monasteries and reformed the educational side of these institutions by the introduction of teachers, English and foreign. The story of Grimbald's visit to Oxford and of the existence there of a community of scholars is, however, not supported by any evidence. The legend was interpolated in an edition of Asser's *Life of Alfred*, based on Parker's text, which Camden published in 1602-3. No MS., or other authority, is known to support Camden's statement. The consequence of the educational and literary activity of Alfred's reign was to transfer the centre of learning from Northumbria to Wessex. The monastic communities of Lindisfarne, Evesham and Croyland had fostered scholarship in the north, and, in the seventh century, Whitby had produced Caedmon. In 674 Benedict Biscop had built the monastery of St. Peter at Wearmouth and, in 682, a second house at Jarrow, at both of which large libraries were collected. The arts of glass-making, gold-work and embroidery were introduced from the continent. Northumbria had thus become "the literary centre of western Europe," producing scholars of the type of Bede, the master of the learning of his day, and Alcuin, the scholarly helper of Charles the Great. But with the appearance of the Danes began the decline of learning in the north. So much did scholarship suffer in consequence of the viking raids that, at the date of Alfred's accession. there was no scholar even south of the Thames who could read the mass-book in Latin. The revival of letters in Wessex was the direct result of the king's enthusiasm and personal efforts, and his educational aims recall irresistibly the work of Charles the Great.

The authorities for the life of Alfred are many, but of unequal value. His own works, reflecting as they do his personal character and convictions, furnish the most important data, the *Chronicle* and the *Life* by Asser ranking next in value. Asser, a Welsh cleric, was, in all probability, educated at St. David's. He had already been in communication with Alfred regarding the defence of his monastery when he was summoned by the king to assist him in his educational schemes. According to his own account, Asser arranged to stay with Alfred for six months of each year, spending the remaining six in Wales. He became the king's most intimate friend and diligently assisted him in his study of Latin. He was eventually appointed bishop of Sherborne, and died some ten years after the king. The authenticity of Asser's book has been much disputed. The unique MS. survives only in charred and illegible fragments, but it is clear from external evidence that Parker's edition (1574) contains large editorial alterations and interpolations from the *Lives of St. Neots*. Formidable evidence in support of the genuineness of the original *Asser* has been collected by Stevenson and others. The Welsh and Latin forms and the scriptural quotations point to the early part of the tenth century, and, at the same time, attest the Celtic nationality of the author. The chronology is based on a primitive version of the *Chronicle*, which the author supplements by details which none but an eye witness could have supplied. The very incompleteness of the book is an argument against its being a forgery. Its abrupt beginning and conclusion, and its awkward combination of extracts from the *Chronicle* with original matter, may have been due to the choice of Frankish models, such as Einhart's *Life of Charles the Great* or Thegan's *Life of Ludwig the Pious*. Asser's book holds a unique position as "the earliest biography of an English layman." Florence of Worcester is valuable as illustrating the genuine text of Asser, since he ignores what was, apparently, interpolated. The later chroniclers, Simeon of Durham and William of Malmesbury, throw occasional light on incidents in the king's career, but, on the whole, are responsible for the growth of the Alfred legend.

The chronological order of Alfred's works is difficult to determine. Depending, as we do, mainly upon internal evidence, there is no absolute test whereby to fix the priority of one work over another. Evidence of style is notoriously untrustworthy. There are, however, a few considerations on the basis of which a general arrangement may be attempted, though scarcely two critics are in entire agreement as to the final order. Of these considerations the most important is ability to reproduce in West Saxon prose the spirit of the Latin original. A comparatively close translation is, in Alfred's case, a sign of the prentice hand; his latest work is marked by great freedom of rendering and large insertions. Some further light is thrown on the problem by the character of the prefaces to the various books. The chroniclers are of little assistance in the determination of the relative order.

The *Handbook* may safely be considered the earliest of Alfred's compilations. Unfortunately, no trace of the book is now to be found, though its existence is attested by external evidence. The circumstances under which the formation of the *Handbook* was begun make it clear that it was essentially a commonplace book of extracts from the Latin Bible and the Fathers. Asser, to whom was due the suggestion that a book of this nature might be of service to the king, describes it as an assemblage of *flosculi*, culled from various sources. These extracts Alfred wrote down in Latin, in the first instance, and, afterwards, began to render them into English. The first entries were made on 11 November, 887, *in venerabili Martini solemnitate*. William of Malmesbury[1] refers to the common-place book, *quem patria lingua Handboc (Encheiridion) i.e., manualem librum appellavit*. Further, there is in Florence of Worcester's *Chronicle* a reference to certain *Dicta regis Aelfredi*, whereby the *Handbook* may possibly be meant. There would, however, be no justification for identifying the *Dicta* with the *Handbook*, were it not for the fact that Malmesbury uses the latter as an authority for the life of Aldhelm. It is quite conceivable that Alfred inserted among his notes an account of Aldhelm, with whose verses he was probably acquainted.

[1] *Gesta Regum Anglorum*, II, § 123.

But no importance whatever is to be attached to Florence of Worcester's suggestion that the *Handbook* was a record of West Saxon genealogy. It is possible that neither chronicler is to be relied upon in this matter. The formation of the *Handbook* was of literary importance merely: it afforded Alfred valuable literary training and indirectly stimulated him to try his hand at more extensive translation.

The translation of Gregory's *Cura Pastoralis* may be considered the first of Alfred's literary works, properly so called. Grein, Pauli and Bosworth awarded first place to *Boethius*, but internal evidence is altogether in favour of the priority of the *Pastoral Care*. The decay of learning consequent upon Danish raids made it imperative that an attempt should be made to revive the education of the clergy. No work of the middle ages seemed better adapted to enlighten the church than Gregory's treatise, designed to serve as a spiritual guide for the conscience of the priest. In *Moralia* Gregory had indulged to the full his passion for allegory; *Cura Pastoralis* is less dominated by the tendency to allegorise, though it contains some gross examples of the practice—the explanation, for example, of Ezekiel's injunction to the priests not to shave their heads. But the allegorical method of the church reformer does not altogether obscure a vigorous and healthy tone, and this in spite of Gregory's expressed contempt for the technical side of letters. *Cura Pastoralis* appealed to Alfred by its spiritual insight; consequently he began to turn into West Saxon "the book called in Latin *Pastoralis* and in English *Hierdeboc*, sometimes word for word, sometimes sense for sense." In so doing he availed himself of the help of his teachers Plegmund and Asser, Grimbald and John, and as he understood their explanations he rendered the matter into English.

The preface which gives this particular account of the origin of the *Pastoral Care* is of great importance in another respect. An earlier passage makes it clear that the present was only the first of a series of books which the king intended to translate, in order that ultimately all the free-born youths of England, who had the necessary leisure, might be instructed in their own tongue. The preface to the *Pastoral Care* is thus a preface to the whole series of translations. At the same time it ranks among the most important of Alfred's original contri-

butions to literature.   It gives an account of the decay of learning in Britain, and sets forth the king's determination to reform
the schools of Wessex.   It defends the use of the vernacular by
showing how the Old Testament was written first in Hebrew,
then translated into Greek and subsequently into Latin, and
how all other Christian nations had turned some portion of
ancient literature into their own tongue.   From a literary point
of view, the preface is the first important piece of prose in
English; linguistically, it is, on account of its age, of unique
value.   A passage in alliterative verse, containing a glowing
tribute to Gregory, "Christ's warrior, the Pope of Rome,"
forms a kind of second preface.   It closes with a reference
to the despatch of a copy to each bishop in the land.

The style of the *Pastoral Care* has just those characteristics
which might have been expected in an early work.   Alfred's
conception of the translator's province never limited him to a
very close rendering; but, compared with his later work, there
are signs of restraint in this effort that suggest inexperience.
The double versions and the anacolutha in the text have given
rise to the ingenious suggestion that the translation was dic-
tated.   A close comparison of the Latin text and the West
Saxon version throws further light on the king's methods.
His English audience is always kept in view, and, for their
benefit, he inserts brief explanatory notes.   Thus, he interprets
"manna" as "the sweet meat which came down from heaven,"
"shittim wood" as "the tree which never decays," "purple"
as "the royal robe."   Occasionally he Teutonises the terms of
the Latin original by identifying Hebrew institutions and
social grades with their nearest analogues in West Saxon civilisation.   *Plateis* he renders by "herestraetum."   David is
described as a "salm-sceop," Uriah as a "thegn."   Blunders
are naturally to be met with, as, for example, in the derivation
of *sacerdotes*—"in English cleansers because they are to act as
guides of believers and govern them."   Compared with later
translations, Alfred's *Pastoral Care* is very close to the original.
The style is somewhat Latinised and abounds in pleonasms
and repetition, and the translation is remarkable for the num-
ber of $\overset{\text{\'a}}{\alpha}\pi\alpha\xi$ $\lambda\varepsilon\gamma\acute{o}\mu\varepsilon\nu\alpha$ it contains.   The copy preserved in
the Bodleian is interesting as containing the name of Werferth,
and it is the actual copy destined for the Worcester see.

The relative positions of *Orosius* and *Bede* are difficult to determine. For a long period the prior position was assigned to *Orosius*, but, latterly, there has been a tendency to reverse the order. The argument based on closeness of translation may, in this case, be fallacious, not only from the fact that the Latin of Orosius presents more difficulties than that of Bede, but because, in the latter case, Alfred would have been far less justified in tampering with his original. Bede's work ranked, in Alfred's day, as a standard history of the early English church; it was a recognised classic. Much of Orosius, on the other hand, was obviously unsuitable for English readers unversed in the outlines of classical history. The comparative closeness of the translation of Bede does not, therefore, necessarily imply early work. Plummer has pointed out that the account of Caesar's invasions was omitted in the first recension of *Bcde*—a fact which can only be understood by assuming that Alfred had already treated these events in detail in *Orosius*.

The *Historia adversus Paganos* of Paulus Orosius, a Spanish ecclesiastic, dates from the fifth century and was looked upon as a standard text-book of universal history. Orosius, as a disciple of Augustine, had already given expression to anti-Pelagian views in an earlier work. His later book, likewise due to the inspiration of Augustine,[1] was an attempt to expound the thesis that the decline of the Roman empire was due to other causes than the rise of Christianity and the neglect of pagan deities.

Alfred's interest in the work of Orosius lay chiefly on the historical and geographical sides, though he did not neglect to draw the moral. He aimed at giving to the English people a compendium of universal history and geography, handling his original with great freedom, introducing alterations and additions, omitting much superfluous detail and making original contributions of great value. The account of the geography of Germania is an interpolation of the greatest importance as a historical document. Further, the accounts of the celebrated voyages of Ohthere and Wulfstan inserted in the volume were taken down from hearsay. The Norwegian Ohthere had voyaged furthest north of all his contemporaries,

[1] Cf. *De Civ. Dei,* III.

reaching a latitude of about 71° 15′.   Passing round the north
of the Scandinavian peninsula, he afterwards explored the
White Sea.   Not till 1553 was this feat eclipsed, by Willoughby.
Ohthere afterwards made a voyage south, from Halgoland
to Haddeby in the Baltic.   From this point Wulstan set out
to explore the great sea, which Ohthere had described as run-
ning for many miles into the land.   For a time he had Wend-
land on his starboard and the Danish islands on his port side.
Continuing past the Swedish provinces of Bleking and Smaland,
he reached the mouth of the Vistula.   He entered the Frische
Haff and sailed up the Elbing to Truso, having accomplished
the voyage in seven days.   On their return both voyagers
recounted their adventures to Alfred, who gave them a sympathetic hearing.   The narrative of Ohthere must have had
particular interest for him, for the spirit of discovery which
animated the Norwegian sailor was akin to that felt by the
West Saxon king.   Alfred had already formed plans for the
development of a navy, and would readily recognise the relation
between the spirit of adventure and the maintenance of sea-
power.   Geographical conditions were largely responsible for
the unrest of the Scandinavians.   The interior of Sweden
was filled with dense pine forests and Norway was, for the
most part, a barren moor.   Hence expeditions, piratical or
otherwise, and the growth of that love for the sea which is
reflected in the northern sagas.   "He alone," says the *Ynglinga Saga*, "had full right to the name of sea-king, who never
slept under sooty beam and never drank at chimney corner."
The narrative of Ohthere's voyage holds a unique position
as the first attempt to give expression to the spirit of discovery.
It is, besides, good literature, and finds an honourable place in
Hakluyt's great collection of voyages.

Alfred was too wise to burden his book with all the geographical detail given by Orosius.   He confined himself to the
essentials of general geography, omitting the descriptions of
northeast Africa and of central Asia and abbreviating other passages.   The mistakes which crept into his version are to be ascribed either to lack of acquaintance with the district described
or to a misunderstanding of the somewhat difficult Latin of
Orosius.   The historical portion of the book is less original
than the geographical.   Alfred omitted a great deal, particu-

larly in the sections dealing with classical mythology. The stories of Philomela, Tantalus and Caligula had little to commend them, and were not inserted in the translation. Many of the moralisings of Orosius were left out, though a number were retained in a paraphrased form. Curiously enough, some of the passages definitely ascribed by Alfred to Orosius are not to be traced in the original. It is possible that, in such cases, Alfred availed himself of materials as yet unknown to us. A more questionable proceeding is the omission of details prejudicial to the reputation of Germanic tribes. The alterations and additions in the historical section are decidedly interesting. There are the usual misunderstandings— the identification of Theseus with the victor of Marathon, of Carthage with Cordova, and the fusion of the consuls Lepidus and Mucius into one under the title of Lepidus Mutius. Wherever possible the king acts as interpreter, substituting, for example, English equivalents for the Latin names of British towns and English names of measures for Latin. The description given by Orosius of the appearances of Commodus in the arena is reduced to the simple statement that the emperor was accustomed to fight duels. Alfred's imagination plays around the details of the plague of frogs in Egypt—"No meat could be prepared without there being as large a quantity of reptiles as of meat in the vessel before it could be dressed." Cleopatra is described as placing the adder against her arm because she thought it would cause less pain there. Interesting accounts are inserted of a Roman triumph and of the temple of Janus. A side glimpse is often to be had of the king's opinions, religious or otherwise. He enlarges on Scipio's love for the fatherland, concluding, "He compelled them to swear that they would all together either live or die in their native land." His admiration is likewise moved by the courage of Regulus, to whom he devotes considerable space. *Orosius* is thus of great value for the light it throws on Alfred's character. He is shown to have been a skilful geographer and an interested, if not a scholarly, student of history. His practical purpose is clearly apparent. Everywhere in dealing with history he endeavours to bring the historical fact into vital relation with current affairs. The military achievements of Greeks and Romans remind him of wars in which he had himself been engaged, and his explanations of manœuvres are generally based on his own experience. Though the hand of Alfred is very apparent in the pages of *Orosius*, there is no good external authority for the authorship. The first to associate his name with this translation was William of Malmesbury.[1]

The translation of Bede's *Historia Ecclesiastica* may be considered next. The original is much less freely rendered than is the case with *Orosius*—a fact which may have been due to the authoritative position occupied by Bede's book. The external testimony of Alfred's authorship is fairly trustworthy. In his *Homily on St. Gregory* Aelfric refers to the *Historia Anglorum*, "which Alfred translated out of Latin into English," and there is further evidence in the Cambridge MS., on the first leaf of which is written, *Historicus quondam fecit me Beda latinum, Aelfred rex Saxo transtulit ille pius.* On the ground of certain Mercian characteristics in the text, however, Miller ventures to doubt the Alfredian authorship, and is led by the fact of certain omissions to fix the locality of the original MS. at Lichfield. On the other hand, Schipper holds to the orthodox view and considers the arguments based on dialect to be unproven. The omissions in Alfred's *Bede* are very considerable, and no attempt is made to supplement the original with southern annals. No account is given of the famous ecclesiastical controversy which took place at Whitby—a fact which seems to Miller to confirm his view that the translator was not a West Saxon but a Mercian, keenly aware of Scotch susceptibilities. Bede's accounts of the great figures of the early churches are retained, though the story of Adamnan is omitted. In the interest of his narrative Alfred omits such documents as letters from popes and bishops, retaining only Gregory's first letter to the monks, and this in *oratio obliqua*. The finest passage in the English version is the account of Caedmon, an excellent piece of early prose, and Caedmon's hymn is inserted in a West Saxon form, of which the original is to be found only in the Moore MS. of Bede's *History*. The style is frequently marred by over-literalness. Latin constuctions are constantly introduced in an altogether un-English fashion, and words are used in an un-English sense as equiva-

---

[1] *Gesta Regum Anglorum*, II, § 123.

lents for Latin terms.   A peculiarity of the style is the employment of two English terms to represent a single term in the
original.   On the whole, the translation cannot rank very
high among Alfred's works, even if it be rightly attributed
to him.

There is no external evidence to enable us to decide the
date of Alfred's code of laws.   The historical introduction,
based on the *Vulgate*, shows considerable independence and
cannot be dated very early.   The composition of the code
may be assigned, provisionally, to the close of Alfred's first
translation period (c. 893), without, however, attaching
much importance to Malmesbury's statement that it was
undertaken "amid the clash of arms."[1]   The code is of a somewhat composite character, and has usually been arranged in
three sections—the introduction, the laws of Alfred proper
and the laws of Ine.   In his monograph entitled *The Legal Code
of Alfred the Great*, Turk points out that this arrangement is
not justified by the MSS.   The introduction consists properly
of two parts—the historical introduction based on the Mosaic
law and the introduction proper.   The insertions from the
Mosaic law give a universal character to Alfred's code.   They
are rendered somewhat freely, large portions of the Latin
text being omitted and other portions altered.   One of the
Mosaic laws ran as follows: "If a man shall deliver unto his
neighbour money or stuff to keep, and it be stolen out of the
man's house, if the thief be found, he shall pay double.   If the
thief be not found, then the master of the house shall come
near unto God (or the judges), to see whether he have not put
his hand unto his neighbour's goods."[2]   This passage Alfred
renders as follows: "If any one entrust his property to his
friend: if he shall steal it, let him pay double; if he know not
who has stolen it, let him excuse himself."   Another Mosaic
law—"If men contend, and one smiteth the other with a stone
or with his fist, and he die not, but keep his bed: if he rise again,
and walk abroad upon his staff, then shall he that smote him
be quit; only he shall pay for the loss of his time, and shall
cause him to be thoroughly healed"[3]—has been much altered
in Alfred's version: "If a man strike his neighbour with a

---

[1] *Gesta Regum Anglorum*, I, § 129.
[2] *Ex*. xxii, 7, 8.   [3] *Ex*. xxi, 18, 19.

stone or with his fist and he may nevertheless go about with a
staff, let him provide him a leech and do his work during the
time that he is not able." The law concerning the first-born
—"the first-born of thy sons shalt thou give unto me"[1]—
naturally finds no place in the West Saxon code. Another
alteration is the substitution of two oxen for five in the
Mosaic ordinance, "If a man shall steal an ox, or a sheep, and
kill it, or sell it, he shall pay five oxen for an ox, and four sheep
for a sheep."[2] A remarkable addition, intended to counter-
act the severity of the Mosaic code as a whole, is that of the
apostolic letter, at the close of which Alfred continues in
his own words—"From this one law a man may learn how
we ought to judge aright. He needs no other law-books; let
him bethink him that he do not to another what he would
not have done to himself."

Alfred's code is, as we have indicated, of a composite
character. He links himself with the church not only by his
insertions from the Mosaic code but by his reference to "the
many synods throughout the world and throughout England,
after they had received the faith of Christ, of holy bishops
and other distinguished counsellors." Some of the synodical
laws may have been embodied in the West Saxon code. Further we find alongside Alfred's own laws those of Ine, of
Offa and of Aethelbriht. The Mercian laws ascribed to Offa
are unfortunately lost, but the Kentish laws of Aethelbriht,
the earliest "dooms" we have, though in a late copy, can be
traced in Alfred's code, where they have been inserted in a revised form. Bede refers to the original Kentish laws as "written
in English and still preserved. Among which the king in the
first place set down what satisfaction should be given by those
who should steal anything belonging to the church, the bishop
and the other clergy" (II, 5). The prominence given to the
church seems to have appealed forcibly to the historian. Aethelbriht's code is mainly taken up with the penalties payable for the
infliction of personal injuries. The compensation for the loss
of an ear is fixed, tariff-like, at 6s., of an eye at 50s., of a nose at
9s. "If one man strike another with the fist on the nose—3s."
Alfred carefully revised each of the penalties before inserting
Aethelbriht's code in his own. The laws of Ine date back

---

[1] *Ex.* xxii, 29.　　　　　[2] *Ex.* xxii, 1.

to the eighth century and are the earliest of West Saxon laws. They are more comprehensive in character than the laws of Kent, but seem by Alfred's date to have received large accretions. Alfred adopted the developed code of Ine apparently without subjecting it to revision. But he connects his own particular code with the earlier one in such a way as to make the one supplementary to the other. One of Ine's laws as it appears in Alfred's text is worth quoting:

If a man burn a tree in a wood and it is made clear who did it, let him pay the full penalty of 60s., because fire is a thief. If a man fell many trees in a wood, and it is found out, let him pay for three trees, each with 30s. He need not pay for more, however many they be, because the axe is an informer and not a thief.

It is possible that some years elapsed before Alfred began his translations of Boethius's *De Consolatione Philosophiae.* Assuming that his energies had been fully employed during the period from 888 to 893 with his early work, he could have had little leisure for any new undertaking before the year 897. The freedom with which the whole of this new task is carried out points to a late period and a mature method. Boethius's book ranked among the most characteristic products of the Middle Ages. Its influence on later literature was immense, and is scarcely to be estimated by the number of translations, numerous though they were. It was done into English, after Alfred's time, by Chaucer and Elizabeth, into German by Notker, into French by Jean de Meun. An early metrical version in Provençal also exists. The influence of Boethius has been traced in *Beowulf;* it permeates Dante and Chaucer. The closing words of the *Paradiso*—"Already my desire and will were rolled, even as a wheel that moveth equally, by the love that moves the sun and the other stars"—owe their origin to the *Consolation of Philosophy.* The book was written while the author was under sentence of death after having fallen into disfavour with the Ostrogothic king Theodric. It is in the form of a dialogue between Boethius and Philosophy, wherein are set forth the consolations associated with the contemplative state of mind. The famous dissertation upon fate and providence is conducted with considerable subtlety; but the atmosphere of the book is religious rather than philosophical, and it is signally free from the technicalities of the schools. Boethius harks back to the early Greek standpoint of Plato, from whom he derives his central doctrine of submissiveness. The finite is to be realised only in the absolute, which is identical with love, and love is realised by faith. The Middle Ages, with their vivid sense of an overruling fate, found in Boethius an interpretation of life closely akin to the spirit of Christianity. The *Consolation of Philosophy* stands, by its note of fatalism and its affinities with the Christian doctrine of humility, midway between the heathen philosophy of Seneca and the later Christian philosophy of consolation represented by Thomas à Kempis. Alfred's religious outlook had much in common with the gentle philosophy of "the last of the Romans," and the translation afforded him considerable opportunity for self-expression. In some passages the king identifies himself with the philosopher and enlarges on metaphysical themes. In others, as in the famous seventeenth chapter, he reflects on such problems as his duty toward the state:

Thou knowest, Reason, that the greed and grandeur of this temporal power have never pleased me much, nor have I longed overmuch for this earthly kingdom: but I desired tools and material for the work which I was ordered to work, in order that I might virtuously and fittingly control the power entrusted to me.

The rendering of Boethius is never close, and the additions give a unique character to the work. The spirit of Alfred's version is naturally more in keeping with Christianity than is the Neo-Platonic doctrine of Boethius. There is definite mention of God and Christ where Boethius speaks of "the good," or "love," or "the true way," or "divine reason"; again, the English version substitutes "angels" for "divine substance." The minor additions are often interesting. The lynx is "an animal that can see through anything—trees or even stones"; the Parcae are "the cruel goddesses who preside over the fates of every man"; Orpheus is "an excellent good harper." Alfred's interest in geography induced him to supply the information that *ultima Thule* is situated "in the north-west of this earth," and Mount Etna in "the island of Sicily." But it is in the expanded passages that the chief value of the book consists. The preface and chapter I, with its interesting account of the Latin author, are wholly original. Chapter XVII, again, is original, save for a few lines. Details concerning Busiris, Regulus and Seneca are inserted, which are only partially translated, and the account of Cicero is a noteworthy addition. It was a happy inspiration that led Alfred to render the Latin *Ubi nunc fidelis ossa Fabricii manent ?*—in the spirit of a Teuton attached to his national legends—"Where are the bones of Weland?" He is much interested in astrology, and refers more than once to "the cold star," Saturn. The reflective passages afford most instructive glimpses into the workings of the king's mind. They are permeated by deep religious fervour: "It is," he writes, "the expectation and fancy of fools that power and wealth are the highest good; but really is quite otherwise." He reflects on the vanity of earthly ambition: "O glory of this world, why do men falsely call thee glory, when thou art not so?" The literary beauty of the similes employed by Alfred has been often noted. Prosperity passes away "like a gust of wind"; blessings flow from the source of all goodness "like waters from the sea." God is likened to a steersman who perceives the oncoming of a storm and makes preparations against it. In an important article, Schepss raised the question as to how far Alfred's interpolations were based on Latin commentaries similar to that of Froumond, or upon scholia such as are to be found in the Munich MS. He pointed out that, in expanding Boethius's account of the giants, who incurred the wrath of Jupiter by assailing heaven, Alfred introduced Nimrod and the Tower of Babel. The hint for this seems to have been derived from the Munich MS. The famous simile of the egg—

Thou, glorious king of hosts, through strong might wonderfully didst establish the earth so firmly that she inclineth not on any side nor may she sink hither and thither any more than she ever did. Yet nothing earthly sustains her, it is equally easy for this world to fall upwards or downwards: likest to that which happens in an egg, the yolk is in the midst yet glideth freely about the egg. So stands the world fixed in its place, while the streams, the play of waters, the sky and the stars and the shining shell move about day by day as they did long ago—

and the other simile, of the wheel, in which God is compared
to the fixed axle round which the felly and spokes turn, are
not wholly original but, together with many other passages,
show the influence of the scholia. It is highly probable that
much in Alfred's work which has hitherto been looked upon as
wholly original will be found to have been based upon similar
sources. The preface, on the genuineness of which some doubt
has been thrown, informs us that Alfred was the translator of
the book and that he rendered his original "sometimes word
for word, sometimes sense for sense, as best he could amid the
manifold occupations of his kingdom." This description of the
king's method is altogether in keeping with that prefixed to the
Pastoral Care. It is worthy of note that, according to William
of Malmesbury,[1] Asser had previously glossed the Latin for the
king's benefit. In view of this statement the present translation was, for a long time, considered to have been the first of
Alfred's undertakings. He may have intended to begin *Boethius* at an early period, but it is certain that the translation
as we now have it is a late piece of work. The language has
given rise to interesting problems. The two chief MSS., the
Bodleian and the Cottonian, contain, according to Sievers, a
large number of Kentisms. These are possibly due to a scribe
of Kentish origin, the whole case being parallel to that of *Bede*.

Much discussion has arisen with regard to the authorship
of the alliterative metres which are to be found in the British
Museum MS. of *Boethius* (Otho A. 6). The younger MS. at
Oxford contains a prose version of these metres. It is generally
agreed that the verse renderings are based, not on the Latin
directly, but on a West Saxon prose version. In the British
Museum MS. the text is preceded by two prefaces, one of
which is in alliterative verse; the other, in prose, attributes the
metres to Alfred. Thomas Wright was the first to doubt
the king's authorship of the metres, but his arguments have
been largely disproved. Leicht was able to bring forward a
more formidable case. While admitting the weakness of
Wright's argument, he contended that the case for Alfred's
authorship rests on an unsound basis. He agreed with Ten
Brink in the opinion that the preface ascribing the verses to
Alfred is not authentic, and maintained that the king, in at-

---

[1] *Gesta Regum Anglorum*, II, § 122.

tempting to render his own prose into verse, would scarcely have clung so closely to his model as is the case. On the other hand, Hartmann has pointed out that Alfred's skill in prose argues no facility in verse-making. The two poems in *Cura Pastoralis* have no more distinction than those in the British Museum MS. Again, there are certain expressions in this MS., not to be found in the Oxford type, which definitely refer to passages in the latter. The author of the verses appears to identify himself with the author of the prose translation. On the whole, the question must be left open, though it would seem that it rests with those who deny the king's authorship to establish their case. It is known that Alfred was an enthusiast in regard to Old English verse, and it is not improbable that he was well acquainted with the verses of his kinsman, Aldhelm. A spirit of emulation may have led him to try his hand at versification.

The West Saxon version of Augustine's *Soliloquia* stands last in order of Alfred's translations, and considerable doubt has been expressed as to its genuineness. Pauli, on the ground that Alfred's name does not occur in the preface, rejects it altogether, and finds justification in the fact that the language is an impure form of West Saxon. Wülker, who formerly identified the *Soliloquies* with the *Handbook*, considers the book to be genuine. He points out that the preface in its present form is mutilated and that the twelfth century MS. is too late to afford any evidence based on style. Judging from the nature of the references to holy orders, the translation appears to have been the work of a layman rather than a monk, and the closing words, whether genuine or not, attribute it to Alfred. The vocabulary of the *Soliloquies* has much in common with that of Alfred's *Boethius*, and there are close resemblances between the two works in thought and style. Some of the original passages seem to have been directly based upon translated portions of Boethius, and original passages in both works sometimes correspond closely. Alfred was attracted to Augustine by the nature of his theme. The Latin work is a treatise on God and the soul, in which much space is devoted to a discussion of immortality. The translation is undertaken quite in accordance with Alfred's customary methods. He renders the first book somewhat closely, but paraphrases the sense and makes a few additions, indulging his taste for simile in a comparison between the soul at rest in God and a ship at anchor, and discoursing at length on the changes that take place in nature, on the likeness between God and the sun and on the relation between king and subject. Book II he renders very freely. He discusses the problem of immortality from an independent standpoint: "Believe thine own reason and believe Christ, the Son of God, and believe all His saints for they were truthful witnesses, and believe thine own soul which ever declares through reason that she is in thee." Book III is based on another source, Augustine's *De Videndo Deo*, supplemented by passages from Augustine's *De Civitate Dei*, Gregory's *Morals* and *Dialogues* and Jerome's *Commentary on Luke*. The dialogue form is continued for some time, though the sources do not justify such an arrangement. The spirit of the whole translation is deeply religious. It is a logical discussion of the nature and future of the soul, in which Augustine's dialectics are rejected in favour of common-sense reasoning. There is a natural connection between the *Soliloquies* and Boethius, since its central theme had already been suggested in the closing pages of the latter. It has already been shown that the preface to the *Pastoral Care* is in the nature of a general introduction to Alfred's translated works; the preface to the *Soliloquies* may be considered an epilogue—the king's farewell to literature—

I gathered me poles and props and bars and handles for each of the tools which I could handle, and bough timbers and bolt timbers for each of the tasks which I was capable of undertaking, the fairest wood, as far as I could bear it away. I came not home with a great burden, since it pleased me not to bring all the wood home, even if I could have carried it. On each tree I saw something which I needed at home. Therefore, I advise every man who is able and has many waggons, that he direct himself to the same wood where I cut the props, and that he procure for himself more, and load his waggons with fair beams, that he may construct many a fair wall, and many a beautiful house, and many a town and dwell there merrily and peacefully, both winter and summer, as I have not done.

With this parable Alfred closes his literary career.

The literature of the reign for which the king was not directly responsible owed at least its inspiration to him. In the monasteries the work of producing MSS. went forward with great activity, but the scribes were engaged in merely copying out books; they did no original work. It had been customary, however, for the monks to keep record of events of outstanding importance. These monastic records were of the briefest possible kind, designed to serve merely as landmarks in the passage of time and not as historical surveys, but in these casual and unsystematic notes Alfred perceived the nucleus for a larger survey of West Saxon history. The change in the tone of the *Chronicle* has been ascribed to Aethelwulf's reign, but it is probable that Alfred was responsible for the systematic revision of the earlier records back to Hengest and Horsa, and his connection with the *Chronicle* is possibly referred to in Gaimar's *Estorie des Engles*, though the allusion is somewhat obscure. The *Chronicle*, as known to us, is a highly composite piece of work, and it consists of various recensions, the relations between which have been carefully worked out by Earle and Plummer.[1] The original nucleus belonged to Winchester, the capital of the West Saxon kingdom. The Alfredian version comes down to 892 only, at which date the first hand in the MS. ceases, and of this portion Alfred may be supposed to have acted as supervisor.

From a historical point of view, the *Chronicle* was the first national continuous history of a western nation in its own language; from a literary point of view, it was the first great book in English prose. The account of the years 893–7 is one of the most vivid in the whole of the annals. The struggle with the Danes and the great series of campaigns extending over the whole of the south of England are described in detail. At one time the king is at Exeter while Aethelred, the ealdorman, is occupied on the Severn, the struggle extending north as far as York and Chester. Alfred's military and naval reforms are enlarged upon, the king's brilliant exploits, and his care for the nation's well-being, inspiring the annalist with the spirit of a historian. The whole narrative is a masterpiece of Old English prose, full of vigour and life.

[1] The different recensions of the *Chronicle* and its further development are dealt with in the chapter that follows.

The West Saxon translation of Gregory's *Dialogues* owed its inspiration directly to Alfred. The authorship of the translation has never been called in question; both Asser and William of Malmesbury attribute it to Werferth, bishop of Worcester, who undertook the task at the king's bidding. The book is partly in dialogue form. Gregory is found by his deacon, Peter, sitting "in a solitary place, very fit for a sad and melancholy disposition." The stories which Gregory proceeds to tell, serve to relieve his mind of its weight of thought. The monk, Martinius, impresses the sign of the cross upon a hearth-cake with a motion of the hand; a sweet fragrance miraculously arises from the grave of count Theophanius; bishop Frigidianus turns the course of the Serchio by marking out its bed with a rake. Book ii is exclusively devoted to St. Benedict. The collection was an attempt to complete the accepted lives of the saints by a recital of miraculous deeds performed in Italy. Towards the end of the book Gregory leaves Italy and tells the story of St. Hermenegild and his brother king Recarede. The preface, in the Oxford and Cambridge MSS., is the work of the king and is thus of particular interest—

I, Alfred, by God's grace, dignified with the title of king, have perceived and often learnt from the reading of sacred books, that we, to whom God hath given so much worldly honour, have particular need to humble and subdue our minds to the divine laws in the midst of worldly cares; accordingly, I besought my faithful friends that they would write down out of holy books concerning the miracles of the saints the following narrative; that I, strengthened in my mind by admonition and love, might think upon spiritual things in the midst of my worldly cares.

The MSS. of the *Dialogues* have given rise to interesting problems. The Cambridge and British Museum types are closely related and stand apart from that of Oxford. From this fact Krebs deduced the theory that the *Dialogues* were translated on two separate occasions. A more careful comparison of the MSS. has shown that they are all derived from a single original, of which the Oxford type represents a revised version.

The West Saxon *Martyrology* may be ascribed to Alfred's reign. Cockayne was of opinion that the oldest MS.—that in the British Museum—dates from the ninth century.

it is noteworthy that the saints referred to belong either to the period preceding the king's reign or to the reign itself. Another proof of the age of the collection is the fact that under 5 August Oswald is described as buried at Bardney, though his body was moved to Gloucester soon after Alfred's death. The story of St. Milus (15 November) seems to have been derived from the east. The *Leech-book* attests Alfred's relations with Elias, the patriarch of Jerusalem, whose rule extended from 897 to 907. The *Martyrology* is incomplete, but it extends from 31 December to 21 December.

Alfred's literary reputation caused a number of other works to be ascribed to him for which there is no trustworthy evidence. Of these the most important is the so-called *Psalter*. William of Malmesbury makes a statement to the effect that Alfred began a translation of the *Psalms*, but was unable to complete it—*Psalterium transferre aggressus vix prima parte explicata vivendi finem fecit.*[1] Curiously enough, an eleventh century MS. in the Bibliothèque Nationale at Paris contains an Old English prose version of the first fifty psalms, followed by an alliterative version of the remainder (psalms li–cl). Wülker conjectures that the prose portions were based on the work of Alfred referred to by William of Malmesbury. Each psalm is preceded by an introduction, in which are set forth the circumstances under which the psalm was written. The translation is free, and the method of rendering one word by two is frequently resorted to. In this latter respect the prose *Psalter* resembles Alfred's *Bede* and *Pastoral Care*.[2] The alliterative portions in the Paris MS. were probably introduced to supplement the deficiencies of the prose version; there can be no doubt that a complete alliterative version of the *Psalms* was in existence when the prose was undertaken.

Alfred has been credited with a collection of *Proverbs* in metrical form. In favour of this there is not the slightest evidence. For centuries he must have had some reputation as a philosopher, and an anonymous collection of maxims would naturally be associated with his name. A treatise on *Falconry* and a translation of Aesop's *Fables* have also been attributed to him, but for neither of these is there any evidence.

---

[1] *Gesta Regum Anglorum*, II. § 123.
[2] But see Bruce's *Anglo-Saxon Version of the Book of Psalms*.

Alfred's literary achievement is of immense importance. The prominence given to the vernacular during his reign made it possible for English literature to develop on its own lines. He was wise enough to limit himself to the work of translation, since he had not, apparently, great creative genius in letters. But the effect of his choice of models was to introduce a large Latin element into Old English prose style. Compared with the abrupt and rugged style of the king Cynewulf episode in the early part of the *Chronicle*, Alfred's prose is that of an accomplished writer: compared with later prose, it is largely tentative. It was not until nearly a century later that more definite results were achieved when Aelfric took up the task left incomplete by the West Saxon king. Apart from the historic estimate, Alfred has some personal claim to recognition as a prose writer. His original passages, however much they may owe to undiscovered sources, embody his own personal convictions, and afford a remarkable proof of his ability to inform with life the materials at his disposal. In literature, personality is of the utmost importance, and Alfred is one of the most personal of writers. He is the embodiment, not only of the intellectual, but of the spiritual, thoughts of his time. His writings constantly reveal his aspirations after truth, and, even in the *Laws*, there is a definitely religious tone. "I have wished," he writes in *Boethius*, "to live worthily while I lived, and to leave to those who should come after me my memory in good deeds." And, in the language of the inscription on the monument erected to his memory at Wantage in 1877, he "found learning dead, and he restored it; education neglected. and he revived it."

CHAPTER VII

FROM ALFRED TO THE CONQUEST

IT seems permissible to treat the year 901, when king Alfred died, as the dividing line between the earlier and later periods of Old English literature.[1] According to this classification, nearly all the poetry composed in this country before the Norman conquest would fall within the first period; while the bulk of the prose writings in the vernacular would be included in the second. It was, indeed, during the tenth and eleventh centuries that our language in its Old English stage attained its highest development as a prose medium. The circumstances of the time were unfavourable to the production of sustained poems. This may be owing to the gradual break-up of Old English tradition and to the influence of another Germanic literature, then at its height, in the English court. The chief poetical fragments that have survived from these years deal with contemporary events, and seem to be the outbreak of emotions too strong to be suppressed.

Like feelings find their expression also in the prose literature of these centuries, which saw not only the rise of the West Saxon kings to full mastery over England, but also the victories of Dane and Norman, and the quenching of all hope of English rule over England until the conquered should absorb the conquerors. There was scarcely a year during this period in which the harassed rulers of the kingdom could afford to lay aside their arms; though during the time of comparative quiet between the death of Aethelstan and the accession of Aethelred England took an active part in the monastic revival which was so marked a feature of contemporary European history. In these times of struggle, letters and learning found, for a time, their grave, and long years of patient struggle were needed to revive them.

[1] See note on p. 497.

The gloomy tale is nowhere better told than in the *Chronicle*, which, written in simple language, alone marks for more than half a century the continuance of literary activity in England.

The beginning of the *Chronicle* is usually ascribed to the influence of Alfred, and it continues for two and a half centuries after that king's reign, long after the last English king had been slain and the old tongue banished from court and school. Its principal recensions[1] differ from one another not in the main story, but in the attention given to various details, and in the length to which they are carried. Owing to the number of hands employed in its composition, the literary merit is very unequal; sometimes the entries consist of a date and the simple statement of an event; at others we find passages of fluent and glowing narrative, as in the record of the war-filled years from 911 to 924. The period from 925 to 975 is very bare, and such entries as exist relate mostly to church matters. It is, however, within this time that the principal poems of the *Chronicle* are inserted. Under 991 is told the story of Anlaf's raid at Maldon in which Byrhtnoth fell. In the years 975–1001 the *Chronicle* is of extreme interest, and the annals for the year 1001 are very full. Some time about the middle, or towards the last quarter, of the eleventh century the present recension of the Winchester chronicle was transplanted to Christ Church, Canterbury, and there completed with Canterbury annals, passages being interpolated in various places from beginning to end from the chronicle kept at St. Augustine's, Christ Church library having been previously burnt. Before this, the notice taken of Canterbury events was so extremely slight that we do not even hear of the murder of archbishop Aelfhēah (St. Alphege) by the Danes.[2] The MS. known as Cott. Tib. A. VI seems to have been originally meant to serve as an introduction to further annals, which, however, were never written; and it is appar-

---

[1] The Winchester or Parker chronicle, in the library of Corpus Christi College, Cambridge; the shorter Abingdon chronicle (Cott. Tib. A. VI); the longer Abingdon chronicle (Cott. Tib. B. I); the Evesham or Worcester chronicle (Cott. Tib. B. IV); the Peterborough chronicle (Bod. Laud. 636).

[2] The recension under notice is a copy of the original Winchester chronicle, which latter was also the source of the original Abingdon chronicle. Hence the agreement with Tib. A. VI, and Tib. B, I. up to 892. Naturally, it does not incorporate the Mercian chronicle, but maintains a kind of separate parallelism from 894–915.

ently a copy of the original Abingdon chronicle (itself a copy
of the original Winchester, written at Abingdon), which did
not reach beyond 977. The MS. under consideration is shown
by a mass of internal and external evidence to have been
written about 977, the year to which its annals reach. It may
fitly be called the *shorter* Abingdon chronicle to distinguish it
from the *longer* Abingdon chronicle referred to below, with
which it has much in common;[1] both, for example, bodily
insert the Mercian annals (sometimes called the chronicle of
Aethelflaed). These extend from 902–925, and tell, with some
detail, of the warlike feats of the Lady of Mercia. It may be
noted, in passing, that these Mercian annals occur in the so-
called Worcester chronicle,[2] where, however, they are distributed, with some omissions, amongst other matter. These
Mercian annals are the greatest interest, both in origin and
history. Their chronology differs considerably from that of
other chronicles. Perhaps the original document, or some
copy of it, in which they were contained, is to be traced under
the record *Cronica duo Anglica* in the *Catalogi veteres librorum
Ecclesiae Dunelmi*, where we also find the record of *Elflēdes Boc*
in the same place. This at once suggests to us the existence
of these annals in a book of Aethelflaed, telling of her
fight for English freedom. Thus the inscription and
record bring us into close connection with what may
well have suggested and stimulated the heroic poem of
Judith.[3]

The (*longer*) Abingdon chronicle is so called because, from
its references to the affairs of that monastery, it is supposed
to have been written there. This longer chronicle is not expanded from the shorter, nor the shorter extracted from the
longer. Both have a number of independent annals up to
the very year 977 where the common original ended. It may
be surmised that the author of the recension under notice
found the original Abingdon ready up to 977 (when the troubles
consequent on Edgar's death may have accounted for many
things), and further annals up to 1018, to which he made later
additions. The MS. tells of the election of Siward, abbot
of Abingdon, as archbishop of Canterbury in 1044, the

---

[1] Cott. Tib. B. i   [2] Cott. Tib. B. iv.   [3] See p. 142.

appointment of Aethelstan as his successor to the abbacy,
Aethelstan's death in 1047 and archbishop Siward's return
to the monastery after his retirement from office in
1048.

In 892, a copy of the southern chronicle was sent to a northern cloister, and there was revised with the aid of the text of
Bede's *Ecclesiastical History*.   There seems, also to have been
a northern continuation of Bede's *History*, and, from this, were
woven into the chronicler's text annals 737–806.   Fifteen of
these annals are wholly, and sixteen partly, Northumbrian.
That these annals were taken from some such source seems to
be proved by their being found also in other works.   The
chronicler then followed southern sources until 904, when he
began to weave into his text the book of Aethelflaed, mingling
with it southern and northern records.   From 983–1022, he
returned to his Abingdon source.   After this he struck out on
his own line.   From the original thus created was copied the
extant MS. commonly known as the Worcester or Evesham
chronicle,¹ which shows especial acquaintance with the midlands and north.   The close connection between Worcester
and York is shown by the fact that the archbishop of York is
mentioned simply as "the archbishop."   The chronicle shows
strong feeling on the subject of Godwin's outlawry, and in
every way supports that nobleman.   Alone amongst the chronicles it tells the sad tale of the battle of Hastings.   The original
from which the above chronicle was copied, seems also to
have been the basis for that patriotic Kentish chronicle, now
lost, which was the chief source both of the Peterborough
chronicle up to 1123 and the rescension known as Cott. Dom.
A. VIII, 2.

The Peterborough chronicle² is the longest of all, extending
to the year 1154.   In 1116 the town and monastery of Peterborough were destroyed by a terrible fire, which left standing
only the monastic chapterhouse and dormitory, and when,
in 1121, the rebuilding was completed, the annals contained
in this chronicle were undertaken to replace those lost in the
fire.   They were based on the lost Kentish chronicle, which
must have been forwarded to Peterborough for that purpose.

---

¹ Cott. Tib. IV.   ² Bod. Laud. 636.

This original Kentish chronicle is full of patriotic feeling and shows great knowledge of southern affairs from Canute's death, the burial of Harold Harefoot (the record of which it alone rightly tells) and the viking raid on Sandwich, to the feuds between English and Norman in the reign of the Confessor. It relates count Eustace's broils with the English of Canterbury and Dover, and the flight of archbishop Robert, leaving his pallium behind him, an annal recorded with dangerously schismatic glee. The scribe had lived at the court of William the Conqueror, and had, therefore, seen the face of the great enemy of the English. The entries for the tenth century are very meagre; but from 991 to 1075 they are much fuller and contain, among other contemporary records, the story of the ravages of Hereward. Towards the end of the chronicle, which is written in a somewhat rough and ready manner, occurs the famous passage, so often quoted by historians, telling of the wretchedness of the common folk during the reign of Stephen and its civil wars.

From the lost Kentish chronicle is derived the recension known as F or Cott. Domitian A. VIII, 2, seemingly written by one hand in the twelfth century, and of interest because of its mixed use of Latin and English. In this it indicates the approach of the employment of Latin as the general literary vehicle of English culture. There is great confusion in its bilingual employment of Latin and English; sometimes English is the original and Latin the copy, at other times the process is reversed; finally, in some passages, Latin and English become ludicrously mixed. Two other recensions exist as mere fragments: one, of three damaged leaves, in a hand of the eleventh century, is bound up with a copy of Bede's *Ecclesiastical History*[1]; and the other[2] consists of a single leaf. The manuscript to which the former of these fragments belonged was edited by Wheloc in 1644 before it was consumed in the Cottonian fire.

The following table adapted from Plummer shows the relations of the various MSS. to each other, the extant MSS. being indicated by initial letters;

[1] Cott. Oth. B. XI, 2.   [2] Cott. Tib. A. III, fol. 175.

Original Winchester

(A) Winchester   Original Abingdon

(B) (*shorter*) Abingdon   (C) (*longer*) Abingdon   Original Worcester

Lost Kentish   (D) Worcester

Lost enlarged Kentish   (F) MS. Cotton Dom. A. VIII, 2.

(E) Peterborough

The *Chronicle* is of inestimable value as an authority for
the history of the time.   The impression it leaves on the reader
is one of almost unrelieved gloom.   Records of harrying with
fire and sword occur on almost every page, and, whether the
English ealdormen or the Danes "possess the place of slaughter," the wild lawlessness and the contempt for human life
which prevailed during the greater part of the period are plainly
visible.   Sometimes the chronicler displays bitter indignation
at the misgovernment of the country, as when he tells how
Aethelred and his ealdormen and the high witan forsook the
navy which had been collected with immense effort by the
people and "let the toil of all the nation thus lightly perish."
But the entries are usually of an entirely impersonal kind; the
horror and desolation, the fiery signs in the heaven, and the
plagues that befell men and cattle upon earth, are recorded
without comment; such misfortunes were too common to call
for special remark in the days of the long struggle between
Dane and Englishman.

It has already been said that this portion of the *Chronicle*
contains several fragments of verse.   These will be noticed
later.   Here, it may, however, be remarked that some passages
written as prose are based on songs which have been inserted,
after some slight modification, by the scribe; and, towards the
end of the Peterborough chronicle, there occur some long
stretches of rhythmic prose almost akin to the sung verse of
the people.   These may be either a development of the loose
rhythm of Aelfric's prose, or may, possibly, result from the
incorporation of ballads and their reduction to prose.   The
subject is, however, still too obscure to admit of any very
definite statement on this point, and most of what has been
said on this subject seems far removed from finality.

From this brief description of the manuscripts of the *Chronicle* we must turn to the homilists, who showed especial vigour between 960 and 1020. The development reached in style and in literary tradition is at once apparent; it had its origin, doubtless, in the religious revival of the tenth century, which emanated from Fleury, and was identified in England with the names of Dunstan, Aethelwold and Oswald, the "three torches" of the church.

At the beginning of the tenth century, English monasticism and, therefore, the state of learning in England, were in a deplorable condition, from which all the efforts of king Alfred had been unable to lift them. There were religious houses, of course, but most of these seem to have been in the condition of Abingdon when Aethelwold was appointed abbot—"a place in which a little monastery had been kept up from ancient days, but then desolate and neglected, consisting of mean buildings and possessing only a few hides." To the influence of the Benedictine reformers we owe much of the prose literature of the tenth and eleventh centuries. The great bond thus knit once more between English literature and the literature of the continent ensured our share in what was then living of classical and pseudo-classical lore.

With the accession of Edgar (959) better times dawned. On the death of Odo, Dunstan became archbishop, and, in 961 Oswald, Odo's nephew, was consecrated to the see of Worcester. His appointment was followed in 963 by that of Aethelwold, abbot of Abingdon, to the see of Winchester, and the three bishops set about a vigorous ecclesiastical reform. During the reigns of Edgar and his sons no fewer than forty monasteries for men were founded or restored, and these were peopled chiefly by monks trained at Abingdon or Winchester.

The most famous school of all was that founded at Winchester by Aethelwold, one of the most distiguished of the pupils of Dunstan, and himself an enthusiastic teacher, who did not scorn to explain the difficulties of Donatus and Priscian to the postulants and other youthful frequenters of the Benedictine school. The most important of his scholars was Aelfric, the greatest prose writer in the vernacular before the Conquest.

The inhabitants of the newly restored monasteries naturally required instruction in the Benedictine rule, and to this neces-

sity is due the version of the rule which Aethelwold drew up under the title *Regularis Concordia Anglicae Nationis Monachorum
Sanctimonialiumque*.   In the beginning of this he stated that
the work had the sanction of the king, and that it was framed
at a council at Winchester.   The name of the writer is nowhere
given, and, were it not that Aelfric, in his *Letter to the Monks of
Eynsham*, says that the source of his information is bishop
Aethelwold's *De Consuetudine*, and quotes long passages from
the *Regularis* (evidently the same work), we should be ignorant
of the authorship.[1]

But it was not enough to multiply copies and commentaries
of the *Rule* in Latin.   Many of the newly admitted postulants
and novices were quite ignorant of that language, and, therefore, king Edgar further entrusted Aethelwold with the task of
translating the *Rule* into English, giving him in acknowledgment the manor of Southborne, which he assigned to the newly
restored monastery at Ely.   There are several MSS. containing
an Old English version of the *Rule*, and in one of them[2] it is
followed by a historical sketch of the monastic revival of the
tenth century, which recounts Edgar's share in the movement,
his refounding of Abingdon and his command to translate
into English the *Rule*.   Schröer thinks that this tractate
is by the author of the foregoing version of the *Rule;* but,
since the writer calls himelf everywhere "abbot," and not
"bishop," if it is by Aethelwold he must have made it between
959, the year of Edgar's accession, and 963, when he became
bishop of Winchester.

It is possible that the *Blickling Homilies*, so called because
the MS. is preserved at Blickling Hall, Norfolk, were also due
to this religious revival.   They are nineteen in number, but
several are incomplete, and some are mere fragments.   The
earlier homilies are sermons, properly so called; but the later
are largely narrative in character, and are based on legendary
sources.

The style of these homilies stands midway between the
style of Alfred and that of Aelfric; it is more developed than
the one, more primitive than the other; it is rude, vehement

---

[1] Miss Bateson, *Rules for monks and secular canons after the revival under
king Edgar, Eng. Hist. Review*, 1894.
[2] Faustina A. x.

and homely, more indulgent of legend and shows the primitive love for recitative; the syntax is clumsy, and the vocabulary often archaic. On the other hand the treatment is sometimes very poetical, though this characteristic appears rather in simile and metaphor than in rhythm of structure. "The redness of the rose glitters in thee, and the whiteness of the lily shines in thee," says Gabriel to Mary; and Heaven is pictured as a place where there "is youth without age; nor is there hunger nor thirst, nor wind nor storm nor rush of waters." The palm branch in the hand of the angel who announces to the Virgin her approaching death is "bright as the morning star," and the Lord appears to Andrew with a face "like that of a fair child." Equally poetical are the passages that deal with more sombre themes, such as doomsday, the lamentation of the lost at the harrowing of hell and the vision of St. Paul of the souls clinging to the cliffs from which the devils sought to drag them away. Morris has pointed out that there is a good deal of similarity between this last passage and the well-known lines in *Beowulf* which describes the "rimy groves" which grew above the abyss where Grendel had his home. But exactly similar descriptions are found in all other versions of this aged legend.[1] Aelfric, it is true, rejected the legend on critical grounds, but the coming centuries were to see it become the basis of a masterpiece of the world's poetry. Comparisons of these Old English legends with their sources and cognate branches lead to the conclusion that the poetic element which was inherent in them could scarcely be destroyed altogether, however poor the translation might be.

The probable date of these homilies is towards the close of the third quarter of the tenth century; they refer to the universal belief, based on a misunderstanding of the Talmudic metaphor prevailing throughout the *Revelation of St. John*, that the year 1000 would see the end of the world; and one of them, the eleventh, contains a statement to the effect that it was composed in 971. This date cannot be accepted as indisputably that of the whole collection; the passage may be an interpolation, and, moreover, there is nothing to prove that all the homilies were composed at the same time, or by one writer.

---

[1] Cf. the Provençal.

During these years Aelfric was growing up in the monastery school at Winchester. The exact year of his birth is not known, but, as he himself tells us that he spent many years as a pupil of Aethelwold, who died in 984, we may, perhaps, put the date at about 955. It is worth noticing that, in his *Life of St. Swithun*, Aelfric describes with some detail the translation of the relics of that saint to the restored cathedral at Winchester, and, as this took place in 971, he was probably then a postulant. We know that he was a priest, and over thirty years of age, when, in 987, he was sent to the abbey of Cerne in Dorsetshire to instruct the brethren in the Benedictine rule, that is to say, when he was novice-master of Cerne abbey.

It was soon after this that Aelfric composed his first homilies, in two series, each of which has a Latin preface addressed to Sigeric, archbishop of Canterbury. As Sigeric's years of office extended only from 989 to 995, and as he was absent in Rome during the first two or three of these years, the homilies were probably composed between the years 990 and 995. The second series is more exactly dated by a reference in the Latin preface to the Danish attack on Southampton in 994, so that we may assign the first collection to the years 990 to 993.

In addition to the Latin prefaces, there is prefixed to each series a statement in English composed much later, probably after 1016, recounting the reasons which had induced the author to turn them from Latin into the vernacular. In the first, he explains that he has done it for the sake of unlearned men, who, especially at this time, when the end of the world is approaching, need to be fortified against tribulation and hardship; and, remembering the injunctions of Christ, Aelfric believed it to be his duty also to teach the ignorant. The English preface to the second series is much shorter, simply stating the author's reasons for dividing the homilies into two books, and giving the sources in general terms.

According to the original plan each collection was to consist of forty sermons, and each was to cover the whole of the church year, the second treating of such Sundays and feast-days as were not mentioned in the first. But neither in the manuscripts nor in Thorpe's edition does the number of homilies correspond with this scheme; for, while the first series contains forty, the

second has forty-five, of which the last six do not belong to the
original collection. This gives only thirty-nine; but if the
two sermons for mid-Lent Sunday are counted separately we
arrive at the proper number. The two series were designed to
give alternate sermons for the greater feast-days, the first
series being simple, doctrinal and instructive, the second dis-
cursive, historical and more elaborate, with much narrative.[1]

Although the subjects of the sermons are appropriate to
the days for which they were intended, there is also an attempt
to give a large survey of biblical and ecclesiastical history.
Thus, the first homily of the first series, *De Initio Creaturae*,
treats not only of creation, but relates the stories of the fall,
the flood, the dispersal of tongues, the patriarchs and the
Mosaic law. Then follows another, *De Natale Domini*, which
gives the life of Christ from His birth to His ascension. The
second series treats more particularly of the history of the apostles, the origin of monastic life, the foundation of the English
church under Gregory the Great and its expansion in the days
of St. Cuthbert. The didactic element is less pronounced in
the second part than in the first, and, while the first part seems
to have been intended for the instruction of the ignorant in the
primary facts of their belief, the second is devoted mainly
to the exposition of the teaching of the church. It is in this
second series that we find the famous sermon on the Eucharist
which, owing to the difficulty of expressing in the unaccustomed
English tongue the undeveloped and indefinite standpoint of
the period, has led to much controversy, based on the mistake
of reading into the tenth century the ideas of modern times.
The reformers gave us our first editions of this sermon in the
form of controversial pamphlets.

[1] The manuscripts of these homilies vary much in arrangement of matter,
and it has been supposed that three recensions existed. The first answers to
Thorpe's edition of the Cambridge MS., in which the two parts are kept
asunder and all the prefaces are retained, although other matter is also found.
The second is represented by such MSS. as C.C.C.C. 188, which has only the
first set of sermons, no prefaces, some sermons divided and the homily on the
nativity of Our Lady following that on the birth of St. John. It has also a
new sermon for a confessor's feast, with the statement that, although the
author had written it for another (Aethelwold, bishop of Winchester, 1007–
1013), yet he was to have a copy of it himself. Hence this recension dates
after 1007. Thirdly, there are several MSS. in which both parts are recast
together in the order of the church year, with additional sermons.

The chief sources of these sermons were, as the homilist himself tells us, the works of St. Augustine, St. Jerome, St. Gregory, Bede, Smaragdus and Haymo. Förster regards the homilies of St. Gregory as the groundwork. Additional sources are Alcuin, Gregory of Tours and Rufinus, the *Vitae Patrum* of Ratramnus, and many others. The English song on St. Thomas he did not use, and he rejected St. Paul's vision in favour of English works on St. Peter and St. Paul. But all these are treated very freely, and, although Aelfric was often hampered by the inadequacy of the language to express abstract ideas, his skill as a teacher is especially visible in the lucidity with which he explains the mysteries of their religion to his ignorant audience.

The treatment, throughout, is highly poetical; alliteration abounds, and ten of the homilies are in a rhythm identified by Einenkel and Trautmann as the four-beat verse of the Old High German poet Otfried, though the reality of this identification is doubtful. These are the homilies on the Passion, the invention of the cross, Joshua's victories, St. James the Just, Clement, Alexander, St. Martin, St. Cuthbert, Irenaeus and that on love. Of the three senses of Scripture, the mystical is most delighted in, and symbolism is prominent. Similar feeling and outlook is reflected in most Middle English homilies. Thus, the dead skins in which our first parents were clad after the fall betokened that "they were then mortal who might have been immortal, if they had kept that easy commandment of God." Such a use, in the lengths to which it was then carried, although faithfully reflecting the ideas of the early and subsequent centuries of the Middle Ages, is strained to the modern mind and to the modern reader. Aelfric's imagination is better seen in the tender and pathetic passages describing the slaughter of the Innocents or the solitary sojourn of St. Cuthbert on the island of Lindisfarne.

Aelfric's next works, though equally significant of his zeal as a teacher, were much less ambitious. They consisted of a Latin grammar, a Latin-English vocabulary and a Latin colloquy or dialogue, intended to instruct the novices at Winchester in the daily speech of the monastery. The *Grammar*, like so many of Aelfric's works, has two prefaces, one in

English and one in Latin, the former explaining that the book is based on the greater and lesser Priscian, to the end that, when "tender boys" have mastered the eight parts of speech in the grammars of Donatus (the shorter of which was the general medieval text-book), they may proceed to perfect their studies both in Latin and English; while the latter tells how the grammar was undertaken after the two books of eighty sermons, because grammar is the key to the understanding of those books. He insists, also, on the fact that the maintenance of religion depends on the encouragement of learning, and reminds his readers of the evil years before Dunstan and Aethelwold, when there was scarcely an English priest who could write or even read a Latin letter.

In many of the MSS. which contain the grammar it is followed by a Latin-English *Vocabulary*, the earliest of its kind extant, arranged according to subjects, not alphabetically, and largely derived from the etymologies of St. Isidore. That it is Aelfric's is proved not only by its inclusion in the manuscript containing the grammar, without any pause between them, but also by the presence of many words characteristic of his vocabulary.

The *Colloquy*, of which only two MSS. exist, is exceedingly interesting both in method and in theme. It is in the form of a conversation between the teacher, a novice and a number of other persons representing the various occupations of the day. The ploughman tells how he leads his oxen to the field, while the neatherd, like Caedmon in Bede's famous story, takes them at night to the stable and stands watching over them for fear of thieves. The shepherd guards his sheep against the wolf and makes butter and cheese. The hunter captures harts and hares and is rewarded by the king with horses and collars, while the merchant trades in palls and silks, gold and precious stones, strange garments, perfumes, wine and oil, ivory, brass, tin, glass and silver. Last of all, the novice describes the division of his day, and how, if he sleeps through the bell for nocturnes, his comrades awaken him with rods. The authorship is proved by a note in one of the MSS.: *Hanc sententiam latini sermonis olim Aelfricus Abbas composuit, qui meus fuit magister, sed tamen ego Aelfricus Bata multas postea huic addidi appendices.* The colloquy has an Old English gloss, which is certainly not the work of Aelfric. The additions made by Aelfric's disciple to the text, with the object of providing more matter for practice, in every way destroy the simplicity and neatness of the original.

In one MS. of Aelfric's *Grammar* we meet the famous version of the *Distichs of Cato*. Hence, there has been a certain tendency to ascribe these also to Aelfric. They are marked by clearness of expression and show great sense of adaptability. They seem to be a combination of two translations, one to distich 68, the other to the end. Two of the distichs are taken from Aelfric's *Deuteronomy*, and the fact that one of the three MSS. in which these distichs are contained also includes the *Grammar*, both works being written in one hand, places them, at any rate, in close connection with Aelfric's school.[1] It is, perhaps, best to regard them as the result of Aelfric's influence.

These school-books were followed in 996 or 997 by a third series of homilies, *The Lives*, or *Passions of the Saints*. These homilies, also, are introduced by two prefaces, one in Latin explaining the origin and occasion of the work, while the other is an English letter addressed to the ealdorman Aethelweard, the father of the founder of Cerne abbey.

Thou knowest, beloved [says Aelfric in the letter] that we translated in two former books the passions and lives of the saints whom the English nation honours with festivals: now, it has seemed good to us that we should write this book concerning the sufferings and lives of the saints whom monks in their offices[2] honour among themselves.

The Latin preface further states that only such lives have been chosen from the *Vitae Patrum* as are suitable for narration to the lay attendants at monastic services.

The best manuscript of this work[3] contains thirty-three lives, six general homilies and a narrative without title on the legend of Abgarus, thus, like the two previous series, comprising forty sermons in all. They are arranged in the order of the

[1] The MS. is Trin. Coll. Camb. R. 9.
[2] *i.e.* the customary Divine Hours, daily chanted by the monks in choir, a public service which the secular clergy could not, of course, maintain. The office-books for the two, probably, also differed.
[3] Cott. Jul. E. VII.

church year, beginning with an address on the nativity of
Christ, ending with the life of St. Thomas (21 December) and
including an interesting Rogation Sunday homily on auguries,
witchcraft, etc., and one (25 August) in which we have an
early appearance of the devil of the later mysteries.

Besides the *Vitae Patrum*, which is the only source mentioned by Aelfric in his preface, other authorities cited are
Ambrosius, Augustine, Jerome, Terentian, Abbo of Fleury,
Bede and St. Oswald. The story of St. Swithun is partly
based on a letter of Lanferth, but owes still more to local
tradition.

These homilies exhibit the style of Aelfric in its maturity;
only one, that on the Nativity, is in prose; the others are in the
loose alliterative rhythm which he had already used in some
of his previous sermons. In the long run, this excessive
recourse to alliteration became an obstacle to clear expression
and was alien to the true development of prose; but the monotonous rhythm, so closely akin to the ballad verse of the common people was, no doubt, very attractive to lay audiences.
The *Lives*, since they deal with fact and not theory, throw less
light on Aelfric's doctrine than the earlier homilies; but, on the
other hand, they provide many valuable side-lights on contemporary manners, and on the life of the homilist himself.
The most interesting of all are those of the English saints, St.
Oswald, St. Edmund and St. Swithun. In the first two we
see portrayed the ideal king of the Old English, protector and
benefactor of his people. Oswald breaks in pieces the silver
dish on which his meat is served, and commands Aidan to distribute the pieces among the suppliants for his charity; St.
Edmund after his subjects have been slaughtered by the Danes
no longer desires life. "This I wish in my mind, that I should
not be left alone after my dear thanes, who in their very beds,
with their wives and children, have, by these sea-goers, suddenly been slain." In the life of St. Swithun we have reminiscences of the happy time under king Edgar, "when the kingdom still continued in peace, so that no fleet was heard of save
that of the folk themselves who held this land."

The date of these *Lives* is known almost to the very year.
They are not dedicated, like the others, to archbishop Sigeric,
because he had died in 995; and they cannot have been written

earlier than 996, because in the sermon on Ash Wednesday Aethelwold, who was canonised in that year, is spoken of as "the holy bishop who now worketh miracles." But, as Aelfric says that he borrowed his homily on St. Edmund from Abbo of Fleury's life of that saint (986), which came into his hands a few years after it was written, they cannot well be much later than 997.

Appended to the best MSS. of the *Lives of the Saints* is an English version of Alcuin's *Interrogationes Sigewulfi Presbyteri in Genesin*. It begins with a preface and introduction on Alcuin and the Latin text, which consisted of a series of catechetical answers to questions on *Genesis*, asked by Alcuin's friend, Sigewulf. Then follow the translated *interrogationes*, abridged from a hundred and seventy-eight to forty-eight essentials. The first fifteen are on the moral law of the Creator and His creatures; the next five, relating to the material creation, contain an insertion on the planets, derived from Bede by Aelfric, who was devoted to the study of astronomy; then come four on the manifestations of the Trinity in nature. These are succeeded by a series on man's creation in the divine image and his end, followed by others on the origin of evil. Last of all are questions on the ages of the world, and the whole is concluded by a creed and the doxology. Aelfric is nowhere stated to be the author, but the similarity of the translation to his acknowledged work in style, structure and rhythm enables us to ascribe it to him with some confidence.

Two other works, closely connected in style and theme, also unsigned, but attributed to Aelfric on the ground of style and diction, were probably composed soon after the *Lives of the Saints*. These are a translation of the *Hexameron* of St. Basil, and a version of the *De Temporibus* of Bede. The former, which is a sermon on the six days of creation, the fall of the angels, the day of rest, the expulsion from Paradise and the atonement of Christ, is by no means a literal translation, but is partly original, and partly derived from Bede's *Commentary on Genesis*. It is found in the best MSS., refers to former sermons and has Aelfric's loose alliterative rhythm. It shows a close resemblance to the version of *De Temporibus*, which, as the compiler distinctly states, is not to be considered a homily. It is, indeed, a scientific treatise, adapted from Bede, but showing much independent learning in the matter of astronomy, the entry on the feast of the circumcision telling how the ancient year-systems began and were reckoned.   It is almost certainly Aelfric's, and was, probably, written between 991 and 995.

So far, all Aelfric's works had been either of a homiletic or an educational character; but now, at the request of the ealdorman Aethelweard, he embarked somewhat reluctantly on the task of rendering the scriptures into the vernacular. For Aelfric had now spent the best years of his life in the service of the church and education, bringing nearer to his people the truths and sources of their religion and morality.   He was now in advanced middle life, and felt keenly that these labours withdrew him from further study and from the contemplation of the supernatural, towards which his age, profession and, above all, the grievous state of earthly affairs, that seemed indeed to foretoken the end of the world, now drew him.   At the same time, he had a mass of homiletic material ready, and, at a time when scarce anyone could read, he felt that the living voice of the preacher should be mainly used with the people.   Hence, we find his version of the Bible esentially meant to be preached rather than read; he wrote for those who should teach the as yet unlettered people.   The version was intended to be of the nature of a homily, and was not meant to be an accurate version of Holy Writ.   Name lists, genealogies and difficult passages were left out.

Aelfric's principal achievement in this department was editing the paraphrase of the first seven books of the Bible. It is certain, however, that his hand is not to be traced throughout.   In the prefatory letter, which he addressed to Aethelweard, he reminds his friend how he had said that he need not labour any further in the book of *Genesis* than the story of Isaac, since another had translated it from that point to the end.   In the MS. in the Cambridge University Library only chapters i—xxiv of *Genesis* are given, and Dietrich has observed that the style thenceforward to the end of *Leviticus* is essentially different.   In the fourth book of Moses Aelfric's style is once more recognisable, and alliteration again occurs. It is possible that Aelfric may have worked over another translation of the books of *Numbers* and *Deuteronomy;* but he himself tells us, in *De Veteri et de Novo Testamento*, that he had trans-

lated *Joshua* and *Judges* at the request of Aethelweard.   The
book of *Judges* was added afterward; it was probably intended
originally to be included, like the homily on the *Maccabees*,
in the series of *Saints' Lives*.   It is composed entirely in Aelfric's
usual rhythm, and ends with a short notice of the good kings
Alfred, Aethelstan and Edgar, who put to flight the Danes and
fostered religion and learning.   With the exception of *Daniel*
the work consists merely of extracts.   Since the *Lives* were
written in 996, and other homiletic work had followed, these
paraphrases seem to date from 997, and, in their completed
state, from 998.   It is important to note in them that Aelfric
merely signs himself as monk.   They were, probably, the last
work done for Aethelweard, who is not heard of after 999.
But Aelfric's close friendship with his son continued and bore
important fruit in later years.

Three other biblical paraphrases or homilies may be traced
to Aelfric.   In his tractate on the Old Testament he observes
that he formerly made in English a discourse or short exposition of *Job*, and also that he had turned into English the book
of *Esther*.   The MS. of *Job* is lost, but a copy printed by L'Isle
in 1638 shows unmistakable signs of Aelfric's workmanship,
and the theme resembles that of his other works; thus, a passage on Antichrist is strongly reminiscent of some sentences
in the preface to the first series of homilies, and the whole
treatment corresponds to that of the thirty-fifth homily of the
second series.   *Esther*, which also exists only in L'Isle's transcript, seems originally to have belonged to the *Saints' Lives*.   It
is a series of extracts in Aelfric's customary alliterative rhythm.

Aelfric also mentions, in the same place, a work on the
apocryphal book of *Judith*, but without claiming the authorship.   "It is also," he says, "arranged in English in our manner,
as an example to you men, that you should defend your land
with weapons against the hostile host."   These words were
formerly supposed to refer to the beautiful poem *Judith*, which
is found in a fragmentary state in the *Beowulf* MS.; but
Assmann has shown that an Old English version of the story
contained in two MSS.[1] has all the characteristics of Aelfric's
style.   Moreover, it contains many passages parallel with
others in his preface to the Old Testatment.

[1] Corpus Christi Coll. 303 and Cott. Oth. B. 10.

About the year 998, Aelfric was asked by bishop Wulfsige of Sherborne to compose a pastoral for him. It was written in the bishop's name, and, after a short preface addressed to Wulfsige, admonishing him to reprove his clergy more frequently for their neglect of the ecclesiastical canons, it treats of celibacy, clerical duties, synods and the Benedictine rule, ending with a warning against clerical attendance at lykewakes. This concludes the first part. The second is entirely concerned with the rite of the presanctified and the proper length of time for the reservation of the sacrament, and expresses the same views that Aelfric had already advanced in the homilies, based upon St. Augustine (probably the *Enarratio* in *Psalm* xcviii), through the famous Ratramnus, opponent of Paschasius Radbertus, abbot of Corby. It thus shows Aelfric as a keen follower of contemporary "science" abroad. Aelfric sided, seemingly, against Radbertus; his opinions are nowhere exactly reflected to-day, though the obscure Augustinian "spiritual," rendered in English "gāstlīce," did the good service of giving us editions of him in the sixteenth century, when he was quoted by Foxe and others. It is an anachronism to impute any fully developed modern opinion to the tenth century.

About the same time must be dated Aelfric's *Advice to a Spiritual Son*, translated from St. Basil's work with the same title. The author is not expressly named, but, from internal evidence, we know that he was a Benedictine monk, and that he had already written about Basil. It speaks of St. Basil's *Hexameron* in almost the very words Aelfric used earlier; it contains passages on St. Basil closely resembling some in the *Interrogationes Sigewulfi Presbyteri;* and, inclusive of the preface, it is composed in Aelfric's loose rhythm. The subject is the admonition of a spiritual father to his son to lead a righteous life.

In a manuscript in the Bodleian,[1] under the general heading *Sermones Lupi*, occurs a homily *On the sevenfold gifts of the Holy Ghost*, which, owing to its presence in that manuscript, was formerly ascribed to Wulfstan. But that Aelfric composed a homily on this subject we know from his own statement[2]: "Sevenfold gifts he giveth yet to mankind, concerning

[1] Junius 99.
[2] *De Veteri et de Novo Testamento*, Preface.

which I wrote formerly in a certain other writing in the English speech." This homily is seventh from the superscription, which only seems to apply to those immediately following it (two in number). We are, therefore, as Napier in his work on Wulfstan pointed out, justified in rejecting the ascription of the seventh homily to Wulfstan, and it may be by Aelfric.

In 1005 Aelfric was called from Wessex to Mercia. The thane Aethelmaer, who had formerly invited him to Cerne, and for whom so many of his works had been composed, had recently acquired two estates in Oxfordshire, which he, in turn, presented to his newly founded abbey of Eynsham. These are interesting on account of their connection with the hero of Maldon, himself a patron of learning, who had fallen some fourteen years before, fighting against the Danes.[1] Hither Aethelmaer retired for the rest of his life, and hither he summoned Aelfric as first abbot. The monastery followed the Benendictine rule, and it was for the instruction of its inmates that Aelfric wrote, soon after his instalment there, the Latin *Letter to the Monks of Eynsham*, to which reference has already been made. His object was to give an account of the rule as practised at Winchester, and he says that the source of his information is bishop Aethelwold's *De Consuetudine Monachorum*, by which title, as we have already seen, he refers, in all probability, to Aethelwold's *Regularis Concordia*.

It is in the preface to this letter that Aelfric speaks of the years spent by him in the school of Aethelwold, and, as a further acknowledgment of the debt he owed his great master, he composed soon afterwards, in Latin, his *Vita Aethelwoldi*. In the preface to this *Life*, Aelfric calls himself abbot and alumnus of Winchester, and, greeting Kenulph, bishop of Winchester, and the brethren of the monastery there, he says that it now seems right to him to recall to men's memory some of the deeds of their father and great teacher, St. Aethelwold (d. 984), who had been dead for twenty years. Since Kenulph was not appointed to the see till 1006, and died either the same year or the next, the *Life* must have been finished about this time. Of the two recensions of the *Life*, one, by Aelfric alone, shows his usual characteristics; the other is apparently Aelfric's life

[1] See p. 144.

"written over" by Wulfstan, precentor of Winchester, with additional matter concerning posthumous miracles.

Besides these Latin works, in the first year of his office as abbot, Aelfric wrote an English letter addressed to a thane called Wulfgeat, "at Ylmandun," a place which has been identified with Ilmington, about thirty miles from Eynsham. It begins with a six-line address to Wulfgeat, in which Aelfric refers to former English writings, lent to the thane, and to his promise to lend him more. Since he calls himself abbot, and since in 1006 Wulfgeat fell into disgrace and lost all his possessions, being supplanted by Eadric the famous traitor, the letter was evidently written in 1005 or 1006.

It was probably two or three years after this that Aelfric composed his treatise on the Old and the New Testaments— *De Veteri et de Novo Testamento*.   It begins with a long address to Sigferth or Sigweard, a thane living at Easthealon, the modern Asthall, which is only twelve miles distant from Eynsham.   Aelfric begins by saying that Sigferth had very often asked him for English books, but that he would not grant his request till the thane had proved his sincerity by good deeds. But since he had complained to Aelfric that he could not obtain his works, the abbot had written this especially for him. The tractate, which is based on St. Augustine's *De Doctrina Christiana*, is, in substance, a popular introduction to the contents of the Bible, and falls into two parts.   The first, on the Old Testament, is especially valuable because, in the course of his summary of the various books, Aelfric gives the particulars to which we have already referred, concerning his translations from the Bible.   The second part, on the New Testament, begins with the story of John the Baptist, treats of the four Gospels, the *Acts of the Apostles*, the epistles and the book of *Revelation*, and, after certain allegories, some words on the duties of the three stations of life—workers, praying folk and fighters—and a description of the capture of Jerusalem by Titus, ends with an admonition against the Teutonic habit of setting folk to drink beyond their measure—a native pleasantry which, it seems, Sigferth had endeavoured to impose upon Aelfric when visited by him.

It was to the same nobleman that Aelfric, about the same time, addressed his letter on the celibacy of the clergy, for

Sigferth entertained among his household an anchorite who affirmed that the marriage of mass priests (*i.e.* full priests as distinguished from "preostas," a generic name including deacons and minor orders as well) was permissible. But Aelfric, though loth to differ from this "good friend," if he were a God-fearing man, could not refrain from pointing out that the earlier usage of the church required celibacy from all the clergy, and the letter is a prolonged argument on this theme.

Aelfric's last important work was a pastoral letter written for Wulfstan, who, from 1002 to 1023, was archbishop of York, and, till 1016, held also the see of Worcester, being thus a neighbour of the abbot of Eynsham. It falls into two parts, of which the first speaks of the three periods of the law, and goes on to the theme already treated in the letters to Wulfsige and Sigferth. The subject of the marriage of the clergy is reviewed from a historical standpoint, and the letter further admonishes the clergy on the celebration of the Eucharist, as their great function, and treats of the seven grades of holy orders. The second part deals with the use of the holy oils and the administration of the last sacraments to the dying. Mass was not to be said in laymen's houses, nor churches used for worldly purposes. The work must have been composed after 1014, since it contains a quotation from Aethelred's laws of that date; and, probably, before 1016, when Wulfstan's connection with Worcester came to an end. The epistles were written in Latin and translated into English by Aelfric himself, at Wulfstan's request, in the following year.

Aelfric's life was now drawing to a close. The exact date of his death is not known, but he died, probably, soon after 1020. His last years were passed in times not favourable for literary work. They were eventful years for England, for they witnessed the Danish sack of Canterbury in 1011, the murder of St. Alphege by the Danes at Greenwich, the flight of Aethelred before Sweyn, the strife of Edmund Ironside and Canute and Canute's final triumph.

Aelfric was not only the greatest prose writer, he was also the most distinguished English-writing theologian, in his own time, and for five centuries afterwards. Yet he was in no sense an original thinker; his homilies, as he frankly states, are borrowed from others, and in them he reflects the thought of the west, especially the teachings of St. Augustine its great Father. His chief object was to convey to the simple and unlearned the teaching of the Fathers; and in this he was pre-eminently successful. If Dunstan and Aethelwold first kindled the flame, it was Aelfric who, through dark years of strife and warfare, when men's thoughts were absorbed by the pressing anxieties of their daily life, kept the lamp alight and reminded them of spiritual ideals. His influence lasted long after his death, as is shown by the many late manuscripts of his writings, some of which date from the twelfth century; and if it had not been for his faithful, modest labour, the difficulties of Lanfranc and Anselm would have been even greater than they were.

As he himself tells us, he took Alfred for his model, but, in ease and grace, his style far surpasses that of his great predecessor. Both Aelfric and Wulfstan write and translate in a free style, but it is no longer the gossiping colloquialism of Alfred. English had become a literary language, polished in the cloisters with long use as a vehicle for translation and original works. In the cloisters Latin was still a living language, and hence Latin constructions became common. The necessity of having to express difficult ideas in a form intelligible to ignorant men helped Aelfric in his choice of words and in his effort after lucidity, while, with the instinct of a true teacher, he refused to be led astray by the example of Latin syntax and preferred simple constructions. Unfortunately, as time went on, he deferred more and more to the preferences of his audience, and debased his prose by throwing it into the rhythmical alliterative form so popular with the vulgar. Perhaps it was felt that a more pompous, rhetorical style than that of ordinary speech should be used in treating of solemn themes. However that may be, the later, florid manner which Aelfric affected in the *Saints' Lives,* and in some of his other treatises, is distinctly inferior to that of the first two series of homilies. His prose is seen at its best in simple narrative, and, to appreciate the difficulties under which he laboured, the homilies on the Eucharist and on the Creation (both philosophic subjects) should be read together. The first is confused and complex, compared with the flowing ease of the great Father upon whose work it was based and, obviously, the language was not, at this time, equal to abstruse metaphysical speculation.

The second, which deals with a simpler subject, is clear and comprehensive.   Aelfric shows power in his treatment of pathos as well as of philosophy, when both are simple; as may be seen in the homilies on the Holy Innocents and on the Creation. But, whatever his theme, he is always logical and persuasive, and the "sweet reasonableness" of his methods especially distinguishes his sermons from the fiery denunciations, and the direct, strenuous language, of his contemporary and friend archbishop Wulfstan, who goes to the point without any of the abstract moralising to be found in Aelfric. Wulfstan delivers his Christian doctrine as a statement of facts, and his phrases have a legal smack about them; while Aelfric loves what has some philosophy in it, for even his simplicity is often profound.   In a word, Wulfstan is a judge and legalist, Aelfric a contemplative student.

This difference in tone is explained partly by temperament, partly by the circumstances of their lives.   Aelfric, following the quiet industrious routine of duty behind the shelter of the abbey walls, heard only the rumours of the strife that raged without; Wulfstan, absorbed in practical, political life, was brought face to face with the anguish and the practical needs of the time.   He was already bishop of Worcester when, in 1002, he was appointed, also, to the see of York.   In 1014 he assisted in the compilation of the laws of Aethelred, drawn up at the synod of Eynsham; he died on 28 May, 1023.   Thus, his period of office coincided with that of the most disastrous and devastating invasions of the country.

It is extremely difficult to determine exactly which of the homilies in the Bodleian[1] are really Wulfstan's.   Owing to the superscription at the beginning of the first, *Hic incipiunt sermones Lupi*, all were ascribed to him by Wanley.   Napier has pointed out, however, that this heading was, probably, taken from another manuscript of the archbishop's sermons, which were copied into a miscellaneous collection containing many others, of which the authorship is uncertain, or certainly not his.   Of the fifty-three homilies in the Bodleian MS. only five are indisputably by Wulfstan.   There are two immediately following the superscription, dealing with the Bible story,[2]

and with the catholic faith[1]; next follows a sermon[2] of which
only parts are by Wulfstan, and which Napier, rejecting the
passages he considers unauthentic, has divided into four portions[3]: on the Christian life, on Christ's death, on Christ as the
true friend and on the duties of Christians. Then comes the
famous *Address to the English*[4], and last of all a short exhortation[5] with the superscription *Sermo Lupi*, on the duty of Christians, full of metrical fragments, which can be separated from
the context and show signs of sung verse united by alliteration
or assonance. Of the remaining homilies, some, which occur
in the same order in various manuscripts, are, possibly, by
Wulfstan; many, such as the paraphrase of the poem called *Be
Domes Daege*, and *The Address of the Soul to the Body*, must be
entirely rejected; while others[6] appear also among the *Blickling
Homilies* or the works of Aelfric. It is noteworthy that the
homilies referred to above as possibly by Wulfstan are very
similar in phraseology to the Old English laws drawn up at
the council of Eynsham in 1014; and, as we know from his own
statement that Wulfstan was responsible for the Latin paraphrase of these statutes, it is probable the English version was
his also.

Of the five homilies which certainly can be ascribed to
Wulfstan, the most powerful is the one entitled in the Bodleian
MS. *Sermo Lupi ad Anglos quando Dani maxime persecuti sunt
eos, quod fuit in die Aethelredi regis*, to which another MS. adds
more explicitly that this was in *anno millesimo xiiii ab incarna-
tione Domini nostri Jesus Christi*, and another, in *anno millesimo
viii*. But it is, indeed, applicable to any year in the ill-fated
reign of Aethelred. The vices, evil deeds and cowardice of the
English are scourged with a heavy hand; the English are
likened to the Britons whom they have turned out, and are
threatened with the same fate. The archbishop's passionate
patriotism breaks forth in the burning words with which he
describes the desolation and demoralisation of the people, scattered like frightened sheep before the onset of the heathen,
without a single leader to rally them to resistance. Villages
are destroyed by fire, the new ministers are stripped of their

---

[1] Wanley 2, Napier 3. [2] Wanley 4. [3] Napier XIX, XX, XXI, XXII.
[4] Wanley 5, Napier 33. [5] Wanley 6, Napier 34. [6] XLIX, LIV and LV.

holy things; father is turned against son and brother against brother; even the ancient bond of thane and thrall becomes loosened in this time of universal disintegration. And, like some Hebrew prophet, Wulfstan refuses to believe that the Almighty would have laid so heavy an affliction upon an innocent people; he sees in the crimes of the nation the cause, rather than the effect, of the long strife; this evil has come upon them for their sins; they have provoked the wrath of Heaven, and unless they repent and reform, a worse evil shall befall them. But there is still room for penitence, and the sermon ends on a gentler note:

"Let us creep to Christ," says the preacher, "and call upon Him unceasingly with trembling hearts, and deserve His mercy; let us love God and His laws, and faithfully perform what our sponsors promised for us at our baptism. Let us order rightly our words and our deeds, and keep faith with one another without guile, and frequently think upon the great judgment that awaits us all; and protect ourselves against the flaming fire of hell; and let us earn for ourselves the glory and the joy which God has prepared for those who do His will on earth. So God help us. Amen."

Here and there are traces of metrical character, sometimes assonant, sometimes alliterative, which may have been part of some pessimistic folk-ballads on England's downfall.

Wulfstan's style is much more vehement than that of Aelfric. He is preacher rather than teacher, appealing more to the emotions than to the reason of his hearers, fertile in concrete illustrations, and avoiding the subtle symbolism in which Aelfric delighted. His sentences, though not deficient in lucidity, are very long; synonym is heaped on synonym and clause upon clause; yet the chanting sense of rhythm is always present; epithets are balanced, and the effect is often heightened by the use of antithesis. But, as might be expected from one whose life was so much absorbed by the administration of public affairs, his style is that of the rhetorician rather than of the philosopher.

In addition to the homilies already mentioned, several isolated tracts of the same nature by unknown authors survive. Among these may be noted the *Life of St. Guthlac* and of *St. Swithun*, the former translated from the Latin of Felix of

Croyland, and, on the ground that one MS.[1] is in the same handwriting as Aelfric's Pentateuch[2], often attributed to him; the latter a mere fragment, which is also supposed by some scholars to be his.   There are also the *Life of St. Neot*, and *of St. Mary of Egypt*, which may, possibly, be his.

Another renowned contemporary of Aelfric was the monk Byrhtferth, whose writings are chiefly concerned with mathematics.   He lived about 980, and is said to have been a pupil of Abbo.   Leland says he was called Thorneganus.   He seems to have known some of Dunstan's earlier disciples, and to have lived at Canterbury for a time.   His reputation as an English writer rests on his *Handboc* or *Enchiridion*, a miscellany preserved in only one MS.[3]   It begins with a descriptive calendar, and then follow short treatises of a mathematical and philological nature.   After these come three theological tracts, on *The Ages of the World*, *The Loosing of Satan* and *The Seven Sins*. The collection concludes with two homilies, one entitled *Ammonitio Amisi paet is freondlic mynegung*[4], and the other on the four cardinal virtues.   The sermon on the loosing of Satan seems to indicate that it was composed towards the close of the tenth century, and this date is corroborated by what other information we possess about the author.[5]

Like Aelfric, Byrhtferth was a product of St. Aethelwold's monastic reform, but his scientific leanings differentiated him remarkably from the greater homilists.

Besides these homilies and scientific treatises, there were composed, during the tenth century, three English versions of the Gospels, known as the Lindisfarne, Rushworth and West Saxon glosses.   The Latin text of the Lindisfarne Gospels[6], contained in a magnificent manuscript, adorned with beautiful illuminations, was written about the year 700; and it was not till at least two hundred and fifty years later, when it had been removed to Chester-le-Street, near Durham, for safety, that the interlinear North Northumbrian gloss was added by

---

[1] Cott. Vesp. D xxi.   [2] Bod. Laud. E. 19.
[3] Oxf. Ash. 328.   [4] reminder.
[5] Besides these English treatises Byrhtferth was also responsible for Latin commentaries on Bede's *De Temporum Ratione* and *De Natura Rerum* and two essays entitled *De Principiis Mathematicis* and *De Institutione Monachorum;* a *Vita Dustani* has also been attributed to him.
[6] Cott. Nero D. iv.

Aldred, a priest of that place. The gloss gives many variant English equivalents for the Latin words. Aldred himself, however, seems to have written only the latter part of the gloss, that beginning at *St. John* v, 10, in a new hand, though the earlier portion was, probably, made under his supervision. The gloss is of the greatest importance from a philological point of view, since it is our most valuable authority for the Northumbrian dialect of the middle of the tenth century.

Equally interesting are the Rushworth Gospels.[1] The Latin text, which differs very slightly from that of the Lindisfarne MS., was, perhaps, written in the eighth century, while the gloss dates from the second half of the tenth. It falls into two distinct portions, the first of which, in the dialect of North Mercia, was written by Farman, a priest of Harewood, seven miles north-east of Leeds. This portion, which includes the gospel of *St. Matthew* and part of chapters i and ii of *St. Mark*, begins as a gloss, and, later, becomes again a gloss, but, in the main, it is a fairly free version of the Latin text. The second part, in a dialect which has been called South Northumbrian by Lindelöf, was written by Owun, and shows, very strongly, the influence of the Lindisfarne glosses, which must have been before the writer as he worked, since he often goes astray from the Latin text to follow Aldred's version. It seems probable that Farman, who was a good Latin scholar, had made his gloss as far as *St. Mark* ii, 15, when the Lindisfarne MS. came into his hands. He then entrusted the task to Owun, who was a less accomplished linguist, and who, whenever he was confronted by a difficulty, resorted to the Lindisfarne gloss for its solution. It may be that Farman chose Owun as one knowing a dialect closely akin to that of Lindisfarne.

There also exists in six MSS. a West Saxon version of the Gospels, which, owing to a note in one MS.[2]—*ego Aelfricus scripsi hunc librium in monasterio Baðhonio et dedi Brihtwoldo preposito*—was formerly ascribed to Aelfric of Eynsham. If we suppose this Brihtwold to be the same as the bishop of that

---

[1] So called because the MS. in which they are contained was formerly owned by J. Rushworth, clerk of the House of Commons during the Long Parliament.

[2] Corpus Christi College, Cambridge, cxl.

name, who held the see of Sherborne from 1006-1046, as he is here called *prepositus*, we may conclude that the Corpus MS. was written before 1006. It certainly belongs to the first quarter of the eleventh century and is not of Aelfric's authorship, for it in no wise agrees with his description of his own work on the New Testatment. He tells us that he had translated pieces from the New Testament; but this is a full version. The other MSS. are later, and one of them, in the Cambridge University Library, contains also the apocryphal *Gospel of Nicodemus*, which provided legendary material for later medieval homilists and for the growth of the Arthurian legend in respect of Joseph of Arimathaea.

The early Christian legends, indeed, and more particularly such as mark the continuance of Jewish traditions and the gradual diffusion of Christianity in the east, seem to have had a special attraction for English writers of this period. There are two legends connected with the Holy Rood—one with the growth of its wood, the other with the history of the cross after the crucifixion. The legend of the Holy Rood itself is the same as the original story of Cynewulf's poems. It will be remembered that St. Helena was reputed to be of British origin.

The oldest English version of the legend of the growth of the wood is found in a MS. in the Bodleian (343), which contains also fifty-one homilies by Aelfric. The manuscript dates only from the twelfth century, but as the other contents are copies of eleventh century originals, it is reasonable to suppose that the cross legend also was composed at an earlier period. This theory is borne out by the language, which Napier considers too archaic for the twelfth century. From a literary point of view, as well as linguistically, the version is of the greatest interest, as showing the development of English prose. In its original eleventh century form, it represented, perhaps, the best tradition of the literary West Saxon language developed in the cloisters, and the grace and ease of the story show considerable mastery of the art of narrative.

The theme ultimately depends on the Jewish legends contained in the *Book of Adam* and the *Book of Enoch*, and it had originally no connection with Christianity. The story frequently occurs in medieval literature (as, for instance, in the *South English Legendary* and the *Cursor Mundi*), and a brief outline of it may therefore be given here. Unfortunately the earlier part of the legend in its Latin form, treating of the history of the rood to the time of Moses, is missing in the English text. The story shapes itself as follows: Adam being on the point of death, Eve and Seth go to Paradise to ask the guardian angel for the healing oil of life. Seth, as fallen man, is denied entrance to Paradise, and instead of the oil the angel gives him three pips of cedar, cypress and pine. When Seth returns to his father, he finds Adam already dead; he places the three pips under Adam's tongue, and, God having given Adam's body to Michael, it is buried by the four archangels in Paradise. The pips fructify in the ground, and from them spring three rods, which remain green until the time of Moses. The Old English version begins at this point and tells how Moses, having led the children of Israel over the Red Sea, lies down to rest, and, in the morning, finds that three rods have sprung up, one at his head, and one at each side. With these rods he makes sweet the bitter waters, and the host continues its journey to Arabia. Hither David, whom the legend represents as contemporary with Moses, is sent to demand the rods, and it is revealed to him in a vision that they betoken the Trinity.[1] He carries them to Jerusalem, where there is a pit of water so bitter that none can taste of it. The rods are placed in it, and they join together into a mighty tree, the growth of which is marked by silver rings. After the death of David, Solomon attempts to use the tree for the building of the Temple; but, owing to the fact that it continually alters in length, this proves impossible, and it remains untouched within the sanctuary. Finally, when the Jews seek for a tree on which to crucify Christ, they remember this rood, and use part of it for the cross.

The legend of the finding of the cross by St. Helena is entirely Christian in origin, and is cognate to the version in *The Golden Legend* of Jacobus a Voragine, and in the Bollandist *Acta Sanctorum* for the fourth of May, and it is the same theme as that treated so beautifully by Cynewulf in his *Elene*.

---

[1] "Cypressus tacnæð þone fæder; Cedrus tacæð þone sunæ; Pinus tacnæð þone halʒæ gast."

An important legend cycle, to which attention has recently
been drawn, is that of the letter sent from Heaven on Sunday
observance. It is found in Old English in four of Wulfstan's
homilies, and in two separate versions (C.C.C.C. 140 and 162).
Of the legends printed by Cockayne, that of Jamnes and
Mambres has quite a modern "psychical" flavour. The fact of
its being a mere fragment, and breaking off when just about
to become dull, saves it in the eyes of all lovers of ghost-tales.

In addition to other legends of a sacred character there are
others of a more worldly nature, the most remarkable being
the (suppositious) *Letter from Alexander to Aristotle*,[1] *The
Wonders of the East*[2] and the story of *Apollonius of Tyre*.[3]
The first two are closely connected with the eastern legend
of Alexander the Great, which had taken shape before the
Christian era in a work known as the *pseudo-Kallisthenes*, which
was translated into Latin before 340 by the so-called Julius Valerius. The two Alexander legends, as we have them, are
very faithful translations from Latin originals, each chapter of
The Wonders of the East being preceded by a copy of the text
on which it is founded. They are important in the history
of literature as proving the interest taken by the educated
clergy of the eleventh century in the Latin legend cycles.
Rather later than these two works, and also of eastern origin,
is the Old English version of *Apollonius of Tyre*, of which
only half is extant, a version of the same theme as that treated
in the 153rd chapter of the *Gesta Romanorum*. It tells of the
wooing of the king of Antioch's daughter by Apollonius of
Tyre, and how her father, to prevent her marriage, required
her suitors to solve a riddle or to be beheaded. The early
appearance of this legend in the vernacular is especially interesting, since Gower's version of the story in his *Confessio
Amantis* provided the theme for *Pericles of Tyre*. The presence
of these legends in Old English is peculiarly significant as indicating the oncoming flood of foreign literature. Hitherto, the
priest had been the story-teller, after the heroic minstrelsy of
earlier days had passed away; henceforth, the lighter touch of
the deliberate tale-teller was to be heard in English.

From these we must turn to consider the quasi-scientific

[1] MS. Vitell. A. xv.   [2] Cott. Tib. B. v.   [3] C.C.C.C. S. 18.

works of this period, which have all been printed by Cockayne in his *Leechdoms, Wortcunning and Starcraft in Early England*. As might be expected, they have little literary value, but are extremely interesting from a historical standpoint, since they throw many valuable side-lights on the manners and social conditions of the time. Cockayne's collection begins with the *Herbarium* that passes under the name of Apuleius, a work stating the various ills for which each plant is a remedy. It appears in four MSS., the one printed by Cockayne[1] dating from the first half of the eleventh century. Following this is an English version of the *Medicina de quadrupedibus* of Sextus Placidus, about whom nothing is known, which describes the various kinds of animals and the use of their bodies in medicine.

Even more interesting is the leech-book in Cockayne's second volume.[2] The author was evidently acquainted with the Greek and Latin authorities on medicine, for the work is full of their prescriptions, and Helias, patriarch of Jerusalem, is mentioned as having sent such prescriptions to King Alfred.

Lastly, Cockayne printed in his third volume two collect-tions of miscellaneous recipes[3], and a number of prognostications, interpretations of dreams and a horologium.[4] The first collection is extremely interesting on account of the heathen nature of many of the prescriptions, which require for their efficacy the repetition of charms. Some of these are mere gibberish, in which, however, fragments of Greek, Latin and Hebrew may be traced; others, such as the celebrated charm against the stitch, show close connection with Scandinavian mythology; while in some, such as the charm to bring home straying cattle, there is a curious mingling of Christian nomenclature and heathen superstition. All these works are deeply tinged with poetic feeling; and the desire to propitiate the powers that distribute storm and sunshine is visible throughout. The date of these compositions is not known, but most of the manuscripts belong to the eleventh century.

From the foregoing survey of English prose literature

[1] Cott. Vitell. C. III.　　　　[2] Printed from MS. Reg. 12 D. XVI.
[3] MS. Harl. 585 and MS. Harl. 6258.　　[4] Chiefly from MS. Cott. Tib. A. III.

during the eleventh century it is clear that the language had attained considerable development as a literary medium. In the hands of Aelfric its vocabulary becomes less concrete, its construction more logical, and, though it was still seen to best advantage in simple narrative, it was moulded by him with fair success to philosophic requirements. But, in the years that followed the Norman conquest, the development of English prose met with a great check, and four hundred years elapsed before the vernacular was again employed with the grace and fluency of Aelfric.

The decline of Old English poetry cannot be so directly attributed to the Norman conquest. During the course of the tenth and eleventh centuries the classical rhetorical metre had already begun to deteriorate, and was being gradually replaced by the sung metre of the popular ballad. For the whole of our period we have only two great poems, the fragment of *Judith* in the Beowulf MS. and the East Anglian poem of Byrhtnoth's death at Maldon. Both poems deal with the struggle against the same foe and both are in the alliterative rhetorical metre. *Judith* contains a fair number of lines which are undoubtedly clear types of sung verse, such as is found in the thirteenth century in Layamon's *Brut*. *The Battle of Maldon* also contains two much alike.[1] The adoption of this metre, which, although ancient, here exhibits what are practically its first known traces in Old English literature, is carried to much greater lengths in the poems embedded in the *Chronicle;* and some observations upon this new metre called the "sung" or four-beat verse, as opposed to the declamatory or two-beat metre of the older poems, will be found in an appendix at the end of the volume.

The first poem in the *Chronicle* occurs under the year 937, and celebrates the glorious victory won by Aethelstan at Brunanburh. It is a markedly patriotic poem and shows deep

---

[1] But the reader must be cautioned against assuming that every rimed verse was also sung verse. The shorter types of rimed verse in such poems as *Judith* and *The Battle of Maldon* were almost certainly not. The only sure criteria are (1) conformity to the metrical schemes given in the Appendix, (2) a tendency to neglect the rhetoric stress and turn the two-beat rhythm into a four-beat, as shown by the riming use of syllables not carrying the full stress. Examples are: *Judith*, l. 231, (écgùm gecóstè) slógon *éornòstè;* *Maldon*, l. 309, Býrhtwold *mǎpĕlòdè* bórd hǎfĕnòdè.

feeling; its brilliant lyrical power, and the national enthusiasm evident throughout, have made it familiar, in one form or another, to all lovers of English verse. Great care was taken with the metre, which is the ancient rhetorical line.

Under the year 942 another poem in alliterative rhetorical metre occurs. It consists only of a few lines, and its subject is the liberation of the five boroughs, Leicester, Lincoln, Nottingham, Stamfordand Derby, "which were formerly Danish, constrained by need in the captive bonds of the heathen," by Edmund, son of Edward the Elder. It has little poetic value; but it is distinguished by the same intense patriotism as is the verse on the battle of Brunanburh.

The first poem in sung verse contained in the *Chronicle* is that for 959, on the accession of King Edgar. It contains forty-nine half lines, making twenty-four and a half full lines, connected, of which only about eight show alliteration. The lines are connected in the earlier form of rimeless rhythm, not strictly alliterative, though assonance is sometimes found. Metrically, it is our best preserved example. The theme is the prosperity of Edgar; how his wise rule was honoured far and wide, how he established peace in the land and how he was rewarded by God with the willing submission of kings and earls. Of one fault, however, says the chronicler, he was too often guilty, namely that he loved foreign ways and enticed outlanders into his dominions. The poem ends with a prayer that God may be more mindful of the king's virtues than of his evil deeds, and that they may shield his soul from harm on its long journey hence.

The delight of the English in the peaceful rule of Edgar is still further shown by a poem in the old rhetorical metre which is variously given in the different recensions of the *Chronicle* under the years 972, 973 and 974, and relates the coronation of Edgar. The Peterborough chronicle has some lines which have been written as verse, but scansion seems to raise insurmountable difficulties. It can only be scanned on the assumption that we have an attempt to combine two-stress lines with four-stress rhythm, or an attempt to put a ballad into the form of the "higher" poetry. They tell how kings came from afar to do homage to Edgar, and how there was no fleet so daring as to threaten his dominions, or host so strong as to ravage the land while he ruled over it.

Another interesting ballad poem, on the troubles caused by Aelfhere and other rebels in the reign of Edgar's son Edward, is found in the MS. known as Cott. Tib. B. IV. It is of nineteen half lines, or nine and one-half full lines. The linking system seems to be mostly alliteration, but rime and assonance show themselves most clearly where alliteration becomes absent or weak, as in

> Godes wiþersǎecan
> Godes lage brǎecon

and

> mynstra tostaencton,

and

> munecas todraefdon.

The verse is sung ballad-verse, and the alliteration what would be called irregular in rhetorical verse. It is uncertain whether what seems an opening verse really belongs to the song.

The murder of Edward, son of Edgar, at Corfesgeat, is related in a peculiarly distinctive poem, which is quite clearly in sung verse, and shows traces of strophic arrangement. A later hand has tampered greatly with the original poem; some lines have, obviously, been lengthened, and the last six printed as verse do not scan as such, being, possibly, only rhythmic prose added afterwards. They are exactly like the irregular lines on Edgar's death. Probably the chronicler took a popular ballad or ballads, broke it up, and attempted to destroy its sing-song character by the addition of end verses. This, and the strophic character of the original or originals, would account for its metrical variety and uncertainty. In several places we meet with half line tags, generally trimetric, once certainly in full tetrameter. The poem declares that no worse deed than the murder of Edward had ever been committed among the English since the invasion of Britain; men murdered him, but God glorified him; and he who was before an earthly king is now, after death, a heavenly saint. His earthly kinsmen would not avenge him, but his heavenly Father has avenged him amply, and they who would not bow to him living now bend humbly on their knees to his dead bones. Thus, we may perceive that men's plans are as naught before God's. The words "Men murdered him, but God glorified him," are alliterative, and seem like a refrain; and the whole poem is, metrically, one of the most interesting of the series.

There is a long interval before the next verses, which tell of the siege of Canterbury, and the capture of archbishop Aelfhēah (Alphege) in 1011. They consist of twelve half lines of sung verse, and are, evidently, a quotation from some ballad commemorating these disasters. They lament the imprisonment of him who was erstwhile head of Christendom and England, and the misery that men might now behold in the unhappy city whence first came the joys of Christianity. There are some difficulties in scansion, and the variant readings in certain MSS.[1], though they can be restored to something like proper metrical harmony, show what mishandling these songs underwent when written down by the scribes.

The metre of the next poem is much better preserved. It is of the same Layamon sung verse type, but shows a regular union of each two half lines by rime and assononce. Where this fails, we can at once suspect that the scribe has tampered with the original version. The assonance is wholly south-eastern. Its subject is the capture and cruel fate of the actheling Alfred, and it shows a strong spirit of partisanship against Godwin. This is led up to by the prose account telling how Alfred came to Winchester to see his mother, but was hindered and captured by Godwin. The poem relates how Godwin scattered Alfred's followers, killing some and imprisoning others, and how the aetheling was led bound to Ely, blinded aboard ship and given over to the monks. It gives us the important architectural statement (since the old minster long has perished) that he was buried at the west end in the south porch "close to the steeple." The story is told in twenty couplets of sung half lines (40 half lines). The few lines that do not rime can easily be restored.[2]

---

[1] Cott. Tib. B. iv., and Bodl. Laud. 636.

[2] At the end we have the following: They buried him

> "ful wurðlice | swa he wyrðe waes (no rime)
> aet þam Westende | þam styple fulgehende (rimes)
> on þam suðportice | seo saul is mid Criste" (no rime) .

Now *on þam suðportice* rimes with *ful wurðlice*, although it does not rime in its present place. It also would then follow on in sense. *Seo saul is mid Criste* needs a rime in *-iste* and what better one can be than *oð þa aeriste* ? This rime was possibly removed because, on a fullstop being lost in the last

Many of the features of this poem are paralleled in another on a like theme, the arrival of Edward Aetheling, son of Edmund Ironside, in England in 1057, his illness and his death, without seeing his kinsman the king. The story is that of the death of the last of the kingly line. The poem is in sung verse, the half lines being mainly arranged in pairs of one short and one fuller half line, a combination which is the great feature of this poem, whose strophic connection depends absolutely neither on rime or assonance, but rather on rhythm. The poem is in four uneven tirades. The first two are ended by a single half line as a tag (no. 1, of 3 full lines + tag; no. 2, of 5 full lines + half line tag). The last two tirades (no. 3, of 3 full lines; no. 4, of 4 full lines) are without half line tags. The tags may here have been lost in copying.

It is noticeable that all these poems in sung verse, which seem to be based on popular ballads, are characterised by deep patriotic feeling. This, however, is wanting in the alliterative rhetorical lines on the death of Edward the Confessor, which merely tell how he had reigned for twenty-four years and had governed illustriously Welsh, Scots, Britons, Angles and Saxons.

Another passage in sung verse dealing with the marriage of Margaret, the sister of Edward Aetheling, to Malcolm of Scotland, and recording her distaste for marriage and her desire for convent life, seems to be in ten sung half lines, of which the first four have been completely wrecked. The last four are perfect and of great interest. Less obscure are the fragments on the marriage of earl Ralph of Norwich, the first couplet of which

> þaer waes þaet bryd ealo
> þaet waes manegra manna bealo.

shows, unmistakeably, its ballad origin.

The last verses of this class are those on the reign of William the Conqueror. Earle arranged some twelve lines as poetry, but the whole passage claims similar treatment, since, in the

---

line, the first half verse would apply to the soul, and smack of heresy to the monk. We may then read:

> "ful wurðlice | on þam suðportice.
> aet þam Westende | þam styple fulgehende
> oðða aeriste | seo saul is mid Criste"

which changes the architectural sense.

portion which he has printed as prose, there occur examples
of full rime and also of full assonance, connecting the half lines
in the passages he has not so written. The whole passage
seems to be derived from at least two ballads against the Norman conqueror. The first begins "He ríxade òfer Énglaelànd"
and tells of the king's intimate acquaintance with his dominions, so that he knew the owner of every hide of land and how
much it was worth; then, how he conquered Wales and Scotland and, if he had lived two years longer, would have won
Ireland, also, without weapon strife. This, which is unrimed,
is followed by the passage "Cástelas hè lēt wýrceàn," which is
invaluable because of its strong Kentish assonances. These
lines tell, in bitter words, of the king's oppression, of his heavy
taxation, and of the terrible game laws, drawn up to preserve
those "tall deer" which he loved as greatly as though he were
their father. This last part is 38 lines long, divided into 19
couplets linked by rime or assonance, the nineteenth being
either marred in transcription or a monastic addition in rime.
The spelling often hides the dialectical completeness of the
assonance. After this sung ballad follows a passage of rhythmical prose, in which the compiler states that he has written
these things about the king, both good and evil, that men may
imitate the goodness and wholly flee from the evil. It would
seem that the chronicler had to be original in telling of the
Conqueror's virtues; but, for the vices, he had plenty of popular material at hand. The unhappy people were in no mood
to exalt his virtues, and, for the description of these, the chronicler was forced to rely on his own literary resources.

The verses in the *Chronicle* have little literary merit, with
the exception of the poem on the battle of Brunanburh, and
this seems to have been strongly influenced by the epic of
Judith. Of this latter, unfortunately, only a beautiful fragment, consisting of some 350 lines survives.[1] *Judith* was,
perhaps, composed as a eulogy of Aethelflaed, queen of Mercia,
who fought nobly against the Danes in the first quarter of the
tenth century. It has been attributed to Caedmon; but its
use of rime and the character of its language has led some critics
to place the poem comparatively late. The use of rime, however, is no conclusive argument. It recounts, in vigorous

[1] Cott. Vitell. xv.

language, the deeds of the Apocryphal heroine, and dwells especially on the way in which her deed stired up the timorous Jews to more courageous patriotism. It is noteworthy that Aelfric himself had written a homily on Judith, to teach the English the virtues of resistance to the Danes. This homily must have been written earlier, and, perhaps, it influenced the writer of *Judith* to choose her as a national type in the fight for God and fatherland. The poem, as we have it, begins at the end of the ninth canto; cantos x, xi and xii are preserved in full, but the earlier part of the poem is entirely wanting. This loss, however, is the less to be regretted since the remaining cantos, containing the crisis of the story, are, probably, the finest of all, and deal with a complete episode, to which the fragment of canto ix, telling of the faith of the heroine and the invitation to the feast of Holofernes, serves as introduction. Canto x describes, with all the delight of Old English poets in such pictures, the banquet in the Assyrian camp, the deep bowls of wine borne along the benches, and the shouts and laughter of the revellers. Darkness descends, and the warriors bring the maiden to their master's tent. Overcome with wine, he falls into a deep slumber, and the heroine, with a supplication to heaven for help draws the sword from its sheath. She hales the heathen towards her by his hair, and smites twice with her weapon, till his head rolls upon the floor. In canto xi, we read how Judith and her maid steal from the camp with the head of Holofernes, and return to Bethulia, where their kinsmen are waiting for them on the wall. As soon as the two approach, men and women hasten together to meet them, and Judith bids her servant uncover the trophy and exhibit it to the warriors. Then, with passionate words, she exhorts them to attack the camp, to bear forth shields and bucklers and bright helmets among the foe. So, at dawn of day, they set out, the wolf and raven rejoicing in the tumult, and the dewy-feathered eagle singing his war-song above them, their sudden onset on the camp disturbing the enemy, drowsy with mead. The next canto relates how the terrified Assyrians hasten to tell their leader of the assault, and how, when they find only his dead body, they, "sorrowfully minded, cast down their weapons, and turn, sad at heart, to flight." The poem ends with the entire overthrow of the Assyrians, the return of the conquerors with their booty to Bethulia, and Judith's praise of the Almighty for the triumph of her stratagem.

From this sketch of the poem it will be seen that it is closely allied in theme to those of Cynewulf and his school, and this led to the assumption of Ten Brink and others that it was composed in the early part of the ninth century. A close investigation of its diction by Gregory Foster led him to place it a century later; and, if, as he thinks, it was composed to commemorate the valiant deeds of Aethelflaed, the Lady of Mercia, who wrested the five boroughs from the Danes, it was probably written about 918. But nothing can be said with certainty on the subject.

As poetry, this fragment stands in the front rank of Old English literature, with *Beowulf* and *Elene* and *Andreas*. In wealth of synonym it is equal to the best poems of Cynewulf, while the construction of the sentences is simpler, and the narrative, in consequence, less obscure. An impression of intensity is produced by the heaping of synonyms in moments of stress, as in the prayer of Judith, and in the fierce lines which describe the onset against the Assyrians; while a sense of dramatic fitness is shown in the transitions, the divisions of the cantos and the preparation for each great adventure. The tragedy is alive, and the actors play their parts before our eyes.

The patriotic feeling which probably gave rise to *Judith* was certainly responsible for the second great poem of our period, the *Battle of Maldon*, sometimes called *Byrhtnoth's Death*. The manuscript of this poem[1] was destroyed by the Cottonian fire; but it had, fortunately, been printed by Herne in 1726, and it is from his text that our knowledge of the poem is derived. It celebrates the death of the great ealdorman Byrthnoth, who was connected by close ties of kinship with Aethelmaer, the friend of Aelfric; it was, indeed partly by means of legacies left by him that Aethelmaer was enabled to support so generously the monastic revival, and it is, therefore fitting that he should be commemorated by one of the finest poems in Old English. In the poem before us he stands out as the ideal leader of men, admirable alike in his devotion to his king, his simple piety and his sense of responsibility towards

[1] Oth. A. XII.

his followers. He died as became a member of the race that thirsts for danger,[1] almost the last of the warriors of that time who maintained the noble tradition of the days of Alfred. In less than twenty years after this date, the chronicler tells a pitiful story of divisions between those who should have united to lead the people to battle, and of forced payment of the shameful tribute which Byrhtnoth refused.

It was in the year 991 that the Northman Anlaf sailed with ninety-three ships to the coast of England, and after harrying Stone, Sandwich and Ipswich, came to Maeldune (now Maldon) on the banks of the river Panta or Blackwater. The stream divides here into two branches, and, leaving their ships at anchor in one of them, the Danes drew up their forces on the intervening piece of land. The poem, the beginning and end of which are lost, opens with the directions of Byrhtnoth to his men, and tells how, after marshalling his troops, he exhorted them to stand firm, taking his place among the band of his immediate followers. At that moment there appeared on the other side of the stream the viking herald, who said that he was sent by the seamen to announce that, if Brythnoth would buy off the assault with tribute, they would make peace with him and return to their own land. But Byrhtnoth scornfully rejected the offer, saying that he would give tribute, indeed, but it should be the tribute of the sharp spear and the ancient sword, and their only booty would be battle. With this message he bade his men advance to the edge of the stream; but, owing to the inflowing flood after the ebb, neither army could reach the other, and they waited in battle array till the tide's going out. Then Byrhtnoth, overweeningly daring, trusting too much in his own strength, allowed the enemy to cross by the bridge (probably one of stepping-stones which would be covered at high tide), and the fight became fierce. "The time had come for the fated men to fall; then was a tumult raised, the raven, eager for carrion, hovered in the air, and on earth was a great cry." On every side fell the heroes; a kinsman of Byrhtnoth was wounded, and, at last, the brave earl himself was slain by a poisoned spear. With his last words he exhorted his men to resistance, and died commending his soul to God. True to the noble traditions of the

[1] Tacitus, *Hist.* v, 19.

heroic age, Aelfnoth and Wulfmaer shared his faith and fell, hewn down by the heathen beside their lord. Then cowards began to flee and seek safety in the woods, forgetting the brave words they had spoken when feasting in the mead-hall. But Aelfwine, the son of Aelfric, shouted to those fleeing, reminding them of their vows, and declaring that none among his race should twit him with flight, now that his prince lay fallen in battle, he who was both his kinsman and his lord. His brave words were taken up by Offa and Dunnere; and the warriors advanced to a fresh attack. The appearance amongst the defending ranks of Aeschere, son of Ecglaf, a Northumbrian hostage is of great interest, as it seems, for a moment, to give us a vivid glance of the political troubles of the land. The poem ends by telling how Godric exhorted his comrades and fought fiercely against the heathen till he too fell.

This brief outline may, perhaps, give some idea of the great interest of the poem, whose every word is filled with deep hatred against the marauding foe, and with dignified sorrow for the loss of beloved friends. The verse is as noble as the deed and instinct with dramatic life. In it we see the heroic feeling of the earlier national poetry, full of the Teutonic theme of loyal friendship and warlike courage. And not until many hundreds of years have elapsed do we find its equal in tragic strength. It is from this stirring narrative, from Wulfstan's address to the English and from the bitter records in the *Chronicle*, that we realise the degradation of the country during the unhappy reign of Aethelred.

The remaining poems of our period in the old alliterative metre are of a didactic character. Among them may be mentioned the *Menologium* or poetical calendar, which is prefixed to a version of the *Chronicle*.[1] It is an interesting metrical survey of the progress of the year, with special mention of the saints' days observed by the church, preserving some of the Old English names of the months, such as Weodmonað (August), Winterfylleð (October) and Blōtmonað (November), and retaining traces of heathen times, though the whole is Christian in basis. Its value, as poetry, depends on the tender feeling for nature shown in such passages as those which describe the coming of May, tranquil and gentle, with blossom-

[1] Cott. Tib. B. 1.

ing woods and flowers, or winter, which cuts off the harvest with the sword of rime and snow, when all is fettered with frost by the hest of the Creator, so that men may no longer haunt the green meadows or the flowery fields.

Of more literary value is the poem entitled *Be Domes Daege*,[1] a free version of the Latin poem *De Die Judicii*, by some scholars ascribed to Bede and by others to Alcuin. The 157 lines of the Latin original are expanded to 304 by the translator, whose imaginative gift is especially visible in the way he enlarges on a hint from his source. The opening passage is extremely beautiful. It tells how, as the author sat lonely within a bower in a wood where the streams murmured among pleasant plants, a wind suddenly arose that stirred the trees and darkened the sky, so that his mind was troubled, and he began to sing of the coming of death. He describes how he wept and lay upon the earth, beating his breast for sorrow, and he calls upon all his fellow sinners to confess their sins with tears and to throw themselves on the mercy of Christ. Then comes another highly imaginative passage, describing the terrors that will foretell the second advent. "All the earth shaketh, and the hills also quiver and fall; the gates of the mountains bend and melt, and the terrible tumult of the stormy sea fearfully frights the minds of men." Then the Lord shall come with hosts of angels, the sins of all shall be revealed and fire shall consume the unrepentant. The poem ends with a passage, partly borrowed from the Latin, on the joys of the redeemed. They shall be numbered in heaven among the angels, and there, amidst clusters of red roses, shall shine for ever. A throng of virgin souls shall wander there, garlanded with flowers, led by that most blessed of maidens who bore the Lord on earth.

The translation is one of the finest in Old English. It is far more powerful than its Latin original, and many of the most beautiful passages are new matter put in by the Old English translator; for example, the lengthening of the opening, telling of the woodland scene, the section of the terrors of judgment and hell, and the whole passage describing Mary leading the flower-decked maiden throng in Heaven.

[1] Found in a unique manuscript in the library of Corpus Christi College, Cambridge.

In the same manuscript occurs another poem to which its editor, Lumby, gave the title of *Lār*, and which he ascribed to the author of the previous poem.   It has, however, none of the imaginative power of *Be Domes Daege*, and consists simply of eighty lines of exhortatory verse addressed by one friend to another, bidding him work, fear God, pray, give alms and go to church in cold weather.   And, since the length of life is unknown, and the enemies of man are ever at hand to assail him, they must be routed by earnest prayer and meditation, and the abandonment of all bad habits.   The low poetical worth of this piece would seem to show that it was not by the translator of *Be Domes Daege*.

Next follow in the manuscript some curious verses, of which each line is half in Latin and half in English, and which were formerly also attributed to the author of *Be Domes Daege*. The poems, however, differ so much in merit that this theory must certainly be rejected.   The further theory that the invocation of saints in these verses shows that it was not by the author of *Be Domes Daege* is, however, scarcely sound, for it disregards contemporary theology and overlooks the English verses in praise of the Virgin added by the translator of that poem.   Hence our truest warrant for attributing these verses to a different author lies rather in the beauty and dignity of *Be Domes Daege*.   The hymn in question is an ingenious piece of trickery, like many a Provençal poem of later date.   It opens with a prayer for God's mercy on the reader, and then goes on to speak of the incarnation, ending with an invocation to Mary and the saints.   These verses, however, are of inestimable value metrically, since they show, by their Latin equivalents, the two-beat characters of the rhetorical verse, just as similar Old German poems show, by their far greater length in the Latin portions, the four-beat characters of Germanic sung verse.

More interesting are the eleventh century metrical versions of the *Psalms*, in a manuscript in the Bibliotheque Nationale. This MS. contains only *Psalms* 1 to cl, but Bouterwek discovered further fragments in a Benedictine office, which partly fill up the gaps, and point to the existence of a complete metrical version of the *Psalter* in Old English.   Taken altogether, however, this Benedictine office is merely a heap of fragments.

The translation is, as a rule, good, when play is given to love of nature or to feeling, common in Old English poetry. An isolated version exists of *Psalm* 1 in Kentish dialect,[1] which was formerly supposed to belong to the eighth century, but which is shown, by its language, to be two hundred years later. It was not, apparently, one of a series, but was complete in itself, being rounded off at the close by a short hymn-like passage on David's sin and his atonement.

A gloomy poem on *The Grave*, "For thee was a house built Ere thou wast born," etc., written in the margin of a volume of homilies in the Bodleian[2] and known to all readers of Longfellow and many beside, need not detain us long. It is, probably, of later date than any of the poems already referred to and shows signs of the coming metrical change.

Last, there must be mentioned a poem on the city of Durham, which, though not composed within our period, is the latest in classical rhetorical metre that is known to exist, and is, therefore, most suitably described in this place. One version[3] was printed by Hickes in his *Thesaurus* (1703–05), and another copy occurs at the close of a manuscript of the *Historia Ecclesia Dunelmensis* of Simeon of Durham in the University Library, Cambridge. The poem, which contains twenty long lines, falls in two parts, the first eight describing the city on the hill, surrounded with steep rocks, girdled by the strong flowing river, and full of many kinds of fish, and environed by forests in whose deep dells dwell countless wild beasts; while the last twelve tell of the wonderful relics preserved there, memorials of Cuthbert and Oswald, Aidan and Eadberg, Eadfrith and bishop Aethelwold, as well as of the famous writers Bede and Boisil, which, amidst the veneration of the faithful, awaited in the minster the doomsday of the Lord. It is this catalogue of saints which enables us to fix the date of the poem, for the translation of their relics to the new cathedral took place in 1104, and the poem follows closely the order of enumeration found in Simeon of Durham's description of that ceremony.[4] Although it is written in a trained archaistic attempt at West Saxon spelling, yet we catch many clear

[1] Cott. Vesp. D. v. 1.
[2] NE. F. 4, 12.
[3] Cott. Vitt. D. 20.
[4] *Capitula de Miraculis et Translationibus S. Cuthberti*, Cap. **VII.**

glimpses of south-eastern twelfth century phonology in its faulty attempts at correctness.

After 1100, English poetry ceases to exist for nigh a hundred years, although fragments remain to bear witness to that popular verse which was to keep in the west midlands and north some continuity with the old poetry—for the sung rhythm never died out amongst the common folk, and rose ever and anon to such songs as that of *The Pearl*, to heroic lays of Arthur, Alexander and Troy and, in our own days, has been revived in the rhythm of the mystic *Christabel*.

English prose was wrecked for many a hundred year Centuries elapsed before Aelfric had his equal again.

CHAPTER VIII

The Norman Conquest

THE Norman conquest of England, from a literary point of view, did not begin on the autumn day that saw Harold's levies defeated by Norman archers on the slopes of Senlac. It began with the years which, from his early youth onwards, Edward the Confessor, the grandson of a Norman duke, had spent in exile in Normandy; and with his intimacy with "foreigners" and its inevitable consequences. The invasion of Norman favourites, which preceded and accompanied his accession to the throne, and their appointments, for a time, to the chief places in church and state, led to the tightening of the bonds that bound England to the Roman church, and paved the way for the period of Latin influence that followed the coming of William, Lanfranc and Anselm.

The development of the old vernacular literature was arrested for nearly a hundred and fifty years after Hastings; and, as the preservation of letters depended on ecclesiastics, professed scholars and monastic chroniclers of foreign extraction, the literature of England for practically a couple of centuries is to be found mainly in Latin. Happily for England, her connection with the continent became intimate at a time when Paris, "the mother of wisdom," was about to rise to intellectual dominance over Europe.

Of the national vernacular literature of France, at the time of the Conquest, little was transplanted to English soil; but, in the two centuries that followed, the cultivation of romance, aided by "matter" that had passed through Celtic hands, flourished exceedingly among the Anglo-Norman peoples and became a notable part of English literature.

The development of Old English literature, as we have said, was arrested. It was by no means, as some have urged, lifeless before this break in its history; and speculation would be futile as to what might have been its future, had there been no Norman conquest. Where so much has been lost, there is no safety in sweeping generalisations, based upon what is left. As a whole, the evidence which we possess shows Old English literature to have been richer than that of any other European nation during the period of its most active life; and, though there was, apparently, throughout Christian Europe, a lowering of letters, in which England shared, during "the gloom and iron and lead" of the tenth century, yet the lamps of learning and of literature, though low, were not extinguished in this island. It was the age of Dunstan, a lover of ballads and music and illuminated missals and precious jewels and letters, a learned saint, a dreamer of dreams, a worker in metal, the reformer of Glastonbury, a statesman and teacher who "filled all England with light." It was, as we have seen, the age of Aelfric, in whose hands Old English prose had been fashioned from the condition in which we find it in the early days of the *Chronicle*, and in the days of Alfred, into an instrument capable of expressing different kinds of thought in ways of lightness and strength. And it was the age, certainly, of *The Battle of Maldon* and of Brunanburh, and, possibly, of *Judith* also. Old English poetry had proved itself capable of expressing with notable aptitude, and with grave seriousness, the nobler views of life.

A period of warfare with the Danes follows, during which monasteries like that of Cerne, in Dorset, are sacked, and literature wanes; but there is evidence that the national spirit, fostered by the beneficent rule of Canute, was strong in England in the days preceding the coming of the Conqueror; and it is but reasonable to assume that this spirit would not have withered away and become a thing of naught, had Harold won, instead of lost, the battle of Hastings. The main stream of its literary expression was dammed at that time, and portions of it were turned into other, and, so far as we can now see, into better, because more varied, channels; but, when the barriers were gradually broken down, and the stream regained freedom of action, it was not the source that had been vitally altered—this had only been changed in ways that did not greatly modify its main character—but, between altered banks, and in freshly wrought-out channels, the old waters ran, invigorated by the addition of fresh springs.

Into what the folk-songs, of which we have faint glimmerings, were about to develop, had there not been an interregnum, we know not; but the literary spirit of the people, though they were crushed under their Norman masters, never died out; it had little or no assistance at first from the alien lettered classes; and, when it revived, it was "with a difference."

There had not been wanting signs of some coming change. Already, in pre-Conquest days, there had been a tendency to seek some "new thing." A growing sense of the existence of wonderful things in the east, of which it was desirable to have some knowledge, had led an unknown Englishman to translate the story of *Apollonius of Tyre* into English. The marvellous deeds of the *Lives of the Saints* had already proved that a taste for listening to stories, if not, as yet, the capacity to tell them with conscious literary art, grace and skill was in existence. And, in addition to this, we learn from the list of books acquired by Leofric for Exeter cathedral, sixteen years only before the battle of Hastings, that the love for books and learning which had inspired Benedict Biscop and Dunstan had by no means died out; of some sixty volumes, many were in English and one is the famous "mycel Englisc boc" "of many kinds of things wrought in verse," from which we know much of the little we do know concerning Old English literature.

The facility with which Englishmen adopted what Normans had to give was, in some measure, due to the blood-relationship that already existed between the two races. Scandinavian seafarers, mated with women of Gaul, had bred a race possessing certain features akin to those of the Teutonic inhabitants of England. It was a race that, becoming "French," adapted itself rapidly to its new surroundings, soon forgetting its northern home and tongue; and, when it was master of England, further barriers between race and race were soon broken down. The Norman conquest of England differed altogether from the English conquest of Britain. The earlier conquest was a process of colonisation and gave the land an almost entirely new population, with entirely new thoughts and ways of looking at things, save in the borderlands of the "Celtic fringe"; the later brought a new governing, and then a new trading, class, and added a fresh strain to the national blood without supplanting the mass of the people. Intermarriage, that would begin, naturally enough, among Norman serving-men and English women, spread from rank to rank, receiving its ultimate sanction when Anselm crowned Matilda as Henry's queen. Sooner or later the Norman, whether of higher or of lower degree, adopted England as his country, spoke and acted as an Englishman and, before the great Charter, that is to say, a hundred and fifty years after the battle of Hastings, when the French homes of Normandy and Anjou had been lost, the mixture of the invading race and the conquered people was approaching completion. The more stolid native had been touched with "finer fancies" and "lighter thought"; the natural melancholy of the Old English spirit had been wedded to the gaiety of the Norman; and England . . . in due season was recognised to be

> a wel god land, ich wene ech londe best,
> Iset in the on ende of the worlde as al in the west:
> The see geth him al aboute, he stond as in an yle
> Of fon[1] hii dorre the lasse doute—bote hit be thorȝ gyle
> Of folc of the sulve[2] lond, as me hath iseye ȝwile,[3, 4]

in language that irresistibly recalls the "fortress built by Nature for herself," the "happy breed of men," the "little world," the "precious stone set in the silver sea," the "blessed plot, this earth, this realm, this England," of Shakespeare. So it came to pass that, though, as the immediate result of the Conquest, Norman-French became the exclusive language of the rich and courtly nobles and ecclesiastics, knights and priests, and Latin the exclusive language of learning—the conduits thus formed tending inevitably to trouble the isolated waters—yet the language

> in the country places,
> Where the old plain men have rosy faces,
> And the young fair maidens
> Quiet eyes,

and among the serfs and the outlaws in the greenwood, and "lowe men" generally, was the unforbidden, even if untaught,

---

[1] Of foes they need the less fear—unless it be through guile.
[2] same. [3] formerly. [4] Robert of Gloucester.

English of the conquered race. And, contrary to the expectation and, perhaps, the desire of the governing class, it was this language which, in the end, prevailed.

The gain to English literature that accrued from the Norman conquest in three directions is so great as to be obvious to the most superficial observer. The language was enriched by the naturalisation of a Romanic vocabulary; methods of expression and ideas to be expressed were greatly multiplied by the incursion of Norman methods and ideas; and the cause of scholarship and learning was strengthened by the coming of scholars whose reputation was, or was to be, European, and by the links that were to bind Paris and Oxford.

In a less obvious way, it gained by the consequent intercourse with the continent that brought our wandering scholars into connection with the wisdom of the east. It is not to be forgotten, for instance, that, for three or four hundred years, that is to say, from about the ninth to about the twelfth century, Mohammadism, under the rule of enlightened caliphs in the east and in the west, fostered learning and promoted the study of the liberal arts at a time when many of the Christian kingdoms of Europe were in intellectual darkness. Harun ar-Rashid was a contemporary of Alcuin, and he and his successors made Baghdad and the cities of Spain centres of knowledge and storehouses of books. The Aristotelian philosophy, which had so commanding an influence over the whole of the religious thought of the west during the Middle Ages, was known prior to the middle of the thirteenth century, chiefly through Latin translations based upon Arabic versions of Aristotle; and the attachment of the Arabs to the study of mathematics and astronomy is too well known to call for comment. Our own connection with Mohammadan learning during the period of its European predominance is exemplified in the persons of Michael Scot; of Robert the Englishman or Robert de Retines who first translated the Coran into Latin; of Daniel of Morley, East Anglian astronomer, scholar of Toledo and importer of books; and of Adelard or Aethelard of Bath, who, in many wanderings through eastern and western lands, acquired learning from Greek and Arab, who translated Euclid and who showed his love of the quest for knowledge in other than purely mathematical ways in his philosophical treatise *De Eodem et*

Diverso, an allegory in which Philocosmia, or the Lust of the World, disputes with Philosophia for the body and soul of the narrator.

The Christian learning of the west received fresh impetus in the middle of the eleventh century at the hands of Lanfranc, who made the monastic school at Bec a centre famous for its teaching, and who, when he came to England, to work for church and state, did not forget his earlier care for books and learning. It was under Lanfranc's direction that Osbern, the Canterbury monk, wrote his lives of earlier English ecclesiastics, of St. Dunstan and St. Alphege and St. Odo; and he gave generously to the building of St. Albans, a monastery which, under the abbacy of Lanfranc's well-beloved kinsman Paul, encouraged the spirit of letters in its specially endowed *scriptorium*, and so led the way to the conversion of annalist into historian illustrated in the person of Matthew Paris.

A consideration of the writings of Lanfranc himself falls outside our province; they consist of letters, commentaries and treatises on controversial theology. Prior to his appointment as archbishop of Canterbury, Lanfranc had been mainly responsible for the refutation of the "spiritual" views concerning the Eucharist held by Berengarius, who, following the footsteps of John Scotus (Erigena) opposed the doctrine of Real Presence. Lanfranc's deputation helped largely to strengthen the universal acceptance of the doctrine of transubstantiation throughout the Roman church; and, as the chief officer of the English church, in the years of its renovation under William, his influence could but tend towards placing English religious life and thought and, therefore, English religious literature, more in harmony with the religious system of Europe.

Lanfranc's successor in the see of Canterbury was his fellow-countryman and pupil, Anselm; perhaps less of a statesman, but a greater genius, a kindlier-natured and larger-hearted man and a more profound thinker. As one of the greatest of English churchmen, who fought for the purity and liberty and rights of the English church, we may claim Anselm as English, and we may rejoice at the place given him in the *Paradiso* in the company of Bonaventura and John Chrysostom and Peter "the devourer" of books, but the consideration of his writings, also, falls rather to the historian of religious philosophy.

Inasmuch, however, as the result of Anselm's fight against kingly tyranny led to the charter of Henry I and so prepared the way for the Great Charter that followed a century later he must be mentioned among those who took part in the making of England.

The reflection in English literature of the gradual construction of this new England will be seen more clearly when we have passed through the interval of quiescence that prevailed in vernacular letters after the Conquest. The literature of church and state and scholarship was for those who knew Latin; and the literature that followed the invaders was for those who taught French; the struggle for supremacy between native and alien tongues was fought out; and, when the first writers of Transition English appear, it is seen that the beaten Romance has modified the conquering Teutonic. The early days appear to be days of halting steps and curious experiment; and, naturally, the imitation of foreign models seems greater at first than later, when the naturalisation, or, rather, the blending, is nearer completion. Even the manuscripts of these early days, in their comparatively simple character, show that the vernacular is in the condition of a "poor relation." Writers in English were at school under the new masters of the land, whose cycles of romance, including much that was borrowed from the adopted country, and, therefore, much that was easily assimilated, afforded, both in respect of form and of matter, excellent material for translation for many a year until, in fact, the clipped wings had had time to grow again.

As before hinted, we do not know the extent of what we lost, and we cannot, with any advantage, proceed far on the road of aesthetic comparison between old and new. We must be content, therefore, to recognise to the full the gifts of the Norman race, and these were not confined to the making of literary English. For, as an outward and visible sign, still remaining in many places to testify, with the strengthening of our literature, to the change in art that accompanied the change in blood, and that gave expression to the change in thought, there stand the buildings erected throughout the land, as William of Malmesbury said, "after a style unknown before."

After the axe came the chisel; and this change of tool which helps us to follow the steps that mark the development

of Anglo-Norman architecture, may symbolise the development of language and letters in England under Anglo-Norman
kings, a development that had begun years before the Conqueror had landed. When inflections had been well-nigh
lopped off, and the language had been made more copious by
additions to its ornamental vocabulary, the new "smiths of
song"—whether graceless minstrel or ascetic priest—were
able to give more adequate expression to the work of their
hands and to branch out into less imitative ways. They were
beating out the material in preparation for the coming of
Chaucer.

CHAPTER IX

Latin Chroniclers from the Eleventh to the Thirteenth Centuries

O F all the literary monuments of the remarkable revival of learning which followed the coming of the Normans and which reached its zenith under Henry II, the greatest alike, in bulk and in permanent interest and value, is the voluminous mass of Latin chronicles compiled during the twelfth and thirteenth centuries. So ample is the wealth of this chronicle literature, and so full and trustworthy is its presentment of contemporary affairs, that few periods in our history stand out in such clear and minute relief as that of the Norman and Angevin kings. Priceless as these documents are to the modern historian, they are far from being as a whole, the colourless records which concern the student of political and constitutional movements alone. Many of them may have but little charm or distinction of style, and may appear to be nothing better than laboriously faithful registers of current events. They all, however, after their quality and kind, bear the marks of a common inspiration, and the meanest chronicler of the time felt that, in compiling the annals of his own country, he was working in the tradition of the great historians of antiquity. Some few of the chronicles are real literature, and show that their writers were well aware that history has its muse.

While a scholarly delight and an honest pride in their art were common to all the English chroniclers of the Norman and Angevin period, not a few of them found an additional incentive in royal and aristocratic patronage. Much of the activity of the twelfth century historians was palpably due to the favour shown to men of letters by the two Henrys, and the personal encouragement of princely nobles like earl Robert of Gloucester, and courtly ecclesiastics like Alexander, bishop of Lincoln. Some of the monastic writers enjoyed no such direct patronage; but they were none the less responsive to the demands of the time. They not only felt the impulse of the new learning—they were conscious of living in a great age, and of witnessing the gradual establishment in England of a new and powerful kingdom. Nothing is more significant than the way in which the Anglo-Norman chroniclers, whether native Englishmen or Normans, domiciled in England, reflect the united patriotic sentiment which it was the design of Norman statesmanship to foster. Though composed in a foreign tongue, these chronicles are histories of England, and are written from a national English standpoint. It was under Henry I, whose marriage with Matilda seemed to symbolise the permanent union of the two peoples, that a new sense of national self-consciousness began to grow out of the Norman settlement. A shrewd observer of the next generation, Walter Map, tells us that it was Henry who effectually "united both peoples in a steadfast concord." [1] It was Henry's reign also that witnessed the transfer of the central seat of Norman power from Normandy to England. William of Malmesbury, himself half-Norman, half-English, in his account of the battle of Tinchebray, reminds his readers that it was fought "on the same day on which about forty years before, William had first landed at Hastings"—a fact which the chronicler characteristically takes to prove "the wise dispensation of God that Normandy should be subjected to England on the same day that the Norman power had formerly arrived to conquer that kingdom." [2] In other words, England now became the predominant partner in the Anglo-Norman kingdom, and the twelfth century chroniclers are fully alive to the meaning of the change. As the dreams of a great Anglo-Norman empire began to take shape in the minds of the new rulers of England, and came to be temporarily realised under Henry II, the English historiographers rose to the height of their opportunities with patriotic ardour. No other country produced, during the twelfth and the thirteenth centuries, anything to be compared with the English chronicles in variety of interest, wealth of information and amplitude of range. So wide is their outlook,

---

[1] *De Nugis Curialium*, Dist. v, Cap. v.   [2] *Gesta Regum Anglorum* Bk. v.

and so authoritative is their record of events, that, as Stubbs observes, "it is from the English chroniclers of this period that much of the German history of the time has to be written." [1] The new England had become conscious of her power, and of her growing importance in the international economy of Europe.

In literature the most signal expression of that consciousness is the work of our Latin chroniclers. Thus, however unattractive much of this chronicle literature may be to the ordinary reader, there belongs to all of it the human interest of having been written under the pressure of great events and the stimulus of a glowing national feeling.

Even apart from the patriotic incentives, there were other influences at work during the twelfth century which made for the study and the writing of history. The Norman settlement in England synchronised with a movement which shook all western Christendom to its foundations. The crusades not only profoundly stirred the feelings of Europe—they served indirectly to quicken the imagination and stimulate the curiosity of the western races as nothing had done for centuries. Intercourse with the east, and the mingling together of different tribes in the crusading armies, brought about a "renascence of wonder" as far-reaching in some of its effects as the great renascence itself. The twelfth century is, above all, the age of the birth of modern romance. The institutions of chivalry, the mystic symbolism of the church, the international currency of popular *fabliaux*, the importation of oriental stories of magic and wizardry—all contributed to the fashioning of the fantastic creations of the medieval romances. And of the romantic cycles none came to have so speedy and triumphant a vogue as that which was named, originally in France, "the matter of Britain." This "matter of Britain" had its beginning as a formative influence in European literature, in the work of an Anglo-Norman writer, who, while professing to draw his information from a suspiciously cryptic source and frequently giving obvious rein to his own imagination, assumes none the less the gravity and the deliberate manner of an authentic chronicler. Geoffrey of Monmouth, ambitious of supplying what previous writers had failed to tell about the kings of Britain before the coming of the English, wrote a

[1] *Lectures on Medieval and Modern History*, p. 125.

chronicle which had all the charm and novelty of a romance of adventure. King Arthur, as a romantic hero, is Geoffrey's creation. Hence, the most readable Latin chronicle of the twelfth century is one that has the least real claim to that title. But the *History of the Kings of Britain* is no more to be ruled out of a place in the chronicle literature of England than it is to be ousted from its assured pre-eminence as the fountain-head of Arthurian romance. For Geoffrey's legends not only wrought their spell upon innumerable poets and imaginative writers, but continued for generations to disturb the waters of history, and to mystify a long line of honest and laborious chroniclers.

Geoffrey's *History*, whatever opinion may be held as to its author's methods and motives, well illustrates in its general style and manner the ambitious designs of the greater Anglo-Norman chroniclers. Those of them who aspire to write history, as distinguished from mere contemporary annals, are studious both of literary ornament and of the symmetry and proportion of their narrative. Compiling and borrowing, as Geoffrey professes to do, from previous chroniclers, they all endeavour to impart some new life and colour to their materials. They take the great Bede as their native master in the art of historical writing. But, for their literary models, they look beyond him, and seek, like William of Malmesbury, to "season their crude materials with Roman art." [1] Even minor chroniclers, like Richard of Devizes, who confine themselves to the events of their own time, are fond of adorning their pages with classical allusions or quotations. Henry of Huntingdon is even more adventurous, and enlivens his narrative with frequent metrical effusions of his own. Most of them endeavour, according to their ability, to be readable, arming themselves, as Roger of Wendover does, against both "the listless hearer and the fastidious reader" by "presenting something which each may relish," and so providing for the joint "profit and entertainment of all." [2]

But, far more than their embellishments of style, their fulness and accuracy of detail and their patriotic motives, what gives life and permanent interest to the Anglo-Norman chronicles is the sense which they convey of intimate relation-

---

[1] Preface to *Gesta Regum Anglorum*.   [2] Preface to *Flowers of History*.

ship with great men and great affairs. Even those chroniclers who do not pretend to write history on the larger scale, and only provide us with what Ralph of Diceto, in describing his own work, calls "outlines of histories," *imagines historiarum*, for the use of some future philosophic historian—even they succeed in conveying to us something, at least, of the animation of the stirring age in which they lived. They describe events of which they themselves were eye-witnesses; they preserve documents to which they had special privilege of access; they record impressions derived from direct contact with great statesmen, warriors and ecclesiastics; they retail anecdotes gathered from the cloister, the market-place and the court. For even the monastic chroniclers were not the mere recluses of the popular imagination. They were, in their way, men of the world, who, though themselves taking no active part in public affairs, lived in close intercourse with public men. The great abbeys, such as those of Malmesbury and of St. Albans, were open houses, constantly visited by the mighty ones of the land. William of Malmesbury tells us how his own monastery was distinguished for its "delightful hospitality," where "guests, arriving every hour, consume more than the inmates themselves." [1] Even the most remote of monastic writers, such as William of Newburgh, in his secluded Yorkshire priory, kept in such close touch with contemporary affairs as fully to realise their dramatic significance. "For in our times," he writes in the preface to his *English History*, "such great and memorable events have happened that the negligence of us moderns were justly to be reprehended, should they fail to be handed down to eternal memory in literary monuments." Other monkish writers, like Matthew Paris in a later generation, enjoyed the royal confidence, and occasionally wrote under royal command. Moreover, not all the chroniclers were monks. Henry of Huntingdon, Roger of Hoveden, Ralph of Diceto and the author of the chronicle so long wrongly ascribed to Benedict of Peterborough—not to mention writers like Giraldus Cambrensis and Walter Map, who have left behind them records scarcely distinguishable from contemporary chronicles—were all men who lived in intimate association with the court. So much store, indeed, came, in time, to be

[1] *Gesta Regum Anglorum*, Bk. v.

set upon the records of the chroniclers that they became standard authorities to which kings and statesmen appealed for confirmation of titles and the determination of constitutional claims. The conditions under which they were composed, and the importance which they once had as documents of state, are alone more than sufficient sanction for the provision made by "the Treasury, under the direction of the Master of the Rolls," for the publication of those editions in which they can best be studied by the modern reader.

"Of the several schools of English medieval history," writes Stubbs,[1] "the most ancient, the most fertile, the longest lived and the most widely spread was the Northumbrian." At its head stands the great name of Bede, the primary authority and the pattern of most of the Latin historians of our period. The first conspicuous representative of the northern school of chroniclers in the twelfth century is Simeon, precentor of the monastery of Durham, and he, like so many historiographers after him, makes Bede the foundation of the early part of his history. His second source of information, covering the period from the death of Bede down to the beginning of the ninth century, was the lost Northumbrian annals known to us through Simeon alone. From the middle of the ninth century down to 1121 he borrows his matter almost entirely from the chronicle of Florence of Worcester and the first continuator of the latter. The rest of Simeon's narrative, extending to the year 1129, probably represents his own independent work. Little is known of Simeon's life, and it is impossible to determine whether he was the actual compiler, or merely the editor, of the chronicle which bears his name. His work, however, had a high repute throughout the Middle Ages, and his fame was second only to that of Bede among the writers of the Northumbrian school. Simeon's chronicle was continued down to the close of the reign of Stephen by two priors of Hexham. The elder of the two, Richard, wrote an account of the *Acts of King Stephen, and the Battle of the Standard,* which contains much original information. His son, John, brought the narrative down to the year 1154, and is an independent authority of considerable value. Another north-countryman, the canonised Ailred or Ethelred, a Cistercian

[1] Preface to Roger of Hovede n's *Chronicle, Rolls Series.*

monk of Rievaulx, claims a place among the many chroniclers who wrote of the battle of the Standard. His account is neither so full nor so trustworthy as that of Richard of Hexham, but is somewhat more ambitious, in that it professes to give after the manner of the classical historians, the speeches of the rival leaders before the encounter. For a brief period about the middle of the twelfth century there was, in Northumbria as elsewhere, a curious break in the activity of the chroniclers. But, in the next generation, two writers who worthily uphold the traditions of the northern school appear in William of Newburgh and Roger of Hoveden. William confines himself to his own times; but Roger attempts a comprehensive history of several centuries, and, gathering his materials from the best available authorities, gives us what Stubbs calls "the full harvest of the labours of the Northumbrian historians."

The first Latin chronicler of any importance who belongs to southern England is Florence of Worcester, already mentioned as one of Simeon of Durham's main sources. Florence's work is notable as being the first attempt in England at a universal history beginning with the creation and embracing within its compass all the nations of the known world. But, as the title of his chronicle—*Chronicon ex Chronicis*—frankly indicates, Florence is not much more than a laborious compiler from the works of others; and he took as the basis of the early portions of his narrative the universal chronicle of Marianus Scotus, an Irish monk of the eleventh century. Marianus, in his turn, is, so far as English history is concerned, only a compiler from Bede and the Old English *Chronicle*. He brings his record of events down to the year 1082, but it is so fragmentary and perfunctory in its treatment of English affairs as to give Florence abundant opportunities for interpolation and addition. Florence's account of his own times, which closes with the year 1117, possesses much independent value, and was largely drawn upon by subsequent chroniclers. It is less valuable, however, than its continuation by John, another monk of Worcester, from 1117 to 1141. A second continuation, down to 1152, was based mainly upon the work of Henry of Huntingdon. The task of still further extending Florence's chronicle seems to have become a special concern of the monks of St. Edmundsbury, for it is to two inmates of that house

that we owe two other additions to it which continue the record, without a break, down to the very end of the thirteenth
century.

Neither Simeon of Durham nor Florence of Worcester
can be called a historian in any high sense.   Both are, at best,
but conscientious annalists, making no effort either to present
events in their wider relations of cause and effect, or to adorn
their narrative with any studied literary graces.   The earlier
portions of the chronicle which bears Simeon's name are,
indeed, embellished with frequent poetical quotations, but the
work, as a whole, is as barren of literary ornament as that of
Florence.   Literature of a somewhat richer colour, and history
of a higher order, are found in the writings of two of their contemporaries, one, like them, a pure Englishman, the other a
Norman born on English soil—Eadmer and Ordericus Vitalis.
Eadmer, the follower and intimate friend of Anselm, wrote
in six books a history of his own times down to the year 1122
—*Historia Novorum in Anglia*—which is full of fresh and vivid
detail.   In his preface Eadmer justifies the historian who
confines himself to a narrative of contemporary events; the
difficulty of obtaining an accurate knowledge of the past had
convinced him that none deserved better of posterity than he
who wrote a faithful record of the happenings of his own lifetime.   His immediate purpose, he tells us, is to give an
account of the relations of his master Anselm with William II
and Henry I, and especially of the disputes about the investiture.   But, as he anticipates, his task will oblige him to
illustrate at many points the history of England before, during
and after the investiture quarrel. While the main interest of
Eadmer's work is ecclesiastical, and, in the last two books,
turns largely upon the affairs of the see of Canterbury, it
throws much valuable light upon the general political and
social conditions of the time. Written with what William
of Malmesbury calls "a chastened elegance of style,"[1] Eadmer's
History is distinguished most of all by its design and sense of
proportion.   Eadmer is almost modern in his deliberate limi-
tation of himself to a period and a special subject upon which
he could speak as first-hand authority. His example in this
respect was not without its effect upon more than one his-

[1] Preface to *Gesta Regum Anglorum.*

toriographer of the next generation. Richard of Devizes and the author of the *Acts of Stephen* are chroniclers who make up for the brevity of their narratives by the graphic force which belongs only to a contemporary record. In addition to his *History* Eadmer wrote a Latin life of Anselm, and upon all that concerns the character and the work of that great prelate there is no more trustworthy authority.

Ordericus Vitalis, the son of Norman parents but born in Shropshire in 1075, was a writer of much more ambitious scope than Eadmer. His voluminous *Ecclesiastical History*, borrowing its title from Bede's great work, extends from the beginning of the Christian era down to the year 1141. It is in thirteen books, and represents the labour and observation of some twenty years of the writer's life. It is a characteristic product of the cloister. The church, and all that concerns it, are, throughout, uppermost in Orderic's mind, and determine his standpoint and design as a historian. But he had sufficient curiosity and knowledge of the world to gather and place on record a vast amount of information about mundane affairs. Taken over to Normandy to be educated at the early age of ten, he spent his life as a monk of St. Evroul; but he was not without opportunities of travel, and he paid at least one visit to England for the express purpose of collecting material for his *History*. Although he is often inaccurate in his chronology, and confusing in the arrangement of his matter, Orderic is one of our standard historical authorities for the Norman period. He is especially valuable for the information he gives as to the condition of Normandy itself during the eleventh, and part of the twelfth, century, and his *History* deals even more with continental than with English affairs. Yet he always prides himself upon his English birth; he even called himself an Englishman, and could, in Freeman's words, "at once admire the greatness of the Conqueror and sympathise with the wrongs of his victims." Orderic's very defects of arrangement and order as a chronicler were the result of a curiosity and a range of interest which add much to the value of his work as a minute and varied contemporary record. He tells us much that is not found elsewhere about the social conditions of his time, about the monastic profession and even about the occupations, tastes, pastimes and personal appearance of prominent men.

His style is, in many places, highly rhetorical. Of it, as a whole, "an English reader," writes dean Church, " may best form an idea by combining the Biblical pedantry and doggerel of a Fifth-monarchy pamphlet of the seventeenth century with the classical pedantry of the most extravagant burlesque of Dr. Johnson's English."[1]

Contemporary with Eadmer and Orderic, William of Malmesbury is a much greater historian, and, to the literary student, a far more attractive writer, than either. Milton's opinion, that "both for style and judgment" William is "by far the best writer of all" the twelfth century chroniclers,[2] still holds good. William, as many incidental confessions in his *History* show, had high ambitions as an author, and aspired to restore to the historian's art the dignity and the splendour with which it had been invested by the illustrious Bede. His design is to tell, artistically yet critically, all that is known about his country's history from the first coming of the English and, especially, as he informs us in his preface, to "fill up the chasm of two hundred and twenty-three years" after Bede which Eadmer had left altogether unnoticed in his *Historia Novorum*. William's chronicle is in two parts. The first, divided into five books, is called a *History of the Kings of England*, and extends from A.D. 449 to 1127. The second part, entitled *Historia Novella* or *Modern History*, is in three books, and brings the narrative down to the year 1142. These histories represent but a small portion of William's entire literary work, for he was one of the most prolific writers of his time; his other productions include a history of the prelates of England, a life of St. Wulfstan, and a history of the church of Glastonbury. William of Malmesbury possessed many of the highest qualifications of a historian; he had learning, industry, judgment and a wide knowledge of the world. He was, for his day, a considerable traveller, and was, both by temperament and training, a discriminating as well as an inquisitive student of life and character. He is thus singularly free from the prejudices and the narrow standards of the cloister. Although he himself claims that his mixed blood[3] is a guarantee of his

---

[1] *St. Anslem*, p. 140. [2] *History of England*, Bk. IV, p. 172 (1st ed. 1670).

[3] In the preface to the third book of his *History* William says that "the blood of the two peoples flows in [his] veins," and that he is therefore qualified to "steer a middle course " between racial partisans.

impartiality, he has not escaped the suspicion, among modern
critics, of having been something of a time-server. He had,
however, a thoroughly disinterested love of history as a study
and as an art; and the task of writing the history of England
presented itself to him as a patriotic duty, all the more clearly
incumbent upon him because of the "criminal indolence" of
those who might have continued the work of Bede.[1]

Bede, then, is William's greatest exemplar, and the fount of
his inspiration—Bede, with whom "was buried almost all
knowledge of history down to our own times," and whose
praises William protests that he has "neither the abilities nor
the eloquence" adequately to blazon.[1] For materials of the
earlier portions of his *History* William states[2] that he searched
far and wide; and, while he borrowed from nearly every known
work of his time, he evidently draws upon other sources which
have not been identified. But he by no means borrows indiscriminately. He sifts and selects his material, and cautions
his readers against accepting the testimony of his authorities
too implicitly. That he was not, however, so very much in
advance of his time is shown by the fact that he, in company
with more credulous chroniclers gravely records marvels and
seemingly supernatural occurrences as authentic historical
events. The evidence of a respectable eye-witness is, in most
of these cases, sufficient warrant for unquestioning belief.
Anecdotes, also, of every kind, seem to have had a peculiar
charm for William, and, at the end of his third book, he
quaintly excuses his fondness for including them in his *History*
by saying that, "if I am not too partial to myself, a variety
of anecdote cannot be displeasing to any one, unless he be
morose enough to rival the superciliousness of Cato." To the
modern reader, who looks for literary entertainment as much
as for authentic history, William's ingenuous habits of reminiscence, of quotation, of anecdotal digression and of sententious
comment add much to the personal charm and vivacity of his
narrative.

He is at his best, however, when he brings all his powers
of rhetoric and his faculty of pictorial writing to bear upon the
description of some great event or stirring public movement.
His graphic account of the first crusade, for example, has

---

[1] Bk. I, ch. 3.   [2] Bk. II, prol.

about it a spaciousness and a wealth of colour which all but rival the glowing periods of Gibbon.

This ardent love not only inspired the continental provinces but even all who had heard the name of Christ, whether in the most distant islands or savage countries. The Welshman left his hunting, the Scot his fellowship with vermin, the Dane his drinking-party, the Norwegian his raw fish. Lands were deserted of their husbandmen; houses of their inhabitants; even whole cities migrated. There was no regard to relationship; affection to their country was held in little esteem; God alone was placed before their eyes. Whatever was stored in granaries, or hoarded in chambers, to answer the hopes of the avaricious husbandmen or the covetousness of the miser, all, all was deserted; they hungered and thirsted after Jerusalem alone.

Even this brief passage serves to show that William was a writer who could make the dry bones of history live, and who had an artist's instinct for the salient and significant features of the panorama of events which the historian has to depict upon his canvas. The muse of history needs, for her highest service, the aid of the imagination; and William of Malmesbury's pre-eminence among the twelfth century chroniclers is due to the art which enabled him to give a picturesque setting to his narrative without any sacrifice of accuracy in circumstantial detail. For he still holds his place among historians as a high authority, not quite so impartial, perhaps, as he professes to be in his judgments of individuals, but singularly clear and trustworthy in his presentment of events. William, after all, wrote under the direct patronage of a great noble, and it was only natural that he should have paid some deference to the wishes and interests of earl Robert of Gloucester. Yet, even in the *Historia Novella*, written at Robert's request to describe the struggle between king Stephen and the empress Maud, in which Robert himself played a prominent part, the substantial truth of William's narrative remains unassailed.

Of the early twelfth century chroniclers, Henry of Huntingdon enjoyed, for generations, a popular repute second only to that of William of Malmesbury. Modern criticism, however, has largely destroyed Henry's claims to rank as a first-rate historical authority, and in neither style, accuracy, nor fulness of detail is he worthy of any serious comparison with William. Henry himself appears to have rated his powers at quite as high a value as William's; for he prefaces his chronicle with a floridly rhetorical and ambitious disquisition upon the "prerogatives" of history. But he possessed neither the learning nor the patient industry of William, and his studied endeavours after rhetorical ornament only serve to accentuate his pretentiousness by the side of his great monastic compeer. Henry was a secular clerk, who lived under the patronage, first of Robert Bloet, bishop of Lincoln, and afterwards of his successor, Alexander of Blois. It was, as he tells us, by command of Alexander that he wrote his *History of the English*, and he probably compiled the greater part of it between 1125 and 1130. The work was dedicated to Alexander; and the prefatory letter ends, characteristically, with an invocation in verse both of the Divine blessing and of the approbation of his episcopal patron. The entire *History*, frequently revised and extended, ends with the year 1154. Its earlier portions are borrowed, with many embellishments, from Bede and the Old English *Chronicle*. In many places Henry simply translates from the old English annals, and among his translations is a metrical version, though much curtailed, of the famous song on *The Battle of Brunanburh*. Henry prided himself on his accomplishments in verse, and his *History* is decorated with many poetical passages. Of his work, as a whole, the best that can be said is that it shows some sense of design, and of proportion in its execution; he treats of the history of England up to his time as dividing itself naturally into the four periods of the Roman, the Saxon, the Danish and the Norman occupations. It is when he comes to deal with the Norman dominion and especially with the events of his own time, that he is most disappointing. At the beginning of the seventh book he states that, after having so far relied upon either "ancient writers or common report," he is about to "deal with events which have passed under" his "own observation, or have been told to" him "by eye-witnesses." Neither in the seventh nor in the eighth book do we find much to justify the expectation thus raised. Henry was a facile writer, but a perfunctory historian. "He was ambitious, but not laborious; literary, but not exact; intelligent, but not penetrating. He formed large projects, but was too indolent to execute them satisfactorily."[1] Henry's rhetorical pages are brought to an appropriate close with a glowing peroration, in verse, celebrating the accession of King Henry II. What appears to have been at one time intended to stand as the eighth book of the *History* is a treatise *On the Contempt of the World*—a letter, addressed to a friend named Walter, upon the fortunes of "the bishops and the illustrious men of his age." This work, both the title and the motive of which remind us of more imposing literary achievements by greater men, contains many vivid portraits of Henry of Huntingdon's famous contemporaries.

A chronicler who is as great an authority, for the reign of which he treats, as either William of Malmesbury or Henry of Huntingdon, is the anonymous author of the *Acts of Stephen* (*Gesta Stephani*). Not even William himself surpasses this writer in accuracy and vividness of detail. He is a palpable partisan of Stephen, and has been supposed by some to have been the king's confessor. Nothing, however, better illustrates the general trustworthiness and impartiality of the twelfth century chroniclers than a comparison of the narrative of this historian with those of William of Malmesbury and Henry of Huntingdon. The *Gesta Stephani* covers much the same ground as the *Historia Novella* of William; yet though the two works were composed from opposite standpoints, they differ little in their presentment of the essential facts of the history of the time.

William of Malmesbury claimed, as we have seen, the patronage of Robert, earl of Gloucester; Henry of Huntingdon that of Alexander, bishop of Lincoln. The favour of both these magnates, and, if we are to trust the evidence of a MS. preserved at Berne, that of King Stephen himself, was invoked by the chronicler who enjoys the dubious distinction of having been among British writers the greatest disturber of the waters of history. Could he have foreseen the influence which he was destined to exercise over the poets of England, Geoffrey of Monmouth would doubtless have been quite content with the prospect of forfeiting the confidence of critical historians. Indeed, it is difficult to believe, on any supposition, that the *History of the Kings of Britain* was written as a serious contribution to authen-

[1] Thomas Arnold preface to *Rolls* edition.

tic history. Geoffrey's manner only too obviously betrays
him. Just as William of Malmesbury is anxious to "fill up the
chasm" between Bede and Eadmer, so Geoffrey professes to
explore and map out a still more obscure period, namely that
of "the kings who dwelt in Britain before the incarnation of
Christ," and especially of "Arthur and the many others who
succeeded him after the incarnation." It so happened that a
document was placed in his hands which "set forth the doings
of them all in due succession and order from Brute, the first king
of the Britons, onward to Cadwaladr, the son of Cadwallo, all
told in stories of exceeding beauty." This document was a certain "most ancient book in the British tongue," which was
supplied to him by Walter, archdeacon of Oxford. No other
contemporary chronicler seems to have had access to this mysterious book, and no amount of subsequent research has been
able to discover it. Geoffrey himself evidently looked upon its
contents as his own exclusive secret; for, in the epilogue to his
History, he expressly warns William of Malmesbury and
Henry of Huntingdon, who could write competently enough
about the kings of the English, not to meddle with the kings of
the Britons,"inasmuch as they have not the book in the British
speech which Walter brought over from Britanny."

All this affectation of mystery, however, does not prevent
Geoffrey from openly commending his work to the favourable
notice of the two great men whose confidence and encouragement William and Henry respectively enjoyed. The main
body of his *History* is dedicated to earl Robert of Gloucester,
while the seventh book, consisting of the famous prophecies of
Merlin, is prefaced by an almost fulsomely laudatory letter
addressed to Alexander of Lincoln. Geoffrey was thus determined to lose nothing of the prestige and credit to be derived
from aristocratic patronage; and his dedications only confirm
the assumption that he imitates the practices and assumes the
pose of an authentic chronicler with the deliberate purpose of
mystifying his readers. For Geoffrey's *History* is, on the last
analysis, a prose romance, and, in its Arthurian portions in
particular, a palpable excursion in fiction. One need not
believe that the entire work is, in the words of William of Newburgh, a tissue of "impudent and shameless lies." Even the
reference to "the British book" cannot altogether be re-

garded as a ruse for the deception of the ingenuous reader. Geoffrey doubtless drew upon some documents, possibly Welsh, which have since been lost. He borrowed all he could from Bede and Nennius; he probably borrowed more from floating British traditions. What is even more certain is that he invented a great deal. It is impossible to read the later books of the *History* without feeling that Geoffrey, when he had embarked upon the history of Merlin and of Arthur, was fully conscious of his opportunities of romantic dilatation. Arthur was a British prince capable of being exalted into a heroic figure who should overshadow both Alexander and Charlemagne. These two potentates were already the titular heroes of profitably worked romantic cycles. Why should Britain not have its romantic "matter," as well as Rome and France? Read in the light of the general literary history of its time, and of its immediate and immense popularity, Geoffrey's *History* can be adequately explained only as the response of a British writer, keenly observant of the literary tendencies of the day, to the growing demand for romance. How well he succeeded in his design appears from William of Newburgh's complaint that he had "made the little finger of his Arthur stouter than the back of Alexander the Great."

The *History of the Kings of Britain* was complete in the form now known to us by 1148 at the latest; but there is evidence that it existed in some form as early as 1139. A letter from Henry of Huntingdon, addressed to one Warinus, otherwise unknown, and prefixed to the *Chronicle* of Robert de Monte,[1] gives an abstract of a "big book" by "Geoffrey Arthur," which Henry discovered in 1139 at the abbey of Bec in Normandy. Henry himself had long been anxious to know something about the kings of the Britons; and "to his amazement he found" at Bec "a written record" of their deeds, including the history of Arthur, "whose death the Britons deny, and still continue to look for his return." Henry's letter contains no mention of Merlin; but whether then incorporated in the *History* or not, the *Prophecies* must have been written before 1139, for Ordericus Vitalis quotes from them in the twelfth book (ch. 47) of his *History*, which was composed in 1136 or 1137. By the year 1152 Geoffrey's work seems to have been well

---

[1] *Chronicles of Stephen (Rolls Series)*, IV, 65.

known, and to have won him favour in high places, as he was
then consecrated bishop of St. Asaph. He died in 1155. The
fame of his *History* had spread even before his death; for Wace,
and, probably, Geoffrey Gaimar, had begun to translate it into
Anglo-Norman verse before 1155.

In England a long line of chroniclers, in both prose and
verse, from Layamon and Robert of Gloucester down to Graf-
ton and Holinshed, accepted Geoffrey in all good faith as a
revealer of "the marvellous current of forgotten things";
while a host of poets, great and small, have been constantly
haunted by his fables. Two hundred years after his death
his repute was such that, on the strength of his use of the
Brutus legend, Chaucer gave him a high place in his *Hous of
Fame*. With Homer and Statius, Dares and Dictys and Guido
de Colonna, "English Gaufride" stands on an iron pedestal,

> besy for to bere up Troye.

In a later age both Spenser and Drayton sang his praises;
while even Wordsworth could not withhold a tribute to "the
British record long concealed," where

> We read of Spenser's fairy themes,
> And those that Milton loved in youthful years;
> The sage enchanter Merlin's subtle schemes,
> The feats of Arthur and his knightly peers.[1]

But Geoffrey has exacted still greater homage from the poets.
Lear and Cymbeline and Sabrina, "virgin daughter of Locrine,"
are names that link his memory for ever with the two supreme
poetical geniuses of England. Here, indeed, is a distinction
which the greatest of chroniclers might have coveted; and it is
enough to mark the *History of the Kings of Britain* as the most
significant literary product of the twelfth century.

Geoffrey, however, succeeded in deluding so many honest
chroniclers who followed him that, in modern times, he has
been altogether proscribed from the company of sober historians. Even before the twelfth century was out, his credit had
come to be gravely questioned. Giraldus Cambrensis, who had
himself no mean gift for the artistic manipulation of the legendary and the marvellous, is one of Geoffrey's severest detractors.
According to Gerald, a certain Welshman named Meilyr was

[1] *Artegal and Elidure.*

reported to have an extraordinary familiarity with unclean spirits, and they never responded to his call in greater numbers than when Geoffrey's book was placed on his bosom. Gerald, as is well known, had a strong sense of humour, and, probably all he means to imply is that Geoffrey had over-reached himself in the art of romance. It is otherwise with William of Newburgh. He regarded Geoffrey as one who had deliberately and flagrantly profaned the sacred functions of the historian, and devotes the entire preface of his chronicle to a vehement denunciation of Geoffrey's motives and to an exposure of his fabrications.

This severe preface has contributed as much as anything to the high repute in which William of Newburgh is held as a critical historian. Freeman's description of him as "the father of historical criticism"[1] has often been repeated, but scarcely seems deserved when we compare his actual achievement with that of his greater namesake of Malmesbury. For William of Newburgh belongs to that group of modest chroniclers who are content with treating a limited period, and describe, mainly, the events of their own lifetime. His *History* extends from the Conquest to the year 1198; but the narrative down to the time of Stephen is so compressed as to make the work, in effect, an account of the reigns of Stephen and Henry II. For the latter reign there are few better authorities. His work, as a whole, forms the best single commentary upon the history of the twelfth century left us by any writer of his day. For William's chronicle is no mere bare record of events, but an ordered and critical presentment of the affairs of his time, with due regard to their cause and effect. His remoteness from the court and the metropolis doubtless enabled William of Newburgh to maintain an attitude of impartiality impossible to chroniclers thrown into close contact with the greater actors in the drama of contemporary events. At any rate, the work of no twelfth-century chronicler is marked by a more transparent honesty of purpose, by greater independence of judgment, or by more acute estimates of men and their motives. William writes in a clear, straightforward style; less studious of artistic effect and literary ornament than his namesake of Malmesbury, he is inspired by a similar, if not a greater, desire for accuracy. Like his prede-

[1] *Contemporary Review*, vol. XXXIII (1878), p. 216.

cessor, he venerates the memory and the example of Bede, "whose wisdom and integrity none can doubt" ; and, following that historian's pious motives, he hopes that his own labours will form some "contribution, however scanty, to the treasure-house of the Lord.".

William of Newburgh was a contemporary of the brilliant galaxy of scholars who flourished in the full light of the encouragement given to learning and letters at the court of Henry II. But, living in the comparative seclusion of his monastery, he is not quite of them, and may be regarded rather as a continuator of the honourable traditions of the historical school of the north. In particular, he is one of the most trustworthy authorities for a period of some twenty years, after the turn of the twelfth century, of which we have scarcely any contemporary record.[1] For the English history of the years 1153—4, and especially for the foreign policy of the early years of Henry II's reign, our best contemporary authority is a chronicler who lived and wrote in Normandy, Robert de Monte or, as he calls himself, Robert of Torigni. He compiled a comprehensive record of events from the close of the first Christian century down to 1186, and is indebted for much of his account of purely English affairs to Eadmer and Henry of Huntingdon. The troubles of King Stephen's reign appear to have had a paralysing effect upon the chroniclers in England; and it is not until the height of Henry II's power that they begin once more to give us a full and vivid account of contemporary affairs. The historian's art flourished anew in the warmth of the general enthusiasm for learning which made the England of Henry's time the paradise of scholars. In palace and abbey, in the full glare and bustle of the court no less than in the bookish atmosphere of the monastic cell, men were infected by a common ardour of intellectual enterprise and literary achievement. In close touch with the court were men like Gilbert Foliot and Richard Fitz-Neale; Ralph of Diceto, who was dean of St. Paul's during Fitz-Neale's episcopate, and Ranulf de Glanville, whose name is associated with one of the earliest and most valuable treatises on the laws and customs of England, though the real author of it was, more probably, his nephew, Hubert Walter; Giraldus Cambrensis and Walter Map, Gervase of Tilbury and Peter of Blois. In remoter haunts,

[1] See Stubbs, Preface to Roger of Hoveden, *Rolls Series*, p. xl.

though having frequent opportunities of intercourse with men of action and affairs, were Gervase of Canterbury and Nigel Wireker, John of Salisbury and Richard of Devizes, Benedict of Peterborough and William of Newburgh and Roger of Hoveden. Altogether, there was in the country, as Stubbs says, "such supply of writers and readers as would be found nowhere else in Europe, except in the University of Paris itself."

Several of these names are of the first importance in the list of our Latin chroniclers. That of Benedict of Peterborough is associated with the most authoritative chronicle of the reign of Henry II, but only (as is now known) on the strength of the fact that one of the extant MSS. of the work was transcribed under his order. Benedict, however, was by no means a mere director of other men's literary labours, for he is known to have either written or edited accounts of the passion and the miracles of Becket. The author of the chronicle so long ascribed to him still remains undiscovered. Begun in 1172, the work bears in the main all the marks of a contemporary narrative, and includes several important documents. Stubbs holds that the internal evidence is sufficient to prove not only that the chronicle was not by Benedict, but that it is not the work of a monastic writer at all.

It has not even in its most disjointed portion the disorderly form, the disproportionate details, the unimportant memoranda, the generally undigested character, of monastic annals. It displays no propension to monastic institutions, or to those principles and persons that were especially favoured by monks. The author did not even trouble himself to compose an original account of Becket's martyrdom. Whatever positive indications are to be found point to a member of the king's court rather than to a monk, or even a secular churchman.[1]

Stubbs's conjecture that the chronicle may have been the work of Richard Fitz-Neale, and is a transcript of that writer's lost *Tricolumnis*, "merely altered from its inconvenient tripartite shape" has not found much acceptance among scholars. Fitz-Neale, who was treasurer of England from 1168—98, and bishop of London from 1189—98, is best known as the author of the famous *Dialogus de Scaccario*, or *Dialogue of the Exchequer*. That work, written in the form of a dialogue, in two books,

[1] Preface to edition in *Rolls Series*, p. lvi.

between the master and the pupil, is one of the chief sources of our knowledge of constitutional principles and practice in England before the Great Charter; it "stands out as an unique book in the history of medieval England, perhaps in the history of medieval Europe." [1]

The chronicle ascribed to Benedict forms, with some slight alterations and additions, one of the most substantial portions of the ambitious historical compilation attempted by Roger of Hoveden. The chroniclers generally had little scruple about thus transcribing, and embodying in their own works, the writings of their predecessors; it was, indeed, held among the monastic annalists to be a perfectly legitimate, not to say a necessary, practice. Thus Matthew Paris, the greatest monastic historian of the thirteenth century, makes the compilations of two of his predecessors at St. Albans the nucleus of those parts of his *Chronica Majora* which deals with events before his own time. Roger of Hoveden not only borrowed the so-called Benedict chronicle almost in its entirety, but made use of everything that he could find from the hands of the northern chronicles. In the first part of his work, extending from 732 to 1148, he copies from a Durham compilation, based upon the narratives of Simeon and of Henry of Huntingdon, which is known as the *Historia post Bedam*. His main source from 1148 down to 1169 is the chronicle of Melrose. The third part, extending to the year 1192, is substantially "Benedict of Peterborough," illustrated by several new documents; the final portion, ending with the year 1201, is Roger's own work. Roger was a man of affairs, and had exceptional opportunities for watching the development of public events. He was at one time in attendance upon Henry II in France; he subsequently held public office, as justice itinerant of the forests. It is disappointing, however, to find in Roger's *Chronicle* few of the intimate personal revelations which might be expected in the narrative of one who had such opportunities of intercourse with the leading men of his time. Roger makes up to some extent for this reticence by the compass of his narrative; for the later portions of his chronicle include not only a survey of English affairs during the reign of Henry II and Richard I, but a fairly comprehensive history of Europe during the same period.

[1] Pollock and Maitland's *History of English Law*, vol. 1, 2nd ed. p. 161.

"Well illustrated as the reigns of Henry II and Richard are," says Stubbs,[1] "one side of their character would be imperfectly known, and some of the crises of their policies would be almost inexplicable," without Ralph of Diceto. Ralph was another chronicler whose public life and position brought him into close contact with the great men of his time, and gave him access to the best sources of information. He was for many years archdeacon of Middlesex, and, from the year 1180 until his death, about 1202, held the deanery of St Paul's. "Diceto" appears to have been an artificial Latin name adopted by Ralph to signify his association with some place, probably French, which had no proper Latin name of its own. His chief work is entitled *Imagines Historiarum*, or *Outlines of Histories*, extending from the year 1148 down to 1202. Robert de Monte's chronicle forms the basis of his narrative down to 1172; from that year begin his own original memoranda, which are of especial value as contemporary records from 1183 onwards. Ralph is one of the most sober and straightforward of the chroniclers, and is little given to gossip or rhetorical decoration. His work is somewhat deficient in orderly arrangement, and its chronology is not always to be relied upon. Ralph, however, had much of the insight of the historian who seeks to analyse and to account for, as well as to record, public events and movements, and he was a shrewd judge of character and motive. His chronicle is illustrated by many important contemporary documents, to which his position gave him special means of access.

Of the several other chroniclers who wrote during the latter part of the twelfth, and the opening years of the thirteenth, century, only a passing mention need be made. Gervase of Canterbury, who died about 1210, is chiefly remembered as an ecclesiastical historian, and as one of the standard authorities on the contemporary history of the see to which he belonged. One of his works, entitled *Gesta Regum*, which is of some value as illustrating the reign of John, perpetuates the Brutus legend to which Geoffrey of Monmouth had given so startling a currency. A more important authority for king John's reign is Ralph, abbot of the Cistercian abbey of Coggeshall, whose *Chronicon Anglicanum* (1066—1223) contains, among other things, a full and well-informed account of Richard I's crusade.

[1] Preface to vol. II of edition of Ralph de Diceto in *Rolls Series*.

That crusade has been described by several chroniclers, but by none more graphically than by a monkish writer whose *History of King Richard I* is one of the briefest of the many contemporary narratives penned in the twelfth century. Its author, Richard of Devizes, has, however, stamped upon his modest essay in history the impress of a personality which is altogether absent from many more ambitious productions. His work has a real literary interest, on account both of the author's fondness for classical quotations and rhetorical ornament and of the vivid and picturesque force of his narrative. In a flowery letter of dedication, addressed to Robert, prior of the church of Winchester, Richard states that he has deliberately chosen a limited period for himself, leaving a more comprehensive survey of events to those "who produce greater works." "My narrative," he says, "is for the living"; and he writes with a dramatic instinct and an eye to pictorial effect not unworthy of a modern journalist. No chronicle gives us a more vivid picture of the general social condition of England in Cœur de Lion's time, or of the pageant of events in which the king took paramount part. The persecutions of the Jews, in particular, are described with a terrible faithfulness which reflects the author's own avowed hatred of the race.

Social life in England at the end of the twelfth century, and especially the internal life and economy of the monasteries are portrayed with intimate knowledge in the celebrated chronicle of Jocelin of Brakelond. Jocelin has had the good fortune, denied to the more ambitious chroniclers of great affairs of state, to engage the attention of a brilliant modern writer, and will continue to be known through Carlyle's *Past and Present* to thousands of readers who will never have the curiosity to read his actual Latin record. Quite apart, however, from the adventitious importance it has thus gained, Jocelin's account of the deeds of Abbot Sampson and his community at St. Edmundsbury is of unique historical value for the light it throws upon the organisation of monastic institutions and of their relations to the social and industrial life of the common people.

The life and habits of a different section of society have been illustrated, in an almost equally vivid way, by several of the scholars who flourished in and around the court of Henry II. John of Salisbury and Peter of Blois, Gervase of Tilbury and

Nigel Wireker, and, above all, Walter Map and Gerald of Wales, have left behind them documents which bear, in some respects, even more of the very "form and pressure" of the time than the chronicles themselves. The *Polycraticus* of John of Salisbury, the letters of Peter of Blois, the *Otia Imperialia* of Gervase and the poems of Nigel Wireker, throw a flood of light upon the studies and the pastimes, the intrigues and the scandals, the humours and the passions of those who dwelt in the high places of both state and church. Of all these writers none has contrived to blend information and entertainment more successfully than Giraldus Cambrensis. A scholar trained at Paris, an insatiably curious student of men and books and every form of odd lore, a fighter and an intriguer to his finger-tips, an inveterate gossip, yet a man capable of high ideals and far-reaching schemes of public policy, the intimate friend of kings and statesmen, popes and prelates, yet withal a passionate lover of his own native little Wales—Gerald is one of the most romantic figures in all medieval literature. The most stirring episode in his life was the struggle in which he engaged,[1] "for the honour of Wales"; and is still deservedly beloved among his countrymen as the devoted champion of one of the most creditable of lost causes and impossible loyalties. But his enduring title to fame rests upon the writings which, alike for brilliancy of style and for variety of interest, remain unsurpassed among the Anglo-Norman literature of the twelfth and thirteenth centuries.

A greater renown, however, in literary history generally has been enjoyed by Gerald's friend, and, probably, fellow-countryman, Walter Map. Were it possible to prove to demonstration Map's authorship of the great Arthurian romances so commonly associated with his name, there could be no question about his claim to rank as the greatest literary genius who appeared in England before Chaucer. But the claim made on behalf of Map to the authorship of these imaginative works rests on very slender evidence. Even the authenticity of his equally celebrated Goliardic poems is open to grave question. The *De Nugis Curialium*, or book *Of Courtiers' Trifles*, is, undoubtedly, his. It was probably composed by instalments, and forms a sort of common-place book in which Map seems to have jotted down from time to time, both shrewd reflections upon

[1] *Op.* (Rolls Series), I, 129.

men and things, and pleasant anecdotes to divert the vacant mind. Of the strictly historical portions of the work, the most valuable are the accounts, in the first book, of some of the heretical sects which had sprung up in the twelfth century, and the reflections, which take up the whole of the fifth book, upon the character and achievements of the Anglo-Norman kings. The fourth book includes, in company with some lively tales, the celebrated letter, well known to the Wife of Bath's fifth husband, from Valerius to Rufinus, upon the folly of marrying a wife. The whole work is a medley of such diverse and curious ingredients—satire, gossip, fairy-lore, folk-tales and snatches of serious history—as to make us easily believe that its author was, as Gerald hints, one of the most versatile and witty talkers in the court circles of that eager and inquisitive age.

The thirteenth century is, emphatically, the golden age of the monastic historians. At their head stands Matthew Paris, the greatest of all our medieval chroniclers; but his work only represents the crowning literary achievement of an enthusiasm and an industry that inspired every considerable monastery in the land. The annals, most of them nameless, of Burton, of Winchester, of Waverly, of Dunstable, of Osney, of Worcester—all testify to the assiduity of monkish scribes in compiling, revising, and adding to the stores of historical material accumulated in their respective houses. Invaluable, however, as these chronicles are to the student of political and social history, they possess little interest as literature.

But, at the powerful monastery of St. Albans, there arose a school of historians as brilliant as that which had, in the north, closed with Roger of Hoveden. This school produced in Matthew Paris a writer who, both in his conception of the historian's art and in the force and picturesqueness of his style, surpasses all the chroniclers of the twelfth century. The historians of St. Albans possessed exceptional advantages. The wealth of the abbey, its accommodation and equipment as an ideal home of learning, its position on Watling Street and its proximity to the capital, marked it out as the chief centre of monastic culture in the thirteenth century; and its inmates kept up a constant intercourse with the great men of the day as they passed through it on their way to and from London and the provinces. Nowhere else, perhaps, in the

kingdom could a historian of contemporary events pursue his
task at that time under more favourable conditions.   Moreover, in no other abbey does the writing of history appear
to have been so carefully organised as at St. Albans.   Abbot
Simon, who died in 1183, established in the monastery a regular
office of historiographer.   The first occupant of this office
whose complete work has come down to us was Roger of Wendover; but his chronicle is based upon materials of which an
ample wealth already existed in the abbey.   The actual
nucleus of the early part of Roger's *Flowers of History* is supposed to have been the compilation of John de Cella, who was
abbot of St. Albans from 1195 to 1214.   John's work extended
down to the year 1188, and was revised and continued by Roger
down to 1235, the year before his death.   Roger claims in
his preface to have selected "from the books of catholic writers
worthy of credit, just as flowers of various colours are gathered
from various fields."   Hence he called his work *Flores Historiarum*—a title appropriated in the fourteenth century to
a long compilation by various hands.   Begun at St. Albans
and completed at Westminster, it was based upon the *Chronicle*
of Matthew Paris and continued to the year 1326.   The work
was long ascribed to one Matthew of Westminster, but it is
now known that no actual chronicler of that name ever existed.
Roger of Wendover's work is, however, now valued not so
much for what he culled from previous writers as for its full
and lively narrative of contemporary events, from 1216 to
1235.   Although in accuracy and range and in sublety and
shrewdness of insight he falls far short of his great successor
as historiographer of St. Albans, Roger largely anticipates him
in the fearless candour of his personal and moral judgments.

Matthew Paris became historiographer of St. Albans upon
the death of Roger of Wendover in 1236, and proceeded in his
famous *Chronica Majora* to revise and continue the work of
his predecessor.   Matthew Paris's own narrative is an extraordinarily comprehensive and masterly survey of both English
and continental history during almost an entire quarter of a century.   We know little of the details of the historian's own
life.   He became a monk of St. Albans in 1217, and tradition
ascribes to him not only a high repute for scholarship, but the
possession of varied gifts as an artist.   The most notable

incident in his career was his employment by the pope, in 1248, on a mission of reform to the Benedictine monks of Holm, in Norway, which kept him away from England for some eighteen months. He lived, throughout, in close intimacy with the court, and, notwithstanding his plain-spokenness, enjoyed a share of royal favour. He died in 1259. Courtier and scholar, monk and man of the world, Matthew Paris was, both by training and position, exceptionally well qualified to undertake a history of his own time. Moreover, he had the instinct, the temper and the judgment of the born historian. He took immense pains in the collection and the verification of his facts, and appears to have been in constant communication with a host of correspondents both at home and abroad. Indeed, his work reads like a stately journal of contemporary European events, where everything is marshalled in due order and proportion by a master editorial hand. Great events and small follow each other in quick, though orderly, succession, just as in some modern review of the world's work. Simon de Montfort's preparations for his crusade; a dispute between the scholars and citzens of Oxford; the death of Llywelyn, prince of Wales; the pope's dealings with foreign clerks in England; a great storm; the decapitation of certain robbers; war in Flanders; the burning of heretics by the Milanese; the irruption of the Tartars—such is a brief selection of topics culled at random from a few consecutive pages of Matthew's *Chronicle*. But he is much more than a mere recorder of events. He is a fearless critic and censor of public men and their doings. A thoroughly patriotic Englishman, he is severe upon all misgovernment, openly rebuking the king, denouncing the greed and rapacity of the nobles, protesting indignantly against the extortionate exactions of the pope. He is not, indeed, altogether free from the professional bias of his class; and in nothing is this more apparent than in his obviously prejudiced references to the mendicant orders. But his criticisms as a whole are animated by a transparently honest fervour of moral indignation and by a patriotic jealousy for the honour of England. The pope's emissaries are "harpies and bloodsuckers, plunderers, who do not merely shear, but skin, the sheep." For his complacent acquiescence in the deeds of the papal legates the king is denounced as having become to the clergy "as it were the stalk of a reed—on which those who lean in confidence are wounded by the fragments." The king's own extortionate demands for money from the clergy are no less boldly condemned, while his foolishness and extravagance are constantly censured. These outspoken animadversions did not, however, blind Henry to Matthew's skill as a writer, and the chronicler relates how, during the celebration of the feast of Edward the Confessor, in 1247, the sovereign himself bade him take a seat near the throne and write a full account of the proceedings so that the facts might stand accurately recorded for ever. Matthew was, indeed, a ready and a picturesque writer. Though frequently prolix and rhetorical, he is never tedious or irrelevant. His narrative, as a rule, is wonderfully direct, clear and nervous, while his instinct for order and literary effect is such as to give to his *Chronicle*, as a whole, a unity and a sustained interest which belong to the work of no other English medieval historian.

Matthew Paris quite overshadows every other chronicler of the time of Henry III. But much of the history of Henry's reign would remain obscure were Paris's *Chronicle* not supplemented by the monumental work of Henry of Bracton, or Bratton, on the laws of England. Bracton scarcely belongs to the chroniclers; but his writings throw sufficient light upon the social conditions of his time to entitle him to stand side by side with Matthew Paris as a contributor to the English history of the thirteenth century. Following in the footsteps of Ranulf de Glanville (or Hubert Walter), Henry II's great justiciar, Henry of Bracton compiled, some time between 1250 and 1258, an elaborate treatise on the laws and customs of England. Bracton was one of the many ecclesiastics who held high judicial office under Henry III. He was, in turn, a justice in eyre, a judge of the king's court, a Devonshire rector and archdeacon of Barnstaple. In addition to his legal treatise he left behind him a note-book, containing some two thousand cases taken from the plea rolls of his time, with comments which "to all appearance came from Bracton's hand or from Bracton's head."[1] Indebted though he was for the form and method of this great book to such foreign works as those

---

[1] Pollock and Maitland, *History of English Law*, ed. 1898, vol. i, p. 207.

of the celebrated Italian lawyer Azo of Bologna, Bracton's work, is, in substance, thoroughly English, and is a laborious exposition, illustrated by some hundreds of decisions, of the approved practice of the king's court in England. Bracton died in 1268, leaving his work unfinished, although he appears to have been adding to and annotating it to the very last; but, even as it stands, his treatise is not only the most authoritative English law-book of his time, but, in design and matter, "the crown and flower of English medieval jurisprudence."[1] It "both marks and makes a critical moment in the history of law, and, therefore, in the essential history of the English people."[2]

The art of the historian proper, however, gradually began to decline after the death of Matthew Paris. Among the chroniclers who take us down to the fourteenth century there are few names worthy of a place in a history of literature. Prominent among them are Matthew's own followers at St. Albans, William Rishanger and John of Trokelowe; Nicholas Trivet or Trevet, a Dominican friar, whose works are of considerable historical importance for the reign of Edward I and of additional literary interest in connection with Chaucer's *Man of Law's Tale;* Walter of Hemingburgh, a canon of the Yorkshire priory of Guisburn, who not unworthily continues the work of the northern school; John de Tayster, or Taxster, a monk of St. Edmundsbury, who adds to a compilation from previous chroniclers what seems to be an original narrative for the years 1258–65; and Thomas Wykes, a monk of Osney, whose chronicle extends down to 1289, and is an authority of the first importance "for the whole history of the campaign of Lewes and Evesham, and the events immediately preceding and following them."[3] But these, and other writers, are largely subdued to the monastic atmosphere in which they work, and possess few of the traits of character and style which interest us in the personality of the greater chroniclers. The impulse of the revival of learning had been spent, and neither in literary distinction nor in accuracy and wealth of information are the

---

[1] Pollock and Maitland, *History of English Law*, ed. 1898, vol. 1, p. 206.
[2] *Bracton's Note Book*, ed. Maitland, vol. 1, p. 1.
[3] Luard, *Annales Monastici*, IV (*Rolls Series*).

chroniclers who wrote during the hundred years after
Matthew Paris's death worthy of comparison with their predecessors of the twelfth and early thirteenth centuries. The
best of them are those who by their industry at least, endeavoured down to the end of the fourteenth century to retain
for St. Albans as a historical school the supreme repute which
had been so signally established by Matthew Paris.

CHAPTER X

English Scholars of Paris and Franciscans of Oxford.

Latin Literature of England from John of Salisbury to Richard of Bury

THE University of Paris owed its origin to the cathedral school of Notre-Dame. It was not until the time of William of Champeaux (d. 1121) that this school began to rival the scholastic fame of Chartres. Early in the thirteenth century the schools of Paris were connected with three important churches. On the Ile de la Cité there was the cathedral of Notre-Dame; to the south of the Seine, on rising ground near the site of the present Panthéon, was the collegiate church of Sainte-Geneviève; and, to the east of the walls south of the river, the church of Canons Regular at the Abbey of St. Victor. The schools of Notre-Dame and of Sainte-Geneviève were successively the scenes of the ever-memorable lectures of a famous pupil of William of Champeaux, the eloquent, brilliant, vain, impulsive and self-confident disputant, Abelard (d. 1142). The fame of his teaching made Paris the resort of large numbers of scholars, whose presence led to its becoming the home of the many masters by whom the university was ultimately founded. The earliest trace of this university has been discovered in the passage where Matthew Paris states that his own preceptor, an abbot of St. Albans, had, as a student in Paris, been admitted into "the fellowship of the elect Masters" (c. 1170).[1] In 1136, when John of Salisbury went to Paris, the university was not yet in existence. The first recorded "town and gown" riot, that of 1200, led to the grant of a charter to the resident body of Masters; the approximate

---

[1] *Gesta Abbatum*, I, 217, ed. 1867.

date of the first statutes, ten years later, marks the earliest recognition of the university as a legally constituted corporation, a veritable *universitas;* and, about ten years later still, the Masters of Arts were first organised into four nations, namely, the French, the Normans, the Picards and the English, this last including the Germans and all who came from the north and the east of Europe. In the thirteenth century Paris was still the centre of European culture. It is sufficient to cite as proof a passage from the English encyclopaedist Bartholomew, who flourished in the middle of that century:

Even as Athens shone of old as the mother of liberal arts and the nurse of philosophers, so, in our day, Paris has raised the standard of learning and civilisation, not only in France but all the rest of Europe; and, as the mother of wisdom, she welcomes guests from all parts of the world, supplies all their wants and submits them all to her pacific rule.[1]

The carnival riot of 1229 led to the withdrawal of the resident Masters and Scholars for two years; meanwhile, many of them accepted the invitation of Henry III, and thus reinforced the rising universities of Oxford and Cambridge.

The first important representative of England in the schools of Paris was John of Salisbury. He began by becoming a pupil of Abelard, who had returned to the scene of his early triumphs, and at the age of 57, was now lecturing on the hill of Sainte-Geneviève. That "illustrious and admirable teacher" was discoursing, as of old, on logic; and "at his feet" John of Salisbury "acquired the first rudiments of dialectics, greedily seizing all that fell from his lips." But his brilliant instructor was once more opposed, and once more withdrew from Paris; and the pupil passed into the school of Master Alberic and Robert of Melun. The first was, "in questions, acute and expansive"; the second, "in responses, brief and lucid"; and, if "anyone could have combined the merits of both, he would have been unrivalled in debate."[2] Having thus studied logic for two years (1136-8) in Paris, John of Salisbury spent three years (probably the latter part of 1138, and a large part of 1139 and 1140) working at "grammar," or the scholarly study of Latin literature. The place is not named,

[1] xv, c. 57.   [2] *Metalogicus.* II, 10.

but it has, rightly, been identified as the school of Chartres.[1] In that school the sound and healthy tradition of Bernard of Chartres was still maintained by his pupils. By John of Salisbury's time, Bernard had been succeeded as chancellor of the cathedral school by Gilbert de la Porrée. John of Salisbury learnt rhetoric from Richard L'Évêque, who was "familiar with almost every branch of learning, whose knowledge was even greater than his eloquence, who had more truth than vanity, more virtue than show."[2] He had already attended, with less profit, the somewhat meagre lectures of Bernard's younger brother, Theodoric, who is nevertheless described as "a most studious investigator of the Arts."[3] This description was confirmed in 1888, when he was identified as the author of two large volumes containing a comprehensive *Survey of the Liberal Arts*, written in a bold and clear hand, which may now be seen in the public library of the cathedral town. It may be added that it was between 1134 and 1150, during the time when Theodoric was successively "master of the school" and chancellor, that the south doorway of the west front of the cathedral was adorned with figures of the seven arts, each of them associated with the ancient representative of that art, for example, grammar with Priscian, dialectic with Aristotle and rhetoric with Cicero.

It was probably early in 1141 that John returned to Paris. For a short time he attended not only the lectures of Gilbert, who had lately ceased to be chancellor of Chartres, but also those of Robert Pullen, the future cardinal, who had taught at Oxford in 1133. Socially, he saw much of Adam du Petit Pont, who owed his surname to the school that he had set up on the little bridge between the Ile de la Cité and the Quartier Latin.

John of Salisbury's student life in Paris, and Chartres, and again in Paris, probably extended from early in 1136 to late in 1145. In the spring of 1148 he was present at the council of Rheims. It was there that he was introduced by Bernard of Clairvaux to Theobald, archbishop of Canterbury, an introduction that had an important effect on his literary and ecclesiastical career.

About 1150 he returned to England, and resided mainly at

---

[1] Schaarschmidt, *Joh. Saresberiensis*, p. 22.
[2] *Metalogicus, loc. cit.* [3] *Metalogicus,* 1, 5.

the court of Canterbury, engaged on secretarial and diplomatic work, which frequently took him to the court of Rome. On the most celebrated of these visits, during the winter of 1155-6, his friend the English pope, Hadrian IV, sent Henry II his written authority to extend his rule over Ireland, together with an emerald ring in token of his right.[1]　It was probably John of Salisbury's eager interest in the privileges of the church while he was still in the service of Theobald that led to his soon falling into disfavour with the king. During the enforced leisure of 1159 he revised and completed two of his most extensive works, finishing the *Policraticus* shortly before, and the *Metalogicus* immediately after, the death of Hadrian IV (31 August, 1159). Both of these were dedicated to Becket, the warlike chancellor, with whose aid Henry II was then "fulminating" at the siege of Toulouse.[2]　When Becket became archbishop in 1162, John of Salisbury entered his service, and, soon afterwards, composed a *Life* of archbishop Anselm with a view to the canonisation which was not conceded until three centuries later. On the king's return, early in 1163, John of Salisbury found it safest to leave the country, staying for six or seven years with Peter de la Celle, then abbot of Rheims, under whose roof he wrote the *Historia Pontificalis*. His exile, like that of Becket, lasted till late in 1170. On the fatal 29th of December he was at Canterbury with the archbishop, who unhappily disregarded the counsels of moderation suggested by his devoted friend. They entered the cathedral together. In the face of the murderous attack on the archbishop's person, John of Salisbury seems to have fled at first, but to have soon returned to the post of peril. He was probably present at the end. He was certainly believed by his friend Peter to have been " sprinkled with the precious blood of the blessed martyr." [3]

He immediately urged the inclusion of his master's name in the calendar of martyrs, wrote his *Life*, and loyally served his successor. In 1176 his devotion to the memory of St. Thomas and his friendship with the archbishop of Sens led to John of Salisbury being made bishop of Chartres. For the last four years of his life he was the most prominent personage

---

[1] *Metalogicus*, IV, 42.　　　　[2] *Policraticus*, VIII, 25.
[3] Petrus Cellensis, *Ep.* 117.

in the place where he had spent three of the most successful years of his youth. In the necrology of his cathedral church he is described as *vir magnae religionis, totiusque scientiae radiis illustratus*.

His *Letters* give abundant proof of his wide influence as a sagacious counsellor, an able politician and a zealous ecclesiastic. They were collected and edited by himself soon after 1170. Of the 326 comprised in the modern editions, some were written after the above date, and some by other writers. His *Entheticus*, an elegiac poem of no less than 1852 lines, was, apparently, intended as an introduction to *Policraticus*, which is now preceded by a short set of verses bearing the same title as the above poem. In both of these poems, which are written in a strong and solid but not particularly elegant style, Becket is warmly eulogised. He is the king's right hand, the embodiment of all excellence, the refuge of the oppressed, the light of the church, the glory of the nation.[1]

The *Policraticus* is a work in eight books. The primary title has led to its being regarded as a "statesman's handbook." The alternative title, *De Nugis Curialium, et Vestigiis Philosophorum*, is suggestive of a satire on the vanities of courtiers, followed by a set treatise on morals; but the latter half deals with the principles of government, and with matters of philosophy and learning, interspersed with many digressions. It is, in fact an "encyclopaedia of miscellanies," reflecting the cultivated thought of the middle of the twelfth century. It includes an interesting chapter on Aristotle,[2] and a satirical account of the scholastic controversies of the age.

The *Metalogicus*, in four books, contains a defence of the method and use of logic, vindicating the claims of "grammar," and pleading for an intelligent study of logic. It includes an analysis of the whole series of Aristotle's treatises on that subject, being, in fact, the earliest work in the Middle Ages in which every part of the *Organon* is turned to account.

The *Historia Pontificalis* is only preserved in an incomplete form in a single manuscript at Bern; it was not printed until 1886, and was not identified as the work of John of Salisbury until 1873. It gives an account of the ecclesiastical history of the years 1148 to 1152 but is really as much a satire as a history.

[1] Migne, *P. L.* cxcix, 379, 993.   [2] VII, 6.

In his attitude towards the ancient classics, John of Salis-·
bury is far from regarding Aristotle as infallible; he is opposed
to Plato, though he is fully conscious of Plato's greatness.
His favourite author is Cicero, and the purity of his own Latin
prose has been justly praised.   Caesar and Tacitus he knows
solely by name; but in all the literature accessible to him he is
obviously the best read scholar of his time.   A humanist two
centuries in advance of his age, he is eager to give the widest
possible interpretation to "whatsoever things were written
aforetime for our learning."[1]

In his day the first period in the medieval study of logic
was drawing towards its close, and with the degenerate type
of the professional dialectician he has no sympathy.   The earliest of all the medieval theories on the nature and the functions of the state is due to John of Salisbury.   He is the first
of modern writers on the philosophy of politics, and he founds
his own theory on the records of the Old Testament and on the
annals of the ancient Roman empire.

As a representative of literature and learning, Peter of Blois
is only a pale reflection of John of Salisbury.   Born at Blois,
he was probably educated at Tours; he learnt and taught at Bologna and Paris, settled in England about 1175 as secretary
to Richard of Dover, archbishop of Canterbury, and was successively archdeacon of Bath (c. 1177) and of London (c. 1204).
He was repeatedly entrusted with diplomatic duties by Henry
II, and the *Letters* ascribed to him purport to have been originally collected at the request of the king.   But some of them
—for example, those on the capture of Damietta in 1219—
could not possibly have been written during the life of the king,
who died in 1189, or during that of Peter of Blois, who died
in or before 1212.   Peter of Blois, on his appointment as secretary to the archbishop in 1175, obviously made a diligent
study of the *Letters* of John of Salisbury, who had edited his
Letters soon after 1170, while Peter did not begin to edit his
own until 1181, the year after John of Salisbury's death.
Many of Peter's *Letters* are enriched with quotations from the
classics, but most of those quotations are borrowed from John
of Salisbury.   Thus, in a letter to the archdeacon of Nantes,
we have a list of ancient grammarians, and a second list of

[1] Cf. Prologue to *Policraticus*, VII.

ancient historians.[1] Both of these are borrowed from John of Salisbury;[2] but, while John of Salisbury modestly refers his readers to Tacitus, without professing to have read that author, Peter of Blois pretends to have "frequently looked into" Tacitus,—an author never mentioned by such well-informed contemporaries as Giraldus Cambrensis and Ralph of Diceto. Criticised for his constant quotations, he defends a manner of composition which places him "like a dwarf on the shoulders of giants"[3]; but this very comparison is tacitly taken from John of Salisbury, who honestly quotes it from Bernard of Chartres.[4] It is improbable that Peter was ever an actual pupil of the scholar to whom he owed so much of his borrowed erudition; but, curiously enough, he held preferment at Chartres, and also at Salisbury. His brief *Sermons* call for no comment. Of his few poems the longest deals with the sacraments in twenty-six chapters of riming hexameters; while two others, written in a different metre, have for their themes the life of the clergy, and the conflict between the flesh and the spirit.

Walter Map, who was born about 1137 on the marches of Wales, and accordingly called England his mother, and the Welsh his fellow-countrymen, studied in Paris from about 1154 to 1160. He returned to England before 1162, was frequently one of the king's itinerant judges, and, after holding other preferment, was appointed archdeacon of Oxford in 1197. About 1209, when Giraldus published the second edition of his *Conquest of Ireland*,[5] Walter Map was no longer living.

Map was the author of an entertaining miscellany in Latin prose, *De Nugis Curialium*, a work in a far lighter vein than that of John of Salisbury, who had adopted this as an alternative title of his *Policraticus*. But, even in this lighter vein, Map has often a grave moral purpose. Stories of the follies and crimes of courts, and a lament over the fall of Jerusalem are here followed by an account of the origin of the Carthusians, the Templars and the Hospitallers, with reflections on their growing corruption, and a violent attack on the Cister-

---

[1] *Ep.* 101. [2] *Policraticus*, VIII, 18.
[3] *Ep.* 92. [4] *Metalogicus*, III, 4.
[5] V, 410.

cians, together with notices of heretics and of hermits. In the second book we have anecdotes of the Welsh, with a collection of fairy-tales; in the third, a series of highly romantic stories; in the fourth, the "Epistle of Valerius dissuading from marriage the philosopher Rufinus" (sometimes erroneously ascribed to St. Jerome); and, in the fifth, an invaluable sketch of the history of the English court from William Rufus to Henry II. Walter Map's "courtly jests" are mentioned by Giraldus Cambrensis, who, in his latest work, describes Map as a person of distinction, endued with literary skill and with the wit of a courtier, and as having spent his youth (and more than his youth) in reading and writing poetry.[1] Giraldus sends his friend a set of Latin elegiacs, with a present of a walking-stick, and he has fortunately preserved the twelve lines of his friend's reply in the same metre.[2] This reply is almost the only certainly genuine product of Map's muse that has survived. Of his poems against the Cistercian monks, only a single line is left: *Lancea Longini, grex albus, ordo nefandus.*[3] His notorious antipathy to the Cistercian order has led to his being regarded as the author of another poem entitled *Discipulus Goliae episcopi de grisis monachis.*[4] The worldly, and worse than worldly bishop Golias is the theme of other poems, in accentual riming metres, ascribed to Map, notably the *Apocalypse,* the *Confession* and the *Metamorphosis* of Golias. The *Apocalypse* is first assigned to him in a Bodleian manuscript of the fourteenth century. Here there is no attempt to dramatise the character of Golias; we have simply an apocalyptic vision of the corruptions of the church set forth in 110 riming quatrains of accentual dactyls in lines of the type: *Omnis a clericis fluit enormitas.* In the accentual trochaics of the *Confession,* the bishop is dramatically represented as remembering "the tavern that he has never scorned, nor ever will scorn until the angels sing his requiem." Then follow the four lines, which are better known and more misunderstood than any in the poem:

> *Meum est propositum in taberna mori:*
> *Vinum sit appositum morientis ori,*
> *Ut dicant cum venerint angelorum chori,*
> *"Deus sit propitius huic potatori!"*

[1] IV, 140. [2] I, 363.
[3] *Latin Poems,* p. xxxv. [4] *Ib.,* p. 54.

These lines, with part of the subsequent context, were at an early date extracted from their setting and made into a drinking-song; but it cannot be too clearly stated that they were originally meant for a dramatic representation of the character of the degenerate "bishop." It is a mistake to regard them as reflecting in any way on the habits of the reputed author, who has been erroneously described as the "jovial archdeacon" and the "Anacreon of his age." Giraldus, in the very same work in which he lauds the literary skill and the wit of his friend, quotes for reprobation, and not for imitation, a series of calumnious passages, including the above lines with their immediately previous context.[1] He is clearly quite innocent of ascribing these lines to his friend. The whole of the *Confession* is also preserved in the celebrated thirteenth century Munich MS. of the *Carmina Burana*, formerly belonging to the Benedictine monastery of Benedictbeuern in the Bavarian highlands. It forms part of the vast number of anonymous Latin rimes known from 1227 onwards by the name of *Goliardi*. The character of Bishop Golias may possibly have assumed dramatic form in the age of Walter Map, but the name was certainly three centuries older. As early as the time of Gautier, archbishop of Sens (d. 923), a sentence of condemnation is passed on the *clerici ribaldi, maxime qui vulgo dicuntur de familia Goliae.*[2]

Map is credited in certain MSS. with the authorship of the "original" Latin of the great prose romance of *Lancelot du Lac*, including the *Quest of the Holy Grail* and the *Death of Arthur;* but no such "Latin original" has yet been found. A version of the *Quest* in French prose is assigned to "Maistres Gualters Map," and is described as "written by him for the love of his lord, King Henry, who caused it to be translated from Latin into French." In certain manuscripts, all the four parts of the romance of *Lancelot* are ascribed to Map; and Hue de Rotelande (*c.* 1185), a near neighbour and a contemporary of Map, after describing in his *Ipomedon* a tournament, which is also an incident in *Lancelot*, excuses his romance-writing in the words: "I am not the only man who knows the art of lying; Walter Map knows well his part of it."[3] Such is the evidence, slight as

[1] IV, 293.   [2] Labbé's *Concilia*, 1671, IX, 578.
[3] H. L. D. Ward's *Catalogue of Romances*, I, 734–41.

it is, for ascribing to Map any share in the great cycle of romance surveyed in other chapters.[1] We have already seen that there is very little reason for accepting him as the author of any part of the large body of accentual Latin poetry which passes under his name. The only thirteen lines of Latin verse which are certainly genuine products of his pen are written in hexameters and pentameters of the strictly classical type.

A century before the time of Map, Godfrey, a native of Cambrai, and prior of St. Swithin's, Winchester (d. 1107), had written Latin epigrams after the manner of Martial. He is, in fact, repeatedly quoted as "Marcial" by Gower. The 238 ordinary epigrams of his first book are followed by nineteen others, which have a historic interest, in so far as they refer to royal or ecclesiastical persons of the day. The Anglo-Norman poet Reginald, a monk of St. Augustine's, Canterbury (*fl.* 1112), wrote a lengthy poem in leonine hexameters on the life of the Syrian hermit St. Malchus. In the next half century, Lawrence, the Benedictine monk who became prior and bishop of Durham (d. 1154), composed a popular summary of Scripture history in nine books of elegiac verse. Henry of Huntingdon (d. 1155) has preserved in the eleventh book of his *Historia Anglorum*, the Latin epigrams and other minor poems that he had learnt to compose as a pupil of the monks of Ramsey. A little later, Hilarius, who is supposed to have been an Englishman, and was a pupil of Abelard about 1125, wrote in France three Latin plays on sacred themes, the earliest of their kind. The *Raising of Lazarus* and the *Image of St. Nicholas* are partly written in French; the *Story of Daniel* in Latin only. He is also the author of twelve interesting sets of riming lyrics, in Latin, interspersed with a few lines of French, the most graceful poem in the series being addressed to an English maiden bearing the name of Rose. About the same time the Cistercian monk Henry of Saltrey (*fl.* 1150), wrote a Latin prose version of the legend of the *Purgatory of St. Patrick*. A life of Becket, now only known through the Icelandic *Thomas Saga*, was written by Robert of Cricklade, chancellor of Oxford (1159) and prior of St Frideswide's, who dedicated to Henry II his nine books of *Flores* from the *Natural History* of the elder Pliny.

[1] See especially *post*, Chapter XII.

One of Map's younger contemporaries, Gervase, the author the *Otia Imperialia*, a native of Tilbury on the coast of Essex, was brought up in Rome; he lectured on law at Bologna, and probably died in England. The above work was written about 1211 to amuse the leisure hours of the German emperor, Otto IV. It is a miscellaneous collection of legendary tales and superstitions. The theme of the first three books and many of the quotations are borrowed, without acknowledgment, from the *Historia Scholastica* of that omnivorous compiler Petrus Comestor. The third book tells us of werewolves and lamias and barnacle-geese and other marvels, and also of the enchantments ascribed to Vergil at Naples.

Another of Map's contemporaries, Nigel Wireker, precentor of Christ Church, Canterbury (d. 1200), was the witty author of the *Speculum Stultorum*, a long elegiac poem on the adventures of the donkey " Burnellus," or " Brunellus," a diminutive of " Brown" (just as "donkey" is a diminutive of "dun"). The name is borrowed from the scholastic logic of the day, in which it represents any particular horse or ass, as opposed to the abstract idea of either of those animals.[1]

The author himself explains that the ass of his satire is a monk who, discontented with his condition, wants to get rid of his old stump of a tail, and obtain a new and longer appendage by becoming a prior or an abbot. Brunellus, then, finding his tail too short, consults Galen on his malady, and is, ultimately, sent off to Salerno with a satirical prescription, which he is to bring back in glass bottles, typical of the vanity and frailty of all human things. On his way there and back he is attacked by merchants and monks and mastiffs, and is thus robbed of all his scanty goods, and half of his diminutive tail. Ashamed to return home, and having an immense capacity for patient labour, he resolves on becoming a member of the English school in the university of Paris. Then follows a satire on the idleness and extravagance of some of the English students at that seat of learning. After spending seven years in studying the liberal arts and thus "completing" his education, he finds on leaving Paris that he has even forgotten the name of the place. However, he succeeds in recalling one syllable, but that is enough, for he has learnt in his time that

[1] Immanuel Weber, *De Nigello Wirekero*, Leipzig Dissertation, 1679.

"the part may stand for the whole." Passing from the liberal
arts to theology, the hero of the story tries all the monastic
orders in their turn, and ends in resolving to found an order of
his own. Meeting Galen once more, he begins discussing the
state of the church and the general condition of society, and
urges Galen to join his new order, when, suddenly, his old
master, Bernard, appears on the scene, and compels him to
return to his first allegiance as an ordinary monk. Chaucer,
in *The Nonne Preestes Tale*, recalls one of the stories he had
"rad in daun Burnel the Asse."[1]

The *Architrenius* or "Arch-Mourner" of the Norman satir-
ist Jean de Hauteville (*fl.* 1184), who was born near Rouen
and passed part of his life in England, has only a slight connection with our present subject. The pilgrim of that satire
pays a visit to Paris, and describes the hardships of the students
and the fruitlessness of their studies; he afterwards arrives
at the hill of Presumption, which is the haunt of all manner
of monks and ecclesiastics, as well as the great scholastic
doctors and professors. The seven liberal arts are elaborately
described in the *Anti-Claudianus* of the Universal Doctor,
Alain de Lille (1114–1203). This fine poem, and the mingled
prose and verse of the *De Planctu Naturae*, were familiar to
Chaucer. Alain probably passed some time in England
with the Cistercians at Waverley in Surrey (1128), and he is the
reputed author of a commentary on the prophecies of Merlin.

Alain's contemporary Geoffrey de Vinsauf (*fl.* 1200), who
was educated at St. Frideswide's, Oxford, and travelled in
France and Italy, dedicated to Innocent III his *Poëtria Nova*,
an *Art of Poetry* founded partly on Horace, and recommending
the ancient metres in preference to the modern rimes, with
examples of the various kinds of composition. In the same
period Alexander Neckam, of St. Albans, distinguished himself in Paris in 1180, and, late in life, became abbot of Ciren-
cester. He is the author of an amusing treatise *De Naturis
Rerum*, with many anecdotes of animals, and with an attack
on the method of teaching logic in the university of Paris.
In his lengthy elegiac poem *De Laudibus Divinae Sapientiae*
he traverses much of the same ground. He further describes
the chief seats of learning in his day, summing up in a single

---

[1] *Canterbury Tales*, 15318.

couplet the four faculties in the university of Paris, the *paradisus deliciarum:*

> *Hic florent artes; coelestis pagina regnat;*
> *Stant leges; lucet jus; medicina viget.*[1]

Joannes de Garlandia, who studied at Oxford and Paris (1204), was an Englishman by birth, but regarded France as the land of his adoption. His two principal poems, *De Mysteriis* and *De Triumphis Ecclesiae*, are earlier than 1252. His *Ars Rhythmica* quotes whole poems as examples of the rules of rhythm. His prose works include three *Vocabularies*, one of which, with its interlinear French glosses and its reference to the tricks played by Parisian glovers on inexperienced students, was clearly written for use in the university of Paris.

Later in the same century, a chaplain of Eleanor of Provence, queen of Henry III, named John Hoveden (d. 1275), wrote a number of poems in riming quatrains. The longest of these consists of nearly 4000 lines of meditation on the life of Christ. This was translated into French. His most popular poem, that beginning with the line *Philomela, praevia temporis amoeni*, was translated into German and Spanish and, about 1460, into English.

Latin verse was one of the early amusements of the keen and active Noman-Welshman Giraldus Cambrensis, who was born at the castle of Manorbier, which he dutifully describes as "the sweetest spot in Wales."[2] The grandson, on his mother's side, of Nest, "the Helen of Wales," he celebrated the exploits of her heroic descendants, the Geraldines, in one of his earliest works, the *Conquest of Ireland*. He had himself inherited some of Nest's beauty; he tells us that, in his youthful days, an abbot of the Cistercian order once said of him in the presence of Baldwin, then bishop of Worcester, "Is it possible that Youth, which is so fair, can ever die?"[3] He received his early education from two of the chaplains of his uncle, the bishop of St. David's. After continuing his studies at St. Peter's abbey, Gloucester, he paid three visits to Paris, spending three periods of several years in its schools, and giving

---

[1] P. 453 ed. Wright, in *Rolls Series*, 1863.
[2] VI, 93.   [3] IV, 104.

special attention to rhetoric. We have his own authority for the fact that, when his lecturers desired to point out a model scholar, they mentioned Gerald the Welshman.[1]

As archdeacon of Brecon (1175–1203) he was an ardent reformer of ecclesiastical abuses in his native land, and his great disappointment in life was that he never became (like his uncle) bishop of St. David's. On the first of several occasions when he was thus disappointed, he returned to Paris, and there studied for three years, besides lecturing with great success on canon law (1177–80). Visits to Ireland followed in 1183 and 1185, when he was in attendance on prince John. After the prince's return Gerald stayed till Easter, 1186, collecting materials for his two works on Ireland. The *Topography* was completed in 1188. In the following year he resolved on reciting it publicly at Oxford, "where the most learned and famous of the English clergy were then to be found." He read one of the three divisions of the work on each of three successive days. "On the first [he informs us] he received and entertained at his lodgings all the poor of the town; on the next, all the doctors of the different faculties, and such of their pupils as were of fame and note; and, on the third, the rest of the scholars with the soldiers and the townsmen." He complacently assures us that "it was a costly and noble act; a revival of the bygone ages of poetry"; and (he proudly adds) "neither present nor past time could furnish any record of such a solemnity having ever taken place in England."[2]

Meanwhile, in 1188, Baldwin, archbishop of Canterbury, had been sent to Wales to preach the coming crusade. Riding in full armour at the head of the procession, with the white cross gleaming on his brestplate, he was accompanied by Ranulf de Glanville, chief justiciar of England, and attended by a young man of slender figure, delicate features and beetling eyebrows, a man of learning and wit, and with no small share of self-conceit, "the leader of the clergy of St. David's, the scion of the blood-royal of Wales." The archbishop's exhortations produced little effect on the common people, until he prompted Gerald to take up the preaching. At Haverford Gerald discoursed in Latin and also in French. Although the crowd understood neither language, they were moved to tears

[1] I, 23.   [2] I, pp. xlvii, 72 f.

by the magic of his eloquence and no less than two hundred joined the standard of the cross. [1]   It was pleasantly remarked soon afterwards that if Gerald had only discoursed in Welsh not a single soldier would have failed to follow that banner. Three thousand recruits were enrolled; the archbishop and the chief justiciar had taken the cross at Radnor; and both of them kept their vow and died in 1190 in the course of the crusade.   Gerald, meanwhile, had been appointed to write its history in Latin prose, and the archbishop's nephew, Joseph of Exeter, to write it in verse.   Joseph had already composed an epic on the Trojan war, England's solitary Latin epic, which was long attributed to Cornelius Nepos, notwithstanding its dedication to the archbishop of Canterbury.   He celebrated the crusade in his *Antiocheis*, now represented by a solitary fragment on the *Flos Regum Arthurus*.   Gerald, however, neither went on the crusade, nor wrote its history; he paid his fine and he stayed at home to help the king to keep the peace in his native land, and to write the *Itinerary* and the *Description of Wales*.

When the bishopric of St. David's once more fell vacant, Gerald struggled for five years to win the prize of his ambition, paying three visits to Rome, in 1199, 1201 and 1203, without success.   But he was considered by himself and his fellow-countrymen to have waged a glorious contest.   "Many and great wars," said the prince of Powys, "have we Welshmen waged with England, but none so great and fierce as his, who fought the king and the archbishop, and withstood the might of the whole clergy and people of England, *for the honour of Wales*." [2]

He had already declined two other bishoprics in Wales and four in Ireland.   When the see of St. David's was again vacant, in 1214, he was passed over.   He probably died in 1223, and was buried in the precincts of the cathedral church, for whose independence he had fought so long.   The dismantled tomb which is shown as his probably belongs to a later time.   He deserves to be commemorated in that cathedral by the couplet which he placed above his archidiaconal stall, and also enshrined in one of his "epitaphs":

---

[1] I, pp. xlix, 76.   [2] I, 129—III, 210.

Vive Deo, tibi mors requies, tibi vita labori;
Vive Deo; mors est vivere, vita mori.[1]

The first volume of the Rolls edition of Giraldus includes
two autobiographies and two lists of his writings. Only the
most important need here be noticed. The earliest of his
works is the *Topography of Ireland*. The first book gives an
account of its physical features, and its birds and beasts; the
second is devoted to the marvels of the country, and the third
to the early history, followed by a description of the manners,
dress and condition of the inhabitants. One of the MSS. in
the British Museum has in the margin many curious coloured
drawings of the birds and beasts described by the author.[2] It
is to this work that we owe almost all our knowledge of medieval Ireland.

It was followed by the *Conquest of Ireland*, a narrative of
the events of 1169–85. This is marked by a simpler style and
a more sober judgment than the *Topography*, and is, in fact, a
historical monograph of considerable value. But there is much
bias, and some unfairness; and an air of unreality is produced
by the Irish chiefs, who have Greek patronymics, and harangue
their troops with quotations from Ovid and Caesar. Towards the close the author cites the ominous Irish prophecy
that "scarcely before the Day of Judgment will Ireland be
wholly subdued by the English."[3]

The *Itinerary of Wales* takes us on a tour of one month in
the south, and only eight days in the north. Apart from its
topographical and ecclesiastical interest, it introduces us to
Gerald as a student of languages. He tells us of a priest who,
in his boyhood, paid a visit to fairy-land, and learnt the language, which proved to be akin to Greek; and he gives us one
or two specimens in the words for "salt" and "water," adding
the equivalents in Welsh, English, Irish, German and French.[4]
It was this passage that once prompted Freeman to call Gerald
the "father of comparative philology."[5] In his own Latin
Gerald has no hesitation in using *werra* for "war," and *knip-*

---

[1] I, 364, 382.
[2] Bibl. Reg. 13 B VIII (*c.* 1200), copied in J. R. Green's *Short History*, ill.
ed. p. 225.
[3] v, 385.   [4] VI, 77.
[5] *Norman Conquest*, v, 579; cf. *Comparative Politics*, 486.

ulus for "pen-knife."[1]   At Cardiff we incidentally learn that
Henry II understood English, but could not speak it.[2]   In the
south our attention is drawn to the vestiges of Roman splendour at Caerleon on Usk, and to the old Roman walls at
Carmarthen.

The companion volume, called the *Description of Wales*,
appeared in two editions (1194, 1215). The author patriotic-
ally ascribes to his fellow-countrymen a keenness of intellect
that enables them to excel in whatever study they pursue.
He extols their set speeches and their songs. He also quotes
examples of alliteration in Latin and Welsh. The following are
the specimens he selects from the English of his day: "god is
to-gedere gamen and wisdom" (it is good to be merry and
wise); "ne halt nocht al sor isaid, ne al sorghe atwite" (it
boots not to tell every woe nor upbraid every sorrow); "betere is
red thene rap, and liste thene lither streingthe" (better is
counsel than haste, and tact than vicious strength)[3]. Elsewhere he tells the story of the Englishwoman who, with her
mistress, had for a complete year attended daily mass, at
which the priest had (besides the oft-repeated *Oremus*)
always used the introit *Rorate coeli, desuper;* on finding that her
mistress had, nevertheless, been disappointed in her desires,
she indignantly said to the priest, "Rorisse þe rorie ne wrthe
nan" (your *rories* and *ories* are all to no purpose).[4] He also
quotes the phrase, "God holde þe, cuning" (God save thee,
king), and the refrain of a love-song, "swete lemman, dhin
are" (sweet mistress, thy favour).[5] He notes that the language of North Wales is purer than that of the South, that the
language of Cornwall and Britanny closely resembles Welsh,
that the language of North Wales is purer than that of the
South, that the language of the south of England (especially
Devonshire) is purer than that of the north and that the English
works of Bede and King Alfred were all written in the southern idiom.[6] He also tells his readers how Wales may be
conquered, how it should be governed and how it is to hold
its own.

The *Gemma Ecclesiastica* was its author's favourite work.
It may, perhaps, be described as a lengthy archidiaconal

---

[1] II, 292.   [2] VI, 64 f.   [3] VI, 188.
[4] II, 128.   [5] VI, 64; II, 120; cf. IV, 209.   [6] VI, 177, f.

charge of an exceptionally learned and lively type.   It certainly
presents us with a vivid picture of the state of morality and
learning in Wales, illustrated by not a few stories of ignorance
of Latin among the inferior clergy.   Thus a priest once interpreted "St. John *ante portam Latinam*" to mean that St. John,
ante, first, *portam*, brought, *Latinam*, the Latin language (into
England).[1]   This ignorance, which even extended to some of
the higher clergy, is, here and elsewhere, attributed to the excessive study of law and logic.[2]

The *Book of his Acts and Deeds*, in the midst of much that
is purely personal, tells the story of the holy hermit who prayed
that he might attain to the mystery of the Latin language.   He
was granted the gift of the Latin tongue, without that of the
Latin syntax; but he successfully overcame all difficulties of
moods and tenses by always using the present infinitive.
Gerald once asked this hermit to pray for him that he might
understand the Scriptures.   The hermit warmly grasped his
hand, and gravely added: "Say not *understand*, but *keep;* it is
a vain thing to *understand* the word of God, and not to *keep*
it."[3]

The work *On the Instruction of a Prince*, completed after
the death of King John in 1216, is divided into three books.
The first, on the duties of the ideal prince, is enriched with
many quotations, the virtue of patience being illustrated by
nine, and the modesty of princes by thirteen.   The second
and third include a history of the life and times of Henry II.
The main interest lies in the sketches of the characters of the
royal family.   Gerald here tells the story of the finding of King
Arthur's body at Glastonbury in a coffin bearing the inscription,
"Here lies buried the famous King Arthur, with Guinevere
his second wife, in the Isle of Avalon."[4]

His other works include a *Life of Geoffrey Plantagenet*, archbishop of York, and several lives of saints, partly suggested by
his stay at Lincoln in 1196–8.   His *Collection of Extracts* from
his own works was, naturally, compiled later in life.   Among
his *Epistles* is one urging Richard I to befriend men of letters.
"without whom all his glory would soon pass away."[5]   His
latest work, the *Mirror of the Church*, depicts the principal

[1] II, 342.   [2] II, 348; III, 29 f.   [3] I, 90 f.
[4] VIII, 126 f.   [5] I, 243.

monastic orders of the time in violent language that, not unnaturally, led the monastic copyists to neglect transcribing, and thus preserving, the author's writings. The only MS. of this particular work that has survived suffered severely in a fire in the Cottonian library; but the sketch of the state of learning with which it opens, had, happily, already been partly transcribed by Anthony Wood. In the last book Gerald adds a description of the churches in Rome, and closes his writings with an impressive picture of the day of doom.

To the end of his life Gerald remained true to his early devotion to literature; and he hopefully looked forward to the appreciation of posterity.[1] Freeman, in estimating the historical value of his writings, justly characterises him as "vain, garrulous" and "careless as to minute accuracy," but as also "one of the most learned men of a learned age," "one who, whatever we may say as to the soundness of his judgment, came behind few in the sharpness of his wits," "one who looked with a keen if not an impartial eye on all the events and controversies of his own time."[2]

Among the "English" students at Paris we may briefly mention Michael Scot, who, probably before 1209, learnt Arabic at Palermo, where he lived at the brilliant court of Frederick II, to whom he dedicated three of his earliest works. Leaving Palermo for Toledo about 1209, he there completed a Latin rendering of two Arabic abstracts of Aristotle's *History of Animals*. In 1223 he returned to Palermo. He was highly esteemed as a physician and an astrologer, and his reputed skill in magic has been celebrated by Dante, Boccaccio and Sir Walter Scott. He is described by Roger Bacon as introducing to the scholars of the west certain of the physical and metaphysical works of Aristotle, with the commentators on the same.[3] He may have visited Bologna and Paris for this purpose about 1232. He probably died before 1235, and tradition places his burial, as well as his birth, in the Lowlands of Scotland.

There is no evidence that Michael Scot was ever a student at Oxford. Like Cardinal Curson of Kedleston (d. 1218), and Alexander of Hales (d. 1245), and the able mathematician

---

[1] V, 212, 411; VI, 7.   [2] VII, p. liii.
[3] *Opus Majus*, III, 66, Bridges.

Johannes de Sacro Bosco—probably of Holywood in Dumfriesshire—(d. 1252), he owed his sole allegiance to Paris.   Stephen
Langton (d. 1228), who, similarly, studied in Paris only, was
restored to England by his consecration as archbishop of Canterbury; his successor, Edmund of Abingdon (d. 1240), owed
his first allegiance to Oxford, and his second to Paris.

We have seen that the university of Paris originated in the
cathedral school of Notre-Dame.   The education of Europe
might have long remained in the hands of the secular clergy,
but for the rise of the new orders of the Franciscans and the
Dominicans in the second decade of the thirteenth century.
The old monastic orders had made their home in solitary
places, far removed from the world, while the aim of the Franciscan order was not to withdraw to the lonely valleys and
mountains but to work in the densely crowded towns—

> *Bernardus valles, montes Benedictus amabat,*
> *Oppida Franciscus.*

The order of the Franciscans was founded at Assisi in 1210;
that of the Dominicans, at Toulouse in 1215; and, at an early
date, both orders resolved on establishing themselves in the
great seats of education.   The Dominicans fixed their head-
quarters at Bologna and Paris (1217), besides settling at Oxford (1221) and Cambridge (1274); while the Franciscans
settled at Oxford and Cambridge in 1224, and at Paris in 1230.
When once these orders had been founded, all the great
schoolmen were either Franciscans or Dominicans.   Intellect-
ually, the dogmatic Dominicans were mainly characterised by
a conservative orthodoxy, while the emotional Franciscans
were less opposed to novel forms of opinion.   In Paris, the
greatest Dominican teachers were Albertus Magnus (1193–
1280) and his favourite pupil, the great Thomas Aquinas
(c. 1225–7–1274), who brought scholasticism to its highest development by harmonising Aristotelianism with the doctrines
of the church.   The Angelic Doctor was the foremost of the
intellectual sons of Saint Dominic, the saint who (in Dante's
phrase) "for wisdom was on earth a splendour of cherubic
light."   Meanwhile, Saint Francis, who was "all seraphic
in ardour," and felt no sympathy whatsoever for the intellectual and academic world, nevertheless counted among his fol-

lowers men of academic, and even more than academic, renown. Foremost of these were Alexander of Hales, Roger Bacon, Duns Scotus and William of Ockham.

Alexander of Hales, a native of Gloucestershire, studied in Paris at a time when the *Physics* and *Metaphysics* were not yet translated into Latin, and also later, when their study had been expressly prohibited (1215). This prohibition lasted until the dispersion of the university in 1229; and (although he may have been lecturer to the Franciscans at an earlier date) it was not until the return of the university in 1231 that he actually joined the order. As one of the leading teachers in Paris, he had a distinguished career. In his scholastic teaching he was an exponenet of realism. He was entrusted by Innocent IV with the duty of preparing a comprehensive *Summa Theologiae;* and the ponderous work, which remained unfinished at his death in 1245, was completed by his pupils seven years later. In its general plan it follows the method of Peter Lombard, being one of the earliest comments on the Master of the Sentences. It was examined and approved by seventy divines, and the author became known as the Irrefragable Doctor; but a still greater Franciscan, Roger Bacon, who describes the vast work as *tamquam pondus unius equi*, declares that it was behind the times in matters of natural science, and was already being neglected, even by members of the author's own order.[1] The MS. of Alexander's *Exposition of the Apocalypse*, in the Cambridge University Library, includes a portrait of the author, who is represented as reverently kneeling in the habit of a Franciscan friar.[2]

St. Francis himself regarded with suspicion the learning of his age. He preferred to have his followers poor in heart and understanding, as well as in their dress and their other belongings. Perfect poverty was, however, obviously incompatible with the purchase of books. A provincial minister of the order, who happened to possess books of considerable value, was not allowed to retain them. In the same spirit, on hearing that a great doctor in Paris had entered the order, St. Francis said to his followers: "I am afraid, my sons, that such doctors will be the destruction of my vineyard." The preaching of

---

[1] *Opus Minus*, 326 f.
[2] Reproduced in J. R. Green's *Short History*, ill. ed., p. 287.

the Franciscans among the common people owed its force less to their learning than to their practical experience. Their care for the sick, and even for the leper, gave a new impulse to medical and physical and experimental science; and they gradually devoted themselves to a more scientific study of theology. In their schools the student was expected to take notes and to reproduce them in the form of a lecture, and this practice, combined with the disputation between the teacher and the learner, brought into play readiness, memory and invention. Speculative theology was, in their hands, modified by the hard facts of practical life. Their sermons, however, not unfrequently appealed to the imagination and the feelings, and did not disdain either the sparkling anecdote or the pleasantly didactic allegory.[1]

In September, 1224, two years before the death of the founder, a little band of nine Franciscans was ferried across the Channel by the monks of Fécamp and found a welcome at the priory of Canterbury. Some of them pressed forward to London, where they were received by the Dominicans, while two of them went on to Oxford. The Dominicans had already settled there in 1221, when the church of St. Edward had been assigned them in the Jewry, in the very heart of the town, and a school of theology had been opened under Robert Bacon. For about a week the two Franciscans "ate in the refectory and slept in the dormitory" of the Dominicans[2]; then they hired a house near St. Ebbe's in the south-west quarter, whence they soon moved to a marshy plot of ground outside the walls. Part of that plot was known as Paradise. In 1245 they were followed by the Dominicans, who left the centre of the town for a suburban spot whose memory is now preserved in the name of Black Friars Road. In olden days, the Trill mill stream flowed past the Grey Friars mill and beneath the "Preachers' Bridge," until it reached the two mills of the Black Friars.

It was probably a migration from Paris that had, meanwhile, made Oxford a *studium generale*, or a publicly recognised place of studious resort. In 1167, John of Salisbury, then in exile owing to his devotion to the cause of Becket, sent a letter

---

[1] Brewer's Preface to *Monumenta Franciscana*, i, xxviii–lv.
[2] *Mon. Franc.* i, 5–9; ii, 9.

to Peter the Writer, stating that "the votaries of Mercury were so depressed, that France, the mildest and most civilised of nations, had expelled her alien scholars"[1]; and, either in 1165 or in 1169, at a time when many Masters and Scholars beneficed in England were studying in Paris, Henry II required all clerks who possessed revenues in England to return within three months. It has been reasonably assumed that many of the students thus expelled or recalled, from Paris migrated to Oxford.[2] But the earliest certain reference to the schools of Oxford belongs to 1189, when "all the doctors in the different faculties," and their more distinguished pupils, and the rest of the scholars, were (as we have seen) entertained by Giraldus Cambrensis on the second and third days of his memorable recitation.[3]

The Franciscan friars of 1224 were well received by the university, and, in those early times, were on excellent terms with the secular clergy. They were men of cheerful temper, and possessed the courtesy and charm that comes from sympathy. From Eccleston's account of the coming of the Friars Minor we learn that, "as Oxford was the principal place of study in England, where the whole body (or *universitas*) of scholars was wont to congregate, Friar Agnellus (the provincial Head of the Order) caused a school of sufficiently decent appearance to be built on the site where the Friars had settled, and induced Robert Grosseteste of holy memory to lecture to them there; under him they made extraordinary progress in sermons, as well as in subtle moral themes suitable for preaching," and continued to do so until "he was transferred by Divine Providence from the lecturer's chair to the episcopal see."[4] He was already interested in them about 1225[5]; and, it was, possibly, before 1231 that he was appointed their lecturer. He was then more than fifty years of age, not a friar, but a secular priest, and one of the most influential men in Oxford. To the friars he was much more than a lecturer; he was their

---

[1] *Ep.* 225 (Migne, *P. L.* cxcix, 253 A).

[2] Rashdall's *Universities of Europe*, II, 329 f.

[3] Giraldus, I, 72 f., 410; III, 92, where "*Magister Gualterus, magister Oxoniensis, archidiaconus*" is probably a mistake for "*Magister Gualterus Mapus, Oxoniensis archidiaconus*" (cf. I, 412).

[4] *Mon. Franc.* I, 37; cf. *ib.* 64–66.   [5] *Ep.* 2.

sympathetic friend and adviser, and, after he had become bishop of Lincoln in 1235, he repeatedly commended the zeal, piety and usefulness of their order. About 1238, he wrote in praise of them to Gregory IX: " Your Holiness may be assured that in England inestimable benefits have been produced by the Friars; they illuminate the whole land by their preaching and learning."[1]

Grosseteste, a native of Stradbroke in Suffolk, was educated at Oxford. It is often stated that he also studied in Paris; but of this there is no contemporary evidence. It is true that, as bishop of Lincoln, he writes to the regents in theology at Oxford, recommending them to abide by the system of lecturing adopted by the regents in theology in Paris, [2] but he says nothing of Paris in connection with his own education. While he was still at Oxford he held an office corresponding to that of the chancellor in Paris, but he was not allowed by the then bishop of Lincoln to assume any higher title than that of *Magister Scholarum*.[3] At Oxford he prepared commentaries on some of the logical treatises of Aristotle, and on the *Physics*, and a translation of the *Ethics*, which appeared about 1244, was known under his name. He himself produced a Latin rendering of the "middle recension of" the *Epistles* of Ignatius, beside commenting on Dionysius the Areopagite, and causing a translation to be made of the *Testaments of the Twelve Patriarchs*, the Greek MS. of which (now in the Cambridge Library) had been brought from Athens by his archdeacon, John of Basingstoke. In his *Compendium Scientiarum* he classified all the departments of knowledge recognised in his day. The printed list of his works extends over twenty-five quarto pages [4]; it includes treatises on theology, essays on philosophy, a practical work on husbandry. Perhaps the most interesting of his works is a poem in 1757 lines in praise of the Virgin and Son, an exquisite allegory called the *Château d'Amour*, originally written in "romance" for those who had *ne letture ne clergie*, and soon translated from French into Latin, and ultimately into English. Robert de Brunne, in his translation of the *Manuel des Pechiez*, tells us of the bishop's love for the music of the harp.

---

[1] *Ep.* 58; cf. *Epp.* 20, 41, 67.   [2] *Ep.* 123.
[3] *Lincoln Register* (Rashdall, II, 355 n. 2).   [4] *Life* by Pegge (1793).

In the opinion of Luard, the editor of his *Letters*, "probably no one has had a greater influence upon English thought and English literature for the two centuries that followed his age." Wyclif ranks him even above Aristotle,[1] and Gower calls him "the grete clerc."[2] Apart from his important position as a patriot, a reformer and a statesman, and as a friend of Simon de Montfort, he gave, in the words of his latest biographer, F. S. Stevenson, "a powerful impulse to almost every department of intellectual activity, revived the study of neglected languages and grasped the central idea of the unity of knowledge." One of the earliest leaders of thought in Oxford, a promoter of Greek learning, and an interpreter of Aristotle, he went far beyond his master in the experimental knowledge of the physical sciences. Roger Bacon lauds his knowledge of science, and he is probably referring to Grosseteste when he says that no lectures on optics "have as yet been given in Paris, or anywhere else among the Latins, except twice at Oxford."[3] Matthew Paris, who resented his zeal for the reform of the monasteries, generously pays the following tribute to his memory:

Thus the saintly . . . bishop of Lincoln passed away from the exile of this world, which he never loved. . . . He had been the rebuker of pope and king, the corrector of bishops, the reformer of monks, the director of priests, the instructor of clerks, the patron of scholars, the preacher of the people, . . the careful student of the Scriptures, the hammer and the contemner of the Romans. At the table of bodily food, he was liberal, courteous and affable: at the table of spiritual food, devout, tearful and penitent: as a prelate, sedulous, venerable and never weary in well-doing.[4]

Grosseteste's friend Adam Marsh, who had been educated under him at Oxford and had entered the priesthood, joined the Franciscan order shortly after 1226. The first four lecturers to the Franciscans in Oxford (beginning with Grosseteste) were seculars; the first Franciscan to hold that office was Adam Marsh,[5] who was probably appointed for the year 1247–8. Provision was then made for a regular succession of teachers, and soon there were fifty Franciscan lectureships in various parts of England. Out of love for Adam Marsh,

---

[1] *Trial*, IV, c. 3.
[2] *Conf. Am.* IV, 234.
[3] *Opera Inedita*, 33, 37, 472.
[4] *Chronica Majora*, v, 407, ed. Luard.
[5] *Mon. Franc.* I, 38.

Grosseteste left his library to the Oxford Franciscans.[1] Like
Grosseteste, he is a friend and adviser to Simon de Montfort,
and faithfully tells him that "he who can rule his own temper
is better than he who storms a city."[2] The king and the
archbishop of Canterbury urged his appointment as bishop
of Ely; but Rome decided in favour of Hugo de Balsham (1257),
the future founder of Peterhouse (1284). In his *Letters* Marsh's
style is less classical than that of Grosseteste; but the attain-
ments of both of these lecturers to the Oxford Franciscans are
warmly eulogised by their pupil Roger Bacon. He mentions
them in good company—immediately after Solomon, Aristotle
and Avicenna, describing both of them as "perfect in divine
and human wisdom."[3] On the death of Alexander of Hales
(1245), Grosseteste was afraid that Adam Marsh would be
captured by Paris to fill the vacant chair.[4] His *Letters*, his
only surviving work, give him no special claim to those scholastic qualities of clearness and precision that were possibly indicated in his traditional title of *Doctor illustris*.

Roger Bacon, a native of Ilchester, was the most brilliant
representative of the Franciscan order in Oxford. He there
attended the lectures of Edmund Rich of Abingdon, who had
studied in Paris, who could preach in French and who was
possibly himself the French translator of his principal Latin
work, the *Speculum Ecclesiae*. Rich was the first in Roger
Bacon's day to expound the *Sophistici Elenchi* at Oxford.[5]
It was probably under the influence of Grosseteste and Marsh
that Bacon entered the Franciscan order, a society which,
doubtless, had its attractions for his studious temperament.
He is said to have been ordained in 1233. Before 1245 he left
Oxford for Paris. He there distinguished himself as a teacher;
but he had little sympathy with the scholasticism of the day,
and he accordingly returned to England about 1250.

. In the order of St. Francis there was room for freedom of
thought, no less than for mystic devotion; but, some seven
years later, so soon as the party of the mystics was represented
in the new general of that body, Bacon fell under suspicion

---

[1] *Mon. Franc.*, I, 185. [2] *Ib.*, I, 264.
[3] *Opus Tertium*, c. 22 f., 25. [4] *Ep.* 334.
[5] *Comp. Theol.* (cp. J. E. Sandys, *History of Classical Scholarship*, I, 592,
ed. 2, 1906).

for his liberal opinions, and, by command of the "seraphic" Bonaventura, was sent to Paris and there kept in strict seclusion for ten years (1257–67). He probably owed his partial release to the good-will of Clement IV, who had heard of the studies of the Franciscan friar before his own elevation to the papal see, and, by a letter written at Viterbo on 22 June, 1266, drew him from his obscurity and neglect by pressing him for an account of his researches. Thereupon, in the wonderfully brief space of some eighteen months, the grateful and enthusiastic student wrote three memorable works, the *Opus Majus*, the *Opus Minus* and the *Opus Tertium* (1267). These were followed by his *Compendium Studii Philosophiae* (1271–2), and by a *Greek Grammar* of uncertain date. In his *Compendium*, he had attacked the clergy and the monastic orders and the scholastic pedants of the day; and, by a chapter of the Franciscans held in Paris in 1278 he was, on these and, doubtless, other grounds, condemned for "certain suspected novelties" of opinion. Accordingly, he was once more placed under restraint; but he had again been released before writing his *Compendium Studii Theologiae* (1292). At Oxford he died, and was buried among the Friars Minor, probably in 1294.

Before entering the order, he had written nothing on science; and, after his admission, he came under the rule that no friar should be permitted the use of writing materials, or enjoy the liberty of publishing his work, without the previous approval of his superiors. The penalty was the confiscation of the work, with many days of fasting on bread and water. He had only written a few "chapters on various subjects at the request of his friends."[1] Possibly, he is here referring to the pages on the secret works of nature and art, on Greek fire, on gunpowder and on the properties of the magnet,[2] on which he had discoursed in letters addressed either to William of Auvergne (d. 1248), or to John of Basingstoke (d. 1252). He was surrounded with difficulties; he found philosophy and theology neglected in the interests of civil law, and despised under the delusion that the world knew enough of them already. He had spent forty years in the study of the sciences and languages, and during the first twenty years specially devoted by him to the attainment of fuller knowledge (possibly before

---

[1] *Opera Inedita*, 13.　　　　[2] *Ib.*, 536 f.

joining a medicant order), he had expended large sums on his learned pursuits. None would now lend him any money to meet the expense of preparing his works for the pope, and he could not persuade any one that there was the slightest use in science.[1] Thankful, however, for the pope's interest in his studies, he set to work with enthusiasm and delight, though he was strictly bound by the vow of poverty, and had now nothing of his own to spend on his literary and scientific labours.

His principal works, beginning with the three prepared for the pope, are as follows:

The *Opus Majus*, which remained unknown until its publication by Samuel Jebb in 1733. It has since been recognised as the *Encyclopédie* and the *Organon* of the thirteenth century. It is divided into seven parts: (1) the cause of human ignorance; (2) the connection between philosophy and theology; (3) the study of language; (4) mathematical science; (5) physics (especially optics); (6) experimental science; and (7) moral philosophy. The part on language was preserved in an imperfect form; that on moral philosophy was omitted in Jebb's edition.

The *Opus Minus* was first published by John Sherren Brewer in 1859 (with portions of the *Opus Tertium* and the *Compendium Studii Philosophiae*). It was written partly to elucidate certain points in the *Opus Majus*, partly to meet the risk of the earlier treatise failing to reach its destination. It enters more fully into an examination of the schoolmen; it exposes the pretensions of the Franciscan Alexander of Hales, and of an unnamed Dominican. It recapitulates the passages in the previous work which the author deems specially important, and discusses the six great errors that stand in the way of the studies of Latin Christendom, namely (1) the subjection of theology to philosophy; (2) the general ignorance of science; (3) implicit trust in the dicta of the earlier schoolmen; (4) exaggerated respect for the lecturers on the *Sentences*, in comparison with the expounders of the text of the Scriptures; (5) mistakes in the Vulgate; (6) errors in the spiritual interpretation of Scripture due to ignorance of Hebrew, Greek, Latin, archæology and natural history, and those

[1] *Opera Inedita.*, 16, 59, 65.

due to misunderstanding of the hidden meaning of the Word of God. After a break, there next follows a comparison between the opinions of French and English naturalists on the elementary principles of matter, and, after a second break, an account of the various metals. Only a fragment, equivalent to some 80 pages of print, has been preserved in a single MS. in the Bodleian.

The *Opus Tertium*, though written later, is intended to serve as an introduction to the two previous works. In the first twenty chapters we have an account of the writer's personal history, his opinions on education, and on the impediments thrown in its way by the ignorance, prejudice, contempt, carelessness and indifference of his contemporaries. He next reverts to points that had been either omitted or inadequately explained in his earlier writings. After a digression on vacuum, motion and space, he dwells on the utility of mathematics, geography, chronology and geometry, adding remarks on accents and aspirates, and on punctuation, metre, and rhythm. A subsequent defence of mathematics, with an excursus on the reform of the calendar, leads to a discourse on chanting and on preaching.

The above three works, even in their incomplete form, fill as many as 1344 pages of print. It was these three that were completed in the brief interval of eighteen months.

The *Compendium Studii Philosophiae*, imperfectly preserved in a single MS. in the British Museum, begins with reflections on the beauty and utility of wisdom. The impediments to its progress are subsequently considered, and the causes of human error investigated. The author criticises the current Latin grammars and lexicons, and urges the importance of the study of Hebrew, adding as many as thirteen reasons for the study of Greek, followed by an introduction to Greek grammar.

The above is only the beginning of an encyclopaedic work on logic, mathematics, physics, metaphysics and ethics. The part on physics is alone preserved, and extracts from that part have been printed.[1]

The *Greek Grammar* may be conveniently placed after the above *Compendium*, and before the next. The author's knowledge of Greek was mainly derived from the Greeks of his own

[1] Emile Charles, 369–91.

day, probably from some of the Greek teachers invited to England by Grosseteste.[1] He invariably adopts the late Byzantine pronunciation; and, in his general treatment of grammar he follows the Byzantine tradition. This work was first published by the Cambridge University Press in 1902.

The *Compendium Studii Theologiae*, Bacon's latest work deals with causes of error, and also with logic and grammar in reference to theology. The above parts are extant in an imperfect form, and only extracts from them have been printed from a MS. in the British Museum.[2] A "fifth part," on optics, is preserved in a nearly complete condition in the same library.

Roger Bacon was the earliest of the natural philosophers of western Europe. In opposition to the physicists of Paris, he urged that "enquiry should begin with the simplest objects of science, and rise gradually to the higher and higher," every observation being controlled by experiment. In science he was at least a century in advance of his time; and, in spite of the long and bitter persecutions that he endured, he was full of hope for the future. He has been described by Diderot as "one of the most surprising geniuses that nature had ever produced, and one of the most unfortunate of men." He left no disciple. His unknown grave among the tombs of the Friars Minor was marked by no monument; a tower, traditionally known as "Friar Bacon's Study," stood, until 1779, on the old Grand Port (the present Folly Bridge) of Oxford. The fact that he had revived the study of mathematics was recorded by an anonymous writer about 1370.[3] A long passage in his *Opus Majus*,[4] on the distance between the extreme east and west of the habitable globe, inserted (without mention of its source) in the *Imago Mundi* of Pierre d'Ailly, was thence quoted by Columbus in 1498 as one of the authorities that had prompted him to venture on his great voyages of discovery. Meanwhile, in popular repute, Friar Bacon was regarded only as an alchemist and a necromancer. During the three centuries subsequent to his death, only four of his minor works, those on *Alchemy*, on the *Power of Art and Nature* and on the *Cure of Old Age*, were published in 1485–1590. Like Vergil, he was

---

[1] *Comp. Phil.* 434. [2] Émile Charles, 410–6.
[3] Little's *Grey Friars at Oxford*, 195 n.
[4] *Opus Majus*, ed. Bridges, 1, xxxiii, 290.

reputed to have used a "glass prospective" of wondrous power, and, like others in advance of their times, such as Gerbert of Aurillac, Albertus Magnus and Grosseteste, to have constructed a "brazen head" that possessed a faculty of speech. The popular legend was embodied in *The Famous Historie of Fryer Bacon*, in Greene's *Friar Bacon and Friar Bungay* (*c.* 1587)[1] and in Terilo's satire of 1604. At Frankfurt, the parts of the *Opus Majus* dealing with mathematics and optics were published in 1614; but a hundred and twenty years passed before a large portion of the remainder was published in England (1733), and the same interval of time preceded the first appearance of the *Opera Inedita* (1859). The seventh part of the *Opus Majus*, that on moral philosophy, was not printed until 1897. But the rehabilitation of Roger Bacon, begun by Brewer in 1859, had, happily, meanwhile been independently completed by Émile Charles in 1861.

Friar Bacon is associated in legend with Friar Bungay, or Thomas de Bungay (in Suffolk), who exemplifies the close connection between the Franciscan order and the eastern counties. Bungay lectured to the Franciscans at Oxford, and afterwards at Cambridge, where he was placed at the head of the Franciscan convent. As head of the order in England, he was succeeded (*c.* 1275) by John Peckham, who had studied at Paris under Bonaventura, had joined the Franciscans at Oxford and was archbishop of Canterbury from 1279 to 1292. At Oxford, a number of grammatical, logical, philosophical and theological doctrines taught by the Dominicans, and already condemned by the Dominican archbishop, Robert Kilwardby (1276), a Master of Arts of Paris, famous as a commentator on Priscian, were condemned once more by the Franciscan archbishop, Peckham (1284). Thomas Aquinas had held, with Aristotle, that the individualising principle was not form but matter— an opinion which was regarded as inconsistent with the medieval theory of the future state. This opinion, disapproved by Kilwardby, was attacked in 1284 by William de la Mare, probably an Englishman, possibly an Oxonian, certainly a Franciscan. Both of them may have owed something to Roger Bacon. They were certainly among the precursors of the type of realism represented by Duns Scotus, the *Doctor subtilis*.

[1] Ed. A. W. Ward (1878), pp. xviii–xxvii.

John Duns Scotus was a Franciscan in Oxford in 1300. There is no satisfactory evidence as to the place of his birth; a note in a catalogue at Assisi (1381) simply describes him as *de provincia Hiberniae*.[1] At Oxford he lectured on the *Sentences*. Late in 1304, he was called to incept as D.D. in Paris, where he probably taught until 1307. Among the scholars from Oxford who attended his lectures was John Canon (*fl.* 1329), a commentator on Peter Lombard, and on Aristotle's *Physics*. Duns Scotus died in 1308, at Cologne, where his tomb in the Franciscan church bears the inscription—*Scotia me genuit, Anglia me suscepit, Gallia me docuit, Colonia me tenet.*

The works ascribed to his pen fill twelve folio volumes in the edition printed at Lyons in 1639. At Oxford, Paris and Cologne he constantly opposed the teaching of Thomas Aquinas, thus founding the philosophical and theological school of the Scotists. But he was stronger in the criticism of the opinions of others than in the construction of a system of his own. While the aim of Aquinas is to bring faith into harmony with reason, Duns Scotus has less confidence in the power of reason; he accordingly enlarges the number of doctrines already recognised as capable of being apprehended by faith alone. In philosophy, his devotion to Aristotle is less exclusive than that of Aquinas, and he adopts many Platonic and Neo-Platonic conceptions. "All created things [he holds] have, besides their form, some species of matter. Not matter, but form, is the individualising principle; the generic and specific characters are modified by the individual peculiarity," by the *haecceitas*, or "thisness," of the thing. "The universal essence is distinct . . . from the individual peculiarity," but does not exist apart from it. With the great Dominicans Albertus Magnus and Thomas Aquinas, the Franciscan Duns Scotus "agrees in assuming a threefold existence of the universal: it is *before* all things, as form in the divine mind; *in* things, as their essence (*quidditas*); and *after* things, as the concept formed by mental abstraction." He claims for the individual a real existence, and he accordingly condemns nominalism.[2]

But, even in the ranks of the realists, the extravagant realism of Duns Scotus was followed by a reaction, led by

---

[1] Little, *loc. cit.* 219 f. Major, *Historia Majoris Britanniae* (1740), 170 f., makes him a native of Duns, W. of Berwick-on-Tweed.

[2] Ueberweg, *History of Philosophy*, E. T. 1, 453 f.

Wyclif, who (for England at least) is at once "the last of the schoolmen" and "the first of the reformers." Later reformers, such as Tyndale (1530), were joined by the humanists in opposing the subtleties of Scotus. The influence of scholasticism in England ended with 1535, when the idol of the schools was dragged from his pedestal at Oxford and Cambridge, and when one of Thomas Cromwell's commissioners wrote to his master from Oxford:

We have set Dunce in *Bocardo*, and have utterly banished him Oxford for ever, with all his blynd glosses. . . . (At New College) wee fownde all the great Quadrant Court full of the leaves of Dunce, the wind blowing them into every corner.[1]

The teaching of Thomas Aquinas was opposed, not only by the Franciscan realist Duns Scotus, but also by another Franciscan, the great nominalist, William of Ockham. Born (*c.* 1280) in the little village of that name in Surrey, he became a B.D. of Oxford, and incepted as D.D in Paris, where he had a strong influence over the opponent of the papacy, Marsiglio of Padua. He was probably present at the chapter of Perugia (1322), and he certainly took a prominent part in the struggle against pope John XXII. He was imprisoned at Avignon for seventeen weeks in 1327, but escaped to Italy and joined the emperor, Lewis of Bavaria, in 1328, accompanying him in 1330 to Bavaria, where he stayed for the greater part of the remainder of his life, as an inmate of the Franciscan convent at Munich (d. 1349). He was known to fame as the Invincible Doctor.

The philosophical and theological writings of his earlier career included commentaries on the logical treatises of Aristotle and Porphyry, a treatise on logic (the Caius College MS. of which concludes with a rude portrait of the author), as well as *Quaestiones* on the *Physics* of Aristotle and on the *Sentences* of Peter Lombard; the first book of his questions on the latter having been probably completed before he left Oxford. In the edition of 1495 his work on the *Sentences* is followed by his *Centilogium theologicum*. The political writings of the last eighteen years of his life include the *Opus nonaginta dierum* (*c.* 1330–3), and the *Dialogue between the master and the disciple on the power of the emperor and the pope* (1333–43).

[1] Layton in Strype's *Ecclesiastical Memorials*, Bk. I, ch. XXIX, *sub finem.*

The philosophical school which he founded is nearly in-different to the doctrines of the church, but does not deny the church's authority. While Scotus had reduced the number of doctrines demonstrable by pure reason, Ockham declared that such doctrines only existed as articles of faith. He opposes the real existence of universals, founding his negation of realism on his favourite principle that "entities must not be unneces-sarily multiplied." Realism, which had been shaken, more than two centuries before, by Roscellinus, was, to all appear-ance, shattered by William of Ockham, who is the last of the great schoolmen.

An intermediate position between the realism of Duns Scotus and the nominalism of William of Ockham was assumed by a pupil of the former and a fellow-student of the latter named Walter Burleigh, who studied at Paris and taught at Oxford. He was the first in modern times who attempted to write a history of ancient philosophy. He knew no Greek, but he, nevertheless, wrote 130 treatises on Aristotle alone, dedicating his commentary on the *Ethics* and *Politics* to Rich-ard of Bury.

Among the opponents of the mendicant orders at Oxford, about 1321, was a scholar of Paris and Oxford and a precursor of Wyclif, named John Baconthorpe (d. 1346), a man of ex-ceedingly diminutive stature, who is known as the Resolute Doctor, and as the great glory of the Carmelites. A volumi-nous writer of theological and scholastic treatises (including commentaries on Aristotle), he was long regarded as the prince of the Averroists, and nearly three centuries after his death his works were still studied in Padua.

Scholasticism survived in the person of Thomas Bradwar-dine, who was consecrated archbishop of Canterbury shortly before his death in 1349. Educated at Merton College, Oxford, he expanded his college lectures on theology into a treatise that gained him the title of *Doctor profundus*. He is respect-fully mentioned by Chaucer in company with St. Augustine and Boëthius:

> But I ne can not bulte it to the bren,
> As can the holy doctour Augustyn,
> Or Boëce, or the bishop of Bradwardyn.[1]

[1] *Canterbury Tales*, 15, 248.

In the favourable opinion of his editor, Sir Henry Savile (1618), he derived his philosophy from Aristotle and Plato. His pages abound with quotations from Seneca, Ptolemy, Boëthius and Cassiodorus; but there is reason to believe that all his learning was gleaned from the library of his friend Richard of Bury, to whom he was chaplain in 1335.

Richard of Bury was the son of Sir Richard Aungerville. Born within sight of the Benedictine abbey of Bury St. Edmunds, he is sometimes said to have subsequently entered the Benedictine convent at Durham. In the meantime, he had certainly distinguished himself in philosophy and theology at Oxford. From his academic studies he was called to be the tutor to prince Edward, the future king Edward III. The literary interests with which he inspired the prince may well have led to Edward's patronage of Chaucer and of Froissart. In 1330 and 1333, he was sent as envoy to the pope at Avignon; and it was in recognition of these diplomatic services that he was made dean of Wells, and bishop of Durham.

He lives in literature as the author of the *Philobiblon*, which was completed on his 58th birthday, 24 January, 1345; and, in the same year, on 14 April, at his manor of Auckland, *Dominus Ricardus de Bury migravit ad Dominum.* In seven of the thirty-five manuscripts of the *Philobiblon* it is ascribed to Robert Holkot, the Dominican (d. 1349). But the evidence is inconclusive and the style of Holkot's *Moralitates* is different from that of the *Philobiblon.* Holkot, who was one of the bishop's chaplains, may well have acted as his amanuensis during the last year of his life, and have thus been wrongly credited with having "composed" or "compiled" the work. The distinctly autobiographical character of the volume is in favour of its having been written by Richard of Bury himself.

The author of the *Philobiblon* is more of a *bibliophile* than a scholar. He has only the slightest knowledge of Greek; but he is fully conscious of the debt of the language of Rome to that of Greece, and he longs to remedy the prevailing ignorance by supplying students with grammars of Greek as well as Hebrew. His library is not limited to works on theology; he places liberal studies above the study of law, and sanctions the reading of the poets. His love of letters breathes in every page of his works. He prefers manuscripts to money, and even "slender pam-

phlets[1] to pampered palfreys." He confesses with a charming
candour: "We are reported to burn with such a desire for
books, and especially old ones, that it was more easy for any
man to gain our favour by means of books than by means of
money"; but "justice," he hastens to assure us, "suffered no
detriment."[2]   In inditing this passage, he doubtless remembered that an abbot of St. Albans[3] once ingratiated himself
with the future bishop of Durham by presenting him with
four volumes from the abbey library, besides selling him thirty
volumes from the same collection, including a large folio MS.
of the works of John of Salisbury, which is now in the British
Museum.

In the old monastic libraries, Richard of Bury, like Boccaccio
at Monte Cassino, not unfrequently lighted on manuscripts lying
in a wretched state of neglect, *murium foetibus cooperti et ver-
mium morsibus terebrati.*[4]   But in those of the new mendicant
orders he often "found heaped up, amid the utmost poverty,
the utmost riches of wisdom."[5]   He looks back with regret on
the ages when the monks used to copy manuscripts "between
the hours of prayer."[6]   He also presents us with a vivid picture of his own eagerness in collecting books with the aid of the
stationarii and *librarii* of France, Germany and Italy.   For some
of his purchases he sends to Rome, while he dwells with rapture
on his visits to Paris, "the paradise of the world," "where the
days seemed ever few for the greatness of our love. *There* are
the delightful libraries, more aromatic than stores of spicery;
there, the verdant pleasure-gardens of all varieties of volumes."[7]
He adds that, in his own manors, he always employed a large
number of copyists, as well as binders and illuminators[8]; and
he pays an eloquent tribute to his beloved books:

Truth, that triumphs over all things, seems to endure more
usefully, and to fructify with greater profit in books. The meaning
of the voice perishes with the sound; truth latent in the mind is only
a hidden wisdom, a buried treasure; but truth that shines forth
from books is eager to manifest itself to all our senses. It com-
mends itself to the sight, when it is read; to the hearing when it is
heard; and even to the touch, when it suffers itself to be trans-

---

[1] §123 (the earliest known example of the word), *panfletos exiguos.*
[2] §§119, 122.   [3] *Gesta Abbatum*, II, 200.   [4] §120.
[5] §135.   [6] §74.   [7] §126.   [8] §143.

cribed, bound, corrected, and preserved. . . . What pleasantness of teaching there is in books, how easy, how secret. How safely and how frankly do we disclose to books our human poverty of mind. They are masters who instruct us without rod or ferule. . . . If you approach them, they are not asleep; if you inquire of them, they do not withdraw themselves; they never chide, when you make mistakes; they never laugh, if you are ignorant.[1]

Towards the close, he confides to us the fact that he had "long cherished the fixed resolve of founding in perpetual charity a hall in the revered university of Oxford, the chief nursing-mother of all liberal arts, and of endowing it with the necessary revenues for the maintenance of a number of scholars, and, moreover, to furnish the hall with the treasures of our books."[2] He gives rules for the management of the library, rules founded in part on those adopted in Paris for the library of the Sorbonne. He contemplated the permanent endowment of the Benedictine house of Durham College in the university of Oxford, and bequeathed to that college the precious volumes he had collected at Bishop Auckland. The ancient monastic house was dissolved, and Trinity College rose on its ruins; but the library built to contain the bishop's books still remains, though the books are lost, and even the catalogue has vanished. His tomb in Durham cathedral, marked by "a faire marble stone, whereon his owne ymage was most curiously and artificially ingraven in brass[3]" has been, unfortunately, destroyed; but he lives in literature as the author of the *Philobiblon*, his sole surviving memorial. One, who was inspired with the same love of books, has justly said of the author—"His fame will never die."[4]

Like the early humanists of Italy, he was one of the new literary fraternity of Europe—men who foresaw the possibilities of learning, and were eager to encourage it. On the first of his missions to the pope at Avignon he had met Petrarch, who describes him as *vir ardentis ingenii, nec litterarum inscius;* he adds that he had absolutely failed to interest the Englishman in determining the site of the ancient Thule.[5] But they were kindred spirits at heart. For, in the same vein as Richard

---

[1] §§ 23, 26. [2] §232.
[3] *Description of Monuments* (1593), Surtees Society, p. 2.
[4] Dibdin's *Reminiscences*, 1, 86 n. [5] *Epp. Fam.*, III, 1.

of Bury, Petrarch tells his brother, that he "cannot be sated with books"; that, in comparison with books, even gold and silver, gems and purple, marble halls and richly caparisoned steeds, only afford a superficial delight; and, finally, he urges that brother to find trusty men to search for manuscripts in Italy, even as he himself had sent like messages to his friends in Spain and France and England.[1]

In the course of this brief survey, we have noticed, during the early part of the twelfth century, the revival of intellectual interests in the age of Abelard, which resulted in the birth of the university of Paris. We have watched the first faint traces of the spirit of humanism in the days when John of Salisbury was studying Latin literature in the classic calm of Chartres. Two centuries later, Richard of Bury marks for England the time of transition between the scholastic era and the revival of learning. The Oxford of his day was still the "beautiful city, spreading her gardens to the moonlight, and whispering from her towers the last enchantments of the Middle Age." "Then flash'd a yellow gleam across the world." Few, if any, in our western islands thought to themselves, "the sun is rising"; though in another land, the land of Petrarch, moonlight had already faded away—"the sun had risen."

[1] *Epp. Fam.*, III, 18.

CHAPTER XI

Early Transition English

THE description which suggests itself for the century from 1150 to 1250, so far as native literature is concerned, is that of the Early Transition period. It marks the first great advance from the old to the new, though another period of progress was necessary to bring about in its fulness the dawn of literary English. The changes of the period were many and far-reaching. In politics and social affairs we see a gradual welding together of the various elements of the nation, accompanied by a slow evolution of the idea of individual liberty. In linguistic matters we find not only profit and loss in details of the vocabulary, together with the innovation in the direction of a simpler syntax, but also a modification of actual pronunciation—the effect of the work of two centuries on Old English speech-sounds. In scribal methods, again, a transition is visible. Manuscripts were no longer written in the Celtic characters of pre-Conquest times, but in the modification of the Latin alphabet practised by French scribes. And these changes find their counterpart in literary history, in changes of material, changes of form, changes of literary temper. Anselm and his school had displayed to English writers a new realm of theological writings; Anglo-Norman secular *littérateurs* had further enlarged the field for literary adventurers; and, since the tentative efforts resulting from these innovations took, for the most part, the form of their models, radical changes in verse-form soon became palpable. The literary temper began to betray signs of a desire for freedom. Earlier limitations were no longer capable of satisfying the new impulses. Legend and romance led on the imagination; the motives of love and mysticism began lightly touching the literary work of the time to finer issues; and such was the

advance in artistic ideals, especially during the latter part of
the period, that it may fairly be regarded as a fresh illustration
of the saying of Ruskin that "the root of all art is struck in
the thirteenth century."

The first half of the period (1150–1200) may be roughly
described as a stage of timid experiment, the second half (1200–
1250) as one of experiment still, but of a bolder and less uncertain kind.   But, before dealing with such literary material as
survives, a word may be said as to the submerged section of
popular poetry.   It is true that little can be said definitely
concerning this popular verse, though Layamon refers to the
making of folk-songs, and both William of Malmesbury and
Henry of Huntingdon mention some with which their age was
familiar.   The ancient epic material must certainly, however,
have lived on.   Such things as the legends of Weland and Offa,
the story of Wade and his boat *Guingelot*, must long have
been cherished by the people at large.   This period was also the
seed-time of some of the later Middle English sagas.   The
stories of Horn and Havelok were silently changing their
Danish colouring and drawing new life from English soil.   The
traditions of Guy of Warwick and Bevis of Hampton were
becoming something more than local; the ancient figure of
Woden was being slowly metamorphosed into the attractive
Robin Hood.   It was, in short, the rough-hewing stage of
later monuments.

With regard to the actual literary remains of the earlier
period, a rough division may be made on the basis of the main
influences, native and foreign, visible in those works.   The
Here Prophecy[1] (*c*. 1190) scarcely falls within the range of a
literary survey, though it is interesting from both linguistic
and historical standpoints.   Among those works primarily
reminiscent of earlier times the *Old English Homilies* are naturally prominent.   Some of them are merely twelfth century
transcriptions of the work of Aelfric;[2] in others foreign influences are seen.   But even then the mould into which the material is run is the same.   The earlier method of conveying

---

[1] See Hales, *Folia Litteraria*, pp. 55–61; H. Morley, *English Writers*, III,
200–1.

[2] See Morris, *Old English Homilies* (preface *passim*) for statements regarding the origin of *De Initio Creaturæ*, the homily for the 4th Sunday after
Pentecost, and the homily for the 5th Sunday in Lent.

religious instruction to English parishioners by means of the homily is still retained. The *Proverbs of Alfred* are also strongly reminiscent of earlier native tradition embodied, not only in the Old English *Gnomic Verses*, but also in the proverb dialogues of Salomon and Marcolf, Adrianus and Ritheus, and in the sententious utterances in which Old English writers so frequently indulged. This Middle English collection of proverbs is preserved in three MSS. of the thirteenth century; but these versions are obviously recensions of an earlier form, dating from the second half of the preceding century. The actual connection of the proverbs with Alfred himself must be accepted with some reserve. His fame as a proverb-maker is implied in the later *Owl and Nightingale* and is even more explicitly maintained elsewhere; *Eluredus in proverbiis ita enituit ut nemo post illum amplius.*[1] But no collection of Alfredian proverbs is known to have existed in Old English; and, since some of the sayings occur in the later collection known by the name of Hendyng, it may well have been that the use of the West Saxon king's name in this collection was nothing more than a patriotic device for adding to popular sayings the authority of a great name. It is noteworthy that the matter of the proverbs is curiously mixed. There is, first, the shrewd philosophy of popular origin. Then there are religious elements: Christ's will is to be followed; the soldier must fight that the church may have rest; while monastic scorn possibly lurks in the sections which deal with woman and marriage. And, thirdly, there are utterances similar to those in Old English didactic works like *A Father's Instruction*, where definite precepts as to conduct are laid down.[2] The metrical form of the *Proverbs* is no less interesting. The verse is of the earlier alliterative type, but it shows precisely the same symptoms of change as that of certain tenth and eleventh century poems.[3] The caesura is preserved, but the long line is broken in two. The laws of purely alliterative verse were no longer followed; an attempt is rather made to place words in the order of thought. There are occasional appearances of the leonine rime and asso-

[1] *Ann. Min. Winton, Anglia Sacra*, 1, 289.
[2] *e.g.* "If thou dost harbour sorrow, let not thine arrow know it; whisper it but to thy saddle-bow, and ride abroad with song."
[3] Cf. *O. E. Chronicle*, 975, 1036.

nance, characteristic of tenth and eleventh century work; but, at best, the structure is irregular. In section xxii. an attempt has apparently been made—possibly by a later scribe—to smooth out irregularities and to approximate the short couplet in rime and rhythm. The reforming hand of the adapter, as in other Middle English poems, is also seen eisewhere; but, these details apart, the work belongs entirely in both form and spirit to the earlier period.

Alongside these survivals of an earlier day there were not wanting signs of a new *régime*. In the *Canute Song* (c. 1167), for instance, can be seen the popular verse striving in the direction of foreign style. The song is of rude workmanship, but the effect aimed at is not an alliterative one. Rime and assonance are present, and the line, as compared with earlier examples, will be seen to reveal definite attempts at hammering out a regular rhythm. In the *Cantus Beati Godrici* (before 1170) is visible a similar groping after the new style. The matter dealt with is interesting as anticipating, in some sort, the Virgin cult of the early thirteenth century. The writer, Godric, was an Englishman who, first a merchant, became subsequently a recluse connected with Carlisle, and latterly with Durham. Three small fragmentary poems have been handed down connected with his name, one of them, it is alleged, having been committed to him by the Virgin Mary as he knelt before the altar. The fragment beginning *Sainte Marie Virgine* is the best of the three. The rhythm, the rimes and, also, the strophic form were clearly suggested by Latin verse, but the diction is almost entirely of native origin. In *Paternoster*, a work which appeared about the same date, or later, in the south, may be seen a definite advance in carrying out the new artistic notions. It is a poem of some 300 lines, embodying a lengthy paraphrase of the Lord's Prayer, each sentence of the prayer affording a text for homiletic treatment. The work is notable as being the earliest example of the consistent use of the short riming couplet in English. The underlying influence is clearly that of some French or Latin model. The diction is native, but it is used with Latin simplicity; the lack of verbal ornament marks a striking departure from the earlier English manner.

By far the most important and interesting work of this period, however, is the *Poema Morale*. It is interesting in itself, interesting also in the influence it exercised upon later writers, and its popularity is fairly established by the seven MSS. which survive, though it might also be added that the most recently discovered of these copies,[1] being, apparently, due to a different original from that of the others, affords additional proof that the work was widely known. The writer opens his sermon-poem in a subjective vein. He laments his years, his ill-spent life, and exhorts his readers to pass their days wisely. He alludes to the terrors of the last judgment. Hell is depicted in all the colours of the medieval fancy, and the joys of Heaven are touched with corresponding charm. And so the reader is alternately intimidated and allured into keeping the narrow way. All this, of course, is well-worn material. The Old English work *Be Domes Daege* had handled a similar theme. The terrors and glories of the hereafter had inspired many earlier English pens, and the poet, in fact, specifically states that part of his descriptions were drawn from books (cf. l. 224). But his treatment of the subject has much that is new. It shows real feeling, though there are also the usual conventionalities; the poem contains ripe wisdom and sage advice. If the description of Hell is characteristically material, Heaven, on the other hand, is spiritually conceived. The verse-form is also interesting. Here, for the first time in English, is found the fourteener line, the catalectic tetrameter of Latin poets. The iambic movement of that line is adapted with wonderful facility to the native word-form, accent-displacement is not abnormally frequent and the lines run in couplets linked by end-rime. The old heroic utterance is exchanged for the paler abstractions of the Latin schools, and the loss of colour is heightened by the absence of metaphor with its suggestion of energy. A corresponding gain is, however, derived from the more natural order of words; and, in general, the merits of the poem are perhaps best recognised by comparing its workmanship with that of the songs of Godric and by noting the advances made upon Old English forms in the direction of later verse.

Mention has already been made of the presence of foreign influences in certain of the twelfth century *Homilies*. Correspondences with the homiletic work of Radulfus Ardens of Ac-

[1] Anna C. Paues, A newly discovered Manuscript of the *Poema Morale*, *Anglia*, xxx (xviii), pp. 217–38.

quitaine (c. 1100) and of Bernard of Clairvaux (1090–1153) point
to the employment of late Latin originals.   Certain quotations
in these *Homilies* are also taken from Horace and Ovid—an
exceptional proceeding in Old English works, though common
in writings of the eleventh and twelfth centuries[1]; and thus the
inference is clear that here Aelfric is not the sole or even the
main influence, but that this is rather supplied by those French
writers whose religious works became known in England after
the Conquest.   The influence of the same Norman school of
theology is, moreover, visible in the *Old Kentish Sermons* (1150–
1200).   They are, in reality, translations of French texts, and
signs of this origin are preserved in the diction employed, in the
use of such words as *apierede*, *cuuenable* and others.

The latter half of the twelfth century was a period of experiment and of conflicting elements.   It was a stage necessarily unproductive, but of great importance notwithstanding,
in the work of development.   Older native traditions lived on;
but access had been obtained to continental learning, and,
while themes were being borrowed from Norman writers, as a
consequence of study of other French works, the riming couplet
and the *septenarius* had by this time been adopted, and an alien
system of versification based on the regular recurrence of accent
seemed in a fair way of being assimilated.   With the attainment
of a certain amount of proficiency in the technique of the new
style, the embargo on literary effort was, in some degree,
removed, and the literature for the first half of the thirteenth
century forthwith responded to contemporary influences.
The age became once more articulate, and the four chief works
of the time are eloquent witnesses of the impulses which were
abroad.   The *Ormulum* is representative of purely religious
tradition, while the *Ancren Riwle* points to an increased interest
in the religious life of women, and also, in part, to new mystical
tendencies.   Layamon's *Brut*, with its hoard of legendary
fancy, is clearly the outcome of an impules fresh to English
soil; while *The Owl and Nightingale* is the herald of the love-
theme in England.

It must be conceded, in the first place, that the general
literary tone of the first half of the thirteenth century was deter-

[1] Vollhardt, *Einfluss der lat. geistlichen Litt. auf einige kleinere Schöpfungen
der engl. Uebergangsperiode*, pp. 6–18.

mined by the prevailing power of the church and the monastery. The intellectual atmosphere of England was mainly cleric, as opposed to the laic independence which existed across the Channel; and this difference is suggested by the respective traits of contemporary Gothic architecture in England and in France. From the eleventh to the thirteenth centuries the power of the pope, so far as western Europe was concerned, was at its height. National enthusiasms aroused by the crusades played unconsciously into the papal hands, and, during this time, more than one pope deposed a ruling monarch and then disposed of his dominions. Theology was the main study at the newly founded universities of Paris and Oxford; it dominated all learning. And, whereas the church, generally, had attained the zenith of its power, its influence in England was visible in the strong personalities of Lanfranc and Anselm, while the religious revival under Henry I and the coming of the friars at a later date were ample evidence of the spirit of devotion which was abroad.

But literature was not destined to remain a religious monotone: other and subtler influences were to modify its character. The twelfth century renascence was a period of popular awakening and the vigorous young nations found scope for their activities in attempting to cast off the fetters which had bound them in the past. As the imperial power declined, individual countries wrested their freedom, and in England, by 1215, clear ideas had been formulated as to the rights of the individual citizens. This groping for political freedom found its intellectual counterpart in France, not only in the appearance of secular *littérateurs* but also in that school of laic architects which proceeded to modify French Gothic style.[1] In England it appeared in a deliberate tendency to reject the religious themes which had been all but compulsory and to revert to that which was elemental in man. Fancy, in the shape of legend, was among these ineradicable elements, long despised by erudition and condemned by religion; and it was because the Arthurian legend offered satisfaction to some of the inmost cravings of the human heart, while it led the way to loftier ideals, that, when revealed, it succeeded in colouring much of the subsequent literature. The *Brut* of Layamon is, therefore, a silent witness to a literary

[1] E. S. Prior, *History of Gothic Art in England*, pp. 21-2.

revolt, in which the claims of legend and fancy were advanced anew for recognition in a field where religion had held the monopoly. And this spirit of revolt was further reinforced by the general assertion of another side of elemental man, viz.: that connected with the passion of love. France, in the eleventh and twelfth centuries, had been swept by a wave of popular love-poetry which brought in its wake the music of the troubadours. Germany, in the twelfth century, produced the minnesingers. The contemporary poets of Italy were also love-poets, and, at a slightly later date, Portugal, too, possessed many of the kind. This general inspiration, originating in France, and passing over the frontiers on the lips of the troubadours (for, in each country, the original form of the popular poetry was one and the same[1]), was destined to touch English soil soon after 1200. Though it failed for some time to secularise English poetry, it imparted a note of passion to much of the religious work; and, further, in *The Owl and Nightingale* religious traditions were boldly confronted with new-born ideas, and the case for Love was established beyond all dispute.

The religious writings of the time may be divided into four sections, according to the aims which they severally have in view. The purport of the first is to teach Biblical history; the second to exhort to holier living; the third is connected with the religious life of women; the last with the Virgin cult and mysticism.

Of the several attempts at scriptural exposition the *Ormulum* is the most considerable. The power of literary appeal displayed in this work is, intrinsically, of the smallest. Its matter is not attractive, its movement is prodigiously monotonous, its very correctness is tiresome; and yet it has an interest of its own, for, in its way, it helps to fill in the details of the literary picture of the time. It was probably written in the first decade of the thirteenth century in the north-east midlands. Its author, Orm, was a member of an Augustine monastery in that district, and, in response to the wishes of his "broþerr Wallterr," he undertook to turn into English paraphrases all the gospels for the ecclesiastical year as arranged in the mass-book, and to add to each paraphrase an exposition

[1] A. Jeanroy, *Les origines de la poésie lyrique en France au Moyen-âge.*

for English readers. The work, as projected, entailed a treatment of 243 passages of Scripture: the result, as extant, embodies only one-eighth of the plan—thirty paraphrases with the
corresponding homilies. In his translation of the scriptural
text Orm faithfully followed his original; for the matter of the
homiletic sections he drew mainly on the *Commentaries* and
Homilies of Bede, though, occasionally, he appears to have
consulted the homiletic work of Gregory as well as the writings
of Josephus and Isidore. It has been usual to point to the
works of Augustine and Aelfric as among the sources; but
definite reasons have been advanced for discountenancing
this view.[1] Traces of originality on the part of Orm are few
and far between. Encouraged by the spirit of his originals,
he occasionally essays short flights of fancy; and instances of
such ventures possibly occur in ll. 3710, 8019, 9390. In a
work so entirely dependent on earlier material it is not strange
to find that the theology was already out of date. Orm is
orthodox; but it is the orthodoxy of Bede. Of later developments, such as the thirteenth century mysticism, he has not a
sign. He combats heresies such as the Ebionite (l. 18,577)
and the Sabellian (l. 18,625), which had disturbed the days of
Bede but had since been laid to rest. In his introduction appear Augustinian ideas concerning original sin; but of the pro-
pitiation theory as set forth by Anselm there is no mention.
His dogma and his erudition are alike pre-Conquest; and in this
sense Orm may be said to stand outside his age and to represent
merely a continuation of Old English thought. Again, he is
only following the methods of the earlier schools in his allegorical interpretation. He is amazingly subtle and frequently
puerile in the vast significance which he gives to individual
words, even to individual letters. Personal names and place-
names furnish him with texts for small sermons, and the frequently indulged desire to extract hidden meanings from the
most unpromising material leads to such an accumulation of
strained conceits as would have made the work a veritable
gold mine for seventeenth century intellect. Most illuminating
as to this fanciful treatment is his handling of the name of Jesus
(l. 4302). Of the human and personal element the work contains but little. The simple modesty of the author's nature is

[1] G. Sarrazin, *Englische Stud.* VI, 1–27.

revealed when he fears his limitations and his inadequacy for
the task.   Otherwise the passionless temperament of the monk
is felt in every line as the work ambles along innocent of all
poetic exaltation, and given over completely to pious moralisings.   He shows a great regard for scholarly exactitude; but
this, in excess, becomes mere pedantry, and, indeed, his scruples
often cause him to linger needlessly over trifles in the text
and to indulge in aimless repetitions which prove exhausting.
As a monument of industry the work is beyond all praise.
Its peculiar orthography, carefully sustained through 10,000
long lines, is the joy of the philologist, though aesthetically it is
open to grave objection.   By his method of doubling every
consonant immediately following a short vowel, Orm furnishes
most valuable evidence regarding vowel-length at a critical
period of the language.   It is doubtful whether he was well
advised in choosing verse of any kind as the form of his ponderous work; but it must, at least, be conceded that the verse
which he did adopt—the iambic *septenarius*—was not the
least suitable for the purpose he had in view.   It was the
simplest of Latin metres, and Orm's mechanical handling certainly involves no great complexities.   He allows himself no
licenses.   The line invariably consists of fifteen syllables and is
devoid of either riming or alliterative ornament.   The former
might possibly, in the author's opinion, have tended to detract
from the severity of the theme; the latter must have appeared
too vigorous for the tone desired.   Except for his versification,
Orm, as compared with Old English writers, appears to have
forgotten nothing, to have learnt nothing.   Equally blind to
the uses of Romance vocabulary and conservative in thought,
Orm is but a relic of the past in an age fast hurrying on to new
forms and new ideas.

Other attempts at teaching Biblical history are to be found
in the *Genesis and Exodus* poems and in the shorter poems called
The Passion of Our Lord and *The Woman of Samaria*.   In the
Genesis and Exodus poems may be seen a renewal of the earlier
method of telling Bible stories in "londes speche and wordes
smale."   They are probably by one and the same author,[1]
who wrote about 1250 in the south-eastern Midlands.   Their

[1] Fritzche, *Angl.* v, 42–92, and Ten Brink, *History of English Literature,*
vol. t. Appendix F.

theme comprises Israelitish history down to the death of Moses. But the poet did not write from the Biblical text; his work is founded almost wholly on the *Historia Scholastica* of Petrus Comestor; although the first 600 lines appear to be drawn from some other source, while in ll. 78 ff. a reminiscence of Philipe de Thaun's *Comput* is found. The poet's aim is to tell a plain story, and it is the simple human items upon which he concen-centrates. He avoids all show of moralising, and consistently passes by the quotations with which his original was abundantly fortified. In each, the earlier epic style has given way to the more businesslike methods of the riming chronicle, and both works are written in a short riming couplet of excellent workmanship. They are of considerable importance in the history of English prosody, since in them the principles upon which that prosody is based clearly emerge. The line is based upon feet rather than accents, and studied variations in the arrangement of the feet produce melody of inconceivable variety in the accentual system with its unlicensed particles. The other two poems deal with New Testament history. *The Passion* is a sketch of the life of Christ with details added concerning the later persecutions under Nero and Domitian. It is, confessedly, a set-off to current narratives of *Karlemeyne and the Duzeper*. *The Woman of Samaria* deals with the episode of Christ's meeting with the woman at the well, and, as in the previous poem, the suitable *septenarius* is employed.

The corresponding section of hortatory writings is of mixed character. It comprises both verse and prose, and its effects are produced in divers manners. Sometimes it is by satire in which prevailing vices are specifically arraigned, elsewhere by stock devices for terrifying evil-doers; or again, the method may be the less aggressive one of allegorical teaching. All these writings have but one aim, that of inculcating holier living. Beginning with the satires, we have in *Hwon holy chireche is under uote* a short poem in septenars, in which the evils of simony within the church, and the general hatred of the church without are lamented. *Sinners Beware*, a more ambitious effort in six-line stanzas (*aabaab*), is directed against the age generally, though worldly priests, a rapacious soldiery, cheating chapmen and haughty ladies are the types directly aimed at. And, again, in a *Lutel Soth Sermun*—a poem in septenars—bad

brewers and bakers, priests' wives and illicit lovers like Malkin
and Jankin are railed against.   While thus assailing the vices
of certain types and classes the writers frequently follow up
their indictment with the argument of terror, after the fashion
of the *Poema Morale*.   Material for thundering of this sort lay
ready to hand in medieval compositions connected with the
subjects of doomsday, death and hell, such as the Old English
Be Domes Daege, *The Address of the Soul to the Body* and *The
Vision of St. Paul*.   In the poem called *Doomsday* and in the
work *On Serving Christ* the first of these themes is logically
pursued.   The clearest use of *The Address* motive appears in
the poem *Death*, the sequence of ideas observed in *The Address*
being here preserved, [1] while, in addition, the theme is slightly
developed.   Other reminiscences of the same motive also
appear in the fragmentary *Signs of Death* and in *Sinners
Beware* (ll. 331 ff.).   Of *The Vision of St. Paul* traces are clearly
seen in *The XI Pains of Hell*.   The depicting of hell was a
favourite medieval exercise, and *The Vision* is found in several
languages.   The archangel Michael is represented as conduct-
ing St. Paul into the gloomy abode, and Dante's journey under
Vergil's guidance is merely a variation of this theme.   *The
Vision* can be traced in the twelfth century homily *In Diebus
Dominicis*, where sabbath-breakers are warned.   In *The XI
Pains of Hell*—a poem in riming couplets—the treatment is
modified by the addition of the popular *Address* element.   A
lost soul describes the place of torment for St. Paul's benefit,
whereas in *The Vision* the description proceeds from the
apostle himself.

Besides satire and arguments of terror, allegory was employed for the same didactic end, notably in the *Bestiary*, *An
Bispel* (a Parable) and *Sawles Warde*, each of which was
based on a Latin original.   The *Bestiary* is founded on the
Latin *Physiologus* of one Thetbaldus, though earlier specimens
had appeared in Old English and Anglo-French.   Of the thirteen animals dealt with, twelve are taken from the work of
Thetbaldus, the section relating to the dove from Neckam's
De Naturis Rerum (1, 56).   The method of teaching is venerable
but effective; the habits of animals are made to symbolise
spiritual truth.   The work does not, however, represent much

[1] *Mod. Lang. Notes* (1890), p. 193.

originality,though the metrical form is a blending of old and new. Its six-syllable couplet is derived either from the Latin hexameters of the original or from Philipe de Thaun's couplet, with which it is identical. But the treatment is far from regular; alliteration, rime and assonance are promiscuously used, and syllabic equivalence is but imperfectly apprehended. Occasionally delightful movements are obtained such as exist in

> Al is man so is tis ern,
>   wuldė ge nu listen,
> old in hisė sinnes dern,
>   or he bicumeð cristen:

> And tus he neweð him ðis man,
>   ðanne he nimeð to kirke,
> or he it biðenken can,
>   hise egen weren mirke. [1]

But the whole seems to point to artistic inconsistencies rather than whimsical handling, though the work is interesting as showing English verse in the process of making. The second work, *An Bispel*, is a free translation of Anselm's *De Similitudine inter Deum et quemlibet regem suos judicantem*. This prose parable relates and explains God's dealings with mankind under the simile of a feast held by a king, to which are invited, by means of five messengers, both friend and foe. The English adapter adds certain details, notably the incident of the five messengers, who are intended to represent the five codes of law. The *Sawles Warde*, a more pretentious allegory of much the same date, is based upon a Latin prose work of Hugo de St. Victor, [2] the elements of which were suggested by *St. Matthew*, xxiv, 43. Wit (judgment) is lord of a castle (the soul of man). His wife (Will) is capricious, and the servants (the five senses) are hard to govern. He therefore needs the assistance of his four daughters (the four cardinal virtues, prudence, strength, temperance and righteousness); but the good behaviour of his household is ultimately assured by the appearance of two messengers, Fear (messenger of death), who paints the terrors of hell, and Love of Life, who describes the joys of heaven. The

---

[1] Ll. 88–95. *tis ern*, this eagle. *dern*, secret. *or*, ere. *tus*, thus. *egen*, eyes.
[2] *De anima*, etc. (Works, Bk. IV, chs. 13–15.) See Vollhart, *Einfluss*, etc., pp. 26 ff.

writer shows some originality in his treatment, and the allegory in his hands becomes rather more coherent and convincing; his characters are more developed, and certain dramatic touches are added here and there. The same motive appears in a short contemporaneous poem called *Wil and Wit*. Other didactic methods which call for brief mention are those in which the joys of heaven are persuasively described, as, for instance, in the poems *Long Life* and *The Duty of Christians*, or in which the dialogue form is used for the first time, as in *Vices and Virtues* (c. 1200)—"a soul's confession of its sins, with reason's description of the virtues."

The third section of the religious writings of this period is wholly concerned with the religious life of women. The twelfth century, the golden age of monasticism, witnessed also an increased sympathy with convent life; and this is evident not only from the letters of Ailred, but also from the increasing frequency with which legacies were left to convent communities, and from the founding of such an order as that of St. Gilbert of Sempringham.[1] Before the Conquest religious women had been by no means a negligible quantity. The revival of interest in their cause, at this later date, was part of that impulse which had inspired, on the continent, the mystical writers St. Hildegard of Bingen, St. Elisabeth of Schönau and the philanthropic zeal of the noble Hedwig. In the thirteenth century, the convent of Helfta in Saxony was the centre of these tendencies; and, though it cannot be said with certainty that England produced any women-writers, yet the attention to practical religion and mystical thought, which had been the subjects of zeal abroad, are tolerably well represented in the writings *for* women in England.

Hali Meidenhad and the *Lives of the Saints* are connected with this movement by the incitement they furnish to convent life. The former, an alliterative prose homily, is based on the text of *Psalm* xlv. 10; but the methods of the writer are entirely wanting in that gentle grace and persuasion which are found elsewhere. He sets forth his arguments in a coarse, repellent manner. Where others dwell on the beauty of cloistered affection, he derides rather gracelessly the troubles of the married state; and, if these troubles are related with something like

---

[1] L. Eckenstein, *Woman under Monasticism*, pp. 213 ff.

humour, it is of a grim kind and easily slides into odious invective. Maidenly ideals are exalted in more becoming fashion in the *Lives of the Saints*, which appeared about the same date. They consist of three rhythmical alliterative prose lives of St. Margaret, St. Katharine and St. Juliana, based on Latin originals. Saintly legends had revived in England in the early thirteenth century, and were already taking the place of the homily in the services of the church. With the later multiplying of themes a distinct falling-off in point of style became visible. Of the three lives, that of *St. Katharine* is, in some respects, the most attractive. As compared with its original, the character of the saint becomes somewhat softened and refined in the English version. She has lost something of that impulsiveness, that hardy revengeful spirit which earlier writers had regarded as not inconsistent with the Christian profession. The English adapter also shows some idea of the art of story-telling, in removing certain superfluous details. But, in all three works, sufficient horrors remain to perpetuate the terrors of an earlier age, and, in general, the saintly heroines are more remarkable for stern undaunted courage of the Judith type than for the milder charms of later ideals. Their aim however is clear—to glorify the idea of the virgin life.

Besides these, there are certain works in which definite instruction as to the secluded life is given for the guidance of those who had already entered upon that career. Early in the thirteenth century the Latin *Rule of St. Benet* (516) was adapted for the nuns of Winteney. The version is clearly based on some masculine text, for occasional masculine forms [1] are inadvertently retained in the feminine version. A chapter is also added "concerning the priests admitted to a convent" (LXII). The aim of the *Ancren Riwle* (anchoresses' rule) is of a similar kind; but this is a work which, owing to its greater originality, its personal charm and its complete sympathy with all that was good in contemporary literature, stands apart by itself as the greatest prose work of the time, and as one of the most interesting of the whole Middle English period. It may, in the first place, be assumed that the English version is the original one, though French and Latin forms are found, and that it appeared in the south of England in the first quarter

---

[1] Cf. ȝear-owne, 139. 2, etc.

of the century. The question of authorship is still unsolved.
Richard Poore, bishop of Salisbury (1217–29) and founder of
its cathedral, is credited with it, and Tarrent in Dorsetshire is
regarded as the site of the anchorhold. The aim of the work is
to provide ghostly counsel for three anchoresses, *i.e.* religious
women, who, after a period of training within a nunnery,
dedicated themselves to a secluded life outside. These recluses often lived in a slight dwelling attached to a church;
and such may have been the conditions of these "three pious
sisters." The work incidentally throws much light upon the
life within an anchorhold, upon the duties of the inmates,
the out-sisters and maids, and their sundry difficulties, whether
of a business, domestic, or spiritual kind. The admonition
imparted was not without precedent. As early as 709 Aldhelm,
in his *De Laudibus Virginitatis*, had depicted the glories of the
celibate life, and about 1131–61 a letter (*De vita eremitica*) was
written by Ailred of Rievaulx to his sister, dealing with similar
matters; since this latter work is quoted in the *Ancren Riwle,*
while the general arrangement of both is the same, there can
be little doubt of a certain degree of indebtedness. The treatise
opens with a preface, which summarises the contents; sections
I and VIII refer to external matters, to religious ceremonies and
domestic affairs; sections II–VII to the inward life. The work
has much that is medieval commonplace, an abundance of well-
digested learning, borrowings from Anselm and Augustine,
Bernard and Gregory, and illustrations which reveal a considerable acquaintance with animal and plant lore. The author
also betrays those learned tendencies which gloried in subtle
distinctions. There is the ancient delight in allegorical teaching: Biblical names are made to reveal hidden truths: a play
upon words can suggest a precept. And, alongside of all this,
which is severely pedantic, there is much that is quaint and
picturesque. Traces are not wanting of a vein of mysticism.
Courtly motives occasionally receive a spiritual adaptation,
and here and there are touches of those romantic conceptions
which were elsewhere engaged in softening the severity of
religious verse. The writer, then, is possessed of the learning
of the age, its methods of teaching, its mystical and romantic
tendencies. And yet these facts are far from altogether explaining the charm of the work, its power of appeal to modern

readers. The charm lies rather in the writer's individuality, in his gentle refinement and lovable nature. The keynote of the whole work seems to be struck in that part of the preface where the sisters, belonging as they did to no order of nuns, are instructed to claim for themselves the order of St. James. The work is animated by the "pure religion and undefiled" of that apostle, and is instinct with lofty morality and infinite tenderness. The writer's instructions as to ceremonies and observances are broad-minded and reasonable; his remarks on love reveal the sweetness and light which dwelt in his soul. The prose style from the historical standpoint is of very great merit. The ancient fetters are not quite discarded; there is still constraint and a want of suppleness; but there are also signs that the limping gait is acquiring freedom. The style, moreover, is earnest, fresh and touched with the charm of the sentiment it clothes. Above all it is naïve: the writer occasionally reaches the heart, while provoking a smile.

Closely connected with this woman-literature are those works which belong to the Virgin cult and those which are touched with erotic mysticism. This section is the outcome of those chivalrous ideals which had dawned in the twelfth century, to soften the harshness of earlier heroics and to refine the relation between the sexes. These new ideals coloured the atmosphere of court life, and the exaltation of woman in its courtly sense found a counterpart in the revived Virgin cult, just as knightly wooing suggested the image of the wistful soul striving for union with the Divine. This erotic mysticism, which was to appear again in Crashaw, Herbert and Vaughan, was merely a phase of those allegorical tendencies of which Dante was the culmination. The pious soul yearning for a closer walk with God now expressed its longings in the language of earthly passion, just as earlier mystics had tried to interpret the Divine nature by the use of more commonplace allegory. And this development was encouraged by the mysticism of Hugo de St. Victor, which influenced both Paris and Oxford; while elsewhere on the continent a school of nuns were producing works laden with passion and breathing an intense emotion.

The Virgin cult is represented in the first place by the prose *Lofsong of ure Lefdi*, a fairly close translation of the poem

Oratio ad Sanctam Mariam of Archbishop Marbod of Rheims (1035-1138), and by *On God Ureisun of ure Lefdi* (A Good Orison of our Lady), a poem in riming couplets, for which no Latin original has yet been found, though it contains suggestions of the work of Anselm.[1]   Other examples of the kind are found in *The Five Joys of the Virgin*, a poem in eight-line stanzas; *A Song to the Virgin*, with Latin insertions; *A Prayer to Our Lady*, a sinner's repentance in interesting four-line stanzas; *A Prayer to the Virgin*, in similar form.   Another side of the Virgin cult is represented by the Middle English versions of the *Compassio Mariae* and the *Assumptio Mariae*, which appeared about the middle of the century.   The former is a west Midland translation of a Latin hymn, and the work is artistically interesting as illustrating how metrical innovation was made. The six-line strophe and the riming formula are taken over from the original, though this identity of form prevents a literal rendering.   The treatment is otherwise not without originality. Alliterative ornament is added, and use is made of a popular piece of medieval fancy, namely the comparison of Christ's birth to a sunbeam passing through glass and leaving it unstained.[2]   *Assumptio Mariae* rests on a venerable legend of the ascension of Mary; it is of eastern origin, but is found in Latin, German and French versions.   The English version is written in short couplets, and appears to be of an eclectic kind.   The episode of unbelieving Thomas is taken from a Latin version; otherwise the poem is strongly reminiscent of Wace's *Vie de la Vierge Marie*.

Erotic mysticism is best represented by the *Luve Ron* of Thomas de Hales, a delightful lyric in eight-line stanzas, written in the earlier portion of the reign of Henry III, and probably before 1240 judging from the allusion in ll. 97 ff.   The writer was a native of Hales (Gloucester), who, after a career at Paris and Oxford, attained considerable distinction as a scholar. The main theme of the work is the perfect love which abides with Christ and the joy and peace of mystic union with Him. The poem is full of lofty devotion and passionate yearning; its deep seriousness is conveyed through a medium tender and refined, and it is, in short, one of the most attractive and

[1] Vollhardt, *Einfluss der lat. geistlichen Litt.* etc., pp. 41 ff.
[2] A. Napier, E.E.T.S. ciii, pp. 75 ff.

impassioned works of the time, as the following extracts suggest:

> Maydè her þu myht biholde,
> þis worldes luue nys bute o res,
> And is by-set so felè-volde.
> Vikel and frakel and wok and les.
> þeos þeines þat her weren bolde
> Beoþ aglyden, so wyndes bles:
> Under molde he liggeþ colde,
> And faleweþ so doþ medewe gres.
>
> .   .   .   .
>
> Hwer is Paris and Heleyne
> þat weren so bryht and feyre on bleo:
> Amadas, Tristram, and Dideyne
> Yseudè and allè þeo:
> Ector wiþ his scharpè meyne
> And Cesar riche of wor [l] des feo?
> Heo beoþ iglyden ut of þe reyne,
> So þe schef is of e cleo. [1]

The three prose prayers, *The Wohung of ure Lauerd*, *On Lofsong of ure Louerde* and *On Ureisun of ure Louerde* belong to the same category as the *Luve Ron*. They are written in alliterative prose, [2] which aimed at obtaining the emphatic movement of Old English verse, and is most effective in recitation, though the absence of metrical rules brings about a looser structure. All three prayers consist of passionate entreaties for closer communion with Christ, and the personal feeling revealed in them illustrates the use of the love motive in the service of religion. But to interpret the love terminology literally and to connect these prayers solely with the devotions of nuns, as one critic suggests, seems to involve a misapprehension of their tone, for it infuses into their being an earthliness quite out of keeping with their rarefied sentiment. Further, these works have some points in common, occasionally literal agreement, with the *Ancren Riwle* and *Hali Meidenhad*, but in all probabilty it is in the works of Anselm and Hugo de

---

[1] Ll. 9–16; 65–72. *o res*, passing, transitory. *frakel*, base. *wok*, feeble. *les*, false. *bles*, blast. *meyne*, might. *feo*, wealth. *schef of þe cleo*, corn from the hill-side.

[2] Cf. Hwa ne mei luue þi luueli leor ?

St. Victor that the sources must be sought, in which case all these English works are distinct and separate borrowings from the same Latin originals.[1]

We come now to that section of the literature of the period which represents a revolt against established religious themes. It has been seen that religious writers occasionally made use of the motives of legend and love, and from this it might be inferred that these were the directions into which the general taste was inclining. At all events these are the lines along which the literary revolt began to develop, Layamon, in the first instance, setting forth in the vernacular legendary material which came to hand. Layamon's *Brut*, written early in the thirteenth century, has come down in two MSS. (A text and B text), belonging respectively to the first and second halves of the thirteenth century. The later version has numerous scribal alterations: there are many omissions of words and passages, the spelling is slightly modernised, riming variants are introduced and foreign substitutes take the place of obsolescent native words. The author reveals his identity in the opening lines. He is Layamon, a priest of Ernley (Arley Regis, Worcester), on the right bank of the Severn, where he was wont to "read books" (*i.e.*, the services of the church). Layamon's ambitious purpose was to tell the story of Britain from the time of the Flood. He is, however, content to begin with the story of Troy and the arrival of Brutus, and to end with the death of Cadwalader, 689 A.D. As regards his sources, he mentions the English book of Bede, the Latin books of St. Albin and St. Austin (by which he probably meant the Latin version of Bede's *Ecclesiastical History*) and thirdly, the *Brut* of the French clerk Wace. Of the first two authorities, however, it is curious to note, he makes not the slightest use. The account of Gregory and the English captives at Rome (ll. 29,445 ff.), which is often quoted in support of his indebtedness to Bede, in reality proves his entire independence, for glaring discrepancies occur between the respective narratives. Elsewhere in the *Brut* Bede is directly contradicted[2] and, in fact, Layamon's assertion of indebtedness, as far as Bede is concerned, can be nothing more than a conventional recognition of a venerable work which dealt

---

[1] Vollhardt, *Einfluss der lat. geistlichen Litt.* etc., pp. 41 ff.
[2] Cf. Layamon, *Brut*, 412; Bede, 1, 3, etc.

with a kindred subject. Convention rather than fact also lay behind his statement that he had consulted works in three different languages.

His debt to Wace, however, is beyond all doubt. Innumerable details are common to both works, and, moreover, it is clear that it is Wace's work rather than Wace's original (Geoffrey of Monmouth's *History of the Kings of Britain*) that has been laid under contribution.[1] In the first place, Wace and Layamon have certain details in common which are lacking in the work of Geoffrey; in the matter of omissions Wace and Layamon frequently agree as opposed to Geoffrey; while again they often agree in differing from the Latin narrative in regard to place and personal names. But if Wace's *Brut* forms the groundwork of Layamon's work, in the latter there are numerous details, not accounted for by the original, which have generally been attributed to Celtic (*i.e.* Welsh) influences. Many of these details, however, have recently been shown to be non-Welsh. The name of Argante the elf-queen, as well as that of Modred, for instance, point to other than Welsh territory. The traits added to the character of Arthur are in direct opposition to what is known of Welsh tradition. The elements of the Arthurian saga relating to the Round Table are known to have been treated as spurious by Welsh writers; Tysilio, in his *Brut*, for instance, passes them over. Therefore the explanation of this additional matter in Layamon, as compared with Wace, must be sought for in other than Welsh material.[2]

Hitherto, when Wace's *Brut* has been mentioned, it has been tacitly assumed that the printed version of that work was meant, rather than one of those numerous versions which either remain in manuscript or have since disappeared. One MS. (Add. 32,125. Brit. Mus.), however, will be found to explain certain name-forms, concerning which Layamon is in conflict with the printed Wace. And other later works, such as the Anglo-French *Brut* (thirteenth or fourteenth century) and the English metrical *Mort Arthur*, both of which are based on unprinted versions of Wace, contain material which is present in Layamon, namely, details connected with the stories of Lear,

---

[1] R. Wülcker, P.B.B. III, pp. 530 ff.

[2] For the main points contained in the discussion of Layamon's sources see Imelmann, *Layamon, Versuch über seine Quellen.*

Merlin and Arthur. Therefore it seems possible that Layamon, like the authors of the later works, used one of the variant texts. Further, the general nature of Layamon's additions appears to be Breton or Norman. The names Argante and Delgan, for instance, are derived through Norman media; the fight between Arthur and Frollo is found in the *Roman des Franceis* (1204) of André de Coutances. But Layamon seems to stand in yet closer relation to Gaimar's *Rhyming Chronicle*, so far as that book can be judged from the related *Münchner Brut*. An explanation of the Carric-Cinric confusion, for instance, would be obtained by this assumption. The representation of Cerdic and Cinric in Layamon as one and the same person[1] might conceivably be due, not to the account in the Old English *Chronicle*, but to some such foreign version as is found in Gaimar (ll. 819 ff.). To Gaimar moreover may probably be attributed several details of Layamon's style—his tendency to employ forms of direct speech, his discursiveness, his appeals to the gods and his protestations as to the truth of his narrative. It is possible that one of the later versions of Wace may have embodied details taken from Gaimar. Waurin's *Chroniques et istoires* (fifteenth century) seems a compilation of this kind, and it is not impossible that Layamon's original may have been a similarly compiled work, with, it should be added, elements taken from contemporary Tristram and Lancelot poems. In any case, the English *Brut* is not based on the printed *Brut* of Wace, but on one of the later versions of which certain MSS. remain and of which other traces can be found. This particular version had probably been supplemented by Breton material introduced through some Norman medium, and, since this supplementary portion is reminiscent of Gaimar, there is reason for supposing that the particular version may have been mainly a compilation of the earlier works of Wace and Gaimar.

This view as to sources must modify, in some degree, the estimate to be formed of Layamon's artistic merits, and must discount the value of some of the additions formerly ascribed to his imagination or research. It will also account for certain matters of style already mentioned. But, when these items have been removed, there still remains much that is Layamon's

[1] Cf. ll. 28,867 ff.

own, sufficient to raise his work far above the rank of a mere
translation. The poet's English individuality may be said to
pervade the whole. It appears in the reminiscences of English
popular legend perceived in Wygar, the maker of Arthur's corse-
let, and in the sea of Lumond, the "atteliche pole," where
"nikeres" bathe. His English temperament appears in the
fondness he betrays for maxims and proverbs, which afford
relief from the mere business of the narrative. The poet is
still in possession of the ancient vocabulary, with its hosts of
synonyms, though the earlier parallelisms which retarded
the movement are conspicuously absent. His most resonant
lines, like those of his literary ancestors, deal with the conflict
of warriors or with that of the elements. In such passages
as those which describe the storm that overtook Ursula (II, 74),
or the wrestling match between Corineus and the giant (I, 79),
he attains the true epic note, while his words gather strength
from their alliterative setting. His verse is a compromise
between the old and the new. With the Old English line still
ringing in his ears, he attempts to regulate the rhythm, and
occasionally to adorn his verse with rime or assonance. His
device of simile was, no doubt, caught from his original, for
many of the images introduced are coloured by the Norman
love of the chase, as when a fox-hunt is introduced to depict
the hunted condition of Childric (II, 452), or the pursuit of a
wild crane by hawks in the fenland to describe the chase after
Colgrim (II, 422). The poet, in general, handles his borrowings
with accuracy, but he has limitations—perhaps shows impa-
tience—as a scholar. Apart from a totally uncritical attitude
—a venial sin in that age—he betrays, at times, a certain ignorance on historical and geographical points. But such anach-
ronisms and irregularities are of little importance in a work of
this kind, and do not detract from its literary merits. Other
verbal errors suggest that the work of translation was to
Layamon not devoid of difficulty. Where Wace indulges in
technical terminology, as in his nautical description of Arthur's departure from Southampton, Layamon here and elsewhere solves his linguistic difficulties by a process of frank
omission.

The interest which the *Brut* possesses for modern readers
arises in part from the fact that much of its material is closely

bound up with later English literature. Apart from the Arthurian legend here appear for the first time in English the story of Leir and Kinbelin, Cloten and Arviragus. But the main interest centres round the Arthurian section, with its haunting story of a wondrous birth, heroic deeds and a mysterious end. The grey king appears in a garment of chivalry. As compared with the Arthur of Geoffrey's narrative, his figure has grown in knightliness and splendour. He is endowed with the added traits of noble generosity and heightened sensibility; he has advanced in courtesy; he is the defender of Christianity; he is a lover of law and order. And Layamon's narrative is also interesting historically. It is the work of the first writer of any magnitude in Middle English, and, standing at the entrance to that period, he may be said to look before and after. He retains much of Old English tradition; in addition, he is the first to make extensive use of French material. And, lastly, in the place of a fast vanishing native mythology, he endows his countrymen with a new legendary store in which lay concealed the seeds of later chivalry.

The Owl and Nightingale, which represents another line of literary revolt, has come down in two MSS., one dating from the first, the other from the second, half of the thirteenth century. Of the two MSS. the earlier (Cotton MS.) is the more trustworthy; the scribe of the other has frequently omitted unimportant monosyllabic words, regardless of scansion, besides having altered inflexional endings and made sundry substitutions in the matter of diction; such alterations are clearly revealed in riming positions. The authorship is a matter of conjecture; Nicholas of Guilford, a cleric of Portisham (Dorset), who is mentioned thrice in the poem, is supposed by some to have been the writer, but the objections to this view are that the allusions are all in the third person, and that lavish praise is showered on his name. On the other hand, since the poem aims incidentally at urging the claims of Nicholas to clerical preferment, the end may have justified the means and may account for the unstinted praise as well as the anonymous character of the work. But the name of John of Guildford must also be mentioned. He is known to have written some verse about this period, and, since the common appellation implies a connection between the two, it may have been that he was the advocate of Nicholas's cause. On internal and external evidence, the poem may, approximately, be dated 1220. The benediction pronounced upon "King Henri" (ll. 1091–2) clearly refers to Henry II; but the borrowings from Neckam make an earlier date than 1200 impossible. The mention of a papal mission to Scotland (l. 1095) may refer to the visit of Vivian in 1174, or to that of cardinal Guala in 1218. The poem was probably written before the year 1227, for at that date the regency ceased, and, with Henry III reigning, the benediction would be ambiguous, not to say ominous. As regards sources, no direct original has been found; the poem embodies the spirit as well as the structure of certain Old French models without being a copy of any one. There are certain details, however, which appear to have been definitely borrowed, and of these the most interesting is the nightingale episode (ll. 1049–62). It is narrated at length in Marie de France's *lai, Laustic* (*c.* 1170), as *une aventure dunt le Bretun firent un lai*, and before the close of the century it appeared in a balder form in Neckam's *De Naturis Rerum*. Its subsequent popularity is attested by its frequent reappearances in both French and English. The episode, as it appears in *The Owl and Nightingale*, is due partly to Marie de France, partly to Neckam. There are further details in the poem which are reminiscent of Neckam's *De Naturis Rerum*, while the description of the barbarous north (ll. 999 ff.). is possibly based on a similar description in Alfred's translation of Orosius. The structure of the poem is of a composite kind. The main elements are drawn from the Old French *débat*, but there is also a proverbial element as well as *Bestiary* details, which, though slight in amount, give a colouring to the whole. Of the various kinds of the Old French *débat*, it is the *tençon* in particular upon which the poem is modelled, for that poem, unlike the *jeu-parti*, has no deliberate choice of sides; each opponent undertakes the defence of his nature and kind. And, in addition to the general structure, the poet has borrowed further ideas from this same *genre*, namely, the appointment of judge, suggested by the challenger and commented upon by his opponent; the absence of the promised verdict; the use of certain conventional figures of the Old French *débat*, such as *le jaloux* (cf. ll. 1075 ff.), *la mal mariée* (cf. ll. 1520 ff.), and the adoption of love as the theme of the whole. The proverbial element is derived from the lips of the people, and, of the sixteen maxims, eleven are connected with the name of Alfred. In representing his disputants as members of the bird world, and in interpreting their habits to shadow forth his truths, the poet has adopted the methods of the *Bestiary*. His use of the motive is, however, so far untraditional in that the nightingale, unlike the owl, did not appear in the ancient *Physiologus*.

The main significance of the poem has been subjected to much misconception. Its ultimate intention, as already stated, seems to have been to suggest to English readers a new type of poetry. To the medieval mind the poetic associations of the nightingale were invariably those of love; according to her own description, her song was one of "skentinge" (amusement), and its aim was to teach the nobility of faithful love. She is, however, induced to emphasise (ll. 1347–1450) the didactic side of her singing, in order to meet more successfully her dour opponent; but the emphasis is merely a *passado* in a bout of dialectics, and, further, no inconsistency is involved with her own statement, "And soth hit is of luve ich singe," when mention is made of the ignorance of the barbarous north concerning those love-songs, or of the wantonness at times induced by her passionate music. Her dignified defence of love (ll. 1378 ff.), moreover, finds a counterpart in many products of the contemporary school of love-poetry. The owl, on the other hand, unmistakably represents a poet of the religious type. Her doleful notes and the essentially didactic character of her songs, her special chants at Christmas, and her duties of bestowing comfort, are all in keeping with her own description of herself when she says:

> Ich wisse men mid mine songe
> That hi ne suneʒi nowiht longe.[1]

As to the writer's personal attitude, he inclines rather to the side of the nightingale. The virtues of the religious school clearly emerge in the course of the debate; yet it cannot but be felt that the poem embodies "a new spirit of opposition to monastic training"[2] only, the contending spirit was the erotic theme and not the secular priest.

[1] Ll. 927–8. *wisse*, direct *suneʒi*, sin.
[2] Courthope, *History of English Poetry*, vol. I, ch. IV.

From the literary point of view the poem forms an interesting contrast with the works of the earlier period. The Old English embroidered diction is replaced by a mode of expression less redundant, more unpretending, more natural. Words are no longer artificially arranged, but follow the order of thought. The similes employed in the place of earlier metaphor are of a colloquial character, effective in their unexpectedness; and the dawn of humour is surely at hand when the owl in her bitterness exclaims to the nightingale,

> þu chaterest so doþ on Irish preost [1];

or when the nightingale hurls back the happy retort,

> þu singest so doþ hen a-snowe.[2]

Moreover the illustrations made use of are no mere reprints of orthodox scenes; they reflect country life and the life of the people which, in modern times, Hardy and Barnes were to illuminate. Freshness and originality, is, however, carried at times to excess in the vituperations in which the disputants indulge, when crudity and naked strength seem virtues overdone. Most interesting, on the other hand, are the signs of an appreciation of the softer side of nature. It was the wilder aspects of nature which had appealed to the earlier school. The present poet saw beauty in the gentle arrival of spring, with its blossoming meadows and flower-decked woodlands, as well as in mellow autumn with its golden hues and fallow tints. The nightingale paints a couple of dainty word-pictures when she describes her coming and going. Upon her arrival, she sings,

> þe blostmè ginneþ springe and sprede
> Boȝe in treo and ek on mede,
> þe lilie mid hire fairè wlite
> Wolcumeþ me, þat þu wite,
> Bit me, mid hire fairè bleo
> þat ich shulle to hirè fleo.
> þe rose also mid hire rude,
> þat cumeþ ut of þe þornèwude,
> Bit me þat ich shullè singe,
> Vor hire luve, onè skentinge.[3]

[1] L. 322.

[2] L. 412. *a-snowe*, in the snow.

[3] Ll. 437–46. *wlite*, beauty. *bit*, bids. *rude*, ruddy, colour. *skentinge* piece for amusement.

Her departure takes place amid other scenes:

> *H*wan is ido vor *h*wan ich com,
> Ich fare aȝen and do wisdom:
> *H*wane mon hoȝeþ of his sheve,
> An*d* falewi cumeþ on grenè leve,
> Ich farè hom an*d* nimè leve
> Ne recche ich noȝt of winteres reve.[1]

Nor is the poem devoid of appreciation of dramatic situation and dramatic methods. The debate is brought to a dramatic climax by the appearance of the wren and his companions, while considerable skill is shown in the characterisation of the two disputants. Brief interludes are introduced for the sake of relief and variety: they also add slight touches by the way to the character sketches. Between the lines may be caught, here and there, glimpses of contemporary life. The festival of Christmas with its carol-services, the *laus perennis* of cathedrals and monasteries, and the daily service of the parish priest, the rampant injustice in the bestowal of livings, the picture of the gambler and the tricks of the ape, all help to give a historical setting. The verse is modelled on French octosyllabics, and the earlier *staccato* movement gives place to a more composed rhythm. As a rule, the rimes are wonderfully correct, and it is instructive to note that the proportion of masculine to feminine rimes is that of 10: 37. This fact is interesting in connection with Chaucerian work, where the fondness for the feminine form, which is less pronounced than in the present poem, has been ascribed to Italian influences. It is obvious that no such influence is at work here; nor can Old French models have suggested the form, the masculine rime being there preferred. It must have arisen from native riming exigencies. Iambic lines had, necessarily, to end with accented riming syllables: but, since the English accent fell on the root syllable in all cases where the riming word was of two syllables, the second would become a sort of light ending and go to form a feminine rime. The poem is, therefore, one of many-sided interest. Its permanent value lies in its oft-sounded note of freedom, in its metrical innovations, its discarding of the artificial for the natural, its grasp

---

[1] Ll. 453-8. *hoȝeþ*, takes thought. *nime leve*, take my leave. *reve*, plunder.

of new methods, its new ideals and in the daring suggestion it makes in connection with love. And, finally, it must be confessed, the poet had travelled well.   Though full of appreciation for a foreign literature, he has not changed "his Country Manners for those of Forraigne Parts"; he has "onely pricked in some of the Flowers of that he had Learned abroad into the Customes of his owne Country."   And in this way more than one of our poets have since that day written.

CHAPTER XII

The Arthurian Legend

"A GRAVE there is for March" (or "Mark")—so runs a stanza in one of the oldest extant Welsh poems[1]—"a grave for Gwythur, a grave for Gwgawn of the Ruddy Sword; a mystery is the grave of Arthur." "Some men say yet," wrote Sir Thomas Malory, many centuries later, "that king Arthur is not dead, but had by the will of our Lord Jesu into another place." The mystery of Arthur's grave still remains unsolved, for

> Where is he who knows?
> From the great deep to the great deep he goes.

Towards the end of the twelfth century, in the very heyday of the British king's renown as a romantic hero, the monks of St. Dunstan's at Glastonbury—at the original instance, it is said, of Henry II—professed to have discovered the mortal remains of Arthur in the cemetery of their abbey church.[2] Some sixty years before, William of Malmesbury had given an account of the discovery in Wales of the grave of Arthur's nephew, Gawain but the grave of Arthur himself was not, he said, anywhere to be found; hence ancient songs[3] prophesy his return. It was thought that the illusory expectations thus cherished by the British Celts could be dispelled by the Glastonbury exhumation. But so sorry an attempt to poison the wells of romance met with the failure it deserved. Arthur lived on, inviolate in fabled Avalon. Graven on no known sepulchre, his name,

[1] A poem, in triplet form, entitled *The Stanzas of the Graves*, preserved in *The Black Book of Carmarthen*, a MS. of the twelfth century.

[2] Giraldus Cambrensis gives the longest account of the affair (*De Principis Instructione*, VIII, 126–9).

[3] *Antiquitas naeniarum. Gesta Regum Anglorum*, Bk. III.

> a ghost,
> Streams like a cloud, man-shaped, from mountain peak,
> And cleaves to cairn and cromlech still.

The memory of no other British hero is so extensively preserved in the place-names of these islands; "only the devil is more often mentioned in local association than Arthur."[1]

The nomenclature of Arthurian fable, which has a voluminous critical literature of its own, does not concern us here. No student of Arthurian origins, however, can fail to be impressed by the strange disproportion between the abundance of Arthurian place-names in the British islands and the amount of early British literature, whether in English or in the insular Celtic tongues, dealing with the Arthurian legend. The early English Arthurian literature, in particular, is singularly meagre and undistinguished. The romantic exploitation of "the matter of Britain" was the achievement, mainly, of French writers—so much so that some modern critics would have us attach little importance to genuine British influence on the development of the legend of Arthur. For, when all is told, Arthurian romance owed its immense popularity in the thirteenth century to its ideal and representative character, and to its superiority over the other stock romantic matters as a *point de repère* for every kind of literary excursion and adventure. Thus, the "matter of Britain" very quickly became international property—a vast composite body of romantic tradition, which European poets and story-tellers of every nationality drew upon and used for their own purposes. The British king himself faded more and more into the background, and became, in time, but the phantom monarch of a featureless "land of faëry," which

> None that breatheth living aire doth know.

His knights quite overshadow him in the later romances; but they, in their turn, undergo the same process of denationalisation, and appear as natives of no known clime or country, moving about in an iridescent atmosphere of fantasy and illusion. The Arthurian fairy-land thus became a neutral territory—an enchanted land where the seemingly incompatible ideals of knight-errantry and the church were reconciled, and where even east and west brought their spoils together as

Dickinson, *King Arthur in Cornwall* (Longmans, 1900), preface, p. vi.

to some common sanctuary. " Pilgrimage and the holy wars, " writes Gibbon, "introduced into Europe the specious miracles of Arabian magic. Fairies and giants, flying dragons and enchanted palaces, were blended with the more simple fictions of the west; and the fate of Britain depended on the art, or the predictions, of Merlin. Every nation embraced and adorned the popular romance of Arthur and the knights of the Round Table; their names were celebrated in Greece and Italy; and the voluminous tales of Sir Lancelot and Sir Tristram were devoutly studied by the princes and nobles, who disregarded the genuine heroes and heroines of antiquity."

Britain, however, claimed the titular hero of the legend; and it was on British soil that the full flower of Arthurian romance in due course made its appearance. Sir Thomas Malory's marvellous compilation superseded, for all time, each and every "French book" which went to its making. And, as Caxton takes occasion to emphasise in his preface to Malory's book, Arthur, as the "first and chief of the three best Christian kings" of the world, deserved "most to be remembered amongst us Englishmen." It so happens, however, that in our own, no less than in Caxton's, time "divers men hold opinion that there was no such Arthur, and all such books as been made of him be but feigned and fables." There is, indeed, much in the history of the legend to justify the attitude of these sceptics. The first great outburst of the popularity of the story was due to a writer who, in the words of one of his earliest critics,[1] "cloaked fables about Arthur under the honest name of history"—Geoffrey of Monmouth. The historical Arthur—assuming that Geoffrey meant all that he wrote about him to be taken as authentic fact—thus made his first considerable appearance in literature under very dubious auspices. The "British book" which Geoffrey professes to have used has never been discovered, and is not unreasonably supposed by many to have been a myth. Thus, they who would substantiate Caxton's assertion that "there was a king of this land called Arthur" have to produce earlier, and more authentic, evidence than anything furnished by Geoffrey.

Old English literature, even the *Chronicle*, knows absolutely nothing of Arthur. Wales, alone, has preserved any record of

[1] William of Newburgh.

his name and fame from a date earlier than the twelfth century. But even Welsh writers of an indisputably early date tell us very little about him, and tell that little in a tantalisingly casual and perfunctory way. Yet it is in a few obscure Welsh poems, in one very remarkable but difficult Welsh prose tale and in two meagre Latin chronicles compiled in Wales, that we discover the oldest literary records of both the historical and the legendary Arthur. A few stubborn critics still maintain, against the opinion of the best Welsh scholars, that the Welsh works in question are not, in substance, earlier than the twelfth century—that, in other words, they contain no fragments of Arthurian lore which can be proved to be older than the date of the MSS. in which they are preserved. None, however, will now dispute the approximate dates assigned by the best authorities to Nennius and the *Annales Cambriae;* and it is in the two Latin documents bearing these names that we have the earliest extant records of a seemingly historical Arthur.

The *Historia Brittonum*, commonly ascribed to Nennius, is a curious compilation, which was put into its present form not later than the first half of the ninth century.[1] About the year 800 a Welshman named Nennius—or, to use the native form, Nynniaw—who calls himself a disciple of Elfod, bishop of Bangor in North Wales,[2] copied and freely edited a collection of brief notes, gathered from various sources, on early British history and geography. Nennius claims, in his preface, after the manner of his kind, to be an original compiler. "I have," he says, "gathered together all I could find not only in the Roman annals, but also in the chronicles of holy fathers, . . . and in the annals of the Irish and English, and in our native traditions." Elsewhere he avows himself a mere copyist, and tells us that he wrote "the 'Cities' and the 'Marvels' of Britain as other scribes had done before him." Arthur appears in both the quasi-historical and the purely legendary parts of Nennius's compilation. In what purports to be the strictly historical part of his narrative Nennius relates how, some time after the death of Hengist, Arthur fought against the English along with

---

[1] Zimmer contends (*Nennius Vindicatus*) that the *History* was completed in 796. Thurneysen would fix the year 826 as the date of its completion (*Zeitschrift für Deutsche Philologie*, Halle, 1897).

[2] As a disciple of Elfod (Elbodugus), Nennius must have lived about 800. His *History*, it may be further noted, was known under his name to the Irish scholar Cormac (831–903).

the kings of the Britons and "was himself their war-leader"
—*ipse dux erat bellorum*—in twelve battles.[1] In the eighth of
these encounters, at the castle of Guinnion, "Arthur bore the
image of the holy Virgin Mary on his shoulders,[2] and the pagans
were put to flight with great slaughter." The ninth battle was
fought at the City of Legions;[3] the twelfth, and last, on Mount
Badon, where "nine hundred and sixty men fell before Arthur's
single onset—*de uno impetu Arthur.*" The prominence given,
even in these brief notices, to Arthur's individual prowess shows
that legend was already busy with his name. The *Marvels
of Britain* gives us nothing but legend; here Arthur is translated altogether into the realm of myth. In the Welsh district
of Buelt,[4] we are told, there is a mound of stones, on the top
of which rests a stone bearing the print of a dog's foot. "It
was when he was hunting the boar Troit that Cabal, the dog of
Arthur the warrior, left this mark upon the stone; and Arthur
afterwards gathered together the heap of stones under that
which bore his dog's footprint, and called it Carn Cabal."
Here we discover an early association of Arthurian fable with
the topography of Britain. Another "Marvel" tells us of a certain stream called "the source of the Amir," which was so
named after "Amir the son of Arthur the warrior," who was
buried near it. The allusion to the hunting of the boar links
Nennius' narrative with what is probably the most primitive
of all the Welsh Arthurian tales, the story of *Kulhwch and Olwen.*[5] In that fantastic fairy-tale the hunting of the *Twrch
Trwyth*, which is Nennius's *porcus Troit*, forms one of the chief
incidents, and the hound Cabal there appears under his Welsh
name of *Cavall*.

The Welsh monk and historian Gildas mentions the battle
of Mount Badon in his *De Excidio et Conquestu Britanniae.*
That battle, according to Gildas, was signalised by "the last,
almost, though not the least, slaughter of our cruel foes, and

---

[1] *Hist. Brit.*, ch. LVI.

[2] Cf. Wordsworth, *Ecclesiastical Sonnets*, I, 10:

> "Amazement runs before the towering casque
> Of Arthur, bearing through the stormy field
> The Virgin sculptured on his Christian shield."

[3] Caerleon, or Caerlleon, upon Usk—a city to which Geoffrey of Monmouth, probably from interested motives, gives great prominence.

[4] Builth (modern Welsh, *Buallt*).

[5] Included in Lady Charlotte Guest's *Mabinogion.*

that was (I am sure) forty-four years and one month after the landing of the Saxons, and also the time of my own nativity." But Gildas makes no allusion at all to Arthur's feats in the battle. Neither does he once mention his name in connection with the general struggle which he describes as being carried on, with varying fortune, against the English. The only leader of the British in that warfare whom Gildas deems worthy of notice is Ambrosius Aurelianus,[1] the last of the Romans, "a modest man, who alone of all his race chanced to survive the shock of so great a storm" as then broke over Britain. The silence of Gildas, who was, presumably, a contemporary of the historical Arthur, would be significant, were it not that he is equally reticent about the achievements of every other native British chieftain. Gildas belonged to the Roman party in the Britain of his time, and to exalt the prowess of any British prince would ill assort with his pious lamentations over the absolute degeneracy of his race.

The battle of Mount Badon, together with another which was destined to overshadow it completely in the later developments of Arthurian story, is recorded, and dated, in *Annales Cambriae*—the oldest extant MS. of which was compiled, probably, in the second half of the tenth century.[2] There, under the year 516, we read: "Battle of Badon, in which Arthur carried the cross of our Lord Jesus Christ on his shoulders, and the Britons were victors." The reference to the carrying of the cross is, of course, an obvious echo of the tradition recorded by Nennius about the image of the Virgin Mary—either, or both, being doubtless the device borne by Arthur on his shield.[3] Of

[1] Ambrosius, transformed by Geoffrey into Aurelius Ambrosius (cf. Tennyson, *Coming of Arthur*, "For first Aurelius lived, and fought and died "), is known in Welsh literature as *Emrys Wledig*. He appears in Nennius as *Embreis Guletic*. *Guletic*, or *Gwledig*, means "over-lord," or "king," and Arthur himself would seem to bear this title in a Welsh poem in *The Book of Taliesin* (No. xv). See Skene, *Four Ancient Books of Wales*, vol. i, p. 227.

[2] The most likely date is 954 or 955. See Phillimore's edition in *Y Cymmrodor*, vol. ix, p. 144.

[3] It is worth noting, as bearing upon the Welsh origin of this tradition, that the old Welsh word for "shield," *iscuit*, would be spelt in exactly the same way as the word for "shoulder." Both Nennius and the writer of the *Annals* appear to have misread it. Geoffrey of Monmouth attempts to put the matter right (*Hist.* ix, ch. iv) in describing Arthur as having "on his shoulders a shield" bearing the Virgin's image; but he, also, confuses Welsh tradition in giving to the shield the name of Arthur's ship, *Priwen* or *Pridwen*.

greater interest is the second entry in the *Annals*. In the year 537 was fought "the battle of Camlan, in which Arthur and Medraut fell." Medraut is the Modred, or Mordred, of romance. The *Annals* tell nothing more about him; but in this bare record lies the germ of the first of the tragic motives of subsequent Arthurian story. Camlan is "the dim, weird battle of the west," where Arthur met "the traitor of his house," and

> at one blow,
> Striking the last stroke with Excalibur,
> Slew him, and, all but slain himself, he fell.

From these meagre notices of the early Latin annalists of Wales we pass to such Arthurian traditions as are found embodied in the songs of the oldest Welsh bards. This, indeed, is a perilous quest, for it is beset with difficult problems of historical and textual criticism upon which scholarship is still far from saying its last word. It may, however, be premised with some confidence that there lived in Wales, in the sixth and seventh centuries, several bards of note, of whom the best known by name are Llywarch Hên, Taliesin and Aneirin. The compositions attributed to these, and other bards of this early period, are found in MSS. the dates of which range from the twelfth to the end of the fourteenth centuries. The oldest of all the MSS. is that known as *The Black Book of Carmarthen*, compiled during the latter part of the twelfth century, the period to which also belongs the oldest known MS. of Welsh prose, that of the Venedotian code of the laws of Wales. *The Book of Aneirin*, which contains the famous *Gododin*, is the next oldest MS., and is probably to be assigned to the thirteenth century. To the thirteenth century, also, belongs *The Book of Taliesin*, while another famous MS., *The Red Book of Hergest*, dates from the end of the fourteenth century. These "four ancient books" [1] constitute, together, our chief available repertory of the early poetry of the Kymry.

Amid much that is undeniably late and spurious, these collections of Welsh poetry contain a good deal that is, in substance, of obviously archaic origin. In many of these poems there is, in words applied by Matthew Arnold to the prose

[1] *The Four Ancient Books of Wales* is the title under which the poems in these MSS. were published, with translations and copious dissertations, by W. F. Skene (Edinburgh, 1868).

Mabinogion, "a *detritus*, as the geologists would say, of something far older"; and their secret is not to be "truly reached
until this *detritus*, instead of being called recent because it is
found in contact with what is recent, is disengaged, and is made
to tell its own story."[1] Nowhere, however, is this *detritus* more
difficult to disengage than in the few poems in which Arthur's
name appears. The most celebrated of these early Welsh bards
know nothing of Arthur. Llywarch Hên and Taliesin never
mention him; to them Urien, lord of Rheged, is by far the most
imposing figure among all the native warriors who fought
against the English. It is Urien with whom "all the bards
of the world find favour," and to whom "they ever sing after
his desire."[2] Neither is Arthur known to Aneirin, who sang
in his *Gododin* the elegy of the Kymric chieftains who met
their doom at Cattraeth. "There are only five poems," writes
Skene,[3] "which mention Arthur at all, and then it is the historical Arthur, the *Gwledig*, to whom the defence of the wall is
entrusted, and who fights the twelve battles in the north and
finally perishes at Camlan." This is not a quite accurate summary of the facts; for these poems, while pointing to the existence of a historical Arthur, embody also a *detritus* of pure
myth.

The most significant, perhaps, of all these references to
Arthur in early Welsh poetry is that already quoted from the
Stanzas of the Graves in *The Black Book of Carmarthen*. The
mystery surrounding his grave at once suggests the existence
of a belief in his return, and William of Malmesbury, as we have
seen, knew, early in the twelfth century, of "ancient songs"
which kept this belief alive. The currency of such a tradition,
not only in Wales, but in Cornwall and Brittany, at the very
beginning of the twelfth century is proved by an account given
by certain monks of Laon of a tumult caused at Bodmin in
the year 1113 by the refusal of one of their number to admit
that Arthur still lived.[4] Another of the *Stanzas of the Graves*
is significant, as containing an allusion both to the battle
of Camlan and to "the latest-left of all" Arthur's knights,
Bedwyr, or Bedivere, who shares with Kai, or Kay, the pre-

[1] *On the Study of Celtic Literature.*
[2] *Book of Taliesin*, XL (Skene, vol. II, p. 186).
[3] *Four Ancient Books of Wales*, vol. I, p. 226.
[4] See Migne, *Patrologia*, 156, col. 983.

eminence among Arthur's followers in the primitive Welsh fragments of Arthurian fable:

> The grave of the son of Osvran is at Camlan,
> After many a slaughter;
> The grave of Bedwyr is on the hill of Tryvan.

Bedwyr and Kai appear together in *Kulhwch and Olwen;* they are there once met with, for example, on the top of Plynlimmon "in the greatest wind that ever was in the world." "Bedwyr," the same story tells us, "never shrank from any enterprise upon which Kai was bound." The pair were united even in their death, for, in Geoffrey's *History*, they perish together in the first great battle with the Romans. Another of Arthur's knights figures as the hero of an entire poem in *The Black Book* —Gereint, the son of Erbin.[1] In this poem Arthur is represented as the leader of a number of warriors, of whom Gereint is the most valiant, fighting at a place called Llongborth:[2]

> At Llongborth saw I of Arthur's
> Brave men hewing with steel,
> (Men of the) emperor, director of toil.
>
> At Llongborth there fell of Gereint's
> Brave men from the borders of Devon,
> And, ere they were slain, they slew.

Here we find Arthur in much the same rôle as that of the *dux bellorum* of Nennius, or the *comes Britanniae*, who held "the place of the *imperator* himself, when Britain ceased to be part of the dominions of Rome."[3]

Arthur, however, appears in a distinctly different character in yet another poem included in *The Black Book*. In *Kulhwch and Olwen*, one of Arthur's chief porters answers to the fearsome name of Glewlwyd Gavaelvawr, or Glewlwyd of the Mighty Grasp. *The Black Book* poem is cast in the form of a dialogue between him and Arthur. Glewlwyd would seem, in the poem, to have a castle of his own, from the gates of which he questions Arthur about himself and his followers. The description given of them by Arthur is noteworthy as

---

[1] *Gereint, the Son of Erbin* is also the title of the Welsh prose romance which corresponds, in its main features, to Chrétien de Troyes's *Erec*.

[2] Supposed by some to be Portsmouth. The Welsh name simply means "ship's port."

[3] Rhys. preface to Dent's edition of *Malory*, p. xxv.

pointing to the existence of an early tradition which made him the head of a sort of military court, and foreshadows, in a rude way, the fellowship of the Round Table. Several of the names found in it connect this curious poem with *Kulhwch and Olwen*. The first, and the doughtiest, of Arthur's champions is "the worthy Kei" (Kai). "Vain were it to boast against Kei in battle," sings the bard; "when from a horn he drank, he drank as much as four men; when he came into battle, he slew as would a hundred; unless it were God's doing, Kei's death would be unachieved."

Arthur recedes still further into the twilight of myth in the only other old Welsh poem where any extended allusion is made to him. The poem in question is found in *The Book of Taliesin*, and is called *Preideu Annwvn*, or the *Harrowings of Hell*. This is just one of those weird mythological poems which are very difficult to interpret, and where, again to quote Matthew Arnold, the author "is pillaging an antiquity of which he does not fully possess the secret." Here Arthur sets out upon various expeditions over perilous seas in his ship *Pridwen;* one of them had as its object the rape of a mysterious cauldron belonging to the king of Hades. "Three freights of *Pridwen*," says the bard, "were they who went out with Arthur; seven alone were they who returned" from Caer Sidi, Caer Rigor and the other wholly unidentified places whither they fared. It is in this poem that the closest parallels of all are found with incidents described in the story of *Kulhwch and Olwen*, and, as a whole, it "evidently deals with expeditions conducted by Arthur by sea to the realms of twilight and darkness." [1] But here the British king is much further removed than in *Kulhwch* from any known country, and appears as a purely mythical hero with supernatural attributes.

The most remarkable fragment—for the tale as we have it is an obvious *torso*—of all the early Welsh literature about Arthur that has come down to us is the prose romance of *Kulhwch and Olwen*. The oldest extant text of it is that of the early fourteenth century MS. known as *The White Book of Rhyderch*,[2] where we find many remarkable archaisms which

[1] Rhys, preface to Dent's *Malory*, p. xxxiv, where the poem's correspondences with *Kulhwch* are pointed out.

[2] In the Peniarth Library. Gwenogvryn Evans has an edition of this MS. in preparation.

have been modernised in the version of *The Red Book of Hergest;* but the original form of the story is assigned, by the most competent authorities, to the tenth century.[1]   It is included in Lady Charlotte Guest's translation of the *Mabinogion;* and, as that translation largely contributed to the fashioning of the most popular presentment of Arthurian romance in modern English poetry, a brief account of the entire series of these Welsh tales may here be appropriately given.   All the tales translated by Lady Guest are taken from *The Red Book of Hergest*, with the exception of *The History of Taliesin.   Taliesin,*[2] in the form we have it, is a compilation of obviously late medieval origin, and it is not found in any MS. of an earlier date than the end of the sixteenth century.   The name *Mabinogion* belongs, strictly speaking, to only four of the twelve stories included in Lady Guest's book.   Each of these four tales is called in Welsh "ceinc y Mabinogi," which means "a branch of the Mabinogi"; and the correct title for the group should be "the four branches of the Mabinogi."   The term *mabinogi* signifies "a tale of youth," or "a tale for the young." The "four branches" are the tales known as *Pwyll, prince of Dyved; Branwen, daughter of Llŷr; Manawydan, son of Llŷr;* and *Math, son of Mathonwy.*   They contain what is probably the most archaic body of Welsh tradition in existence, are largely, if not entirely, mythological in character and suggest many points of analogy with the mythic tales of Ireland.[3] They deal, mainly, with the fortunes of three great families, the children of Dôn, the children of Llŷr and the family of Pwyll.   In these stories, the *Mabinogion* proper, Arthur does not appear at all.

Of the other tales, two—*The Dream of Maxen Wledig* and *Llud and Llevelys*—are brief romantic excursions into the domain of British ancient history, later in date, probably, than Geoffrey's *Historia.*   Arthur does not figure in either.   The remaining five tales, however, are all Arthurian, but form two distinct groups.   In *Kulhwch and Olwen* and *The Dream of Rhonabwy* we have two Arthurian stories of apparently pure

---

[1] Rhys, Dent's *Malory*, p. xxxiv.

[2] Thomas Love Peacock drew most of his matter for *The Misfortunes of Elphin* from this tale.

[3] For a suggestive analysis of the probable origins and mythological significance of the "four branches," see Rhys, *Celtic Folk-lore*, vol. ii.

British origin, in which Arthur is presented in a *milieu* altogether unaffected by the French romances. The second and better known group, consisting of the three tales entitled *The Lady of the Fountain, Geraint, son of Erbin*, and *Peredur, son of Evrawc*, are romances palpably based upon French originals. They correspond, respectively, in their main features, to Chrétien de Troyes's *Le chevalier au lion, Erec* and *Le conte del Graal*.[1]

The *Mabinogion*, as a whole, are the most artistic and delightful expression of the early Celtic genius which we possess. Nowhere else do we come into such close touch with the real "Celtic magic," with the true enchanted land, where "the eternal illusion clothes itself in the most seductive hues."[2] Composed though they were in all probability by a professional literary class, these stories are distinguished by a naïve charm which suggests anything but an artificial literary craftsmanship. The supernatural is treated in them as the most natural thing in the world, and the personages who possess magic gifts are made to move about and speak and behave as perfectly normal human creatures. The simple grace of their narrative, their delicacy and tenderness of sentiment and, above all, their feeling for nature, distinguish these tales altogether from the elaborate productions of the French romantic schools; while in its lucid precision of form, and in its admirable adaptation to the matter with which it deals, no medieval prose surpasses that of the Welsh of the *Mabinogion*. These traits are what make it impossible to regard even the later Welsh Arthurian stories as mere imitations of Chrétien's poems. Their characters and incidents may be, substantially, the same; but the tone, the atmosphere, the entire artistic setting of the Welsh tales are altogether different; and "neither Chrétien nor Marie de France, nor any other French writer of the time, whether in France or England, can for one moment compare with the Welshmen as story-tellers pure and simple."[3]

---

[1] *Le Conte del Graal* is only in part the work of Chrétien.

[2] Renan, *The Poetry of the Celtic Races*. (Trans. Hutchinson.)

[3] A. Nutt, in his edition of Lady C. Guest's *Mabinogion*, p. 352. Cf. Renan: "The charm of the *Mabinogion* principally resides in the amiable serenity of the Celtic mind, neither sad nor gay, ever in suspense between a smile and a tear. We have in them the simple recital of a child, unwitting of any distinction between the noble and the common; there is something of that softly animated world, of that calm and tranquil ideal to which

Kulhwch and Olwen, however, is the only one of these tales
that need detain us here, embodying, as it does, in common
with the Welsh poems already quoted, Arthurian traditions far
transcending in age the appearance of the Arthur of chivalry.
Here, as Matthew Arnold has said in an oft-quoted passage,
the story-teller " is like a peasant building his hut on the site of
Halicarnassus or Ephesus; he builds, but what he builds is
full of materials of which he knows not the history, or knows
by a glimmering tradition merely—stones 'not of this building,'
but of an older architecture, greater, cunninger, more majesti-
cal."   The main theme of the story is the wooing of Olwen, the
daughter of Yspaᵭaden Pen Kawr, by Kulhwch, the son of
Kilyᵭ, and the long series of labours imposed upon the suitor
in order to gain her hand.   Olwen appears to have been well
worth the arduous quest, for " her skin was whiter than the
foam of the wave, and fairer were her hands and her fingers than
the blossoms of the wood anemone amidst the spray of the
meadow fountain," and " four white trefoils sprung up wherever she trod."   Arthur appears, here, not as the ideal British warrior, nor as the hope and future restorer of his race, but
as a fairy king, overcoming uncouth and monstrous enemies
by his own and his followers' magic.   All the same, he is the
lord of what is to the story-teller, in many places, a very de-
terminate realm; for one of the most remarkable features of
Kulhwch and Olwen, as compared with the later Arthurian
tales, is the precision of its topography.   The route of the
boar-hunt, for example—or the hunting of the *Twrch Trwyth*
—may be traced without much difficulty, on our maps.[1]

Even more remarkable, however, than the topographical
detail of the story is the *congeries* of fabulous and fantastic
names grouped in it around the central figure of Arthur.   This
feature, suggesting as it does the Arthurian court of the age of
chivalry, might be taken as evidence of the late redaction of
the tale as we have it, were it not that the story-teller gives
details about most of these strange characters which are evidently drawn from the remnants of some lost saga.   Arthur

Ariosto's stanzas transport us.   The chatter of the later medieval French
and German imitators can give no idea of this charming manner of narration.   The skilful Chrétien de Troyes himself remains in this respect far below the Welsh story-tellers."   *The Poetry of the Celtic Races.*
[1] See Rhys's account of the hunt in *Celtic Folk-lore*, vol. ii, p. 572.

himself is introduced to us in his palace, or hall, called Ehang-wen, and thither Kulhwch comes to crave his help to obtain Olwen; "and this boon I likewise seek," says Kulhwch, "at the hands of thy warriors." These warriors Kulhwch then proceeds to name in seemingly interminable succession. First in the long and weird list come Kai and Bedwyr; others well known to early Welsh tradition include Gwynn and Edern, the sons of Nuđ, Geraint, the son of Erbin, Taliesin, the chief of bards, Manawyđan, the son of Llŷr. But, among the company, there also appear several grotesque figures of whom nothing is known save what the story-teller himself, giving rein, as it would seem, to a deliberately mischievous humour, briefly records. Thus we have, for example, one Sol, who "could stand all day upon one foot"; Gwevyl, the son of Gwestad, who "on the day he was sad, would let one of his lips drop below his waist, while he turned up the other like a cap upon his head"; Clust, the son of Clustveinad, who, "though he were buried seven cubits beneath the earth, would hear the ant fifty miles off rise from her nest in the morning." Even famil-iar Arthurian heroes, like Kai, are dowered with superhuman powers. "Kai had this peculiarity, that his breath lasted nine nights and days under water, and he could exist nine nights and nine days without sleep." "Very subtle was Kai; when it pleased him he could make himself as tall as the highest tree in the forest." We are remote, indeed, in such company as this, from the Knights of the Round Table, but we are not so remote from the fairy world depicted in the "Four Branches of the Mabinogi." The conclusion to which *Kulhwch and Olwen*, and the few poems which mention Arthur, clearly point is that the British king was far better known to early Welsh tradition as a mythic hero than as the champion of the Britons in their wars with the English. There may have been a historical Arthur who was a *comes Britanniae*, or a *dux bellorum*, of the sixth century, and his name, "re-echoed by the topography of the country once under his protection," may have "gathered round it legends of heroes and divinities of a past of indefinite extent."[1] What we do, however, know, is that the Arthur who emerges out of the mists of Celtic tradition at the begin-ning of the twelfth century is an entirely imaginary being, a

---

[1] Rhys, preface to Dent's *Malory* p. xxxvi.

king of fairy-land, undertaking hazardous quests, slaying monsters, visiting the realms of the dead, and having at his call a number of knightly henchmen, notably Kay and Bedivere, who are all but his equals in wizardry and martial prowess. This mythical Arthur—the creation of a primitive imagination altogether unaffected by the sophisticated conceptions of chivalry and of conscious dealers in romantic literary wares— belongs to early Welsh literature alone.

The transformation of the Welsh, or British, Arthur into a romantic hero of European renown was the result of the contact of Norman culture and, as it would seem, Norman diplomacy, with the Celtic races of the west. It was doubtless from Brittany, rather than from Wales, that the Normans derived their first knowledge of the Arthurian stories. Indeed, it is probable that the nameless story-tellers of Brittany fastened upon, and expanded, a number of popular traditions which prefigured the Arthur of romance much more clearly than anything told or written in Wales. The Armorican "Bretons" are probably those whom Wace mentions as "telling many a fable of the Table Round." [1] In Brittany, also, a belief in Arthur's return must long have been current, for Alanus de Insulis records that a denial of it in the second half of the twelfth century would be likely to cost a man his life in the country districts of Brittany. [2] By the middle of the eleventh century the relations between the duchy of Normandy and the Bretons had become particularly close, and the duke of Brittany was one of William the Conqueror's staunchest allies at the time of the invasion of Britain.

It is not, however, to Brittany that the great Latin exploitation of the legend of Arthur, under Norman auspices, belongs, but to a section of Great Britain where the Norman conquerors had, very rapidly, succeeded in establishing intimate relations with the Welsh. By the beginning of the twelfth century the Normans had effected a firm settlement in South Wales. Now, it happens that it was a writer associated, at least by name, with the South Wales border, and claiming the patronage of a princely Norman who held that part of the country in fee, who, most of all, is entitled to be

---

[1] *Roman de Brut*, l. 9994.
[2] *Prophetia Anglicana*, etc. (Frankfort, 1603), Bk. I, p. 17.

called the literary father of Arthurian romance. Robert, earl of Gloucester, and a natural son of Henry I—for there is no evidence in support of the tradition that his mother was the beautiful Nest, the daughter of the Welsh prince Rhys ap Tewdwr—acquired, early in the twelfth century, the lordship of Glamorgan by marriage with Mabel, daughter of Robert Fitz-hamon, conqueror of Glamorgan. Robert, like his father, was a liberal and a diplomatic patron of letters. It was to him that William of Malmesbury, the greatest historian of his time, dedicated his *History*. To him was due the foundation of the abbey of Margam, whose chronicle is a valuable early authority for the history of Wales. On his estates at Torigni was born Robert de Monte, abbot of Mont St. Michel, a chronicler of renown, and a lover and student of Breton legends. Above all, it was under his immediate patronage that Geoffrey of Monmouth compiled his romantic *History of the Kings of Britain*.

Of Geoffrey's personal history we know little. His full name appears to have been, significantly, Geoffrey Arthur. His relentless critic, William of Newburgh, takes "Arthur" to have been a by-name given to him on the score of his Arthurian fabrications; but the truth probably is that Arthur was the name of his father.[1] His connection with Monmouth is obscure; he may have been born in the town, or educated at the priory founded there by the Breton, Wihenoc. He was never, as he is commonly designated, archdeacon of Monmouth, for there was no such archdeaconry in existence. Whether he was by descent a Breton, or a Welshman, we know no more than we do whether the famous "British book," which he professes to have used, was derived from Wales or from Brittany. Neither matter is of much consequence. The "British book" may very well have been an authentic document, since lost, which was placed, as he tells us, at his disposal by his friend Walter, archdeacon of Oxford. Much Welsh and Breton folklore doubtless reached him through monastic channels. Nennius and Bede furnished him with matter which can be clearly traced in his text.[2] There can be little doubt, however, that

---

[1] His name is given as *Gaufridus Arturus* in the list of witnesses to the foundation charter of the abbey of Osney in 1129. See Dugdale, *Monasticon*, VI, p. 251, and Sir F. Madden in *Journal of the Archæological Institute*, 1858, p. 305.

[2] A full, and most suggestive, discussion of the whole subject of Geoffrey's

the main source of the Arthurian portions of his *History* was Geoffrey's own imagination. The floating popular traditions about Arthur, and the few documents which he had to his hand, plainly suggested to him the possibilities of developing a new and striking romantic theme. Geoffrey appears to have gauged the tastes and fancies of the courtly readers of his day with an astuteness worthy of a Defoe. Romance was in demand, and Geoffrey, giving the rein to his faculty for decorative and rhetorical writing, responded to that demand with an address that would have done credit to the most alert of modern novelists. The time-honoured vehicle of the chronicle was turned to new and unexpected uses. Sober and orthodox chroniclers, like William of Malmesbury and Henry of Huntingdon, are deliberately warned off the ground thus opened out for the poet and the romancer. The "kings of the Saxons" were their legitimate subject; the "kings of the Britons" were outside their province, for "the British book" was to them a sealed volume.[1]

Geoffrey's relation to the Latin chroniclers of his time is dealt with in another chapter; here, his contributions to Arthurian story alone claim our attention. The glorification of Arthur in the *History* lends some countenance to the supposition that the work was written with an interested motive. Geoffrey probably aspired, like most of his class, to preferment in the church, and may have hoped that his book would ingratiate him with the earl of Gloucester and with Alexander, bishop of Lincoln, to whom he dedicated, separately, the "*Prophesies of Merlin*." Assuming him to have had such motives, Geoffrey's *History* is interpreted as being a kind of prose epic, intended to celebrate the united glories of the composite Anglo-Norman empire which attained its widest extent under Henry II.[2] It did, indeed, provide a hero in whom Norman and Saxon, Welshman and Breton, could take common pride. Moreover, the ancient birthright and the essential homogeneity of the various races embraced in the

sources is given in *The Arthurian Material in the Chronicles* by R. H. Fletcher (*Harvard Studies in Phil. and Lit.*, vol. x, 1906).

[1] See the epilogue to Geoffrey's *History*.

[2] This hypothesis is advanced with much ingenuity, and plausibility, in the epilogue to what is the best English translation of Geoffrey's *History*, by Sebastian Evans, London, 1903.

Angevin empire were attested by an account of their descent from a branch of the Trojan stock celebrated in the *Aeneid*. Brutus, whose eponymous connection with the country had already been suggested by Nennius, became for Britain what Aeneas was for Rome. Geoffrey's chronicle is thus the first *Brut*, the first elaborate, and possibly "inspired," adaptation of the Brutus legend for the glorification of Britain; and, in time, all records of the early British kings, whether in prose or verse, which had this mythic starting-point, came to be called *Bruts*—presumably in imitation of the title of Vergil's epic.

Apart, however, from its Trojan prelude, and its possible political or diplomatic motive, there is little real analogy between Geoffrey's *Brut* and the *Aeneid*. For Arthur, after all, and not Brutus, is Geoffrey's ultimate hero. The *flos regum* of early Britain, the warrior who vindicates the essential valour of the British people, and who not only triumphs over his insignificant enemies in Britain itself, but conquers a great part of Europe and forces even the once victorious Romans to pay tribute to a British king, is Arthur. In him was fulfilled the prophecy that "for the third time should one of British race be born who should obtain the empire of Rome." Thus, Geoffrey brings all his powers of rhetoric, and all his imagination, to bear upon his delineation of Arthur and his exploits. The first six books of the *History* tell, with many embellishments of style and with incidental references to contemporary events elsewhere, inserted, as so many grave guarantees of authenticity, the story of Arthur's kingly predecessors. At the close of the sixth book the weird figure of Merlin appears on the scene; and Geoffrey pauses to give, in an entire book, the fantastic prophecies attributed to that wonder-working seer. Romance, frank and undisguised, now usurps the place of sober, or affected, history. Merlin's magic arts are made largely contributory to the birth of "the most renowned Arthur." Uther and Gorlois and Igerna and the castle of Tintagol, or Tintagel, now take their place, for the first time, in the fabric of Arthurian story.

Uther, with Merlin's assistance, gains admission to Igerna's castle in the semblance of her lord, Gorlois, and begets Arthur; upon the death of Gorlois, Uther takes Igerna for his lawful queen, and Arthur of due right succeeds to the throne. Crowned by Dubricius, "archbishop of the City of Legions," at the early age of fifteen, Arthur at once begins his career of conquest. The Saxons, Scots and Picts are encountered and vanquished at the river Duglas; afterwards, with the aid of his cousin, king Hoel of Brittany, Arthur subjugates the entire island and divides Scotland among its original rightful rulers, Lot and his two brothers, Urian and Augusel. Lot, we are told by the way, "had, in the days of Aurelius Ambrosius, married Arthur's own sister, who had borne unto him Gawain and Mordred." Having restored the whole country to its ancient dignity, Arthur "took unto himself a wife born of a noble Roman family, Guanhumara, who, brought up and nurtured in the household of duke Cador, surpassed in beauty all the other women of the island." Ireland and Iceland are next added to his conquests, while tribute is paid and homage made to him by the rulers of the Orkneys and of Gothland. His court now is the centre of a brilliant assemblage of knights, his fear "falls upon the kings of realms oversea" and his "heart became so uplifted within him" that "he set his desire upon subduing the whole of Europe unto himself." [1] Norway, Dacia and Gaul fall in quick succession under Arthur's sway; Normandy is made over to "Bedwyr, his butler," and Anjou to "Kay, his seneschal." Returning to Britain, Arthur next holds high court at Caerleon-upon-Usk, then a city whose "kingly palaces" vied in magnificence with those of Rome itself.

At that time was Britain exalted unto so high a pitch of dignity as that it did surpass all other kingdoms in plenty of riches, in luxury of adornment, and in the courteous wit of them that dwelt therein. Whatsoever knight in the land was of renown for his prowess did wear his clothes and his arms all of one same colour. And the dames, no less witty, would apparel them in like manner in a single colour, nor would they deign have the love of any save he had thrice approved him in the wars. Wherefore at that time did dames wax chaste and knights the nobler for their love. [2]

The pomp and colour of the age of chivalry, and its ideals of knightly love, are thus already beginning to qualify imaginative conceptions of the Arthurian court; while the picture of

[1] Bk. IX, ch. XI.
[2] S. Evans's trans. (London, 1903).

Arthur himself, as the head of princely vassals and emulous knights, makes the transition easy to the fellowship of the Round Table, and to all the other accretions of later romances. But Geoffrey does not, any more than the early Welsh poets and story-tellers or the later, and more deliberate, purveyors of fantastic fables, altogether remove his Arthur from wonderland. The British king still slays monsters; by his own hand he kills a Spanish giant at St. Michael's Mount, and a still more formidable foe, the giant "Ritho of Mount Eryri, who had fashioned him a furred cloak of the kings he had slain." Equally marvellous is Arthur's individual might in battle, for, in his encounters with the Romans, "nought might armour avail" his antagonists "but that Caliburn would carve their souls from out them with their blood."

The great battle with the Romans, in which Arthur displayed such prowess, was a fateful one. The British hosts did, indeed, gain the victory; and Hoel and Gawain (Walgainus) performed prodigies of valour second only to those of Arthur himself. But the triumph was obtained at a heavy cost; many illustrious British chieftains, and, above all, the faithful Kay and Bedwyr, were numbered among the slain. The result of the battle was to fire Arthur with the design of marching upon the city of Rome itself. He was already beginning to climb the passes of the Alps, when "message was brought him that his nephew Mordred, unto whom he had committed the charge of Britain, had tyrannously and traitorously set the crown of the kingdom upon his own head, and had linked him in unhallowed union with Guenevere, the queen, in despite of her former marriage."[1] Arthur, taking with him his British warriors only, returns home. Mordred meets him as he lands, and, in the ensuing battle, Gawain and many others are slain. Mordred, however, is driven back, and Guinevere, in terror of her safety, becomes a nun. The final battle is fought at the river Camel in the west country. Mordred is defeated and slain, and most of the leaders on both sides perish. "Even the renowned king Arthur himself was wounded unto death, and was borne thence unto the island of Avalon for the healing of his wounds."

Such, in brief, is the narrative through the medium of

[1] Book x, ch. XIII.

which Arthur made his triumphant entry to the kingship of the most splendid province of medieval romance. Let Geoffrey have the credit which is his due. It is little to the point to seek to minimise his influence upon the rise and growth of Arthurian romance by emphasising his omissions,—that, for example, he knows nothing of Lancelot, of Tristram, of the Holy Grail and of other famous characters and incidents of the fully-developed legend. The salient fact is that, while before the appearance of Geoffrey's *History* Arthur, as a literary hero, is virtually unknown, he becomes, almost immediately afterwards, the centre of the greatest of the romantic cycles. He is, indeed, transformed eventually into a very different being from the warlike British champion of Geoffrey's book; but it is in that book that we obtain our first full-length literary portrait of him, and, in the Mordred and Guinevere episode, that we find the first deliberate suggestion of the love-tragedy which the romancers were so quick to seize upon and to expand. Geoffrey's Arthur is, no doubt, largely a Normanised Arthur, and many of the details and incidents woven into his narrative are derived from his knowledge and observation of Norman manners and Norman pomp[1] ; but his story, as a whole, has, like every vivid product of the imagination, a charm altogether independent of the time and the conditions of its making, and is charged throughout with the seductive magic of romance. Hence the spell which Geoffrey's legends exerted over so many famous English poets, haunted by memories of

> what resounds
> In fable or romance of Uther's son,
> Begirt with British and Armoric knights.

Possibly, no work before the age of printed books attained such immediate and astonishing popularity. To this the number of extant MSS. of the work bears testimony,[2] while translations, adaptations, and continuations of it formed one of the staple exercises of a host of medieval scribes. The sensation created by the book at the time of its first circulation is attested by one of the earliest, if not the earliest of all, writers

[1] See Fletcher, *The Arthurian Material in the Chronicles* (Harvard, 1906), pp. 109 sqq.

[2] The British Museum alone has thirty-five, and the Bodleian sixteen.

who borrowed from it—Alfred of Beverley. In the preface
to his *History*, largely an abridgment of Geoffrey compiled
about 1150, Alfred states that Geoffrey's book was so universally
talked of that to confess ignorance of its stories was the mark
of a clown.

In the epilogue to his *History*, where he bids William of
Malmesbury and Henry of Huntingdon "be silent as to the
kings of the Britons," Geoffrey commits the task of writing
their further history to "Caradoc of Llancarvan, my contemporary." No Latin chronicle bearing Caradoc's name is
known to exist; but certain Welsh compilations, continuing
Geoffrey's narrative down to the year 1156, are, on very
doubtful authority, ascribed to him.[1] Caradoc's authorship
is, however, claimed with more confidence for a work which
embodies a few Arthurian traditions of which Geoffrey seems
to have been ignorant—the Latin *Life of Gildas*. In this
curious production, written either before or shortly after
Geoffrey's death,[2] Arthur is described, first of all, as being
engaged in deadly feud with Hueil, or Huel, king of Scotland
and one of Gildas's twenty-three brothers, whom he finally
kills; he subsequently comes into collision with Melwas, the
wicked king of "the summer country," or Somerset, who had,
unknown to him, abducted his wife, Guenever, and concealed
her in the abbey of Glastonia. Just as the two kings are
about to meet in battle, the monks of Glastonia, accompanied
by Gildas, intervene and succeed in persuading Melwas to restore Guenever to Arthur. This would seem to be the earliest
appearance of the tradition which makes Melwas (the Mel-
lyagraunce of Malory) an abductor of Guinevere. Other
Latin lives of Welsh saints, written not long after the *Life of
Gildas*, record traditions about Arthur which are quite independent of Geoffrey,[3] which would seem to indicate that
Geoffrey's direct borrowings of Arthurian stories from Welsh
sources are comparatively slight.

Popular though it immediately became elsewhere, Geoffrey's

---

[1] See the English translation published in 1584 by David Powell.

[2] According to a competent authority, about 1160 (F. Lot in *Romania*,
XXIV, 330). The MS. (at Corpus Christi College, Cambridge) is of the
twelfth century.

[3] See, for example, the *Life of St. Carannog* and the *Life of St. Cadoc* in Rees's
Cambro-British Saints (1853).

History, it is strange to find, seems to have aroused little interest in Wales. An important Welsh translation of it,[1] which was, at one time, supposed to have been its "British" original, was, indeed, made at an early date, but the medieval Welsh bards remained altogether indifferent to Arthurian story. The second great period of Welsh bardic activity extends from the twelfth century down to the death of Prince Llywelyn ap Gruffud in 1282; but we look in vain among the works of the crowd of bards who flourished at this period for any celebration of Arthur and his deeds. There is no Welsh metrical romance, or epic, of Arthur. The medieval bards sing, in preference, of living warriors or of those lately dead, well knowing that such encomiastic poetry brought its ready rewards. It is to her prose story-tellers that Wales owes her one incomparable contribution to Arthurian romance in the native tongue.

The full value of the Arthurian stories as poetic and romantic matter and, in particular, their possibilities of adaptation and expansion as ideal tales of chivalry, were first perceived in France, or, at any rate, by writers who used the French language. Three stages, or forms, in the literary exploitation to which the legends were subjected by French romantic writers, can be clearly traced. First comes the metrical chronicle, in which Geoffrey's quasi-historical narrative appears in an expanded and highly-coloured romantic setting, and of which Wace's *Brut* is the earliest standard example. This was the literary form in which the Arthurian legend made its first appearance in English. Next in order and not much later, perhaps, in their actual origin, come the metrical romances proper. These poetical romances, of which the works of Chrétien de Troyes are at once the typical, and the most successful, examples, are concerned with the careers and achievements of individual knights of the Arthurian court. In them, Arthur himself plays quite

---

[1] *Ystorya Brenhined y Brytanyeit* in *The Red Book of Hergest* (edd. Rhys and Gwenogvryn Evans, Oxford, 1890). Another Welsh chronicle, also at one time supposed to have been Geoffrey's original, is Tysilio's *Brut*, printed in the *Myvyrian Archæology of Wales* as "from *The Red Book of Hergest*." No such chronicle, however, appears in *The Red Book*. Tysilio is supposed to have lived in the seventh century; the chronicle ascribed to him is not found in any MS. earlier than the fifteenth.

a subordinate part; his wars and the complications that led to his tragic end are altogether lost sight of. The third stage is represented by the prose romances, which began to be compiled, probably, during the closing years of the twelfth century, and which underwent a continuous process of expansion, interpolation and redaction until about the middle of the thirteenth century. Many of these prose romances, such as those of *Merlin* and *Lancelot*, give much greater prominence than the poems do to Arthur's individual deeds and fortunes. The most celebrated name associated with the authorship of these prose works is that of Walter Map, who, calling, as he does, the Welsh his "fellow-countrymen," [1] brings Wales and the Angevin court, once more, into touch with the development of the Arthurian legend.

The Norman clerk, Wace, was the first French writer who turned Geoffrey of Monmouth's fabulous chronicle to profitable poetical uses. Geoffrey Gaimar, an Anglo-Norman writer who lived in the north of England, had, probably, anticipated Wace's design; [2] but no copy of Gaimar's translation has been preserved. Wace's poem was completed in 1155, and, according to Layamon, [3] was dedicated to queen Eleanor, the wife of Henry II—another fact which indicates the interest taken by the Anglo-Norman court in the literary exploitation and the dissemination of British legends. Wace was a courtly writer, and in his narrative Arthur appears as the flower of chivalry, the ideal knightly warrior of the Norman imagination. Although his poem is based, in substance, entirely on Geoffrey's *History*, Wace is far from being a mere servile translator of Geoffrey. He dresses up Geoffrey's matter with a wealth of picturesque detail and of colour all his own. Moreover, he seems to have had access to romantic traditions, or stories, quite unknown to Geoffrey. The Round Table, for example, is first heard of in Wace—and of it, as he says, "the Bretons tell many a fable." It was made by Arthur in order to settle all disputes about precedence among his

---

[1] *De Nugis Curialium*, Dist. ii, ch. xx.

[2] Gaimar had probably completed his work by 1150. His lost *History of the Britons* formed a prelude to his *L'Estorie des Engles*, which has been preserved (ed. Hardy and Martin, *Rolls Series*, 1888–9).

[3] Layamon states that Wace "gave" his book to "the noble Eleanor, who was the high king Henry's queen," *Brut*, ll. 42, 43.

knights. [1] Wace also amplifies Geoffrey's account of the passing of Arthur. The British king is not merely left in Avalon "to be cured of his wounds"; he is still there, the Bretons await him, and say that he will come back and live again. [2] Wace's poem, as a whole, thus represents an intermediate stage between the chronicles and the pure romances. It must have contributed powerfully to the popularity of "the matter of Britain," by putting it into a form and a language which commanded a much larger constituency of readers than would be attracted by any Latin prose narrative, however highly coloured or agreeably written.

Above all, Wace's *Brut* is of signal interest to English readers as forming the basis of the solitary contribution of any consequence made by an English writer to the vast and varied mass of Arthurian literature before the fourteenth century. Layamon, however, is a very different poet from Wace. While not indifferent to romance, as several significant additions to the Arthurian part of his story will show, Layamon wrote his *Brut* as a frankly patriotic English epic. Wace's work is almost as artificial and exotic a product as the poetical romances; it was designed as a contribution to the polite literature of the Norman aristocracy. Layamon, dwelling in seclusion on the banks of the Severn, where "it was good to be," was fired by an ambition "to tell the noble deeds of England," and to tell them in the English tongue. His poem is the first articulate utterance of the native English genius reasserting itself in its own language after the long silence which succeeded the Conquest. Although he borrows most of his matter from Wace, Layamon, in manner and spirit, is much nearer akin to the robust singers of the Old English period than to the courtly French poet. The simple force and vividness of the primitive English epic reappear in descriptions of battle scenes and of heroic deeds. Even the poet's diction is scrupulously pure English. And Arthur, who, in the hands of the professional romancers, had already become all but an alien to his fatherland, is restored to his rightful place as the champion of Britain, and the great Christian king who

> Drew all the petty princedoms under him,
> Their king and head, and made a realm, and reign'd.

[1] Ll. 9994–10,007.   [2] L. 13,685.

Arthur, therefore, was to Layamon, primarily, the ideal British hero—an actual king of England, whose character and prowess deserved the veneration of his countrymen altogether apart from the glamour with which romance had enshrouded his name. But Layamon was a poet; and upon him, as upon the rest, the romantic glamour works its inevitable spell. Elfland claims Arthur, both at his birth and at his death. Elves received him into the world; they gave him gifts, to become the best of knights and a mighty king, to have long life and to be generous above all living men.[1] At his passing, Arthur says he will go to Argante (Morgan *le fay*), the splendid elf; she will heal him of his wounds, so that he will return again to his kingdom.[2] Again, Arthur's byrnie was made for him by Wygar, the elvish smith,[3] his spear by Griffin of the city of the wizard Merlin (Kaermerðin).[4] Caliburn, his sword, was wrought in Avalon with magic craft;[5] the Round Table by a strange carpenter from beyond the sea.[6] Nowhere, however, does Layamon's poem breathe more of the spirit of pure romance than in the passages which describe Arthur's last battle and fall. The encounter took place at Camelford (Camlan) "a name that will last for ever."[7] The stream hard by, "was flooded with blood unmeasured." So thick was the throng that the warriors could not distinguish each other,[8] but "each slew downright, were he swain, were he knight." Modred and all his knights perished and "there were slain all the brave ones, Arthur's warriors, high and low, and all the Britons of Arthur's board." Of all the two hundred thousand men who fought none remained, at the end of the fight, save Arthur and two of his knights. But Arthur was sorely wounded, and, bidding the young Constantine, Cador's son, take charge of his kingdom, he consigns himself to the care of Argante, "the fairest of all maidens," who dwells in Avalon. Thence, cured of his wounds, he will come again to "dwell with the Britons with mickle joy."

Even with the words there came from the sea a short boat

---

[1] Ll.19, 254 sqq. (Madden's ed.).　　[2] Ll. 28,610 sqq.　　[3] L. 21,133.
[4] L. 23,783.　　　[5] L. 21, 135.　　　[6] L. 22,910.　　　[7] Ll. 28,533 sqq.
[8] Cf. Tennyson, *Passing of Arthur:*
　　　"For friend and foe were shadows in the mist,
　　　And friend slew friend not knowing whom he slew."

borne on the waves, and two women therein, wondrously arrayed: and they took Arthur anon, and bare him quickly, and softly laid him down, and fared forth away. Then was brought to pass that which Merlin whilom said, that there should be sorrow untold at Arthur's forth-faring. The Britons believe yet that he is alive, and dwelleth in Avalon, with the fairest of all elves, and ever yet the Britons look for Arthur's coming. Was never the man born, nor ever of woman chosen, that knoweth the sooth, to say more of Arthur. But whilom there was a seer hight Merlin; he said with words—and his sayings were sooth—that an Arthur should yet come to help the Britons.

In this passage, as in many others, Layamon supplies several details not found in Wace, and his poem throughout bears abundant evidence that he drew upon a fund of independent traditions gleaned from many fields. Among the most interesting of Layamon's additions to, and amplifications of, Wace's narrative are his accounts of Arthur's dream shortly before his last return to Britain, and of the origin and the making of the Round Table. The dream,[1] of which neither Geoffrey nor Wace knows anything, foreshadows the treachery of Modred and Guinevere, and disturbs Arthur with the sense of impending doom. The occasion of the institution of the Round Table is, as in Wace, a quarrel for precedence among Arthur's knights; but the description of the actual making, and of the properties, of the Table is all Layamon's own. It was while he was in Cornwall, after the quarrel among his knights, that Arthur met the man from oversea who offered to "make him a board, wondrous fair, at which sixteen hundred men and more might sit."[2] Its huge size notwithstanding, and though it took four weeks to make, the board could, by some magic means, be carried by Arthur as he rode, and set by him in what place soever he willed. Like Wace, Layamon evidently knew stories about the Round Table of which the origin has never been traced; for "this was that same table" he says, "of which the Britons boast"—the Britons, who tell "many leasings" of king Arthur, and say of him things "that never happened in the kingdom of this world."[3] So it would appear that Layamon, had he pleased, could have told us much more of Arthur. Even as it stands, however,

---

[1] See ll. 28,020 sqq.   [2] See ll. 22,910 sqq.   [3] L. 22,987.

his poem is a notable contribution to Arthurian story, and has the unique distinction of being the first celebration of "the matter of Britain" in the English tongue.

When we pass from the metrical chronicles to the pure romances, both verse and prose, we all but part with the traditional British Arthur altogether. Not only are we suddenly transported into the "no man's land" of chivalry, but we find ourselves surrounded by strange apparitions from regions Geoffrey and his translators never knew. In the romances, the Arthurian court serves but as a convenient rendezvous for a

> moving row
> Of magic shadow-shapes that come and go

in quest of adventures which bear little or no relation to the British king. Characters, of whom the chroniclers tell us nothing, and who were themselves the heroes of quite independent legends, now make a dramatic entry upon the Arthurian stage. Tristram and Lancelot and Perceval play parts which divert our attention quite away from that assigned to Arthur himself. Thus, a complete history of Arthurian romance involves a series of enquiries into the growth of a number of legends which have, for the most part, only the most artificial connection with the original Arthurian tradition. Some of these legends are as archaic, and as purely mythical, as the primitive fables about the British Arthur, and were probably current in popular lays long before the latter half of the twelfth century. A full account of the romances in which they were embodied and enriched during the age of chivalry belongs to the history of French and German, rather than to that of English, literature. Not until the fourteenth century do we come across a single English writer whose name is to be mentioned in the same breath with those of Chrétien de Troyes and the authors of the French prose romances, or of Wolfram von Eschenbach, Gottfried von Strassburg and Hartmann von Aue. Here, only the briefest review can be attempted of the main features of the subsidiary legends which were imported, by these and other writers, into the vast Arthurian miscellany.

Of all such legends, the most intimately connected with Arthur himself is the story of Merlin. In Welsh tradition, Merlin, or Myrđin, is a figure very similar to Taliesin—a wizard bard of the sixth century, to whom a number of spurious poetical compositions came, in course of time, to be ascribed. His first association with Arthur is due to Geoffrey of Monmouth, who identifies him with the Ambrosius of Nennius and makes of him both a magician and a prophet; to his magic arts, as we have seen, the birth of Arthur was largely due. His character is further developed in a Latin hexameter poem, *Vita Merlini*, composed, probably, about the year 1148 and attributed by several competent authorities to Geoffrey. This poem, however, presents us with a conception of the mage which is not easy to reconcile with the account given of him in Geoffrey's *History*, and suggests many points of analogy with certain early Welsh poems in which Merlin figures, and with which Geoffrey could hardly have been acquainted.[1] Merlin makes his first appearance in French romantic poetry in a poem of which only a fragment has been preserved, supposed to be by Robert de Borron, and dating from the end of the twelfth century. Upon this poem was based the French prose romance of *Merlin*, part of which is assigned to Robert de Borron, and which exists in two forms—the first known as the "ordinary" *Merlin*, and the other as the *Suite de Merlin*. For Robert de Borron the enchanter's arts are but so many manifestations of the powers of darkness; Merlin himself becomes the devil's offspring and most active agent. From the *Suite de Merlin*, of which Malory's first four books are an abridged version, was derived one of the minor offshoots of Arthurian romance, the striking story of Balin and Balan. The earliest romance of Merlin in English is the metrical *Arthour and Merlin*, translated from a French original at the beginning of the fourteenth century. This work, however, is not so well known as the great prose *Merlin*, a translation from the French made about the middle of the fifteenth century.

No knight of the primitive Arthurian fellowship enjoyed a higher renown than Arthur's nephew, Gawain. Under the name of Gwalchmei, Gawain figures prominently in the Welsh

[1] These resemblances are pointed out in what is the fullest account of the Merlin saga in English, *Outlines of the History of the Legend of Merlin*, by W. E. Mead (Part IV of H. B. Wheatley's edition of the prose *Merlin* in the E.E.T.S. series.)

Triads and in the *Mabinogion*; while as Walgainus he is one
of Arthur's most faithful and doughty lieutenants in the
wars recounted by Geoffrey. So great was the traditional
fame of Gawain that William of Malmesbury thought it worth
while to record the discovery of his grave in Pembrokeshire;
and there is some evidence that his name was well known
even in Italy by the beginning of the twelfth century.[1] He
was, probably, the centre of a cycle of adventures quite independent of, and quite as old as, the original Arthur saga. He
is certainly the hero of more episodic romances than any
other British knight,[2] and, in the general body of Arthurian
romance, none is so ubiquitous. In Chrétien de Troyes's *Conte
del Graal*, and in Wolfram von Eschenbach's *Parzival*, Gawain
is almost as important a personage as Perceval himself. In
the German poem *Diu Krône*, by Heinrich von dem Türlin, he,
and not Perceval, is the actual achiever of the Grail quest.
It is curious, however, to note that no other knight undergoes
so marked a transformation of character in his progress through
the romances. In the *Mabinogion*, and the earlier stages
of the legend generally, Gawain appears as the paragon of
knightly courtesy—the gentleman, *par excellence*, of the
Arthurian court. In some of the later romances, particularly
in the more elaborate versions of the Grail legend, as in Malory
and Tennyson,

> A reckless and irreverent knight is he.[3]

Before Malory's time, however, Gawain is uniformly presented
in English literature in a flattering light, and no Arthurian
hero was more popular with English writers.[4] The finest
of all Middle English metrical romances, *Sir Gawayne and
the Grene Knight*, dealing with incidents derived, apparently,
from a primitive form of the Gawain legend, portrays him in
his original character as a model of chivalry and of all the
knightly graces.

In the full-orbed Arthurian cycle the most dramatic feature

[1] Zimmer, *Göttingische Gelehrte Anzeigen*, 1890, No. 20, p. 831.

[2] Gaston Paris gives summaries of a number of these in *Histoire Littéraire
de la France*, vol. xxx.

[3] Tennyson, *The Holy Grail*, 852.

[4] See the *Sir Gawayne* romances, ed. Madden, Bannatyne Club (London,
1839).

of the story which centres around the fortunes of Arthur himself is the love of Lancelot for Guinevere. The story of Lancelot is a comparatively late, and, to all appearance, a non-Celtic,
graft upon the original Arthurian stock. Whether, as some
surmise, its motive was originally suggested by the Tristram
legend or not, it remains as an obvious embodiment of the
French ideal of *amour courtois*, and is thus the most significant
example of the direct influence of the conceptions of chivalry
upon the development of Arthurian story. Lancelot first
appears as the lover of Guinevere in Chrétien's *Chevalier de la
Charrette*, a poem written at the instance of Marie of Cham-
pagne, who took a lively interest in the elaboration of the
theory and practice of "courtly love." Hence it came about
that, as Chaucer tells us, women held "in ful gret reverence
the boke of Lancelot de Lake."[1] The book to which Chaucer,
like Dante in the famous passage about Paolo and Francesca,
refers is, doubtless, the great prose romance of *Lancelot*,
traditionally associated with the name of Walter Map. The
Lancelot is a vast compilation, of which there are three clear
divisions—the first usually called the *Lancelot* proper, the
second the *Quest of the Holy Grail* and the third the *Morte
Arthur*.[2] In the MSS. these romances are persistently attributed to Walter Map; one version of the *Quest* is described as
having been written by him "for the love of his lord, king
Henry, who caused it to be translated from Latin into French."
A passage in Hue de Rotelande's poem, *Ipomedon*, following
the description of a tournament which bears some resemblance
to incidents recorded in *Lancelot*, has been taken to furnish
additional evidence of Map's authorship.[3] The main difficulty
about assigning these romances to Map is that of reconciling
the composition of works of such size with his known activity
as a courtier and a public man. Nor, apart from one or two
fairy-stories included in it, does what may be called his common-place book, *De Nugis Curialium*, afford any indication of
the life-long interest which Arthurian romance must have had

[1] *Nonne Prestes Tale*, 392

[2] See Ward, *Catalogue of Romances in the British Museum* (vol. I, pp. 345
sqq.), for an account of some of the MSS.

[3] See *ante*, Chapter x, p. 211. For a full discussion of the problems suggested
by this passage, see Ward, *Catalogue of Romances in B. M.* (vol. I, p. 734) and
Miss J. L. Weston's *The Three Days' Tournament* (Nutt, 1902).

for one capable of so imposing a contribution to its literature as the great prose *Lancelot*.

The ascription to Walter Map of the prose *Quest of the Holy Grail* links his name with the most intricate branch of Arthurian romance. The Grail saga, in its various ramifications and extensions, is the most difficult to interpret, and to account for historically, of all the constituent elements of the "matter of Britain." None, at any rate, affords a better illustration of the way in which that matter came to be "subdued to what they worked in" by a particular group of romantic hands. Just as the ideals of courtly chivalry shape and colour the story of Lancelot, so do the ascetic proclivities of a monastic cult assert themselves in the gradual unfolding of the legend of the Holy Grail. The original hero of the Grail quest appears to have been Gawain; but he is soon displaced by the central figure of the existing versions of the story, Perceval. Perceval, in his turn, is superseded by one who "exemplifies, in a yet more uncompromising, yet more inhuman, spirit, the ideal of militant asceticism,"[1] Lancelot's son, Galahad. The earlier versions of the legend, however, know nothing of Galahad, nor is there any reason for assuming that the primitive forms of the story had any religious motive. In the Grail literature which has come down to us, two distinct *strata* of legend, which are, apparently, independent of each other in their origin, are to be clearly traced. They are distinguished as the "Quest" proper, and the "Early History of the Holy Grail."[2] The best-known versions of the "Quest" are the *Conte del Graal*, of which the earlier portions are by Chrétien de Troyes, the *Parzival* of Wolfram von Eschenbach and the Welsh *Mabinogi* of Peredur. Of the "Early History" the chief versions are the *Joseph of Arimathea* and *Merlin* of Robert de Borron, and the *Quête del St. Graal* attributed to Map.[3] In the "Quest" forms of the legend the interest turns mainly upon the personality of the hero, Percival, and upon his

[1] A. Nutt, *The Legends of the Holy Grail* (Popular Studies in Mythology, Romance and Folklore, 1902), p. 72.

[2] This is the classification made by Alfred Nutt, our chief English authority on the Grail legends.

[3] Other versions of the Grail legend are those known as the *Grand St. Graal*, the *Didot Perceval* and *Perceval le Gallois*. The latter, a thirteenth century prose romance, has been excellently translated by Sebastian Evans under the name of *The High History of the Holy Grail*.

adventures in search of certain talismans, which include a sword, a bleeding lance and a "grail" (either a magic vessel, as in Chrétien, or a stone, as in Wolfram). The "Early History" versions dwell, chiefly, upon the nature and origin of these talismans. The search for the talismans is, in the "Quest" stories, connected with the healing of an injured kinsman, and with the avenging of the wrong done to him. In the fifteenth century English metrical romance of *Sir Percyvelle*, the vengeance of a son upon his father's slayers is the sole argument of the story.

The Grail cycle, in its fully developed form, would thus seem to comprise stories of mythical and pagan origin, together with later accretions due entirely to the invention of romancers with a deliberately ecclesiastical bias. The palpably mythical character of the earlier "Quest" versions points to their being of more archaic origin than the "Early History" documents, and they are almost certainly to be traced to Celtic sources. "The texture, the colouring, the essential conception of the older Grail Quest stories can be paralleled from early Celtic mythic romance, and from no other contemporary European literature."[1] These tales, however, proved susceptible of being used, in the late twelfth and early thirteenth centuries, for religious purposes; thus, the Grail came to be identified with the cup of the Last Supper, which Pilate gave to Joseph of Arimathea, and in which Joseph treasured the blood that flowed from Christ's wounds on the Cross. The cup was brought by Joseph to Britain, and its story is thus connected with an old legend which attributed to Joseph the conversion of Britain to Christianity. The traditions concerning this evangelisation of Britain appear to have been especially preserved in documents kept at the abbey of Glastonbury; and Glastonbury, associated as it was even with Avalon itself, came, as we know, to have a significant connection with Arthurian lore by the end of the twelfth century. The glorification of Britain manifestly intended by this particular use of the Grail legend suggests, once again, the interest taken by the Angevin court in the diplomatic possibilities of adroit literary manipulation of the Arthurian traditions. And if, indeed, Henry II can be proved to have

[1] Nutt, *Legends of the Holy Grail*, p. 59.

had anything to do with it at all, an argument of some plausibility is established in support of the MS. record that the courtier Walter Map did, "for the love of his lord, king Henry," translate from Latin into French *The Quest of the Holy Grail.*

There remains one other famous legend to be noticed, which has attached itself to the Arthurian group, and which in its origin and character is the most distinctively Celtic of them all. The story of Tristram and Iseult is the most purely poetical, and probably the oldest, of the subsidiary Arthurian tales. Above all its scene, its character and its *motif* mark it out as the one undoubted and unchallenged property of "the Celtic fringe." Ireland and Wales, Cornwall and Brittany, all claim a share in it. Tristram appears, under the name of Drystan son of Tallwch, as a purely mythical hero in a very old Welsh triad, which represents him as the nephew, and swineherd, of Mark—March ab Meirchion—protecting his master's swine against Arthur's attempt to get at them.[1] Mark, in the earliest poetical versions of the tale, is king of Cornwall. Iseult, the primal heroine, is a daughter of Ireland, while the other Iseult, she of the White Hands, is a princess of Brittany. The entire story breathes the very atmosphere, and reflects the dim, mysterious half-lights, of the western islands beaten by the grey, inhospitable sea—the sea, which, in the finest rendering of the legend in English poetry, keeps up a haunting choral accompaniment to Iseult's anguish-stricken cries at Tintagel, when

> all their past came wailing in the wind,
> And all their future thundered in the sea.[2]

Coloured by scarcely any trace of Christian sentiment, and only faintly touched, as compared with the story of Lancelot, by the artificial conventions of chivalry, the legend of Tristram bears every mark of a remote pagan, and Celtic, origin. Neither in classical, nor in Teutonic, saga is there anything really comparable with the elemental and overmastering passion which makes the story of Tristram and Iseult, in tragic interest

---

[1] See Rhys, *The Arthurian Legend*, p. 13, where it is said of March, or Mark, that he was "according to legends, both Brythonic and Irish, an unmistakable prince of darkness."

[2] Swinburne, *Tristram of Lyonesse.*

and pathos, second to none of the great love-tales of the world.

The Tristram legend was preserved, in all probability, in many detached lays before it came to be embodied in any extant poem. The earliest known poetical versions of the story are those of the Anglo-Normans, Béroul (c. 1150) and Thomas (c. 1170), of which we possess only fragments, and which were the foundations, respectively, of the German poems of Eilhart von Oberge and of Gottfried von Strassburg. A lost *Tristan* poem is also ascribed to Chrétien de Troyes, and is supposed by some to have been used by the writer, or writers,[1] of the long prose *Tristan*, upon which Malory largely drew. As it passed through the hands of these writers, the Tristram story, like the rest, was subjected to the inevitable process of chivalric decoration; but it has managed to preserve better than the others its bold primitive characteristics. Its original existence in the form of scattered popular lays is, to some extent, attested by one of the poems of Marie of France—*Le Chèvrefeuille* (The Honeysuckle)—recording a pretty stratagem of Tristan during his exile from King Mark's court, whereby he succeeded in obtaining a stolen interview with Iseult. Nor was it the Tristram legend alone that was thus preserved in popular lays from a period anterior to that of the great romantic efflorescence of Arthurian story. Many isolated poems dealing with characters and incidents subsequently drawn into the Arthurian medley must have been based upon traditions popularised by the rude art of some obscure minstrels, or story-tellers, "Breton" or other. One of the best known examples of such poems is Marie of France's lay of *Lanval*, a Celtic fairy-tale quite unconnected, originally, with the Arthurian court. Even more ambitious works, such as the *Chevalier au Lion*, or *Yvain*, and the *Erec*, of Chrétien, were almost certainly founded upon poems, or popular tales, of which the primitive versions have been irretrievably lost. For the Welsh prose romances of *The Lady of the Fountain* and of *Geraint*—the heroes of which, Owein and Geraint, correspond respectively to Chrétien's Yvain and Erec—while resembling the French poems in their main incidents, cannot be satisfactorily accounted for except on the supposition that the

---

[1] The names, almost certainly fictitious, of Luces de Gast and of Hélie de Borron are associated with the authorship of the prose *Tristan*.

stories embodied in them originally existed in a much older and simpler form than that in which they are presented by Chrétien.

In this necessarily cursory review of an extensive and complicated subject, a good deal has been claimed for Celtic sources and Celtic influence; and it may not be out of place to conclude with an attempt to summarise, very briefly the actual debt of English literature to the early literature of the Celtic peoples. Upon few subjects has there been, in our time, so much vague and random writing as upon so-called Celtic "traits" and "notes" in English imaginative literature. Renan and Matthew Arnold, in two famous essays, which in their time rendered a real service to letters by calling attention to the buried literary treasures of Wales and Ireland, set a fashion of speculating and theorising about "the Celt" as perilous as it is fascinating. For, after all, no critical method is more capable of abuse than the process of aesthetic literary analysis which seeks to distinguish the Celtic from the other ingredients in the genius of the greater English writers, and which sounds Shakespeare, or Byron, or Keats for the Celtic "note." While there is no difficulty about admitting that the authentic literature of the Celts reveals a "sentiment," a "natural magic," a "turn for style," and even a "Pindarism" and a "Titanism," [1] which are all its own, it is a very different matter to assign a Celtic source to the supposed equivalents of these things in later English poetry. An example of the peculiar dangers besetting such speculations is furnished by Matthew Arnold's own observations about Macpherson and the Celtic "melancholy." The Ossianic poems, whatever their original Gaelic sources may have been, reflect far more of the dour melancholy peculiar to the middle eighteenth century than of anything really characteristic of the primitive Celtic temperament. Matthew Arnold is, indeed, able to parallel the laments over the desolation of the halls of Balclutha and so on, with extracts from the old Welsh poet Llywarch Hên. But even Llywarch's anguish as he contemplates the vanished glories of the hall of Kyndylan is by no means peculiar

[1] These are some of Matthew Arnold's "notes" of the Celtic genius in *The Study of Celtic Literature.*

to the Celt.   The same melancholy vein is found in the early
poetry of other races; it appears in the Old English poems
of *The Seafarer* and *The Wanderer*, and even in the ancient
poetry of the east, for

> They say the Lion and the Lizard keep
> The Courts where Jamshyd gloried and drank deep,
>   And Bahrám, that great Hunter—the Wild Ass
> Stamps o'er his Head but cannot break his Sleep.

The direct influence of Celtic literature upon that of England amounts, on any strict computation, to very little.   And
this is only natural when we remember that the two languages
in which the chief monuments of that literature are preserved
—Welsh and Irish—present difficulties which only a few very
intrepid English linguists have had the courage and the
patience to surmount.   Thus it happens, for example, that the
greatest of all the medieval Welsh poets—Davyđ ap Gwilym,
a contemporary of Chaucer—is only known to English readers
by fragmentary notices, and indifferent translations, supplied
by George Borrow.   A few tantalising, and freely translated,
scraps—for they are nothing more—from the Welsh bards are
due to Gray; while Thomas Love Peacock has treated, in
his own peculiar vein of sardonic humour, themes borrowed
from ancient Welsh poetry and tradition.   Above all, there remains the singularly graceful translation of the Welsh *Mabinogion* by Lady Charlotte Guest.   The literature of Ireland
has, at a quite recent date, been much better served by translators than that of Wales, and several admirable English
versions of Irish poems and prose tales are making their
influence felt upon the literature of the day.   So far, however,
as the older Celtic literature is concerned, it is not so much
its form that has told to any appreciable extent upon English
writers as its themes and its spirit.   The main channel of this
undoubted Celtic influence was that afforded by the Arthurian
and its kindred legends.   The popularity of the "matter of
Britain" came about at a time when there was, comparatively,
much more intimate literary commerce between the European
nations than there is now.   The Normans succeeded in bringing
Britain and France at least into much closer contact than has
ever existed between them since; and it was France that

controlled the literary destinies of Europe during the great romantic period of the twelfth and thirteenth centuries. It would be rash to endeavour to apportion between the south of France and the northern "Celtic fringe" their respective contributions to all that is denoted by the ideals of chivalry. But, in the mist which still overhangs the subject, we do seem to discern with fair distinctness that it was the conjunction of these apparently diverse racial tendencies, directed by the diplomatic genius of the Normans, that gave us our vast and picturesque body of Arthurian romance. Through all the various strains of Arthurian story we hear

> the horns of Elfland faintly blowing;

and it is quite possible that, to the Celtic wonderland, with its fables of "the little people," we owe much of the fairy-lore which has, through Shakespeare and other poets of lower degree, enriched the literature of England. Chaucer, at any rate, seemed to have very little doubt about it, for he links all that he knew, or cared to know, about the Arthurian stories with his recollections of the fairy world:

> In th' olde dayes of the king Arthour,
> Of which that Britons speken greet honour,
> Al was this land fulfild of fayerye:
> The elf-queen, with hir joly companye
> Daunced ful ofte in many a grene mede.

So let us believe, with the poets, and leave the British Arthur in his unquestioned place as the supreme king of fairy-land.

CHAPTER XIII

Metrical Romances, 1200-1500

I

Men speke of romances of prys,
Of Horn child and of Ypotys,
Of Bevis and sir Gy,
Of sir Libeux and Pleyn-damour;
But sir Thopas, he bereth the flour
Of royal chivalry.

Sir Thopas.

IT is hard to understand the process of change that made so much difference between Old and Middle English story-telling. At first, one is inclined to account for it by the Norman conquest, and, no doubt, that is one of the factors; the degradation of the English and their language naturally led to a more popular and vulgar sort of narrative literature. *Beowulf* was composed for persons of quality, *Havelok* for the common people. Old English narrative poetry was, in its day, the best obtainable; English metrical romances were known by the authors, vendors and consumers of them to be inferior to the best, *i.e.* to the French; and, consequently, there is a rustic, uncourtly air about them. Their demeanour is often lumbering, and they are sometimes conscious of it. The English look to the French for instruction in good manners and in the kinds of literature that belong properly to a court. In the old times before the Conquest they had the older courtliness which was their own, and which is represented in the Old English epic remains, *Beowulf*, *Waldhere* and other poems.

But it will not do to regard the Conquest as a full and complete explanation of the difference, because the same kind

of change is found in other Teutonic countries, where there
was no political conquest. In Denmark and Sweden and
Germany and the Netherlands there are to be found rhyming
romances of the same sort as the English, written about the
same time. In Germany, it is true, the romantic school of
the early thirteenth century is much more refined than anything in England before the days of Chaucer and Gower; but
besides the narrative work of the great German poets of that
time there are many riming tales that may very well be compared with English popular romances; while in Denmark and
Sweden there is a still closer likeness to England. There the
riming narrative work is not a bit more regular or courtly
than in England; there is the same kind of easy, shambling
verse, the same sort of bad spelling, the same want of literary
standard. But in those countries there was no Norman conquest; so that it will not do to make the political condition of
the English accountable for the manners of their popular
literature. The Norman conquest helped, no doubt, in the
depression of English literature, but like things happened in
other countries without a foreign conqueror. Just as all the
Teutonic languages (except that of Iceland) pass from the
Old to the Middle stage, so in literature there is a parallel movement in Germany, England, and Denmark from an earlier to
a later medieval type. In all the Teutonic countries, though
not at the same time in all, there was a change of taste and
fashion which abandoned old epic themes and native forms
of verse for new subjects and for riming measures. This
meant a great disturbance and confusion of literary principles
and traditions; hence, much of the new literature was experimental and undisciplined. It took long for the nations to
find a literary standard. The Germans attained it about 1200;
the English in the time of Chaucer; the Danes and Swedes not
until long after the close of the Middle Ages. The progress from
Old to Middle English narrative verse is not to be understood
from a consideration of England alone; it is part of a general
change in European fashions, a new mixture of Teutonic and
Roman elements, not to speak of Celtic and oriental strains
in the blending.

In the history of English narrative poetry there is a great
gap of two centuries between *The Battle of Maldon* and Laya-

mon's *Brut*, with very little to fill it or even to show what sort
of things have been lost, what varieties of story-telling amused
the English in the reign of Harold Godwinsson or of Henry
I. In France, on the other hand, these centuries are rich
in story books still extant; and, as the English metrical romances depend very largely upon the French, the history of
them may to some extent be explained from French history;
though often more by way of contrast than of resemblance.

In France, the twelfth century witnessed a very remarkable change of taste in stories which spread over all Europe
and affected the English, the Germans, and other peoples in
different ways. The old national epics, the *chansons de geste*,
were displaced by a new romantic school, which triumphed
over the old like a young Olympian dynasty over Saturn and
his peers, or like the new comedy of the restoration over the
last Elizabethans. The *Chansons de geste* were meant for
the hall, for Homeric recitation after supper; the new romances were intended to be read in my lady's bower; they
were for summer leisure and daylight, as in the pretty scene
described by Chrétien de Troyes in his *Chevalier au Lion*, and
translated into English:

> Thurgh the hal sir Ywain gase
> Intil ane orcherd, playn pase;
> His maiden with him ledes he:
> He fand a knyght, under a tre,
> Opon a clath of gold he lay;
> Byfor him sat a ful fayr may;
> A lady sat with tham in fere.
> The mayden red, at thai myght here,
> A real romance in that piace,
> But I ne wote of wham it was;
> Sho was but fiftene yeres alde.
> The knyght was lorde of al that halde,
> And that mayden was his ayre;
> She was both gracious gode and fayre.[1]

These French romances were dedicated to noble ladies, and
represented everything that was most refined and elegant in
the life of the twelfth century. Furthermore, like other late
romantic schools, like Scott and Victor Hugo, authors travelled

[1] *Ywain and Gawain*, ll. 3081 sqq.

wide for their subjects. The old French poet's well-known division of stories according to the three "matters"—the "matter of France," the "matter of Britain" and the "matter of Rome the great"[1]—very imperfectly sums up the riches and the variety of French romantic themes, even when it is understood that the "matter of Rome" includes the whole of antiquity, the tales of Thebes and Troy, the wars of Alexander. It is true that (as in later romantic schools) the variety of scene and costume does not always prevent monotony. The romantic hero may be a knight of king Arthur's court, may take his name from Protesilaus or Palaemon or Archytas; the scene in one story may be Logres or Lyonesse, in another Greece or Calabria; it does not really make much difference. So Mrs. Radcliffe's heroes, or Victor Hugo's, are of the same sort, whether their scene be in the Pyrenees or in Italy. But, nevertheless, the freedom of wandering over the world in search of plots and characters was exhilarating and inspiriting in the twelfth century in France; there was great industry in fiction, a stirring literary competition. The following ages very largely lived on the products of it, to satisfy their own wants in the way of romance.

The leaders of this school, Benoit de Ste. More and Chrétien de Troyes, with their followers, were courtly persons, authors of fashionable novels, bent on putting into their work the spirit and all the graces of gentle conversation as it was then understood, more particularly the refinements of amatory sentiment, such as was allegorised in the next century in *The Romaunt of the Rose*. This sort of thing could not be equally appreciated or appropriated in all countries. Some people understood it, others could not. The great houses of Germany were very quick to learn from French masters and to rival them in their own line. Hartmann von Aue translated Chrétien freely—the romance of Enid, the tale of Yvain. Wolfram von Eschenbach in his *Parzival* may borrow the substance, but the rendering, the spirit, is his own, removed far from any danger of comparison with the French school, because it has a different kind of nobility. In England things were

---

[1] *Ne sont que trois matières à nul home attendant,*
De France et de Bretaigne et de Rome la grant.
Jean Bodel, *Chanson de Saisnes.*

otherwise, and it was not till the age of Chaucer and Gower that there was any English narrative work of the finer sort with the right courtly good manners and a proper interest in sentimental themes. The English of the thirteenth and fourteenth centuries were generally unable to make much of the "finer shades" in their French authors. They can dispose of romantic plots and adventures, they are never tired of stories; but they have difficulty in following the eloquent monologues of passionate damsels; the elegant French phrasing annoying them just as one of the later French successors of Chrétien, the heroic romance of *Le Grand Cyrus*, affected Major Bellenden. Even the more ambitious of the English romances generally fall far short of the French and cannot keep up with their elaborate play of rhetoric and emotion. There is only one English version of a romance by Chrétien, *Ywain and Gawain*. This is comparatively late; it belongs to the time of Chaucer; it is not rude; on the contrary, it is one of the most accomplished of all the riming tales outside the work of Chaucer and Gower. But it cuts short the long speeches of the original. Chrétien's *Yvain* (*Le Chevalier au Lion*) has 6818 lines; the English version 4032. Hartmann, on the other hand, spins his story out to 8166 lines, being thoroughly possessed with admiration of the French ways of thinking. The English romances of *Ipomedon* (there are two in rime, besides a prose version) show well the difficulties and discrepancies as will be explained later.

William of Palerne is an example of a different sort, showing how hard it was for the English, even as late as the middle of the fourteenth century, to understand and translate the work of the French romantic school. The English poet takes up the French *Guillaume de Palerme*, a sophisticated, sentimental story written in the fluent, unemphatic, clear style which perhaps only Gower could rightly reproduce in English. This is turned into alliterative verse, with rather strange results, the rhetoric of the English school being utterly different from the French: quaint in diction, inclined to be violent and extravagant, very effective in satirical passages (as *Piers Plowman* was to show) or in battle scenes (as in the *Morte Arthure*), but not well adapted for polite and conventional literature. The alliterative poets were justified when they took their own way and did not try to compete with the French. Their greatest work in romance is *Sir Gawayne and the Grene Knight*, written by a man who understood his busness and produced new effects, original, imaginative, without trying to copy the manner of the French artists.

At the same time, while the great, the overruling, French influence is to be found in the ambitious literary work of Chrétien de Troyes and his peers, it must not be forgotten that there was also a simpler but still graceful kind of French romance with which the English translators had more success. This is best represented in the work of Marie de France; and, in English, by the shorter romances which profess to be taken from Breton lays, such as *Launfal, Orfeo* and the *Lai le Freine*. Here, the scale is smaller, and there is no superabundance of monologue and sentimental digression. The clear lines of the original could be followed by the English without too much difficulty; for the English, though long inferior to the French in subtlety, were not bunglers, except when they ventured on unfamiliar ground without the proper education.

Briefly and roughly, the history of the English romances might be put in this way: About the year 1200 French literature came to dominate the whole of Christendom, especially in the matter of stories; not only sending abroad the French tales of Charlemagne and Roland, but importing plots, scenery and so forth, from many lands, Wales and Britanny, Greece and the further east, and giving new French forms to them, which were admired and, as far as possible, borrowed by foreign nations, according to their several tastes and abilities. The English took a large share in this trade. Generally speaking, their taste was easily satisfied. What they wanted was adventures: slaughter of Saracens, fights with dragons and giants, rightful heirs getting their own again, innocent princesses championed against their felon adversaries. Such commodities were purveyed by popular authors, who adapted from the French what suited them and left out the things in which the French authors were most interested, viz. the ornamental passages. The English romance writers worked for common minstrels and their audiences, and were not particular about their style. They used, as a rule, either short couplets or some variety of that simple stanza which is better known to most readers from *Sir Thopas* than from *Horn Childe* or *Sir Libeaus*. *Sir Thopas* illustrates and summarises, in parody, all the ways of the popular romance for a long time before Chaucer and for long after his death. Of course there are many differences in particular cases, and *Sir Thopas*, with all his virtue, does not so far outshine the others as to make them indistinguishable. *Beves* is not exactly the same kind of thing as *Sir Guy*, and the story of *Sir Libeaus* has merits of its own not to be confounded with those of the other heroes. Nevertheless, they are all of one kind, and their style is popular and hackneyed. The authors were well enough pleased to have it so; they did not attempt to rival their eminent French masters.

But there were exceptions. One finds ambition at work in English poets even in days when French literature might have appeared so strong and so exalted as to dishearten any mere English competitor. The English *Sir Tristrem* is a specimen of literary vanity; the English author is determined to improve upon his original, and turns the simple verse of his French book into rather elaborate lyrical stanzas. And, again, it was sometimes possible for an Englishman to write gracefully enough without conceit or emphasis; as in *Ywain and Gawain*, already quoted. And the alliterative romances are in a class by themselves.

Chaucer and Gower disturb the progress of the popular romance, yet not so much as one might expect. Chaucer and Gower, each in his own way, had challenged the French on their own ground; they had written English verse which might be approved by French standards; they had given to English verse the peculiar French qualities of ease and grace and urbanity. A reader to whom the fifteenth century was unknown would, naturally, look for some such consequences as followed in the reign of Charles II from the work of Dryden and his contemporaries—a disabling of the older schools, and a complete revolution in taste. But, for whatever reason, this was not what actually followed the age of Chaucer. The fifteenth century, except for the fact that the anarchy of dialects is reduced to some order, is as far from any literary good government as the age before Chaucer. It is rather worse, indeed, on account of the weaker brethren in the Chaucerian school who only add to the confusion. And the popular romances go on very much as before, down to the sixteenth century, and even further. The lay of the last minstrel is described by Sir Walter Scott, in prose, in a note to *Sir Tristrem:*

Some traces of this custom remained in Scotland till of late years. A satire on the Marquis of Argyle, published about the time of his death, is said to be composed to the tune of Graysteel, a noted romance reprinted at Aberdeen so late as the beginning of the last century. Within the memory of man, an old person used to perambulate the streets of Edinburgh singing, in a monotonous cadence, the tale of Rosewal and Lilian, which is, in all the forms, a metrical romance of chivalry.

It is possible to classify the romances according to their sources and their subjects, though, as has been already remarked, the difference of scenery does not always make much difference in the character of the stories. The English varieties depend so closely on the French that one must go to French literary history for guidance. The whole subject has been so clearly summarised and explained in the *French Medieval Literature* of Gaston Paris [1] that it is scarcely necessary here to repeat even the general facts. But of course, although the subjects are the same, the English point of view is different; especially in the following respects:

The "matter of France" includes the subjects of the old French epics. These, being national, could not bear exportation so well as some of the other "matters." It is only in France that the *Song of Roland* can be thoroughly understood and valued. Yet Roland and Charlemagne were honoured beyond the Alps and beyond the sea. The *Karlamagnus Saga* is a large book written in Norway in the thirteenth century, bringing together in a prose version all the chief stories of the cycle. One section, *Olif and Landres*, was found "in the English tongue in Scotland" by a Norwegian envoy who went there in 1284 after the death of king Alexander III. Roland was almost as popular in Italy as in France. He appears also in English, though not to very great advantage. The favourite story from the French epics was that of Oliver

---

[1] *La Littérature française au moyen âge* (with bibliography); also *Esquisse historique de la litt. fr. au moyen âge*; English translation of this latter, Dent. 1903.

and Fierabras, where the motive is not so much French patriot-·
ism as the opposition between Christian and infidel.

In the "matter of Britain" the English had a better right
to share. They accepted at once the history of Geoffrey of
Monmouth and made king Arthur into an English national
hero, the British counterpart of Charlemagne. The alliterative
Morte Arthure, derived from Geoffrey, is a kind of political
epic, with allusions to contemporary history and the wars of
Edward III, as George Neilson has sufficiently proved.[1] This
touch of allegory which one need not be afraid to compare
with the purpose of the *Aeneid* or of *The Faerie Queene*, makes
it unlike most other medieval romances; the pretence of
solidity and historical truth in Geoffrey is not suitable for
mere romantic purposes. Quite different is the Arthur who
sits waiting for adventures, being "somewhat child-geared,"
as the poet of *Sir Gawayne* says. In most of the stories Arthur
is very unlike the great imperial monarch and conqueror
as presented by Geoffrey and his followers. He has nothing
particular to do, except to be present at the beginning and
end of the story; the hero is Sir Perceval, Sir Ywain, Sir Gawain,
or the Fair Knight Unknown (Sir Libeaus); unfortunately
not Sir Erec (Geraint) in any extant English poem before
Tennyson. In this second order, the proper Arthurian romances as distinguished from the versions or adaptations of
Geoffrey, England had something to claim even before the
English rimers began their work; for some of the French poems
certainly, and probably many now lost, were written in
England. This is a debatable and difficult part of literary
history; but, at any rate, it is plain that the more elaborate
French Arthurian romances were not the only authorities
for the English tales. Chrétien's *Yvain* in translated into
English; but the French romance of *The Fair Unknown* is
probably not the original of the English story of *Sir Libeaus*,
which, like the old Italian version, would seem to have had
a simpler and earlier form to work upon. Likewise, the English *Sir Percevall* must, surely, come from something older
and less complicated than Chrétien's *Conte del Graal*. It is
at least a fair conjecture that these two romances belong to an
earlier type, such as may have been hawked about in England

---

[1] *Huchown of the Awle Ryale*, Glasgow, 1902, pp. 59–66.

by French or French-speaking minstrels; and, without any
conjecture at all, they are different in their plots (not merely
in their style) from the French work of Renaud de Beaujeu
in the one case, and Chrétien de Troyes in the other. *Sir
Gawayne and the Grene Knight*, again, cannot be referred to
any known French book for its original; and, in this and other
ways, the English rendering of the "matter of Britain" goes
beyond the French, or, to be more precise, is found to differ
from the existing French documents.

The "matter of Rome the great," that is, classical antiquity,
is well represented in English. There are several poems in
rime and alliterative verse on Alexander and on Troy, some
of them being fragmentary. The tale of Thebes, though often
referred to, does not appear fully told till Lydgate took it up,
nor the romantic version of the *Aeneid* (*Roman d'Énéas*) before
Caxton's prose.

The classification under the three "matters" of France,
Britain and Rome is not exhaustive; there are many romances
which fall outside these limits. Some of them are due to
French invention; for the twelfth century romantic school was
not content always to follow merely traditional fables; they
drew largely on older stories, fairy tales and relics of mythology;
but, sometimes, they tried to be original and at least succeeded
in making fresh combinations, like a modern novelist with his
professional machinery. Perhaps the English poet of *Sir
Gawayne* may have worked in this way, not founding his poem
upon any one particular romance, but taking incidents from
older stories and arranging them to suit his purpose. In
French, the *Ipomedon* of Hue de Rotelande is an excellent
specimen of what may be called the secondary order of romance, as cultivated by the best practitioners. The author's
method is not hard to understand. He is competing with
the recognised and successful artists; with Chrétien de Troyes.
He does not trouble himself to find a Breton lay, but (like
an Elizabethan dramatist with no Spanish or Italian novel at
hand) sets himself to spin his own yarn. He has all the proper
sentiments, and his rhetoric and rimes are easy work for him.
For theme, he takes the proud young lady and the devoted
lover; the true love beginning "in her absence," as the Irish
story-teller expressed it, before he has ever seen the princess;

telling of his faithful service in disguise, his apparent slackness in chivalry, his real prowess when he "bears the gree" in three days of tournament, with three several suits of armour, the white, the red and the black. The incidents are not exactly new; but it is a good novel of its kind, and successful, as the English versions prove, for longer than one season. Hue de Rotelande takes some trouble about his details. He does not (like Chrétien in his *Cligès*) attach his invention to the court of Arthur. He leaves Britain for new ground, and puts his scene in Apulia and Calabria—which might as well have been Illyria or Bohemia. And he does not imitate the names of the Round Table; his names are Greek, his hero is Hippomedon. In the same way Boccaccio, or his lost French original, took Greek names for his story of Palamon, and let it grow out of the wars of Thebes. So also Parthenopex de Blois, who was translated into English (*Partonope*), is Parthenopaeus. *William of Palerne*, without his classical prestige of name, is another example of the invented love-story, made by re-arranging the favourite commonplaces. Another sentimental romance, *Amadas and Ydoine*, was well known in England, as is proved by many allusions, though no English version is extant; the poem was first composed, like *Ipomedon*, in Anglo-French.[1]

Further, there were many sources besides Britain and Rome for authors in want of a plot. The far east began very early to tell upon western imaginations, not only through the marvels of Alexander in India, but in many and various separate stories. One of the best of these, and one of the first, as it happens, in the list of English romances is *Flores and Blancheflour*. It was ages before *The Arabian Nights* were known, but this is just such a story as may be found there, with likenesses also to the common form of the Greek romances, the adventures of the two young lovers cruelly separated. By a curious process it was turned, in the *Filocolo* of Boccaccio, to a shape like that of Greek romance, though without any direct knowledge of Greek authors. *The Seven Sages of Rome* may count among the romances; it is an oriental group of stories in a setting, like *The Arabian Nights*—a pattern followed in the *Decameron*, in *Confessio Amantis* and in *The Canterbury Tales*.

[1] Gaston Paris in *An English Miscellany*, Oxford, 1906, p. 386.

Barlaam and Josaphat is the story of the Buddha, and *Robert of Sicily*, the " proud king," has been traced back to a similar origin. *Ypotis* (rather oddly placed along with Horn and the others in *Sir Thopas*) is Epictetus; the story is hardly a romance, it is more like a legend. But the difference between romance and legend is not always very deep; and one is reminded that Greek and eastern romantic plots and ideas had come into England long before, in the Old English *Saints' Lives*.

There is another group, represented, indeed, in French, but not in the same way as the others. It contains *The Gest of King Horn* and *The Lay of Havelok the Dane*; both of these appear in French, but it is improbable that any French version was the origin of the English. These are northern stories; in the case of *Havelok* there is fair historical proof that the foundation of the whole story lies in the adventures of Anlaf Cuaran, who fought at Brunanburh; " Havelok," like "Aulay," being a Celtic corruption of the Scandinavian Anlaf or Olaf.

In *Horn* it is not so easy to find a definite historical beginning; it has been suggested that the original Horn was Horm, a Danish viking of the ninth century who fought for the Irish king Cearbhall, as Horn helped King Thurston in Ireland against the Payns, *i.e.* the heathen invaders with their giant champion. Also it is believed that Thurston, in the romance, may be derived from the Norwegian leader Thorstein the Red, who married a granddaughter of Cearbhall. But, whatever the obscure truth may be, the general fact is not doubtful that Horn's wanderings and adventures are placed in scenery and conditions resembling those of the ninth and tenth centuries in the relations between Britain and Ireland. Like *Havelok*, the story probably comes from the Scandinavian settlers in England; like *Havelok*, it passed to the French, but the French versions are not the sources of the English. There must have been other such native stories; there is still an Anglo-Norman poem of *Waldef* extant, *i.e. Waltheof*, and the story of *Hereward the Wake* is known, like that of *Waltheof* also, from a Latin prose tale. The short tale of *Athelston* may be mentioned here, and also the amazing long romance of *Richard*

Cœur de Lion, which is not greatly troubled with the cares of the historian.

The varieties of style in the English romances are very great, under an apparent monotony and poverty of type. Between *Sir Beves of Hamtoun* and *Sir Gawayne and the Grene Knight* there is as wide an interval as between (let us say)" Monk" Lewis and Scott, or G. P. R. James and Thackeray. There are many different motives in the French books from which most of the English tales are borrowed, and there are many different ways of borrowing.

As regards verse, there are the two great orders, riming and blank alliterative. Of riming measures the most usual are the short couplet of octosyllabic lines and the stanza called *rime couée, rithmus caudatus*.

King Horn is singular in its verse, an example of one stage in the development of modern English metres. It is closely related in prosody to Layamon's *Brut*, and might be described as carrying through consistently the riming couplet, which Layamon interchanges with blank lines. The verse is not governed by the octosyllabic law; it is not of Latin origin; it has a strange resemblance to the verse of Otfried in Old High German and to the accidental riming passages in Old English, especially in the more decrepit Old English verse:

> Thanne him spac the godĕ king:
> Wel bruc thu thi nevening;
> Horn thu go wel schüllè
> Bi dalĕs and bi hüllè;
> Horn thu ludĕ sunè
> Bi dalĕs and bi dunè;
> So schal thi namĕ springè
> Fram kyngè to kyngè,
> And thi fairnessè
> Abutĕ Westernessè,
> The strengthe of thine hondè
> In to evrech londè.[1]

There is no other romance in this antique sort of verse. In the ordinary couplets just such differences may be found as in modern usage of the same measure. *Havelok* and *Orfeo*, *King Alisaunder* and *Ywain* have not exactly the same effect.

[1] Ll. 205 sqq.

Havelok, though sometimes a little rough, is not unsound; the poem of *Ywain and Gawain* is nearly as correct as Chaucer; *The Squire of Low Degree* is one of the pleasantest and most fluent examples of this verse in English. There is a pause at the end of every line, and the effect is like that of some ballads:

> The squyer her hente in armes two,
> And kyssed her an hundreth tymes and mo.
> There was myrth and melody,
> With harpe, gytron and sautry,
> With rote, ribible and clokarde,
> With pypes, organs and bombarde,
> With other mynstrelles them amonge,
> With sytolphe and with sautry songe,
> With fydle, recorde and dowcemere,
> With trompette and with claryon clere,
> With dulcet pipes of many cordes,
> In chambre revelyng all the lordes,
> Unto morne that it was daye.[1]

Besides the short couplet different types of common metre are used; very vigorously, with full rimes, in *Sir Ferumbras*—

Now bygynt a strong batayl betwene this knyghtes twayne,
Ayther gan other hard assayle bothe wyth myght and mayne;
They hewe togadre wyth swerdes dent, faste with bothen hondes,
Of helmes and sheldes that fyr outwent, so sparkes doth of brondes:[2]

and without the internal rime, in *The Tale of Gamelyn*, the verse of which has been so rightly praised.[3]

Sir Thopas might be taken as the standard of the *rithmus caudatus*, but *Sir Thopas* itself shows that variations are admitted and there are several kinds besides, which Chaucer does not introduce.

In later usage this stanza is merely twofold, as in Drayton's *Nymphidia* or in *The Baby's Début*. In early days it was commonly fourfold, *i.e.* there are four *caudae* with the same rime:

> And so it fell upon a daye
> The palmare went to the wode to playe,
> His mirthes for to mene;

[1] Ll. 1067 sqq.   [2] Ll. 602 sqq.
[3] Saintsbury, *English Prosody*, i, p. 195.

> The knightes brake up his chamber dore
> And fand the gold right in the flore
>   And bare it unto the quene;
> And als sone als scho saw it with sighte,
> In swoning than fell that swete wighte
>   For scho had are it sene!
> Scho kissed it and said, "Allas!
> This gold aughte Sir Isambras,
>   My lord was wont to bene." [1]

Sometimes there are three lines together before each *cauda*, as in *Sir Perceval* and *Sir Degrevant* and others:

> Lef, lythes to me
> Two wordes or thre
> Off one that was fair and fre,
>   And felle in his fighte;
> His righte name was Percyvelle,
> He was fosterde in the felle,
> He dranke water of the welle,
>   And yitte was he wyghte!
> His fadir was a noble mane
> Fro the tyme that he begane;
> Miche worchippe he wane
>   When he was made knyghte;
> In Kyng Arthures haulle,
> Beste by-luffede of alle,
> Percyvelle they gane hym calle,
>   Who so redis ryghte.

While as this example shows, there are different lengths of line, they are not all in eights and sixes. *Sir Libeaus*, particularly, makes very pretty play with a kind of short metre and a peculiar sequence of the rimes:

> That maide knelde in halle
> Before the knightes alle
>   And seide: My lord Arthour!
> A cas ther is befalle,
> Worse withinne walle
>   Was never non of dolour!
> My lady of Sinadoune
> Is brought in strong prisoun
>   That was of greet valour;

---

[1] *Sir Isumbras*, ll. 641 sqq.

> Sche praith the sende her a knight
> With harte good and light
>   To winne her with honour,[1]

The *cauda* is usually of six syllables, but there is a variety
with four, found in part of *Sir Beves*:

> That erl is hors began to stride
> His scheld he hang upon is side
>   Gert with swerd;
> Moste non armur on him come
> Himself was boute the ferthe some
>   Toward that ferd.
>
> Allas that he nadde be war
> Of is fomen that weren thar
>   Him forte schende;
> With tresoun worth he ther islawe
> And i-brought of is lif-daw
>   Er he hom wende.[2]

The *rime couée* is a lyrical stanza, and there are other
lyrical forms. One of the romances of *Octavian* is in the old
Provençal and old French measure which, by roundabout
ways, came to Scotland, and was used in the seventeenth
century in honour of Habbie Simson, the piper of Kilbarchan,
and, thereafter, by Allan Ramsay, Fergusson and Burns, not
to speak of later poets.

> The knyght was glad to skape so,
> As every man is from hys foo;
> The mayster lette ten men and moo
>   That ylke day,
> To wende and selle that chyld hem fro
>   And that palfray.[3]

The riming *Mort Arthur* is in a favourite eight-line stanza.
Sir Tristrem, in most ways exceptional, uses a lyrical stave,
like one of those in the collection of Laurence Minot, and
very unlike anything that was permissible in the French
schools of narrative at that time. It may be remembered,
however, that the Italian romances of the fourteenth century
and later used a form of verse that, at first, was lyrical, the

---

[1] Ll. 145 sqq.   [2] Ll. 199 sqq.   [3] Ll. 379 sqq.

ottava rima; there are other affinities in Italian and English popular literature, as compared with the French, common qualities which it would be interesting to study further. [1]

The French originals of these English romances are almost universally in short couplets, the ordinary verse for all subjects, after the *chansons de geste* had grown old-fashioned. [2] On the whole, and considering how well understood the short couplet was in England even in the thirteenth century, *e.g.* in *The Owl and Nightingale*, it is rather surprising that there should be such a large discrepancy between the French and the English forms. There are many anomalies; thus, the fuller version of *Ipomedon*, by a man who really dealt fairly and made a brave effort to get the French spirit into English rime, is in *rime couée*; while the shorter *Ipomedon*, scamped work by some poor hack of a minstrel, is in the regular French couplet. It should be noted here that *rime couée* is later than couplets, though the couplets last better, finally coming to the front again and winning easily in *Confessio Amantis* and in *The Romaunt of the Rose*. There are many examples of rewriting: tales in couplets are rewritten in stanzas; *Sir Beves*, in the earlier part, is one, *Sir Launfal* is another. *Horn Childe* is in the *Thopas* verse; it is the same story as *King Horn*, though with other sources, and different names and incidents.

In later times, the octosyllabic verse recovers its place, and, though new forms are employed at the close of the Middle Ages, such as rime royal (*e.g.* in *Generydes*) and the heroic couplet (in *Clariodus* and Sir Gilbert Hay's *Alexander*), still, for simple popular use, the short verse is the most convenient, as is proved by the chap-book romances, *Sir Eger* and *Roswall and Lilian*—also, one may say, Sir David Lyndsay's *Squire Meldrum*. The curious riming alliterative verse of the *Awntyrs of Arthure* and *Rauf Coilyear* lasts well in Scotland; but it had never been thoroughly established as a narrative measure, and, though it is one of the forms recognised and exemplified in King James VI's *Art of Poesie*, its

---

[1] Gaston Paris, *opp. citt.*

[2] There are exceptions; thus the French—or Anglo-Norman—*Beves* is in an epic measure; and, of course, some of the English romances are borrowed from French epics, like *Roland*, and *Sir Ferumbras*, and the alliterative poem of the Swan-Knight (*Chevelere Assigne*) which, though romantic enough in subject, belongs technically, in the original French, to the cycle of Godfrey of Bouillon.

"tumbling verse" is there regarded as most fit for "flytings," which was indeed its usual function in the end of its days.

Alliterative blank verse came up in the middle of the fourteenth century and was chiefly used for romance, *Piers Plowman* being the only considerable long poem to be compared in weight with *The Troy Book* or *The Wars of Alexander*, though there are others of less compass which are still remarkable enough. Where the verse came from is not known clearly to anyone and can only be guessed. The facts are that, whereas the old verse begins to show many signs of decay before the Conquest, and reappears after the Conquest in very battered shapes, in Layamon and *The Bestiary* and *The Proverbs of Alfred*, the new order, of which *William of Palerne* is the earliest, has clearly ascertained some of the main principles of the ancient Teutonic line, and adheres to them without any excessive difficulty. The verse of these alliterative romances and of Langland, and of all the rest down to Dunbar and the author of *Scotish Feilde*, is regular, with rules of its own; not wholly the same as those of old English epic, but partly so, and never at all like the helpless medley of Layamon. It must have been hidden away somewhere underground—continuing in a purer tradition than happens to have found its way into extant manuscripts—till, at last, there is a striking revival in the reign of Edward III. There are some hints and indications in the meantime. Giraldus the untiring, the untamed, with his quick wit and his lively interest in all manner of things, has a note comparing the Welsh and the English love of alliteration—as he compares the part-singing of Wales with that of the north country. He gives English examples:

> Good is togedere gamen and wisdom,

a regular line, like those of the fourteenth century and unlike the practice of Layamon. Plainly, many things went on besides what is recorded in the surviving manuscripts. At any rate, the result in the fourteenth century alliterative poems is a noble one.

The plots of the romances are, like the style of them, not so monotonous as at first appears. They are not all incoherent, and incoherence is not found exclusively in the minstrels' tales; there are faults of composition in some of Chaucer's

stories (*e.g. The Man of Law's Tale*), as manifest as those which
he satirised in *Sir Thopas*. A great many of the romances are
little better than hackneyed repetitions, made by an easy
kaleidoscopic shuffling of a few simple elements. Perhaps
Sir Beves is the best example of the ordinary popular tale,
the medieval book of chivalry with all the right things in it.
It might have been produced in the same way as *The Knight
of the Burning Pestle*, by allowing the audience to prescribe
what was required. The hero's father is murdered, like
Hamlet's; the hero is disinherited, like Horn; he is wooed by
a fair Paynim princess; he carries a treacherous letter, like
Hamlet again, "and beareth with him his own death"; he
is separated from his wife and children, like St. Eustace or
Sir Isumbras; and exiled, like Huon of Bordeaux, for causing
the death of the king's son. The horse Arundel is like Bayard
in *The Four Sons of Aymon*, and the giant Ascapart is won
over like Ferumbras.[1] In the French original there was one
conspicuous defect—no dragon. But the dragon is supplied,
most liberally and with great success, in the English version.
It makes one think of a good puppet-show; for example, the
play of *Don Gayferos*, which drew Don Quixote into a passion.
"Stay, your worship, and consider that those Moors which
your worship is routing and slaying are not real Moors, but
pasteboard!" Saracens are cheap in the old romances; King
Horn rode out one day and bagged a hundred to his own
sword. Yet there are differences; in *Sir Ferumbras*, which
is no very ambitious poem, but a story which has shared with
Sir Beves and *Sir Guy* the favour of simple audiences for many
generations, there is another kind of fighting, because it comes
from the Old French epic school, which gives full particulars
of every combat, on the same scale as the *Iliad*. So far, the
work is more solid than in *Sir Beves*. There are worse things,
however, than the puppet-show of chivalry. The story of
Guy of Warwick, for instance, is something of a trial for the
most reckless and most "Gothic" reader; instead of the
brightly coloured figures of Sir Beves or King Horn and their
adversaries, there is a doleful, stale religion in it, a most

---

[1] A resemblance has been traced between *Sir Beves* and some things in
Firdusi. The east had its books of chivalry like the west, and nearly at the
same time. Cf. Deutschbein, *Englische Sagengeschichte*.

trashy mixture of asceticism (like the legend of St. Alexius),
with the most hackneyed adventures. Not that commonplace
adventures need be dull; sometimes even an increased acquaintance with parallels and variants and so forth may
heighten the interest; as when Horn returns in disguise and
sits down in the "beggars' row." It is natural to think of
the beggars at the foot of the hall in the *Odyssey*; there is the
same kind of scene in an Irish popular tale (*Blaiman* [1]), where
a recognition takes place like that of King Horn. In comparing them, one seems to get, not, indeed, any clear theory
of the way in which the ideas of stories are carried about the
world, but a pleasant sense of the community of stories, so to
speak, and of the relation between stories and real life, in
different ages and places.

Traditional plots like those of the fairy tales appear in medieval romances; not often enough, one is inclined to say, and not
always with any distinct superiority of the literary to the popular
oral version. One example is *Sir Amadas*, which is the story
of the grateful ghost, the travelling companion, *The Old Wives'
Tale*. This story, one of the best known in all languages,
has a strange power to keep its elements free of contamination.
It is found in many mixed forms, it is true, but some of the
latest folklore versions are distinct and coherent. There is
an Irish version (*Beauty of the World*, given by Larminie in
Gaelic and English) which, when compared with *Sir Amadas*,
seems to prove that the authors of the metrical romances might
possibly have done better if they had attended to the narrative,
like the simple tellers of fairy-tales, without troubling themselves as to the rhetoric of the French school. Another example of the same sort can be obtained by comparing *Sir Perceval* with some of the folklore analogues. *Sir Perceval* is
one of the simplest of the old romances: it seems at first almost
like a rude burlesque of the *Conte del Graal*. It is now commonly
thought to be taken from an earlier lost French version of the
same subject. However that may be, it shows the common
roughness of the English as compared with the French tales;
it is full of spirit, but it is not gentle. Percival in this romance
is not like the Percival of Wolfram or of Malory; he is a rollick-
ing popular hero who blunders into great exploits. The style,

[1] Curtin, *Hero Tales of Ireland*.

even for this sort of motive, is rather too boisterous. Again,
in this case, as with *Sir Amadas*, there may be found a traditional oral rendering of some of the same matters which,
in point of style, is better than the English metrical romance.
The scene of the discourteous knight breaking in and insulting
the king is found in the west Highland tale of *The Knight
of the Red Shield*, in Campbell's collection, and it is told there
with greater command of language and better effect.

"Breton lays" have been mentioned; the name meant for
the English a short story in rime, like those of Marie de France,
taken from Celtic sources. Some of these were more complex
than others, but they were never spun out like the romances
of Beves and Guy, and the best of them are very good in the
way they manage their plot. Moreover there is something
in them of that romantic mystery which is less common in
medieval literature than modern readers generally suppose;
it is not often to be found in the professional fiction of the
Middle Ages. But the Breton lays are nearer than other romances to the popular beliefs out of which romantic marvels
are drawn, and they retain something of their freshness. The
best in English are *Sir Orfeo* and *Sir Launfal*. The first of
these, which is the story of Orpheus, is a proof of what can
be done by mere form; the classical fable is completely taken
over, and turned into a fairy tale; hardly anything is left to
it except what it owes to the Breton form (of thought and expression.) It is a story like that of young Tamlane in the
ballad, a rescue from the fairy, for Pluto has become the fairy
king, and everything ends happily; Eurydice is brought back
in safety. There is nothing wrong in the description of it
as a "Breton lay," for it is wholly such a tale as the Bretons,
and many other people, might have told without any suggestion
from Greek or Latin. The English poem (no original is extant
in French) is an utterly different thing from the rambling tales
of chivalry. It has much of the quality that is found in some
of the ballads; and in time, through some strange fortune, it
became itself a ballad, and was found in Shetland, not very
long ago, with a Norse refrain to it. [1]

The different versions of Launfal—*Landavall* in couplets
Launfal Miles of Thomas Chestre, in *rime couée*, and the de-

[1] Child, *Ballads*, No. 19.

generate *Sir Lambewell* of the Percy MS.—have been carefully studied and made to exhibit some of the ordinary processes of translation and adaptation. They come from Marie de France—Thomas Chestre took something from the lay of *Graelent* besides the main plot of *Lanval*. The story is one of the best known; the fairy bride—

> The kinge's daughter of Avalon,
> That is an isle of the fairie
> In ocean full fair to see—

and the loss of her, through the breaking of her command. *The Wedding of Sir Gawain*, which, in another form, is *The Wife of Bath's Tale*, is from the same mythical region, and has some of the same merits.

The romance of *Sir Libeaus*, "the fair unknown," the son of Sir Gawain, is of different proportions, less simple and direct than *Orfeo* or *Launfal*. But it keeps some of the virtues of the fairy tale, and is one of the most pleasing of all the company of *Sir Thopas*. Adventures are too easily multiplied in it, but it is not a mere jumble of stock incidents. It is very like the story of Gareth in Malory, and, along with Gareth, may have suggested some things to Spenser, for the story of the Red Cross Knight. Also, the breaking of the enchantment in the castle of Busirane may owe something to *Sir Libeaus*: there seems to have been an old printed edition of *Libius Disconius*, though no printed copy is extant. The plot is a good one, the expedition of a young and untried knight to rescue a lady from enchantment; it is a pure romance of knight errantry, very fit to be taken as an example of that order, and, possibly, the best of all the riming tales that keep simply to the familiar adventures of books of chivalry. Sir Libeaus takes a long time to reach the palace of the two enchanters—"clerkes of nigremauncie"—who keep the lady of Sinaudon under their spells in the shape of a loathly worm. But the excursion and digressions have some spirit in them, and no confusion.

The elements of the plot in *Sir Gawayne and the Grene Knight* [1] are as ancient and unreasonable as are to be found in

---

[1] See also Chapter xv, where this romance is further considered as part of the work of the author of *Pearl*.

any mythology. No precise original has been found in French; but the chief adventure, the beheading game proposed by the Green Knight to the reluctant courtiers of King Arthur occurs often in other stories. It comes in one of the stories of Cuchulinn in Irish;[1] it comes more than once in the French romances, *e.g.* in *La Mule sans Frein*, one of the best of the shorter stories, a strange old-fashioned chivalrous pilgrim's progress; and this, too, sets out from King Arthur's court, and the hero is Gawain. The beheading "jeopardy" is a most successful piece of unreason: "You may cut off my head, if only I may have a stroke at you some other day." Sir Gawain cuts off the Green Knight's head; the Green Knight picks it up; he summons Gawain to travel and find him by an appointed day, and submit his neck to the return-stroke. This is good enough, one would imagine, for a grotesque romance; one hears the reader quoting *aegri somnia* and reaffirming his contempt for the Middle Ages. Yet this romance of *Sir Gawayne* is very different from the ordinary books of chivalry; it is one of the most singular works of the fourteenth century, and it is one of the strongest, both in imagination and in literary art. The author loses nothing of the fantastic value of his plot; on the contrary, he does everything possible to heighten the effect of it, to a grotesque sublimity; while, at the same time, he is concerned, as Shakespeare often is, to transform the folklore with which he is working, and make it play into his moral scheme. He is a great moralist and he can use allegory; but, in his treatment of this story, his imagination is generally too strong for abstract methods. He succeeds (a very remarkable feat) in making his readers accept strange adventures as part of a reasonable man's life; not smoothing away or suppressing absurdities, but getting out of them everything possible in the way of terror and wonder; and using mockery also, like that of the northern myths of Thor and the giants. Allegory comes in, but accidentally, in the description of Gawain's shield and its device, the "pentangle," with its religious motive—Gawain as the servant of Our Lady; thus adding something more to the complexity of the work. It is a different thing from the simple beauty of the fairy tales; and, on the other hand, the common futilities of the minstrels are kept at a

---

[1] Cf. *Bricriu's Feast*, edited by G. Henderson for the Irish Texts Society.

safe distance by this author. His landscape is not that of the ordinary books; Sir Gawain is not sent wandering in the conventional romantic scenery, but in the highlands of Wales in winter, all well known and understood by the poet, with thorough enjoyment of the season, "the flaky shower and whirling drift." This is not quite exceptional, for, though the winter passages of the Scottish Chaucerians are later, the alliterative poets generally were good at stormy weather; but there is none equal to the poet of *Sir Gawayne* in this kind of description. The three hunting scenes—of the hart, the boar, and the fox—serve to bring out his talent further, while the way they are placed in contrast with the Christmas revels in the castle, shows, at any rate, the writer's care for composition; symmetry of this sort may not be very difficult, but it is not too common at this time. The temptation of Sir Gawain and the blandishments of the lady may have been suggested by the French romance of *Ider*; but, as in the case of the other ordeal—the beheading game—the English poet has given his own rendering.

Sir Tristrem is a great contrast to *Sir Gawayne*, though both works are ambitious and carefully studied. The author of *Sir Gawayne* took some old wives' fables and made them into a magnificent piece of Gothic art; the other writer had one of the noblest stories in the world to deal with, and translated it into thin tinkling rimes.

> Ysonde of heighe priis,
>   The maiden bright of hewe,
> That wered fow and griis
>   And scarlet that was newe,
> In warld was non so wiis
>   Of crafte that men knewe,
> Withouten Sir Tramtris
>   That al games of grewe
>   On grounde.
> Hom longeth Tramtris the trewe.
> For heled was his wounde.

The author is so pleased with his command of verse that he loses all proper sense of his tragic theme. Tristram and Iseult had to wait long for their poet, in England.

The *Tale of Gamelyn* may count for something on the native

English side against the many borrowed French romances.   It
is a story of the youngest son cruelly treated by his tyrannical
elder brother, and coming to his own again with the help of
the king of outlaws.   Thomas Lodge made a novel out of it,
and kept a number of incidents—the defeat of the wrestler
(the "champioun" as he is called), the loyalty of Adam
Spencer and the meeting with the outlaws—and so these
found their way to Shakespeare, and, along with them, the
spirit of the greenwood and its freedom.   The *Tale of Gamelyn*
is *As You Like It*, without Rosalind or Celia; the motive is,
naturally, much simpler than in the novel or the play: merely
the poetical justice of the young man's adventures and restoration, with the humorous popular flouting of respectability
in the opposition of the liberal outlaws to the dishonest elder
brother and the stupid abbots and priors.

> "Ow!" seyde Gamelyn, "so brouke I my bon
> Now I have aspyed that freendes have I non;
> Cursed mot he worthe, bothe fleisch and blood
> That ever do priour or abbot any good!"

The verse is, more or less, the same as that of Robert of
Gloucester, and of the southern *Legends of Saints*; nowhere
is it used with more freedom and spirit than in *Gamelyn*:

> Then seide the maister, kyng of outlawes
> "What seeke ye, yonge men, under woode-schawes?"
> Gamelyn answerde the king with his croune,
> "He moste needes walke in woode that may not walke in towne:
> Sir, we walke not heer non harm for to do,
> But if we meete with a deer to schute therto,
> As men that ben hungry and mow no mete fynde,
> And ben harde bystad under woode-lynde."

Gamelyn is found only in MSS. of *The Canterbury Tales;* Skeat's
conjecture is a fair one, that it was kept by Chaucer among
his papers, to be worked up, some day, into *The Yeoman's
Tale*.

Another romance, less closely attached to Chaucer's work,
the *Tale of Beryn* (called *The Merchant's Second Tale*) is also,
like *Gamelyn*, rather exceptional in its plot.   It is a comic
story, and comes from the east: how Beryn with his merchandise was driven by a storm at sea to a strange harbour, a city

of practical jokers; and how he was treated by the burgesses there, and hard put to it to escape from their knavery; and how he was helped against the sharpers by a valiant cripple, Geoffrey, and shown the way to defeat them by tricks more impudent than their own.

The verse of *Beryn* is of the same sort as in *Gamelyn*, but more uneven; often very brisk, but sometimes falling into the tune of the early Elizabethan doggerel drama:

> After these two brethren, Romulus and Romus,
> Julius Cesar was Emperour, that rightful was of *domus*.

But on the other hand there are good verses like these:

> For after misty cloudes ther cometh a cler sonne
> So after bale cometh bote, whoso bide conne.

There are, obviously, certain types and classes among the romances; medieval literature generally ran in conventional moulds, and its clients accepted readily the well-known turns of a story and the favourite characters. But, at the same time, in reading the romances one has a continual sense of change and of experiment; there is no romantic school so definite and assured as to make any one type into a standard; not even Chaucer succeeded in doing what Chrétien had done two centuries earlier in France. The English romancers have generally too little ambition, and the ambitious and original writers are too individual and peculiar to found any proper school, or to establish in England a medieval pattern of narrative that might be compared with the modern novel.

> Sir Thopas he bereth the flour,

and the companions of *Sir Thopas*, who are the largest group, never think of competing seriously with the great French authors of the twelfth century, the masters, as they must be reckoned, of medieval romantic poetry. The English, like the Italians, were too late; they missed the twelfth century and its influences and ideals, or only took them up when other and still stronger forces were declaring themselves. They failed to give shape in English to the great medieval romantic themes; they failed in *Sir Tristrem*; and the Middle Ages were at an end before Sir Thomas Malory brought out the noblest of all purely medieval English romances, translated from "the French book" that was then nearly three centuries old.

The relation of the romances to popular ballads is not easy to understand.   The romances and their plots go through many transformations; *Horn* and *Launfal* are proof of this. *Horn* turns into a ballad, and so do many others; the ballad of *Orfeo* has been mentioned.   But it will not do to take the ballads in a lump as degenerate forms of earlier narrative poetry, for the ballad is essentially a lyrical form, and has its own laws, independent of all forms of narrative poetry in extant medieval English; and, again, a great number of ballads have plots which not only do not occur in any known romances (which, of itself, would prove little or nothing) but they are plainly not fitted for narrative of any length (*e.g. Lord Randal, Sir Patrick Spens, The Wife of Usher's Well*).   On the whole it seems best to suppose that the two forms of lyrical ballad and narrative romance were independent, though not in antagonism, through all the Middle Ages. They seem to have drawn their ideas from different sources for the most part.   Though almost anything may be made the subject of a ballad, there are certain kinds of plot that seem to be specially fitted for the ballad and much less for the long story; fairy adventures, like that of Tamlane, heroic defences against odds, like that of Parcy Reed and, before all, tragic stories, like Annie of Lochryan or the Douglas tragedy.   The romances, as a rule, end happily, but there is no such law in ballads.   It will be found, too, that the romances which have most likeness to ballads are generally among those of the shorter and simpler kind, like *Orfeo* and the *Lai le Freine*.   The question is made more complicated by the use of ballad measure for some of the later romances, like *The Knight of Curtesy*, a strange version of *The Chevalier de Coucy*.   Of *Robin Hood* and *Adam Bell* and many more it is hard to say whether they are to be ranked with ballads or with romances.   But all this is matter for another enquiry.

CHAPTER XIV

Metrical Romances, 1200—1500

II

THE metrical romances which form during three centuries a distinctive feature of our literature must in no sense be regarded as an isolated phenomenon. They begin under the auspices of the twelfth century renascence. They supply a want while feudalism lasts. And they begin to vanish when feudalism crumbles in the wars of the Roses. It has been already said that legend and love were the two main themes of the twelfth century literary revolt against earlier religious traditions, and it is not without significance that they were precisely the themes of this new creation, the romance. It is true that the crusading zeal, and occasional Christianising tendencies, which characterise some of the romances, still point to militant religious forces, but religion ceases to supply the initial impulse, or to give direction. The *raison d'être* of the romances is of a secular kind. It was felt to be good to indulge the fancy and to hear of love, and so legendary and historical narratives and cheerful love-stories were, from time to time, related with no other motive than the telling of a good tale. The romance, then, obviously forms part of, or is, perhaps, the sequel to, that general emancipatory movement in literature which marked the twelfth century.

But the form and tone of the English romance were determined by more than one consideration. Political and social connections with France and Brittany rendered available a store of French material, and Welsh traditions, through the medium of Brittany, were found to increase that store. The movements of the crusaders brought the west into closer touch with the east. And, amidst all these alien influences, something of what was native still persisted. Nor must internal considerations be entirely forgotten. Neither social nor intellectual development failed to leave its mark upon this branch of literature. Women had come to be regarded as of more importance than ever in the community. The literary tendencies which made for love-tales found their counterpart in the striving towards higher ideals of conduct in relation to woman. Manners became more refined and a code of chivalry was evolved. Heightened sensibility was, moreover, revealed in the increased appreciation of the beautiful—the beauty of womanhood, the beauty of nature, the beauty of noble conduct. And the refinement of fancy made fairyland seem possible.

Jean Bodel's classification of the romances has already been mentioned. Regarding them, however, from the point of view of the motives and influences they embody, it is seen that they fall into certain groups: Carolingian or Old French, Old English, classical, oriental and Celtic.

The Carolingian element is represented in medieval English romance by *Sir Otuel*, *Roland and Vernagu* and *Sir Ferumbras*. The first is an account of a Saracen attack upon France. Sir Otuel is the Saracen emissary who insultingly defies Charlemagne in his own hall and is, in consequence, challenged by Roland. A stiff fight follows; but, in answer to Charlemagne's prayers, a white dove alights upon the shoulders of the Saracen; whereupon he capitulates and undertakes to embrace the Christian faith. *Roland and Vernagu* deals with Charlemagne's exploits in Spain. Its main incident consists of a combat, spread over two days, between Roland and Vernagu, the gigantic black champion of the sultan of Babylon. At one point of the protracted duel the giant is overcome with sleep; and this leads to an exhibition of knightly courtesy. So far from taking advantage of his slumbering rival, Roland seeks to make those slumbers easy by improvising a rough pillow beneath his head. *Sir Ferumbras* relates the capture of Rome by the Saracen hosts and its relief by Charlemagne. The usual combat takes place, this time between Olivier and Ferumbras, son of the sultan of Babylon. The Saracen is, as usual, overcome and accepts Christianity. His sister

Floripas, who is in love with the French Sir Guy, afterwards her husband, assists the Christians, and both brother and sister are subsequently rewarded with territory in Spain.

In these works there is obviously embalmed the fierce heroic temper of the Carolingian era. The animating spirit is that of the crusades. Saracen champions are consistently worsted and forcibly persuaded, after sanguinary combat, of the beauties of Christian doctrine. The chivalrous ideal is still in the making, and the self-restraint and courtesy of Christian heroes are shown to contrast favourably with the brutal manners of Saracen warriors. But chivalry, as such, is still a battle-field grace; its softening virtues have yet to be developed in other spheres of activity. The glory of womanhood lies in ferocity and daring, in a strong initiative, if needs be, in affairs of love. Floripas in *Sir Ferumbras*, for the sake of her love, deceives her father, overpowers her governess and brains a jailor; and other Carolingian heroines like Blancheflour and Guiboux are similarly formidable.

The romances which spring directly from English soil are animated by essentially different motives and reflect a different society from that of the French group. In *Havelok* and *Horn*, in *Guy of Warwick* and *Beves of Hamtoun* there exists primarily the viking atmosphere of tenth century England, though the sagas, in their actual form, have acquired, through alien handling, a certain crusade colouring. In *Horn*, for instance, Saracens are substituted for vikings in plain disregard of historical verisimilitude; and again, in *Guy of Warwick*, the English legend has been invested with fresh motives and relentlessly expanded with adventures in Paynim. After removing such excrescences, however, we shall find something of earlier English conditions. Such situations as they depict, arising out of usurpation on the part of faithless guardians of royal children, spring, in a great measure, out of pre-Conquest unsettlement. They were situations not uncommon in the day of small kingdoms and restless viking hordes. *Havelok* is a tale of how a Danish prince and an English princess came to their own again. The hero, son of the Danish king Birkabeyn, is handed over, by his wicked guardian Godard, to a fisherman Grim, to be drowned. A mystic light, however, reveals Havelok's royal birth to the simple Grim, who saves the situation by crossing to England. They land at Grimsby, a town that still cherishes the name of Havelok and the characters of the tale, in its streets and its seal; and the hero, by a happy coincidence, drifts as a kitchen-boy into the household of Godrich, guardian of Goldburgh. This guardian, however, is no better than Godard, for he has likewise deprived the daughter of the English Aethelwold of her inheritance. Havelok is a strong, handsome youth, who soon becomes famous for feats of strength; whereupon Godrich, who had promised Aethelwold that he would marry Goldburgh to the "best man" in the country, maliciously keeps his promise by forcing her to marry his "cook's knave," a popular hero by reason of his athletic deeds. By degrading Goldburgh into a churl's wife Godrich hopes to make his hold upon her inheritance secure. The princess naturally bewails her lot when led away by Havelok, but she becomes reconciled when mysterious signs assure her, as they had previously assured Grim, of her husband's royal origin. Meanwhile, the faithful Ubbe, who has set matters right in Denmark, appears in England, when all wrongs are righted and the united futures of hero and heroine are straightway assured.

Horn is a viking story plainly adapted to romantic ends. The hero is the youthful son of the king of Suddene (Isle of Man), who, after the death of his father, at the hands of raiding Saracens (vikings), is turned adrift in a rudderless boat. Wind and tide bring the boat with its living freight to the land of Westernesse (Wirral?), where the princess Rymenhild, falling in love with the stranded hero, endeavours, with womanly art, to win his love in return. Horn is knighted through Rymenhild's good offices; but, before he can surrender himself to the pleasant bondage of love, he longs to accomplish knightly deeds. He therefore departs in quest of adventure, but leaves behind him a traitorous companion, Fikenhild, who reveals to the king the secret of the lovers. Horn is banished and only returns on learning that Rymenhild is about to wed. He appears in pilgrim garb, is forgiven, and rescues the princess from a distasteful suitor. But, after marriage, the old knightly instincts again assert themselves; and he crosses to Suddene, which he rids of invaders. The treacherous Fikenhild had, however, in the meantime carried off Rymenhild, and Horn, after avenging this deed, returns once more to his homeland, this time not alone.

In the ponderous but popular *Guy of Warwick* we recognise a tedious expansion of a stirring English legend. Sir Guy was regarded as a national hero, who, by his victory over Colbrand the Dane, had rescued England from the grip of the invader. In the romance this appears—but in company with other episodes which destroy the simplicity of the earlier narrative, confuse its motive and change its colouring. When he first comes on the scene, Guy is madly in love with Felice the beautiful daughter of the earl of Warwick; but his suit is denied on account of his inferiority of standing, for he is but the son of the earl's steward. He, therefore, ventures abroad, and returns in a few years, laden with honours: but only to be repulsed once more by his too scrupulous mistress, who now fears that wedded life may transform her hero into a slothful and turgid knight. Once more he goes abroad; and, after brisk campaigning, he is welcomed on his return by Aethelstan, at whose request he rids Northumbria of an insatiable dragon. After this, Felice can hold out no longer. The lovers are united; but now Guy begins to entertain scruples. The rest of his life is to be spent in hardship and penance, and he leaves again for uncouth lands. He returns in due course to find King Aethelstan hard pressed by the Danish Anlaf; but Guy's overthrow of Colbrand saves the kingdom and he sets out forthwith on his way to Warwick. Disguised as a palmer, he finds his wife engaged in works of charity; but, without revealing his identity, he stoically retires to a neighbouring hermitage, where the much-tried couple are finally united before he breathes his last.

Beves of Hamtoun, like *Horn*, springs from English soil, but the transforming process traced in the one is completed in the other. *Beves* presents almost entirely crusading tendencies, but few traces remain of the earlier form. Beves, who has been despatched as a slave to heathen parts by a treacherous mother, ultimately arrives at the court of the Saracen king Ermyn. Here he is the recipient of handsome favours, and is offered the hand of the princess Josian, on condition that he forsakes the Christian faith. This he refuses to do, but the valour he displays in staggering exploits still keeps him in favour, and Josian, for his love, is prepared to renounce her native gods. The king hears of this, and Beves is committed to a neighbouring potentate, by whom he is kept in a horrible dungeon for some seven years. After a marvellous escape from his terrible surroundings, Beves seeks out Josian, and both flee to Cologne, where they are duly wedded. The hero's career continues to be as eventful as ever; but he is finally induced to turn towards home, where he succeeds in regaining his inheritance, and is recognised as a worthy knight by the reigning king Edgar.

In attempting to estimate the contribution made by these four works to Middle English romance, it must be remembered that, although they originate ultimately from the England of the vikings, of Aethelstan and Edgar, they have all been touched with later foreign influences. In them may be perceived, however, an undeveloped chivalry, as well as reminiscences of Old English life and thought. The code of chivalry is as yet unformulated. In *Havelok* we see the simple ideal of righting the wrong. In *Horn* and *Guy of Warwick* is perceptible a refinement of love which makes for asceticism; but the love details are not, in general, elaborated in accordance with later chivalrous ideals. Rymenhild and Josian both woo and are wooed; but they lack the violence of Carolingian heroines. In Felice alone do we find traces of that scrupulous niceness encouraged in the era of the courts of love. With regard to the existence of earlier English reminiscences, in both *Horn* and *Havelok* can be seen the joy in descriptions of the sea characteristic of Old English verse. Both Guy and Beves, again, have their dragons to encounter after the fashion of Beowulf. The marvellous, which, to some extent, appears in *Havelok*, is of the kind found in Germanic folk-lore; it is distinct in its essence from the product of Celtic fancy. The plebeian elements in the same work, which embody a detailed description of humble life, and which are in striking contrast to the monotonous aristocratic colouring of the romance elsewhere, witness, undoubtedly, to a primitive pre-Conquest community. And, last, Guy's great fight with Colbrand breathes the motive of patriotism—the motive of Byrhtnoth

—rather than the religious zeal which fired crusading heroes in their single combats.

The English medieval romance levied contributions also upon the literature of antiquity. Such levies were due neither to crusading zeal, which loved to recall Charlemagne's great fights against Saracen hosts, nor to the impulse which clung tightly to native history and homespun stories. They were, rather, the outcome of a cherished conceit based on a piece of ingenious etymology, according to which Englishmen, as inhabitants of Britain, held themselves to be of Trojan descent in virtue of Brutus. In this way did the literature of antiquity suggest itself as, to some extent, an appropriate field for the business of romancing. The *Geste Hystoriale of the Destruction of Troy* and *King Alisaunder* may be taken as typical of this class. The former of these consists of an epitome of the well-known story with, however, many modifications characteristic of medieval genius. It sets forth the antique world interpreted in terms of medievalism; Greek warfare, Greek customs and Greek religion alike appearing in the garb of the Middle Ages. And, together with these changes, were tacitly introduced fairy reminiscences and magical details. But, most interesting of all, in the Troy narrative, are those elements of the story of Troilus and Briseida taken over from Benoît de Ste. More, and subsequently moulded into one of the world's greatest stories.

In *King Alisaunder* we see fashioned the historical and legendary hero, his career being supplemented with hosts of fanciful stories drawn from the east. His birth is alike mysterious and marvellous. His youth and manhood are passed in prodigious undertakings. He tames the fiery Bucephalus. He captures Tyre and burns Thebes. Darius falls before him. He advances through Persia and onwards to the Ganges, conquering, on his way, the great Porrus of India. His homeward journey is a progress through wonderland. All the magic of the east lies concentrated in his path; he passes by crowned snakes and mysterious trees, and beholds, in the distance, cliffs sparkling with diamonds. He is ultimately poisoned by a friend and honourably buried in a tomb of gold.

The ruling motive of these classical romances, as compared
with others of their kind, is clearly that of depicting, on a large
scale, the heroic element in humanity and of pointing out the
glories of invincible knighthood. They concern themselves
not with chivalrous love, but with chivalrous valour and knightly accomplishments. Their aim is to point to the more
masculine elements of medieval chivalry. The joy of battle
is everywhere articulate—not least so in the picturesque movements of warlike bodies, and in the varied sounds of the
battlefield. The method of developing this motive is, for
the most part, by bringing the west into touch with the east.
The treasuries of Babylonian and antique fable are ransacked
to glorify the theme of warlike magnificence. The wider
mental horizon and the taste for wonders which attracted
contemporaries in *Mandeville's Travels* are here enlisted in
the work of romance.

Closely akin to the Alexander romance is *Richard Cœur de
Lion*, which may, therefore, be considered here, though its
story is not of either eastern or classical origin. The scheme
in both is much the same. Richard's birth is mysterious
as was Alexander's. In early manhood Richard wrenches
out the lion's heart; Alexander tames Bucephalus. Both
march to the east to perform great things: both are presented
as types of valorous greatness. In the romance Richard
appears as the son of Henry II and the beautiful enchantress
Cassodorien. He is imprisoned in Germany as the result
of an escapade on his way home from the Holy Land, and it is
here that he tears out the heart of a lion set loose in his cell.
The proclamation of a general crusade soon afterwards appeals
to Richard and he joins Philip of France on his way to the
east. The French king is consistently treacherous and jealous,
while Richard is no less hasty and passionate, and, in consequence, ruptures are frequent. After avenging an insult
received from Cyprus, Richard hastens to Syria, where fight
succeeds fight with great regularity and the Saracens under
Saladin are gradually discomfited. At last a truce of three
years is arranged, at which point the romancer is content to
conclude. The romance is one of the most stirring of the
whole group. It deals with the crusades; but its central
theme, like that of the Alexander saga, is the glorification

of the romance of war, the exaltation of the fighting hero. It is, moreover, fiercely patriotic. Scorn is heaped on the braggadocio of the French, and the drawing of Philip's character is far from flattering. On the other hand, Cœur de Lion's haughty arrogance is the glory of Englishmen; on his side fight St. George and big battalions of angels. His humour appears as grim as his blows. He feasts on Saracens and provides the same dish for Saracen ambassadors. The ideal man of action, as here depicted, is one in whom the elements are mixed. He is by no means deficient in knightly instincts and courtesy; but, mingled with these, are coarse-grained characteristics. He is rude and blunt, forceful and careless of restraint—all of which traits represent the English contribution to the heroic picture.

Oriental fable appears in English romance with other effects than were obtained in the work of *King Alisaunder*. The more voluptuous qualities of the east, for instance, are reproduced in *Flores and Blancheflour* and result in a style of romance tolerably distinct. In *The Seven Sages of Rome*, again, the story-book is employed in oriental fashion. The heroine of the first, Blancheflour, is a Christian princess carried off by the Saracens in Spain and subsequently educated along with their young prince Flores. Childish friendship develops into love, and Flores is promptly removed—but not before his lady has given him a magic ring which will tarnish when the giver is in danger. Danger soon threatens her in the shape of false accusation; but this peril, being revealed to Flores by means of his ring, is duly averted, though subsequent treachery succeeds in despatching the princess to Egypt as a slave. Thither Flores pursues her; and, by dint of bribery and strategem, he succeeds in entering the seraglio where she is detained. The inevitable discovery follows, but the anger of the emir having vanished on his learning all the circumstances, the trials of the lovers come to a pleasant end. In this work the central theme is, once again, that of love; but, in the manner of treatment, there are visible certain departures. According to western standards, the tone is, in fact, somewhat sentimental. It is felt that soul-stirring passions are not involved; the whole seems wanting in the quality of hardihood. Flores, for instance, swoons in your true sentimental fashion. He finds heart's-ease in exile by tracing his lady's name in flower designs. He wins his cause by dint of magic and persuasion rather than by the strength of his own right arm. An oriental colouring is also noticeable in the sensuous descriptions of garden and seraglio, as well as in the part played by the magic ring. We have here material and motives which enlarged the domain of the medieval romance, and which appealed to Chaucer when he set about writing his *Squire's Tale*. In *The Seven Sages of Rome* other aspects of the east are duly represented. Diocletian's wicked queen, failing in her attempt to ensnare her stepson Florentine, viciously accuses him of her own fell designs. Whereupon, Florentine's seven tutors plead on his behalf by relating seven tales of the perfidy of woman. The queen, as plaintiff, relates a corresponding number concerning the wickedness of counsellors. The tales are told, the queen is unmasked and duly punished. In an age dedicated by the west to the worship of women we have here represented the unflattering estimate of womankind held by the east. The framework and the device of a series of tales is, likewise, oriental, and so is the didactic tendency which underlies the whole. The aim is to set forth the dangers to which youth is subject, not only from the deceit of men, but, also, from the wiles of women.

Of far greater importance, however, than any of the foregoing influences is that derived from Celtic sources. Stories of Arthur, of Tristram and Gawain, while, in response to formative influences of the time, they present certain details in common with the other romances, have yet a distinct atmosphere, fresh motives and new colouring. Points of similarity exist, but with a difference. The incessant combats of the Carolingian saga find a counterpart in the "derring-doe" of Arthurian heroes. As in *Horn* and *Havelok*, the scene in the Celtic romances is laid in Britain; but the background is Celtic rather than English. Again, just as *King Alisaunder* and *Richard Cœur de Lion* are *magnificats* of splendid heroic figures, so the glorification of Arthur is the persistent theme of this Celtic work. And, last, the love-strain and the magic which came from the east, and were embodied in *Flores and*

Blancheflour, correspond, in some measure, with Celtic passion and Celtic mysticism. For such points of contact the spirit of the age must he held accountable: for such differences as exist, individual and national genius.

The effect of the Celtic genius upon English romance, if, indeed, such a statement may be ventured upon, was to reveal the passions, to extend the fancy and to inculcate sensibility. The Celtic element revealed love as a passion in all its fulness, a passion laden with possibilities, mysterious and awful in power and effect. It opened up avenues to a fairy-land peopled with elvish forms and lit by strange lights. It pointed to an exalted chivalry and lofty ideals, to a courtesy which was the outcome of a refinement of sentiment.

In the romance of Sir Tristram is embodied the Celtic revelation of love. The English poem is based on the version of Thomas, and is distinct from that of Béroul. This story of "death-marked" affection is well known: how Tristram and the fair Iseult are fatally united by the magic love-potion, quaffed in spite of Iseult's approaching union with Mark of Cornwall; how their love persists in spite of honour and duty; how Tristram marries Iseult of the White Hand and comes to lie wounded in Brittany; how his wife, distracted with jealousy, falsely announces the ominous black sail coming over the seas; and how the fair Iseult glides through the hall and expires on the corpse of her former lover. Here we feel that the tragedy of love has been remorselessly enacted. It appears to us as a new and irresistible force, differing alike from the blandishments of the east and the crudeness of the north. A sense of mystery and gloom enfolds it all like a misty veil over cairn and cromlech. The problem is as enduring as life itself. Enchantment is suggested by means of the love-potion, yet the weakness is mortal, as, indeed, is the sombre climax. Passion descends to the level of reality, and the comfortable medieval ending is sternly eschewed. Love is conducted by neither code nor nice theory: it moves, simple, sensuous, passionate, to its appointed end, and relentlessly reveals the poetry of life.

In the romances which deal with the relations between mortal and fairy we find elements of the richest fancy. Here and elsewhere, in this Celtic section, are discovered land-

scapes and scenes which charm the imagination with their
glamour and light.   Fays come and go, wrapped in ethereal
beauty, and horrible spirit-shapes appear to the accompaniment of mad symphonies of the elements.   Knights of faërie
emerge out of weird forbidden tracts, strange enchantments
dictating or following their various movements.   Mystic
commands lightly broken entail tragic penalties, and mortals
become the sport of elvish visitants.

Of the romances which relate to love-passages between
mortal and fairy, *Sir Launfal*, *Sir Orfeo* and *Emarè* may be
taken as types.   In *Sir Launfal*, the hero receives love-favours
from a beautiful fay, but breaks his bond by carelessly betray
ing his secret to the queen.   He is condemned to death and
abandoned by the fay, who, however, relents in time and,
riding to Arthur's court, succeeds in carrying the knight off
to the Isle of Avalon.   *Sir Orfeo* may be briefly described as
a Celtic adaptation of the familiar classical story of Orpheus
and Eurydice.   Queen Heurodys is carried off into fairyland,
in spite of all that human efforts can do.   King Orfeo follows
her in despair, as a ministrel, but his wonderful melodies
at last succeed in leading her back to the haunts of men.
In *Emarè* we have a beautifully told story of the Constance
type, with the addition of certain mystical elements.   The
heroine is a mysterious maiden of unearthly beauty who is
cast off by her unnatural father and drifts to the shores of
Wales, where she wins Sir Cador's love.   After the marriage,
Sir Cador goes abroad, and the young wife is once more turned
adrift by an intriguing mother-in-law.   She reaches Rome
and there, in due course, she is happily discovered by the grief-
stricken Cador.   Other romances relate the deeds of the
offspring of fairy and mortal union as, for instance, *Sir Degare*
and *Sir Gowther*.   The former is an account of a fairy knight
and a princess of Britain.   He is abandoned in infancy by
the princess, who, however, leaves with him a pair of magic
gloves which will fit no hands but hers.   The child in time
becomes a knight, and his prowess in the lists renders him
eligible for the hand of the princess, his mother.   By means
of the gloves, however, they learn their real relationship;
whereupon Sir Degare relinquishes his claim and succeeds
in the filial task of reuniting his parents.   In *Sir Gowther*,

the hero is the son of a "fiendish" knight and a gentle lady whom he had betrayed. The boy, as was predicted, proved to be of a most savage temperament, until the offending Adam was whipped out of him by means of self-inflicted penance. He then wins the love of an earl's daughter by glorious achievements in the lists, and piously builds an abbey to commemorate his conversion.

It is in the Arthurian romances, and more particularly in those relating to Sir Gawain, that we find the loftier ideals of chivalry set forth. Gawain is depicted as the knight of honour and courtesy, of loyalty and self-sacrifice. Softer manners and greater magnanimity are grafted upon the earlier knighthood. Self-restraint becomes more and more a knightly virtue. The combats are not less fierce, but vainglorious boasting gives way to moods of humility. Victory is followed by noble concern for the vanquished. Passing over *Sir Gawayne and the Grene Knight*, which is treated elsewhere, we find in *Golagros and Gawain* these knightly elements plainly visible. The rudeness of Sir Kay, here and elsewhere, is devised as a foil to the courtesy of Gawain. Arthur in Tuscany sends Sir Kay to ask for quarters in a neighbouring castle. His rude, presumptuous bearing meets with refusal, though, when Gawain arrives, the request is readily acceded to. The domains of Golagros are next approached. He is an aggressive knight of large reputation, whom Arthur makes it his business forthwith to subdue. A combat is arranged, in which Gawain proves victor; whereupon the noble Arthurian not only grants the life of the defiant Golagros, but spares his feelings by returning to his castle as if he himself were the vanquished. Matters were afterwards explained, and Golagros, conquered alike by arms and courtesy, becomes duly enrolled in Arthur's train. In the *Awntyrs* [Adventures] *of Arthure at the Terne Wathelyne* we find something of the same elements, together with an exhortation to moral living. The romance deals with two incidents alleged to have occurred while Arthur was hunting near Carlisle. The first, however, is an adaptation of the "Trentals of St. Gregory." A ghastly figure is represented as emerging from the Tarn, and appearing before Guinevere and Gawain. It is Guinevere's mother in the direst torments. The queen thereupon makes a vow

as to her future life and promises, meanwhile, to have masses
sung for her mother's soul. The second incident is of a more
conventional kind, and deals with the fight between Gawain
and Galleroun.

Ywain and Gawain is another romance which embodies
much that is characteristic of Arthurian chivalry. Ywain
sets out on a certain quest from Arthur's court. He defeats
a knight near the fountain of Broceliande, pursues him to his
castle and marries Laudine, mistress of that place. After
further adventures in love and war, in most of which he has
the company of a friendly lion, he falls in with Gawain and,
ignorant of each other's identity, they engage in combat.
The fight is indecisive, and each courteously concedes to
the other the victory—an exchange of compliments which
is speedily followed by a joyful recognition. The *Wedding
of Sir Gawain*, again, points to loyalty and honour, as involving
supreme self-sacrifice. It relates how Gawain, to save Arthur's
life, undertakes to marry the loathsome dame Ragnell. His
noble unselfishness, however, is not unrewarded; the dame is
subsequently transformed into the most beauteous of her kind.
Libeaus Desconus, the story of Gyngalyn, Gawain's son, is
constructed on rather conventional lines. The fair unknown
has several adventures with giants and others. He visits a
fairy castle, where he meets with an enchantress, and rescues
a lady transformed into a dreadful serpent, who, afterwards,
however, becomes his wife. The scene of the *Avowing of
Arthur* is once more placed near Carlisle. Arthur is hunting with Sir Gawain, Sir Kay and Sir Baldwin, when all four
undertake separate vows. Arthur is to capture single-
handed a ferocious boar; Sir Kay to fight all who oppose him.
The king is successful; but Sir Kay falls before a knight who
is carrying off a beautiful maiden. The victor, however,
is afterwards overcome in a fight with Gawain, and then
ensues a significant contrast in the matter of behaviours.
Sir Kay sustains his earlier reputation by cruelly taunting
the beaten knight; while Sir Gawain, on the other hand,
mindful of the claims of chivalry, is studiously kind and con-
siderate towards his fallen foe. The riming *Mort Arthur*,
and the alliterative work of the same name, deal with the
close of Arthur's life. In the first occurs the story of the

maid of Ascolot, and her fruitless love for the noble Lancelot.
The narrative is instinct with the pathos of love, and here,
as in *Tristram*, the subtlety of the treatment reveals further possibilities of the love theme. Lancelot is, moreover,
depicted as Guinevere's champion. The queen is under condemnation, but is rescued by Lancelot, who endures, in consequence, a siege in the Castle of Joyous Garde. The end of
the Arthurian story begins to be visible in the discord thus
introduced between Lancelot and Gawain, Arthur and Modred.
The alliterative *Morte Arthure* is more seriously historical.
Arthur is represented as returning home from his wars with
Lucius on hearing of Modred's treachery. He fights the
traitor, but is mortally wounded, and is borne to Glastonbury,
where he is given a magnificent burial.

In addition to the romances already mentioned as representative in some measure of definite influences at work, there
yet remain certain others which call for notice. We have, in
the first place, a group of some five romances which may be
considered together as studies of knightly character. They
are works which may be said to deal, incidentally perhaps,
with the building up of the perfect knight and Christian hero,
though anything like psychological treatment is, of course,
entirely absent. In *Ipomedon*, we see the knight as a gallant
if capricious lover. Marriage having been proposed between
young Ipomedon, prince of Apulia, and the beautiful queen of
Calabria, the former determines to woo for himself. He arrives
incognito at the court of the queen, wins her favour by manly
exploits, and then departs somewhat capriciously. He is,
however, induced to return on hearing that a tournament is
to be held of which the queen herself is to be the prize. But,
again, his conduct is strange. He loudly proclaims his dislike
for boisterous tournaments, and ostentatiously sets out on
hunting expeditions on the days of the contests. But he
actually goes to a neighbouring hermitage, whence he issues
to the tournament, clad, on successive days in red, white and,
black armour, a favourite medieval method of disguise adopted
by Sir Gowther and others. He carries all before him and then
vanishes as mysteriously as ever, without claiming his prize
nor revealing his identity. Soon afterwards, the queen is

hard pressed by a neighbouring duke, and the hero appears once more to fight her battles, this time disguised as a fool. It is only after further adventures, when he feels he has fooled to the top of his bent, that he declares his love with a happy result. In this stirring romance we see the knight-errant in quest of love. The assumed slothfulness and fondness for disguise were frequent attributes of the medieval hero: the one added interest to actual exploits, the other was an assurance that the love of the well-born was accepted on his own individual merits.

In the beautiful romance of *Amis and Amiloun* we have friendship set forth as a knightly virtue. It is depicted as an all-absorbing quality which involves, if necessary, the sacrifice of both family and conscience. Amis and Amiloun are two noble foster-brothers, the medieval counterparts of Orestes and Pylades, much alike in appearance, whose lives are indissolubly linked together. Amiloun generously, but surreptitiously, takes the place of Amis in a trial by combat, for which piece of unselfishness, with the deception involved in it, he is, subsequently, visited with the scourge of leprosy. Some time afterwards, Amis finds his friend in pitiable plight, but fails, at first, to grasp his identity. It is only after a dramatic scene that the discovery is made, and then Amis, grief-stricken, proceeds to remove his friend's leprosy by the sacrifice of his own children. But such a sacrifice is not permitted to be irrevocable. When Amis and his wife Belisante go to view their slaughtered children, they are found to be merely sleeping. The sacrifice had been one upon which the gods themselves threw incense. The romance, as it stands, is one of the most pathetic and elevating of the whole series.

Knightly love and valour were eloquent themes of the medieval romance: in *Amis and Amiloun*, the beauty of friendship is no less nobly treated. In *Sir Cleges*, the knightly character is further developed by the inculcation of charity, wit and shrewdness. The story is simply, but picturesquely, told. The hero is a knight who is reduced to poverty by reckless charity. When his fortunes are at their lowest ebb he finds a cherry-tree in his garden laden with fruit, though snow is on the ground and the season is yuletide. With this goodly find he sets out to king Uther at Cardiff, in the hope of restoring his fallen fortunes; but court officials bar his way until he has promised to divide amongst them all his reward. The king is gratified, and Cleges is asked to name his reward. He asks for twelve strokes, which the officials, in accordance with the bargain, duly receive, to the unbounded delight of an appreciative court. The identity of the knight then becomes known and his former charity is suitably recognised.

The theme of *Sir Isumbras* is that of Christian humility, the story itself being an adaptation of the legend of St. Eustace. Sir Isumbras is a knight who, through pride, falls from his high estate by the will of Providence. He is severely stricken; his possessions, his children and, lastly, his wife, are taken away; and he himself becomes a wanderer. After much privation nobly endured, he has learnt his lesson and arrives at the court of a queen, who proves to be his long-lost wife. His children are then miraculously restored and he resumes once more his exalted rank.

The Squire of Low Degree is a pleasant romance which does not belie an attractive title. Its theme suggests the idea of the existence of knightly character in those of low estate, a sentiment which had appealed to a conquered English people in the earlier *Havelok*. The humble squire in the story wins the affection of "the king's daughter of Hungary," as well as her promise to wed when he shall have become a distinguished knight. An interfering and treacherous steward is righteously slain by the squire, who then suffers imprisonment, and the king's daughter, who supposes her lover dead, is thereby reduced to the direst straits. She refuses consolation, though the king categorically reminds her of much that is pleasant in life and draws up, in fact, an interesting list of medieval delights, its feasts, its finery, its sports and its music. Persuasion failing, the king is obliged to relent. The squire is released and ventures abroad on knightly quest. He returns, in due course, to claim his own, and a pleasant romance ends on a pleasant note. The story loses nothing from the manner of its telling; it is, above all, "mercifully brief." Its English origin and sentiment, no less than its pictures of medieval life, continue to make this romance one of the most readable of its kind.

Besides these romances which deal, in some sort, with the

knightly character, there are others which embody variations of the Constance theme, namely, *Sir Triamour, Sir Eglamour of Artois* and *Torrent of Portugal*.　Like *Emarè*, they belong to the "reunion of kindred" type—a type which appealed to Chaucer and, still more, to Shakespeare in his latest period. One well-known romance still calls for notice.　This is *William of Palerne*, a tale of love and action which embodies the primitive belief in lycanthropy, according to which certain people were able to assume, at will, the character and appearance of wolves.　The tradition was widespread in Europe, and it still appears from time to time in modern works dealing with ghouls and vampires.　The story relates how William, prince of Apulia, is saved from a murderous attack by the aid of a werwolf, who, in reality, is heir to the Spanish throne.　The werwolf swims with the prince across the straits of Messina, and again renders aid when his *protégé* is fleeing from Rome with his love, Melchior.　William, subsequently, recovers his royal rights, and then helps to bring about the restoration to the friendly werwolf of his human form.

It is striking and, to some extent, characteristic of the age, that, although the field of English romance was thus wide and varied, the personality of scarcely a single toiler in that field has come down to posterity.　The anonymity of the work embodied in our ancient cathedrals is a parallel to this, and neither fact is without its significance.　With the Tristram legend is connected the name of Thomas, a poet of the twelfth century, who is mentioned by Gottfried of Strassburg in the early thirteenth century.　The somewhat misty but historical Thomas of Erceldoune has been credited with the composition of a Sir Tristram story, but this was possibly due to a confusion of the twelfth century Thomas with his interesting namesake of the succeeding century.　The confusion would be one to which the popular mind was peculiarly susceptible.　Thomas the Rhymer was a romantic figure credited with prophetical gifts, and a popular tale would readily be linked with his name, especially as such a process was consistent with the earlier Thomas tradition as it then existed.

In the case of three other romances there seem to be certain grounds for attributing them to a single writer.　All three works, *King Alisaunder, Arthur and Merlin* and *Richard*

Cœur de Lion, are, apparently, of much the same date, and alike hail from Kent. Each is animated by the same purpose —that of throwing on to a large canvas a great heroic figure; there is also to be found in each of them a certain sympathy with magic. The handling of the theme in each case proceeds on similar lines; the close parallel in the schemes of *King Alisaunder* and *Richard Cœur de Lion* has already been noticed; and the narrative, in each, moves along in easy animated style. Moreover, similarities of technique are found in all. The recurrence of similes and comparisons, as well as riming peculiarities in common, suggests the working of a single mind. In *King Alisaunder* and *Arthur and Merlin* appears the device of beginning the various sections of the narrative with lyric, gnomic, or descriptive lines, presumably to arouse interest and claim attention. In *Richard Cœur de Lion* something of the same tendency is also visible, as when a delightful description of spring is inserted after the gruesome account of the massacre of a horde of Saracens. All three works betray a joy in fighting, a joy expressed in vigorous terms. In all is evinced an ability to seize on the picturesque side of things, whether of battle or feasting; Saracens fall " as grass before the scythe"; the helmets of the troops shine "like snow upon the mountains." But if the identity of a common author may thus seem probable, little or nothing is forthcoming as regards his personality. Certain coarse details, together with rude humour, seem to suggest a plebeian pen, and this is, apparently, supported by occasional references to trades. But nothing certain on the subject can be stated. The personality of the poet is, at best, but shadowy, though, undoubtedly, his work is of outstanding merit.

In certain respects these romances may be said to reflect the age in which they were written. They bear witness in two ways to the communistic conception of society which then prevailed: first, by the anonymous character of the writings generally and, secondly, by the absence of the patriotic note. The individual, from the communistic standpoint, was but a unit of the nation, the nation merely a section of a larger Christendom. The sense of individualism, and all that is implied, was yet to be emphasised by a later renascence. It is, therefore, clear that the anonymity of the romances, as in the case of the *Legendaries* and *Chronicle*, was, in part, the outcome of such conceptions and notions. The works represent

> The constant service of the antique world
> When service sweat for duty, not for meed.

And the absence of patriotism from the romances results from the same conditions: national consciousness was not yet really awakened. The mental horizon was bounded not by English shores, but by the limits of the Holy Roman Empire. Cœur de Lion's career alone appealed to latent sympathies; for the rest, the romance is untouched by national feeling. French and other material was adapted without any re-colouring.

The romance also reflects the medieval love of external beauty. The picturesqueness of the actual, of medieval streets and buildings, the bright colours in dress, the love of pageantry and pictorial effects, all helped to inspire, and are, indeed, reflected in, the gay colouring of the romances. If the stories, again, make considerable demands upon the credulity, it was not remarkable in regard to the character of the times. All things were possible in an age of faith: the wisdom of *credo quia impossible* was to be questioned in the succeeding age of reason. Moreover, the atmosphere which nourished the romantic growth was that of feudalism, and an aristocratic note everywhere marks its tone and structure. But it is a glorified feudalism which is thus represented, a feudalism glorious in its hunting, its feasting and its fighting, in its brave men and fair women; the lower elements are scarcely ever remembered, and no pretence is made at holding up the mirror to the whole of society.

Lastly, like so much of the rest of medieval work, the romance moves largely amidst abstractions. It avoids close touch with the concrete: for instance, no reflection is found of the struggles of the Commons for parliamentary power, or even of the national strivings against papal dominion. The problems of actual life are carefully avoided; the material treated consists, rather, of the fanciful problems of the courts of love and situations arising out of the new-born chivalry.

The romance has many defects, in spite of all its attractions and the immense interest it arouses both intrinsically and historically. It sins in being intolerably long-winded and in being often devoid of all proportion. A story may drag wearily on long after the last chapter has really been written, and insignificant episodes are treated with as much concern as those of pith and moment. It further makes demands upon the "painful" reader, not only by its discursiveness and love of digression, but also by the minuteness of its descriptions, relentlessly complete, which leave nothing to the imagination. "The art of the pen is to rouse the inward vision . . . because our flying minds cannot contain a protracted description." This truth was far from being appreciated in the age of the schoolmen, with their encyclopaedic training. The aristocratic tone of the romance, moreover, tends to become wearisome by its very monotony. Sated with the sight of knights and ladies, giants and Saracens, one longs to meet an honest specimen of the citizen class; but such relief is never granted. To these and other shortcomings, however, the medieval eye was not always blind, though romances continued to be called for right up to the end of the fourteenth century and, indeed, after. Chaucer, with his keen insight and strong human sympathies, had shown himself aware of all these absurdities, for, in his *Sir Thopas*, designed as a parody on the romance in general, these are the points on which he seizes. When he rambles on for a hundred lines in *Sir Thopas* without saying much, he is quietly making the first point of his indictment. He is exaggerating the discursiveness and minuteness he has found so irksome. And, in the second place, he ridicules the aristocratic monotone by introducing a *bourgeois* note into his parodied romance. The knight swears an oath on plain "ale and bread": while, in the romantic forest through which he is wandering, lurk the harmless "buck and hare," as well as the homely nutmeg that flavours the ale. The lapse from romance is sufficiently evident and the work silently embodies much sound criticism. The host, with blunt remark, ends the parody, and in him may be seen a matter-of-fact intelligence declaiming against the faults of romance.

But, with all its shortcomings, the romance has a peculiar interest from the modern standpoint in that it marks the beginning of English fiction. In it is written the first chapter of the modern novel. After assuming a pastoral form in the days

of Elizabeth, and after being reclaimed, with all its earlier
defects, in the seventeenth century, romance slowly vanished
in the dry light of the eighteenth century, but not before it
had flooded the stage with astounding heroic plays. The
later novels, however, continued the functions of the earlier
romances when they embodied tales of adventures or tales
of love whether thwarted or triumphant. Nor is Richardson's
novel of analysis without its counterpart in this earlier creation. He treated love on psychological lines. But charming love-problems had exercised the minds of medieval courtiers
and had subsequently been analysed in the romances after
the approved fashion of the courts of love. It is only in the
case of the later realistic novel that the origins have to be
sought elsewhere—in the contemporary *fabliaux*, which dealt,
in a ready manner, with the troubles and the humours of a
lower stratum of life.

CHAPTER XV

Pearl, Cleanness, Patience and *Sir Gawayne*

AMONG the Cottonian manuscripts in the British Museum,
a small quarto volume, numbered Nero A. x, contains
the four Middle English poems known as *Pearl, Cleanness, Patience* and *Sir Gawayne and the Grene Knight*. The
manuscript is in a hand which seems to belong to the end of
the fourteenth or the early years of the fifteenth century;
there are neither titles nor rubrics, but the chief divisions are
marked by large initial letters of blue, flourished with red;
several pictures, coarsely executed, illustrate the poems, each
occupying a full page; the writing is "small, sharp and irregular." No single line of these poems has been discovered in
any other manuscript.

The first of the four poems, *Pearl*, tells of a father's grief
for a lost child, an infant daughter who had lived not two
years on earth. In a vision he beholds his Pearl, no longer
a little child, transfigured as a queen of heaven; from the
other bank of a stream which divides them she instructs him,
teaches him the lessons of faith and resignation and leads him
to a glimpse of the new Jerusalem. He sees his "little queen"
in the long procession of maidens; in his effort to plunge into
the stream and reach her he awakes, to find himself stretched
on the child's grave—

> Then woke I in that garden fair;
> My head upon that mound was laid,
> there where my Pearl had strayed below.
> I roused me, and felt in great dismay,
> and, sighing to myself, I said:—
> " Now all be to that Prince's pleasure." [1]

[1] The renderings into modern English, throughout the chapter, are from
the writer's edition of *Pearl*, 1891.

Naturally arising from the author's treatment of his subject, many a theological problem, notably the interpretation of the parable of the vineyard, is expounded. The student of medieval theology may find much of interest in *Pearl*, but the attempt to read the poem as a theological pamphlet, and a mere symbolical allegory, ignores its transcendent reality as a poet's lament. The personal side of the poem is clearly marked, though the author nowhere directly refers to his fatherhood. The basis of *Pearl* is to be found in that verse of the Gospel which tells of the man "that sought the precious margarites; and, when he had found one to his liking, he sold all his goods to buy that jewel." The pearl was doomed, by the law of nature, to flower and fade like a rose; thereafter it became a "pearl of price"; "the jeweller" indicates clearly enough the reality of his loss.

A fourteenth century poet, casting about for the form best suited for such a poem, had two courses before him: on the one hand, there was the great storehouse of dream-pictures, *The Romaunt of the Rose;* on the other hand, the symbolic pages of Scripture. A poet of the Chaucerian school would have chosen the former; to him the lost Marguerite would have suggested an allegory of "the flour that bereth our alder pris in figuringe," and the Marguerite would have been transfigured as the type of truest womanhood, a maiden in the train of love's queen, Alcestis. But the cult of the daisy seems to have been altogether unknown to our poet, or, at least, to have had no attraction for him. His Marguerite was, for him, the pearl of the Gospel; Mary, the queen of heaven, not Alcestis, queen of love, reigns in the visionary paradise which the poet pictures forth. While the main part of the poem is a paraphrase of the closing chapters of the Apocalypse and the parable of the vineyard, the poet's debt to *The Romaunt* is noteworthy, more particularly in the description of the wonderful land through which the dreamer wanders; and it can be traced here and there throughout the poem, in the personification of Pearl as Reason, in the form of the colloquy, in the details of dress and ornament, in many a characteristic word, phrase and reference; "the river from the throne," in the Apocalypse, here meets "the waters of the wells" devised by Sir Mirth for the garden of the Rose. From these two sources, *The Book of Revelation*, with its almost romantic glamour, and *Romaunt of the Rose*, with its almost oriental allegory, are derived much of the wealth and brilliancy of the poem. The poet's fancy revels in the richness of the heavenly and the earthly paradise; but his fancy is subordinated to his earnestness and intensity.

The chief episodes of the poem are best indicated by the four illustrations in the manuscript.

In the first, the author is represented slumbering in a meadow, by the side of a beflowered mound, clad in a long red gown, with falling sleeves, turned up with white, and a blue hood attached round the neck. Madden and others who have described the illustrations have not noticed that there are wings attached to the shoulders of the dreamer, and a cord reaching up into the foliage above, evidently intended to indicate that the spirit has "sped forth into space."

In the second, there is the same figure, drawn on a larger scale, but without the wings, standing by a river. He has now passed through the illumined forest-land:

> The hill-sides there were crowned
> with crystal cliffs full clear,
> and holts and woods, all bright with boles,
> blue as the blue of Inde,
> and trembling leaves, on every branch,
> as burnished silver shone—
> with shimmering sheen they glistened,
> touched by the gleam of the glades[1]—
>> and the gravel I ground upon that strand
>> was precious orient pearl.
>> The sun's own light had paled before
>> that sight so wondrous fair.

In the third picture, he is again represented in a similar position, with hands raised, and on the opposite side is Pearl, dressed in white, in the costume of Richard II's and Henry IV's time; her dress is buttoned tight up to the neck, and on her head is a crown.

In the fourth, the author is kneeling by the water, and, beyond the stream, is depicted the citadel, on the embattled walls of which Pearl again appears, with her arms extended towards him.

[1] Patches of light.

The metre of *Pearl* is a stanza of twelve lines with four accents, rimed according to the scheme *ababababbebe*, and combining rime with alliteration; there are one hundred and one such verses; these divide again into twenty sections, each consisting of five stanzas with the same refrain—one section exceptionally contains six stanzas. Throughout the poem, the last or main word of the refrain is caught up in the first line of the next stanza. Finally, the last line of the poem is almost identical with the first, and rounds off the whole. The alliteration is not slavishly maintained, and the trisyllabic movement of the feet adds to the ease and music of the verse; in each line there is a well-defined caesura. Other writers before and after the author used this form of metre; but no extant specimen shows such mastery of the stanza, which, whatever may be its origin, has some kinship with the sonnet, though a less monumental form, the first eight lines resembling the sonnet's octave, the final quatrain the sonnet's sestet, and the whole hundred and one stanzas of *Pearl* reminding one of a great sonnet-sequence. As the present writer has said elsewhere—

the refrain, the repetition of the catchword of each verse, the trammels of alliteration, all seem to have offered no difficulty to the poet; and, if power over technical difficulties constitutes in any way a poet's greatness, the author of *Pearl*, from this point of view alone, must take high rank among English poets. With a rich vocabulary at his command, consisting, on the one hand, of alliterative phrases and "native mother words," and, on the other hand, of the poetical phraseology of the great French classics of his time, he succeeded in producing a series of stanzas so simple in syntax, so varied in rhythmical effect, now lyrical, now epical, never undignified, as to leave the impression that no form of metre could have been more suitably chosen for this elegiac theme.[1]

The diction of the poem has been considered faulty by reason of its copiousness; but the criticism does not appear to be just. It should be noted that the author has drawn alike from the English, Scandinavian, and Romance elements of English speech.

The attention of scholars has recently been directed to Boccaccio's Latin eclogue *Olympia*, in which his young

[1] Introduction to *Pearl* (1891).

daughter, Violante, appears transfigured, much in the same way as Pearl in the English poem; and an ingenious attempt has been made to prove the direct debt of the English poet to his great Italian contemporary. The comparison of the two poems is a fascinating study, but there is no evidence of direct indebtedness; both writers, though their elegies are different in form, have drawn from the same sources. Even were it proved that such debt must actually be taken into account in dealing with the English poem, it would not help, but rather gainsay, the ill-founded theory that would make *Pearl* a pure allegory, a mere literary device, impersonal and unreal. The eclogue was written soon after the year 1358.

The second poem in the MS., *Cleanness*, relates, in epic style, three great subjects from scriptural history, so chosen as to enforce the lesson of purity. After a prologue, treating of the parable of the Marriage Feast, the author deals in characteristic manner with the Flood, the destruction of Sodom and Gomorrah, and the fall of Belshazzar. The poem is written in long lines, alliterative and rimeless, and is divided into thirteen sections of varying length, the whole consisting of 1812 lines.

The third poem is a metrical rendering of the story of Jonah, and its subject, too, as in the case of *Cleanness*, is indicated by its first word, *Patience*. Though, at first sight, the metre of the two poems seems to be identical throughout, it is to be noted that the lines of *Patience* divide into what may almost be described as stanzas of four lines; towards the end of the poem, there is a three-line group, either designed so by the poet or due to scribal omission. The same tendency towards the four-lined stanza is to be found in parts of *Cleanness*, more especially at the beginning and end of the poem. *Patience* consists of 531 lines; it is terser, more vivid and more highly finished, than the longer poem *Cleanness*. It is a masterly paraphrase of Scripture, bringing the story clearly and forcibly home to English folk of the fourteenth century. The author's delight in his subject is felt in every line. In *Cleanness*, especially characteristic of the author is the description of the holy vessels—the basins of gold, and the cups, arrayed like castles with battlements, with towers and lofty pinnacles, with branches and leaves portrayed upon them, the flowers being white pearl, and the fruit flaming gems. The two poems, *Cleanness* and *Patience*, judged by the tests of vocabulary, richness of expression, rhythm, descriptive power, spirit and tone, delight in nature, more especially when agitated by storm and tempest, are manifestly by the same author as *Pearl*, to which poem, indeed, they may be regarded as pendants, dwelling more definitely on its two main themes— purity and submission to the Divine will. The link that binds *Cleanness* to *Pearl* is unmistakable. The pearl is there again taken as the type of purity:

How canst thou approach His court save thou be clean?
Through shrift thou may'st shine, though thou hast served shame,
thou may'st become pure through penance, till thou art a pearl.
The pearl is praised wherever gems are seen,
though it be not the dearest by way of merchandise.
Why is the pearl so prized, save for its purity,
that wins praise for it above all white stones?
It shineth so bright; it is so round of shape;
without fault or stain; if it be truly a pearl.
It becometh never the worse for wear,
be it ne'er so old, if it remain but whole.
If by chance 't is uncared for and becometh dim,
left neglected in some lady's bower,
wash it worthily in wine, as its nature requireth:
it becometh e'en clearer than ever before.
So if a mortal be defiled ignobly,
yea, polluted in soul, let him seek shrift;
he may purify him by priest and by penance,
and grow brighter than beryl or clustering pearls.

If there were any doubt of identity of authorship in respect of the two poems, it would be readily dispelled by a comparison of the Deluge in *Cleanness* with the sea-storm in *Patience*. *Cleanness* and *Patience* place their author among the older English epic poets. They show us more clearly than *Pearl* that the poet is a "backward link" to the distant days of Cynewulf; it is with the Old English epic poets that he must be compared if the special properties of these poems are to be understood. But in one gift he is richer than his predecessors—the gift of humour. Earlier English literature cannot give us any such combination of didactic intensity and grim fancy as the poet displays at times in these small epics. One instance may be quoted, namely, the description of Jonah's abode in the whale:

> As a mote in at a minster door, so mighty were its jaws,
> Jonah enters by the gills, through slime and gore;
> he reeled in through a gullet, that seemed to him a road,
> tumbling about, aye head over heels,
> till he staggers to a place as broad as a hall;
> then he fixes his feet there and gropes all about,
> and stands up in its belly, that stank as the devil;
> in sorry plight there, 'mid grease that savoured as hell
> his bower was arrayed, who would fain risk no ill.
> Then he lurks there and seeks in each nook of the navel
> the best sheltered spot, yet nowhere he finds
> rest or recovery, but filthy mire
> wherever he goes; but God is ever dear;
> and he tarried at length and called to the Prince. . . .
> Then he reached a nook and held himself there,
> where no foul filth encumbered him about.
> He sat there as safe, save for darkness alone,
> as in the boat's stern, where he had slept ere.
> Thus, in the beast's bowel, he abides there alive,
> three days and three nights, thinking aye on the Lord,
> His might and His mercy and His measure eke;
> now he knows Him in woe, who would not in weal.

A fourth poem follows *Cleanness* and *Patience* in the MS. —the romance of *Sir Gawayne and the Grene Knight*. At a glance it is clear, as one turns the leaves, that the metre of the poem is a combination of the alliterative measure with the occasional introduction of a lyrical burden, introduced by a short verse of one accent, and riming according to the scheme *ababa*, which breaks the poem at irregular intervals, evidently marking various stages of the narrative. The metre blends the epic rhythm of *Cleanness* and *Patience* with the lyrical strain of *Pearl*. The illustrations preceding this poem are obviously scenes from medieval romance; above one of the pictures, representing a stolen interview between a lady and a knight, is a couplet not found elsewhere in the MS.:

> Mi mind is mukel on on, that wil me noght amende:
> Sum time was trewe as ston, and fro schame couthe her defende.

The romance deals with a weird adventure that befell

Sir Gawain, son of Loth, and nephew of king Arthur, the favourite hero of medieval romance, more especially in the literature of the west and northern parts of England, where, in all probability, traditions of the knight lived on from early times; the depreciation of the hero in later English literature was due to the direct influence of one particular class of French romances. Gaston Paris, in Volume xxx of *L'Histoire Littéraire de la France*, 1888, has surveyed the whole field of medieval literature dealing with Sir Gawain; according to his view, the present romance is the jewel of English medieval literature, and it may, perhaps, be considered the jewel of medieval romance. To Madden belongs the honour of first having discovered the poem, and of having brought it out in his great collection, *Syr Gawayne...Ancient Romance poems by Scottish and English Authors relating to that celebrated Knight of the Round Table*, published by the Bannatyne Club, 1839. The place of *Sir Gawayne* in the history of English metrical romances is treated of elsewhere[1]; in the present chapter *Sir Gawayne* is considered mainly as the work of the author of *Pearl*.

The story tells how on a New Year's Day, when Arthur and his knights are feasting at Camelot, a great knight clad in green, mounted on a green horse, and carrying a Danish axe, enters the hall, and challenges one of Arthur's knights; the conditions being that the knight must take oath that, after striking the first blow, he will seek the Green Knight twelve months hence and receive a blow in return. Gawain is allowed to accept the challenge, takes the axe and smites the Green Knight so that the head rolls from the body; the trunk takes up the head, which the hand holds out while it repeats the challenge to Gawain to meet him at the Green Chapel next New Year's morning, and then departs. Gawain, in due course, journeys north, and wanders through wild districts, unable to find the Green Chapel; on Christmas Eve he reaches a castle, and asks to be allowed to stay there for the night: he is welcomed by the lord of the castle, who tells him that the Green Chapel is near, and invites him to remain for the Christmas feast. The lord, on each of the last three days of the year, goes a-hunting; Gawain is to stay behind with the lady of

[1] See Chapter XIII.

the castle; the lord makes the bargain that, on his return from hunting, each shall exchange what has been won during the day; the lady puts Gawain's honour to a severe test during the lord's absence: he receives a kiss from her; in accordance with the compact, he does not fail to give the kiss to the husband on his return; there is a similar episode on the next day when two kisses are received and given by Gawain; on the third day, in addition to three kisses, Gawain receives a green lace from the lady, which has the virtue of saving the wearer from harm. Mindful of his next day's encounter with the Green Knight, Gawain gives the three kisses to his host, but makes no mention of the lace. Next morning, he rides forth and comes to the Green Chapel, a cave in a wild district; the Green Knight appears with his axe; Gawain kneels; as the axe descends, Gawain flinches, and is twitted by the knight; the second time Gawain stands as still as a stone, and the Green Knight raises the axe, but pauses; the third time the knight strikes him, but, though the axe falls on Gawain's neck, his wound is only slight. Gawain now declares that he has stood one stroke for another, and that the compact is settled between them. Then the Green Knight reveals himself to Gawain as his host at the castle; he knows all that has taken place. "That woven lace which thou wearest mine own wife wove it; I know it well; I know too thy kisses, and thy trials, and the wooing of my wife; I wrought it myself. I sent her to tempt thee, and methinks thou art the most faultless hero that ever walked the earth. *As pearls are of more price than white peas, so is Gawain of more price than other gay knights.*" But for his concealing the magic lace he would have escaped unscathed. The name of the Green Knight is given as Bernlak de Hautdesert; the contriver of the test is Morgan le Fay, Arthur's half-sister, who wished to try the knights and frighten Guinevere; Gawain returns to court and tells the story; and the lords and ladies of the Round Table lovingly agree to wear a bright green lace in token of this adventure, and in honour of Gawain, who disparages himself as cowardly and covetous. And ever more the badge was deemed the glory of the Round Table, and he that had it was held in honour.

The author derived his materials from some lost original; he states that the story had long been "locked in lettered lore." His original was, no doubt, in French or Anglo French. The oldest form of the challenge and the beheading is an Old Irish heroic legend, *Fled Bricrend* (the feast of Bricriu), preserved in a MS. of the end of the eleventh or the beginning of the twelfth century, where the story is told by Cuchulinn, the giant being Uath Mac Denomain, who dwelt near the lake. The Cuchulinn episode had, in due course, become incorporated in Arthurian literature. The French version nearest to the Gawain story that has so far been pointed out was discovered by Madden in the first continuation by Gautier de Doulens of Chrétien's *Conte del Graal*, where the story is connected with Carados, Arthur's nephew, and differs in many important respects from the English version of the romance. There is much to be said in favour of Miss Weston's conclusion that "it seems difficult to understand how anyone could have regarded this version, ill-motived as it is, and utterly lacking in the archaic details of the English poem, as the source of that work. It should probably rather be considered as the latest in form, if not in date, of all the versions." There is, of course, no doubt whatsoever that we have in the French romance substantially the same story, with the two main episodes, namely, the beheading and the test at the castle; our poet's direct original is evidently lost—he no doubt well knew the *Conte del Graal*—but we are able to judge that whatever other source he may have used, he brought his own genius to bear in the treatment of the theme. It would seem as though the figure of Gawain, "the falcon of the month of May," the traditional type and embodiment of all that was chivalrous and knightly, is drawn from some contemporary knight, and the whole poem may be connected with the foundation of the order of the Garter, which is generally assigned to about the year 1345. From this standpoint it is significant that at the end of the MS., in a somewhat later hand, is found the famous legend of the order: *honi soit qui mal (y) penc*; just as a later poet, to whom we are indebted for a ballad of the Green Knight (a *rifacimento* of this romance, or of some intermediate form of it), has used the same story to account for the origin of the order of the Bath. The romance may be taken not to have been written before the year 1345.

The charm of *Sir Gawayne* is to be found in its description of nature, more especially of wild nature; in the author's enjoyment of all that appertains to the bright side of medieval life; in its details of dress, armour, wood-craft, architecture; and in the artistic arrangement of the story, three parallel episodes being so treated as to avoid all risk of monotony or reiteration. As a characteristic passage the following may be quoted:

> O'er a mound on the morrow he merrily rides
> into a forest full deep and wondrously wild;
> high hills on each side and holt-woods beneath,
> with huge hoary oaks, a hundred together ;
> hazel and hawthorn hung clustering there,
> with rough ragged moss o'ergrown all around;
> unblithe, on bare twigs, sang many a bird,
> piteously piping for pain of the cold.
> Under them Gawayne on Gringolet glideth,
> through marsh and through mire, a mortal full lonesome,
> cumbered with care, lest ne'er he should come
> to that Sire's service, who on that same night
> was born of a bride to vanquish our bale.
> Wherefore sighing he said: "I beseech Thee, O Lord,
> and Mary, thou mildest mother so dear!
> some homestead, where holily I may hear mass
> and matins to-morrow, full meekly I ask;
> thereto promptly I pray pater, ave,
>   and creed."
>   He rode on in his prayer,
>   And cried for each misdeed;
>   He crossed him ofttimes there,
>   And said: "Christ's cross me speed!"

But, much as *Sir Gawayne* shows us of the poet's delight in his art, the main purpose of the poem is didactic. Gawain, the knight of chastity, is but another study by the author of *Cleanness*. On the workmanship of his romance he has lavished all care, only that thereby his readers may the more readily grasp the spirit of the work. Sir Gawain may best, perhaps, be understood as the Sir Calidor of an earlier Spenser.

In the brief summary of the romance, one striking passage has been noted linking the poem to *Pearl*, namely, the comparison of Gawain to the pearl; but, even without this reference the tests of language, technique and spirit, would render identity of authorship incontestable; the relation which this Spenserian romance bears to the elegy as regards time of composition cannot be definitely determined; but, judging by parallelism of expression, it is clear that the interval between the two poems must have been very short.

No direct statement has come down to us as to the authorship of these poems, and, in spite of various ably contested theories, it is not possible to assign the poems to any known poet. The nameless poet of *Pearl* and *Gawayne* has, however, left the impress of his personality on his work; and so vividly is this personality revealed in the poems that it is possible, with some degree of confidence, to evolve something approximating to an account of the author, by piecing together the references and other evidence to be found in his work. The following hypothetical biography is taken, with slight modification, from a study published elsewhere.[1]

The poet was born about 1330; his birthplace was somewhere in Lancashire, or, perhaps, a little more to the north, but not beyond the Tweed; such is the evidence of dialect. Additional testimony may be found in the descriptions of natural scenery in *Gawayne*, *Cleanness* and *Patience*. The wild solitudes of the Cumbrian coast, near his native home, seem to have had special attraction for him. Like a later and greater poet, he must, while yet a youth, have felt the subtle spell of nature's varying aspects in the scenes around him.

Concerning the condition of life to which the boy belonged we know nothing definite; but it may be inferred that his father was connected, probably in some official capacity, with a family of high rank, and that it was amid the gay scenes that brightened life in a great castle the poet's earlier years were passed. In later life, he loved to picture this home with its battlements and towers, its stately hall and spacious parks. There, too, perhaps, minstrels' tales of chivalry first revealed to him the weird world of medieval romance and made him yearn to gain for himself a worthy place among contemporary English poets.

The Old English poets were his masters in poetic art;

[1] Introduction to *Pearl*, p. xlvi.

he had also read *The Romaunt of the Rose*, the chief products of early French literature, Vergil and other Latin writers; to "Clopyngel's *clean* rose" he makes direct reference. The intensely religious spirit of the poems, together with the knowledge they everywhere display of Holy Writ and theology, lead one to infer that he was, at first, destined for the service of the church; probably, he became a "clerk," studying sacred and profane literature at a monastic school, or at one of the universities; and he may have received the first tonsure only.

The four poems preserved in the Cottonian MS. seem to belong to a critical period of the poet's life. *Gawayne*, possibly the earliest of the four, written, perhaps, in honour of the patron to whose household the poet was attached, is remarkable for the evidence it contains of the writer's minute knowledge of the higher social life of his time; from his evident enthusiasm it is clear that he wrote from personal experience of the pleasures of the chase, and that he was accustomed to the courtly life described by him.

The romance of *Gawayne* contains what seems to be a personal reference where the knight is made to exclaim: "It is no marvel for a man to come to sorrow through a woman's wiles; so was Adam beguiled, and Solomon, and Samson, and David, and many more. It were, indeed, great bliss for a man to love them well, and love them not—if one but could."

Gawayne is the story of a noble knight triumphing over the sore temptations that beset his vows of chastity: evidently in a musing mood he wrote in the blank space at the head of one of the illustrations in his MS. the suggestive couplet still preserved by the copyist in the extant MS. His love for some woman had brought him one happiness—an only child, a daughter, on whom he lavished all the wealth of his love. He named the child Margery or Marguerite; she was his "Pearl" —his emblem of holiness and innocence; perhaps she was a love-child, hence his *privy* pearl. His happiness was short-lived; before two years had passed the child was lost to him; his grief found expression in verse; a heavenly vision of his lost jewel brought him comfort and taught him resignation. It is noteworthy that, throughout the whole poem, there is no single reference to the mother of the child; the first words when the father beholds his transfigured Pearl are significant:

"O Pearl," quoth I,
"Art thou my Pearl that I have plained,
Regretted by me alone" ["bi myn one"].

With the loss of his Pearl, a blight seems to have fallen on the poet's life, and poetry seems gradually to have lost its charm for him. The minstrel of *Gawayne* became the stern moralist of *Cleanness* and *Patience*. Other troubles, too, seem to have befallen him during the years that intervened between the writing of these companion poems. *Patience* appears to be almost as autobiographical as *Pearl;* the poet is evidently preaching to himself the lesson of fortitude and hope, amid misery, pain and poverty. Even the means of subsistence seem to have been denied him. "Poverty and patience," he exclaims, "are need's playfellows."

Cleanness and *Patience* were written probably some few years after *Pearl;* and the numerous references in these two poems to the sea would lead one to infer that the poet may have sought distraction in travel, and may have weathered the fierce tempests he describes. His wanderings may have brought him even to the holy city whose heavenly prototype he discerned in the visionary scenes of *Pearl*.

We take leave of the poet while he is still in the prime of life; we have no material on which to base even a conjecture as to his future. Perhaps he turned from poetry and gave himself entirely to theology, always with him a favourite study, or to philosophy, at that time so closely linked with the vital questions at issue concerning faith and belief. If the poet took any part in the church controversies then beginning to trouble men's minds, his attitude would have been in the main conservative. Full of intense hatred towards all forms of vice, especially immorality, he would have spoken out boldly against ignoble priests and friars, and all such servants of the church who, preaching righteousness, lived unrighteously. From minor traditional patristic views he seems to have broken away, but there is no indication of want of allegiance on his part to the authority of the church, to papal supremacy and to the doctrine of Rome; though it has been well said recently, with reference to his general religious attitude, that it was evangelical rather than ecclesiastical.

It is, indeed, remarkable that no tradition has been handed

down concerning the authorship of these poems; and many attempts have been made to identify the author with one or other of the known writers belonging to the end of the fourteenth century. Perhaps the most attractive of these theories is that which would associate the poems with Ralph Strode, Chaucer's "philosophical Strode," to whom (together with "the moral Gower") was dedicated *Troilus and Criseyde*. According to a Latin entry in the old catalogue of Merton College, drawn up in the early years of the fifteenth century, Strode is described as "a noble poet and author of an elegiac work *Phantasma Radulphi*." Ralph Strode of Merton is certainly to be identified with the famous philosopher of the name, one of the chief logicians of the age. It is as poet and philosopher that he seems to be singled out by Chaucer. *Phantasma Radulphi* might, possibly, apply to *Pearl;* while *Gawayne and the Grene Knight* might well be placed in juxtaposition to *Troilus*. An *Itinerary of the Holy Land*, by Strode, appears to have been known to Nicholas Brigham; further, there is a tradition that he left his native land, journeyed to France, Germany and Italy, and visited Syria and the Holy Land. His name as a Fellow of Merton is said to occur for the last time in 1361. Strode and Wyclif were contemporaries at Oxford, as may be inferred from an unprinted MS. in the Imperial library in Vienna, containing Wyclif's reply to Strode's arguments against certain of the reformer's views. The present writer is of opinion that the philosopher is identical with the common serjeant of the city of London of the same name, who held office between 1375 and 1385, and who died in 1387. But, fascinating as is the theory, no link has, as yet, been discovered which may incontestably connect Strode with the author of *Pearl*, nor has it yet been discovered that Strode came of a family belonging to the west midland or northern district. The fiction that Strode was a monk of Dryburgh abbey has now been exploded.

Some seventy years ago, Guest, the historian of English rhythms, set up a claim for the poet Huchoun of the Awle Ryale, to whom Andrew of Wyntoun refers in his *Orygynale Cronykil*.[1]

Guest regarded as the most decisive proof of his theory the

[1] See the Chapter on Huchoun in Volume II.

fact that, at the void space at the head of *Sir Gawayne and the Grene Knight* in the MS., a hand of the fifteenth century has scribbled the name *Hugo de;* but little can be inferred from this piece of evidence; while the lines by Wyntoun tend to connect the author with a set of poems differentiated linguistically and in technique from the poems in the Cotton MS. But this is not the place to enter into a discussion of the various problems connected with the identity of Huchoun: it is only necessary here to state that, in the opinion of the writer, the view which would make Huchoun the author of *Pearl, Gawayne and the Grene Knight, Cleanness* and *Patience* is against the weight of evidence. By the same evidence as that adduced to establish Huchoun's authorship of these poems, various other alliterative poems are similarly assigned to him, namely, *The Wars of Alexander, The Destruction of Troy, Titus and Vespasian, The Parliament of the Three Ages, Wynnere and Wastoure, Erkenwald* and the alliterative riming poem *Golagros and Gawain.*

According to this view, *The Parliament of the Three Ages* belongs to the close of the poet's career, for it is supposed to sum up his past course through all his themes—through *Alexander, Troy, Titus* and *Morte Arthure.* But this theory that, on the basis of parallel passages, would make Huchoun the official father of all these poems, in addition to those which may be legitimately assigned to him on the evidence of Wyntoun's lines, fails to recognise that the author of *The Parliament of the Three Ages,* far from being saturated with the *Troy Book* and the *Alexander* romances, actually confuses Jason, or Joshua, the high priest who welcomed Alexander, with Jason who won the golden fleece.

Probably the work of four or five alliterative poets comes under consideration in dealing with the problem at issue. To one poet may, perhaps, safely be assigned the two poems *The Parliament of the Three Ages* and *Wynnere and Wastoure,* the latter from internal evidence one of the oldest poems of the fourteenth century, and to be dated about 1351: it is a precursor of *The Vision of Piers Plowman.*[1] The former poem recalls the poet of *Gawayne,* more especially in its elaborate description of deer-stalking, a parallel picture to the description

[1] See Chapter I, Volume II, *Piers the Plowman,* p. 37.

of the hunting of the deer, the boar and the fox, in *Gawayne*.

The alliterative poem of *Erkenwald* comes nearer to the work of the author of *Cleanness* and *Patience* than any other of the alliterative poems grouped in the above-mentioned list. It tells, in lines written either by this author himself or by a very gifted disciple, an episode of the history of the saint when he was bishop of St Paul's; and, in connection with the date of its composition, it should be noted that a festival in honour of the saint was established in London in the year 1386.

Internal evidence of style, metre and language appears to outweigh the parallel passages and other clues which are adduced as tests of unity of authorship in respect of the *Troy Book*, *Titus*, *The Wars of Alexander* and *Golagros*. For the present, these may be considered as isolated remains which have come down to us of the works of a school of alliterative poets who flourished during the second half of the fourteenth and the early years of the fifteenth century. So far as we can judge from these extant poems, the most gifted poet of the school was the author of *Sir Gawayne and the Grene Knight:* he may well have been regarded as the master, and his influence on more northern poets, and on alliterative poetry generally, may explain in part, but not wholly, the parallel passages which link his work with that of other poets of the school, who used the same formulae, the same phrases and, at times, repeated whole lines, much in the same way as poets of the Chaucerian school spoke the language of their master.

CHAPTER XVI

Later Transition English

I

LEGENDARIES AND CHRONICLERS

IT is significant, both of the approaching triumph of the vernacular, and of the growing importance of the lower and middle classes in the nation, that some of the chief contributions to our literature during the two generations immediately preceding that of Chaucer were translations from Latin and Norman-French, made, as their authors point out, expressly for the delectation of the common people. Not less significant are the facts that much of this literature deals with the history of the nation, and that now, for the first time since the Conquest, men seemed to think it worth while to commit to writing political ballads in the English tongue.

The productions of this time, dealt with in the present chapter, fall into two main classes, religious and historical, the former comprising homilies, saints' lives and translations or paraphrases of Scripture, and the latter the chronicles of Robert of Gloucester, Thomas Bek of Castleford and Robert Mannynge, the prophecies of Adam Davy and the war songs of Laurence Minot. The two classes have many characteristics in common, and, while the homilists delight in illustrations drawn from the busy life around them, the historians seldom lose an opportunity for conveying a moral lesson.

The earliest of the three chronicles mentioned above was written about 1300, and is generally known by the name of Robert of Gloucester, though it is very uncertain whether he was the original author of the whole work. It exists in two versions, which, with the exception of several interpolations in one of them, are identical down to the year 1135. From this

point the story is told in one version, which may be called the
first recension, in nearly three thousand lines, and in the
other, the second recension, in rather less than six hundred.
From an investigation of the style it has been supposed that
there was a single original for lines 1–9137 of the Chronicle,
that is to say, to the end of the reign of Henry I, composed
in the abbey of Gloucester, and that, at the end of the thirteenth
century, a monk, whose name we know from internal evidence
to have been Robert, added to it the longer continuation.
This must have been made after 1297, as it contains a reference
to the canonisation of Louis IX of France, which took place
in that year. Then, in the first half of the fourteenth century,
another writer found the original manuscript, added the
shorter continuation, and also interpolated and worked over
the earlier part.

In any case there can be little doubt that the Chronicle
was composed in the abbey of Gloucester. The language is
that of south Gloucestershire; and Stow, who may have had
access to information now lost, speaks in his Annals (1580) of
the author as Robert of Gloucester, or Robertus Glocestrensis.
The detailed acquaintance with local affairs shown by the writer
of the longer continuation proves that he lived near the city,
while we have his own authority for the fact that he was
within thirty miles of Evesham at the time of the battle so
ably described by him. But, in the earlier part of the Chronicle, also, there are traces of special local knowledge, which,
apart from the dialect, would point to Gloucester as the place
of its origin.

The poem begins with a geographical account of England,
borrowed from Geoffrey of Monmouth, Henry of Huntingdon
and the life of St. Kenelm in the South English Legendary.

Next, Nennius, or, perhaps, Geoffrey of Monmouth, is
followed for the genealogy of Brutus, the legendary founder
of Britain; and, from this point down to the English conquest,
Geoffrey of Monmouth is the chief authority. The compiler
is, however, by no means a slavish translator, and he treats
his original with considerable freedom. Thus, he sometimes
elaborates, giving the speeches of historical personages in a
fuller form, while, on the other hand, he frequently omits long
passages. But the episodes which stand out in the memory

of the reader—the stories of Lear, of the "virgin-daughter of Locrine" and of Arthur—are also those which arrest us in the Latin original.

Although it has sometimes been stated that the author of this part of the *Chronicle* was indebted to Wace, it seems very doubtful whether the work of his predecessor was known to him. Such lines as those which hint at the high place taken by Gawain among Arthur's knights, or make mention of the Round Table may be due to verbal tradition, which was especially rife in the Welsh marches. The coincidences are certainly not striking enough to justify the assertion that the Gloucester *Chronicle* owed anything to the *Geste des Bretons*, though Aldis Wright has shown that the writer of the second recension was acquainted with Layamon's version of Wace's poems.

For the history of England under the Old English and Norman kings, the chief authorities consulted were Henry of Huntingdon and William of Malmesbury, the former being followed in the narration of events, and the latter in the descriptions and anecdotes of famous characters. Occasionally, other sources are drawn upon; for instance, the story of the duel between Canute and Edmund Ironside is from the *Genealogia Regum Anglorum* of Ailred of Rievaulx, and another work by the same author, the *Vita Edwardi Regis et Martyris* is, probably, the chief authority for the life and death of Edward the Confessor. For the reigns of Henry II and Richard I the life of Thomas à Becket in the *South English Legendary*, and the *Annales Waverlienses* supplied some material, the former furnishing almost word for word the accounts of the constitutions of Clarendon and of the death of the saint. Some passages seem to depend on folk-songs; and there are others, such as the account of the misfortunes which befell the duke of Austria's land in revenge for his imprisonment of Richard I, that may be due to tradition. On the whole, however, the *Chronicle* does not supply much that is fresh in the way of legendary lore.

From the beginning of the reign of Henry III, the poem becomes valuable both as history and literature. The writer, whom we may now certainly call Robert, was, as we have seen, either an eye-witness of the facts he relates, or had heard of them from eye-witnesses. He had, moreover, a distinct narrative gift, and there are all the elements of a stirring historical romance in his story of the struggle that took place between the king and the barons for the possession of Gloucester. Not less graphic is the description of the town and gown riot in Oxford in 1263. We are told how the burgesses shut one of the city gates; how certain clerks hewed it down and carried it through the suburbs, singing over it a funeral hymn; how, for this offence, the rioters were put in prison, and how the quarrel grew to such a height that the citizens came out armed against the scholars. Robert relates with evident enjoyment the discomfiture of the former, and the vengeance taken by the clerks on their foes—how they plundered their shops, burned their houses and punished the mayor, who was a vintner, by taking the bungs from his casks and letting the wine run away. But, he adds, when the king came and heard of all this mischief, he drove the clerks out of the town, and forbade their returning till after Michaelmas.

Picturesque as such passages are, they are less valuable than the powerful description of the battle of Evesham and the death of Simon de Montfort, a passage too well known to call for further reference.

The form of this *Chronicle* is no less interesting than its theme. Its metre is an adaptation of the two half-lines of Old English poetry into one long line, one of its nearest relations being the *Poema Morale*. In spite of the well-marked caesura, a relic of the former division into halves, the line has a swinging rhythm especially suited to narrative verse, and the poem is of metrical importance as showing the work of development in progress. [1]

It was not long after Robert had added his continuation to the Gloucester *Chronicle* that Thomas Bek of Castleford composed a similar work in the northern dialect. The unique MS. of this chronicle is preserved at Göttingen, and is as yet inedited. The work contains altogether nearly forty thousand lines, of which the first twenty-seven thousand are borrowed from Geoffrey of Monmouth, while the remainder, extending to the coronation of Edward III, are derived from sources not

---

[1] See Saintsbury, *History of English Prosody*, i, 67.

yet defined. The metre is the short rimed couplet of the French chroniclers.

Mention has already been made of the *South English Legendary*, a collection of versified lives of the saints in the same dialect and metre as those of the Gloucester *Chronicle*. The fact that certain passages from these lives are incorporated in the *Chronicle* has led to the conclusion that one person was responsible for both; but, as we have seen, the *Chronicle* is probably the work of three hands, if not of more, and it is impossible to say anything more definite about the authorship of the *Legendary* than that it had its origin in the neighbourhood of Gloucester towards the end of the thirteenth century, and that more than one author was concerned in it. The oldest manuscript (Laud 108 in the Bodleian) was written after 1265, and is dated by its editor, Horstmann, as belonging to the years 1280–90.

It is probable, however, that it had been in hand a considerable time. As the number of saints' days increased, it was found convenient to have at hand homiletic material for each festival; and, as no single monastic library would contain manuscripts of all the independent lives required, these had to be borrowed and copied as occasion served. This was a task too great for any one man, and it is most probable that the monks at Gloucester had been gathering the legends together for some years, and that a number of them contributed towards the first redaction. This would partly account for the unequal merit of the lives, some of which display much more literary and poetic feeling than others. But, in considering this point, it must be remembered that the charm of any particular story depends largely on its original source; even the clumsy pen of a monkish translator could not wholly disguise the beauty of such legends as that of St. Francis.

Although the collection is of the most varied description, and comprises the lives of saints of all countries and of all ages down to the time of compilation, the best-told legends are those of native saints; and, as the style of these is not unlike that of the author of the longer continuation of the Gloucester *Chronicle*, it is possible that they may be by him. Among them may be especially mentioned the very vivid account of the career and murder of St. Thomas of Canterbury, which displays considerable dramatic power, and the life of St. Edmund of Pontigny (archbishop Edmund Rich, who died in 1240), which treats of events that were still fresh in men's minds and, like the Gloucester *Chronicle*, betrays a great admiration for Simon de Montfort. The same predilection, it may be noted, is evident in the life of St. Dominic, where Sir Simon, "that good and gracious knight," is commended for having lent his support to the order of preaching friars.

Some of the lives, such as those of St. Kenelm and St. Michael, are made the vehicle of secular instruction, and contain curious geographical and scientific disquisitions, the latter being especially valuable for its light upon medieval folk- and devil-lore and for its cosmology. The most interesting of all the lives are those connected with St. Patrick and St. Brendan. The story of Sir Owayn's visit to purgatory shows all the characteristic Celtic wealth of imagination in the description of the torments endured. Nothing could be more terrible than the lines which describe him as "dragged all about in a waste land, so black and dark that he saw nothing but the fiends, who drove him hither and thither and thronged around him." And, on the other hand, nothing could be more charming in its strange mystic beauty than the story of St. Brendan's sojourn in the Isle of Birds, and his interview with the penitent Judas, permitted, in recompense of one charitable deed, to enjoy a little respite from the pains of hell.

While the monks of Gloucester were thus busy with hagiology, similar activity was exhibited in the north of England, according to Horstmann in the diocese of Durham, though the prevalence of midland forms in the texts points to a district further south. There exists in many manuscripts, the earliest of which, in the Royal College of Physicians at Edinburgh, seems to have been written at the beginning of the fourteenth century, a cycle of homilies, in octosyllabic couplets, covering the whole of the Sundays in the church year. Two of the later manuscripts (Harleian 4196 and Tiberius E. VII), both written about 1350, contain also a cycle of legends for use on saints' days.

Considerable diversity is shown in the recensions of the homilies: the Edinburgh MS. opens with a prologue, in which the author, like so many writers of the time, carefully explains that his work is intended for ignorant men, who cannot understand French; and, since it is the custom of the common people to come to church on Sundays, he has turned into English for them the Gospel for the day. His version, however, is not a close translation; it resembles *Ormulum* in giving first a paraphrase of the Scripture, and then an exposition of the passage chosen; but, in addition to this, there is also a *narracio*, or story, to illustrate the lesson and drive the moral home. These stories are often quite short, sometimes mere anecdotes, and are derived from the most diverse sources: sometimes from saints' lives, sometimes from Scripture and sometimes from French *fabliaux*. The homilist is an especial lover of the poor, and one of his most striking sermons is that for the fourth Sunday after Epiphany, on the subject of Christ stilling the waves. The world, says he, is but a sea, tossed up and down, where the great fishes eat the small; for the rich men of the world devour what the poor earn by their labour, and the king acts towards the weak as the whale towards the herring. Like Mannyng of Brunne, the writer has a special word of condemnation for usurers.

The Harleian manuscript is, unfortunately, imperfect at the beginning, so that it is impossible to say whether it ever contained the prologue; while the MS. Tiberius E. vii was so badly burned in the Cottonian fire that the greater part of it cannot be deciphered. These manuscripts, however, show that the homilies had been entirely worked over and rewritten in the half century that had elapsed since the Edinburgh version was composed. The plan of paraphrase, exposition and narration is not always followed, and, so far as Easter Sunday, the stories are taken chiefly from Scripture. From this point, however, they depend on other sources, and they are especially interesting when compared with the contents of other northern poems of the same period. The legend of the Holy Rood, for instance, which runs like a thread through *Cursor Mundi*, is given at great length, and so, also, is the graphic story of Piers the usurer, which occurs in *Handlyng Synne*. Among the stories is the well-known legend of the monk who was lured by a bird from his monastery, and only returned to it after three hundred years, when everything was changed, and no one knew him.

The legends which follow these homilies are much more restricted in scope than those of the southern collection, and are confined chiefly to lives of the apostles or of the early Christian martyrs, St. Thomas of Canterbury being the only English saint represented. But, while the Gloucester *Legendary* seems to have been intended only as a reference book for the preacher, the northern series shows the lives in a finished form, suitable for reading or reciting in church. The verse is polished, limpid and fluent, betraying, in its graceful movement, traces of French influence, while, at the same time, it is not free from the tendency to alliteration prevalent in northern poetry. The writer had a genuine gift of narration and possessed both humour and dramatic power, as is shown by the story of the lord and lady who were parted by shipwreck and restored to one another by the favour of St. Mary Magdalene; and, like most medieval homilists, he excels in the description of horrors—of fiends "blacker than any coal," and of dragons armed with scales as stiff as steel. Sometimes, a little homily is interwoven with the story; and one passage, which rebukes men for slumbering or chattering in church, resembles a similar exhortation in *Handlyng Synne*. The section on the "faithful dead," also, seems to be in close dependence on that work. Three of the stories told occur in close juxtaposition in Mannyng's book; and a reference to the story of Piers the usurer, which is mentioned but not related, probably because it had already found a place in the homilies, points to the conclusion that the compiler was well acquainted with the work of his predecessor.

The desire to impart a knowledge of the Scriptures to men who could understand only the vernacular likewise prompted the author of the *Northern Psalter*, a translation of the *Psalms* in vigorous, if somewhat rough, octosyllabic couplets, composed about the middle of the reign of Edward II. One of the three manuscripts in which it exists belonged to the monastery of Kirkham, but the language is that of a more northerly district, and the author probably lived near the Scottish border.

Further evidence of literary activity in the north of England during this period is given by *Cursor Mundi*, a very long poem, which, as its name implies, treats of universal rather than local history, and, like the cycles of miracle plays which were just beginning to pass out of the hands of their clerical inventors into those of laymen, relates the story of the world from the creation to the day of doom. It opens with a prologue, which is, practically, the author's "apology" for his undertaking. Men, he says, rejoice to hear romances of Alexander and Julius Cæsar, of the long strife between Greece and Troy, of king Arthur and Charlemagne. Each man is attracted by what he enjoys the most, and all men delight especially in their "paramours"; but the best lady of all is the Virgin Mary, and whosoever takes her for his own shall find that her love is ever true and loyal. Therefore, the poet will compose a work in her honour; and, because French rimes are commonly found everywhere, but there is nothing for those who know only English, he will write it for him who "na Frenche can."

With this explanation the author embarks on his vast theme, which he divides according to the seven ages of the world, a device copied from Bede. He describes the creation, the war in heaven, the temptation of Eve, the expulsion from Paradise, the history of the patriarchs and so on through the Bible narrative, sometimes abridging, but more often enlarging, the story by long additions, drawn from the most diverse authorities, which add greatly to the interest of the narrative. One of the most interesting of these additions is the legend of the Holy Rood: this is not told in a complete form in one place, but is introduced in relation to the history of the men who were connected with it. In place of the prophecies there are inserted two parables, probably from Grosseteste's *Château d'Amour;* and the poet then goes on to tell with much detail of the youth of Mary, the birth of Christ and His childhood. Then follow the story of His life as given by the evangelists, His death and descent into hell, the careers of the apostles, the assumption of the Virgin and a section on doomsday. The author concludes with an address to his fellow-men, begging them to think upon the transitory nature of earthly joys, and a prayer to the Virgin, commending his work to her approval.

The humility betrayed in the concluding lines is all the more attractive because, as his poem shows, the writer was an

accomplished scholar, extremely well read in medieval literature. His work, indeed, is a storehouse of legends, not all of
which have been traced to their original sources. His most
important authority was the *Historia Scholastica* of Peter
Comestor; but he used many others, among which may be
mentioned Wace's *Fête de la Conception Notre Dame*, Grosseteste's *Château d'Amour*, the apocryphal gospels, a south
English poem on the assumption of the Virgin ascribed to
Edmund Rich, Adso's *Libellus de Antichristo*, the *Elucidarium*
of Honorius of Autun, Isidore of Seville and the *Golden Legend*
of Jacobus a Voragine.

The popularity of *Cursor Mundi* is witnessed by the large
number of manuscripts in which it is preserved, and it has
many qualities to account for this. In the first place, the
author never loses sight of his audience, showing great skill
in appealing to the needs of rude, unlettered people whose
religious instruction must, necessarily, be conveyed by way
of concrete example. He has a keen eye for the picturesque;
his description of the Flood, for instance, may be compared
with the famous passage in the alliterative poem, *Cleanness*,
and he lingers over the episode of Goliath with an enjoyment
due as much to his own delight in story-telling as to a knowledge of what his hearers will appreciate; there is a strong
family likeness between the Philistine hero and such monsters
as Colbrand and Ascapart. The strong humanity which
runs through the whole book is one of its most attractive
features, and shows that the writer was full of sympathy for
his fellow creatures.

The whole poem shows considerable artistic skill. In
spite of the immense mass of material with which it deals,
it is well proportioned, and the narrative is lucid and easy.
The verse form is generally that of the eight-syllabled couplet;
but, when treating of the passion and death of Christ, the poet
uses alternately riming lines of eight and six syllables; and
the discourse between Christ and man, which follows the
account of the crucifixion, consists largely of six-lined mono-
rimed stanzas.

Of the author, beyond the fact that he was, as he himself
states, a cleric, nothing whatever is known. Hupe's theory,
that his name was John of Lindebergh, which place he iden-

tifies with Limber Magna in Lincolnshire, is based on a mis-
reading of an insertion in one of the manuscripts by the scribe
who copied it; and all that can be affirmed with any confidence is that the author lived in the north of England towards
the end of the thirteenth or beginning of the fourteenth century. Some of the later manuscripts show west midland
and even southern peculiarities, but this is only another
testimony to the wide-spread popularity of the poem.

The most skilful story-teller of his time was Robert
Mannyng of Brunne, who, between 1303 and 1338, translated into his native tongue two poems written in poor French
by English clerics. These two works were William of Wadington's *Manuel des Pechiez*, written, probably, for Norman
settlers in Yorkshire, and a chronicle composed by Peter of
Langtoft, a canon of the Augustinian priory of Bridlington.

Unlike most monastic writers, Mannyng supplies some
valuable information about himself. In the prologue to
Handlyng Synne, his version of the *Manuel des Pechiez*, he tells
us that his name is Robert of Brunne, of Brunnëwake in Keste-
vene, and that he dedicates his work especially to the fellowship of Sempringham, to which he had belonged for fifteen
years. He also tells us the exact year in which he began his
translation—1303. This information is supplemented by some
lines in his translation of Langtoft's chronicle. Here he adds
that his name is Robert Mannyng of Brunne, and that he
wrote all this history in the reign of Edward III, in the priory
of Sixille. We gather, also, from an allusion in the narrative,
that he had spent some time at Cambridge, where he had met
Robert Bruce and his brother Alexander, who was a skilful
artist.

These particulars have been elucidated by the labours of
Furnivall. Brunne was the present Bourne, a market town
thirty-five miles to the south of Boston in Lincolnshire;
Sempringham, where was the parent house of the Gilbertine
order, is now represented by a church and a few scattered
houses; Sixille, or Six Hills, is a little hamlet not far from
Market Rasen, and here, too, was a priory of the Gilbertines.

Of William of Wadington, the author of the *Manuel des
Pechiez* very little is known. In the prologue to his work,

however, he begs his readers to excuse his bad French, because he was born and bred in England and took his name from a town in that country. The apology is not altogether superfluous, for his grammar is loose, and forms that were archaic even in the thirteenth century are of frequent occurrence. His versification is also poor, and, though his normal form is the octosyllabic couplet, he does not hesitate to introduce lines of six, or even of ten syllables. His English audience, however, was not critical, and the popularity of the manual is attested by the number of manuscripts, fourteen in all, which have survived. Most of these belong to the thirteenth century, and Mannyng's translation, as we have seen, was begun in 1303.

The English version begins with an introduction of the usual style, setting out the plan of the work, and stating the object of the author in making the translation. He has put it into English rime for the benefit of ignorant men, who delight in listening to stories at all hours, and often hearken to evil tales which may lead to their perdition. Therefore, he has provided them in this book with stories of a more edifying description.

His instinct for selecting what he feels will interest the unlearned is at once revealed by his omission of the long and dull section in which Wadington dwells on the twelve articles of faith. Theory attracts him little, and he proceeds at once to the first commandment, illustrating it by the dreadful example of a monk, who, by his love for an Eastern woman, was tempted to the worship of idols. Then comes a notable passage, also in Wadington, against witchcraft, and, in expansion of this, is given the original story of how a witch enchanted a leather bag, so that it milked her neighbour's cows, and how her charm, in the mouth of a bishop (who, of course, did not believe in it), was useless. Thus he treats of the ten commandments in order, keeping fairly closely to his original, and generally following Wadington's lead in the stories by which he illustrates them. This occupies nearly three thousand lines, and the poet then enters upon the theme of the seven deadly sins.

Mannyng seems to have found this a congenial subject, and the section throws much light on the social conditions

of his time.　Tournaments, he says, are the occasion of all
the seven deadly sins, and, if every knight loved his brother,
they would never take place, for they encourage pride, envy,
anger, idleness, covetousness, gluttony and lust.　Furthermore, mystery plays—and these lines are highly significant
as throwing light on the development of the drama at the
beginning of the fourteenth century—are also occasions of
sin.　Only two mysteries may be performed, those of the
birth of Christ and of His resurrection, and these must be
played within the church, for the moral edification of the
people.　If they are presented in groves or highways, they
are sinful pomps, to be avoided as much as tournaments;
and priests who lend vestments to aid the performance are
guilty of sacrilege.

One of the best stories in the book, the tale of Piers, illustrates the wickedness and repentance of one of the hated tribe
of usurers.　It is also in illustration of this sin that the grotesque story occurs of the Cambridge miser parson who was
so much attached to his gold that he tried to eat it, and died
in the attempt.

In respect of the sin of gluttony, not only the rich are to be
blamed; most people sin by eating too much; two meals a day
are quite sufficient, except for children, and they should be
fed only at regular hours.　Late suppers, too, are to be avoided,
especially by serving men, who often sit up and feast till
cockcrow.　People should not break their fast before par-
taking of the "holy bread," or dine before they hear mass.

The seven deadly sins being disposed of, there follows
a long section on sacrilege, in which Mannyng departs freely
from his original.　He says, indeed, that he will deal with
some vices coming under this head as William of Wadington
teaches him; but the lines following, in which he apologises
for "foul English and feeble rhyme," seem to show that he
was conscious of some audacity in taking so many liberties
with the French poem.　However this may be, the account
of the reproof that a Norfolk bondsman gave a knight who
had allowed his beasts to defile the churchyard, which is not
in the *Manuel des Pechiez*, and is, evidently, a true story, is
very characteristic of the attitude of the Gilbertines to the
privileged classes.　The order was, as its latest historian has

pointed out, essentially democratic in its organisation, and the fearlessness of monk towards prior is reflected in the approval that Mannyng tacitly bestows on the thrall's behaviour.

The churchyard was not only desecrated by use as a pasture. It was the meeting-place of youths and maidens for games and songs, and this gives occasion for the grim legend, borrowed from a German source, of the dancers and carol singers who, on Christmas night, disturbed the priest in his orisons. Notwithstanding the fact that his own daughter was tempted to join the frivolous company, he punished them with his curse; so that the intruders were doomed to pursue their dance through rain and snow and tempest for ever. There is something very charming in the snatch of song—

> By the leved wood rode Bevolyne,
> Wyth him he ledd feyrë Merswyne,
> Why stondë we? Why go we noght?

and very grim is the irony that dooms the dancers to repeat the last line in the midst of their involuntary perpetual motion. These qualities are, of course, inherent in the story, but it loses nothing in Mannyng's narration.

The discussion of the sin of sacrilege brings the author to line 9492, and now, following Wadington, he enters on the explanation of the seven sacraments. But, as the French version supplies few stories in illustration of these, Mannyng makes up the deficiency by several of his own. Then follows a passage on the necessity of shrift, the twelve points of shrift and the graces which spring from it, all treated with comparative brevity and with little anecdotal illustration.

It is impossible for any short account of *Handlyng Synne* to convey an adequate idea of its charm and interest. Mannyng excels in all the qualities of a narrator. He combines, in fact, the *trouvère* with the homilist, and shows the way to Gower's *Confessio Amantis*. Thus, he differs from the antiquary Robert of Gloucester by being one of the earliest of English story-tellers. He had a vivid imagination which enabled him to see all the circumstances and details of occurrences for which his authority merely provides the suggestion, and he fills in the outlines of stories derived from Gregory or Bede with colours borrowed from the homely life of England in the fourteenth century. He delights, also, to play upon the emotions of his audience by describing the torments of the damned, and his pictures of hell are more grim and more grotesque than those of Wadington. He shows a preference for direct narration, and, where the French merely conveys the sense of what has been said, Mannyng gives the very words of the speaker, in simple, colloquial English. Homely expressions and pithy proverbs abound throughout, and the work is full of telling, felicitous metaphors, such as "tavern is the devyl's knyfe," or "kerchief is the devyl's sail," or "to throw a falcon at every fly."

Simplicity is, indeed, one of the most striking features of Mannyng's style. Writing, as he says, for ignorant men, he is at some pains to explain difficult terms or to give equivalents for them. Thus, when he uses the word "mattock," he remarks, in a parenthesis, that it is a pick-axe; and, in the same way, the term "Abraham's bosom" is carefully interpreted as the place between paradise and hell. And, in his anxiety that his hearers shall understand the spiritual significance of religious symbols, he calls to his aid illustrations from popular institutions familiar to all. Baptism, he says, is like a charter which testifies that a man has bought land from his neighbour, confirmation is like the acknowledgment of that charter by a lord or king.

In dwelling on the personal relations of man to God, Mannyng, like the author of *Cursor Mundi*, often shows much poetic feeling. While he paints in sombre tones the dreadful fate of unrepentant sinners, he speaks no less emphatically of the love of God for His children and the sacrifice of Christ. His simple faith in the divine beneficence, combined with an intense sympathy for penitent man, lends a peculiar charm to his treatment of such stories as those of the merciful knight and Piers the usurer.

Apart from its literary qualities, *Handlyng Synne* has considerable value as a picture of contemporary manners. Much of what is said on these points is borrowed from Wadington, but still more is due to Mannyng's personal observation. In his attacks on tyrannous lords, and his assertion of the essential equality of men, he resembles the author of *Piers Plowman*.

The knight is pictured as a wild beast ranging over the country; he goes out "about robbery to get his prey"; he endeavours to strip poor men of their land, and, if he cannot buy it, he devises other means to torment them, accusing them of theft or of damage to the corn or cattle of their lord. Great harm is suffered at the hands of his officers; for nearly every steward gives verdicts unfavourable to the poor; and, if the latter ask for mercy, he replies that he is only acting according to the strict letter of the law. But, says Mannyng, he who only executes the law and adds no grace thereto may never, in his own extremity, appeal for mercy to God.

But, if Mannyng is severe on tyrannous lords, he shows no leniency to men of his own calling. The common sins of the clergy, their susceptibility to bribes, their lax morality, their love of personal adornment, their delight in horses, hounds and hawks, all come under his lash, and, in words which may not have been unknown to Chaucer, he draws the picture of the ideal parish priest.

Although the order to which Mannyng belonged was originally founded for women, they receive little indulgence at his hands. Indeed, he surpasses William of Wadington and the average monastic writer in his strictures on their conduct. God intended woman to help man, to be his companion and to behave meekly to her master and lord. But women are generally "right unkind" in wedlock; for one sharp word they will return forty, and they desire always to get the upper hand. They spend what should be given to the poor in long trains and wimples; they deck themselves out to attract masculine attention, and thus make themselves responsible for the sins of men. Even when the author has occasion to tell the story of a faithful wife who made constant prayer and offerings for the husband whom she supposed to be dead, he adds, grudgingly,

> This woman pleyned (pitied) her husbonde sore,
> Wuld Gode that many such women wore!

For the ordinary amusements of the people Mannyng has little sympathy; he looks at them from the shadow of the cloister, and, to him, "carols, wrestlings, and summer games" are all so many allurements of the devil to entice men from heaven. The gay song of the wandering minstrel and the loose tales of ribald jongleurs who lie in wait for men at tavern doors are as hateful to him as to the author or authors of *Piers Plowman;* even in the garlands with which girls deck their tresses he sees a subtle snare of Satan. Towards children he shows some tenderness, recognising their need for greater physical indulgence than their elders; but he upholds the counsel of Solomon to give them the sharp end of the rod, so long as no bones be broken.

Mannyng's mode of translation renders a precise estimate of his indebtedness to Wadington somewhat difficult. A hint from his original will sometimes set him off on a long digression, at other times he keeps fairly close to the sense, but interweaves with it observations and parentheses of his own. He does not always tell the same tales as Wadington, but omits, substitutes or adds at will; the fifty-four stories in the *Manuel des Pechiez* are represented in *Handlyng Synne* by sixty-five. Many of his additions are taken from local legends, and it is in these that his skill as a narrator is most apparent. Unhampered by any precedent, the stories move quietly and lightly along, and may almost challenge comparison with those of Chaucer.

The verse of *Handlyng Synne* is the eight-syllabled iambic metre of the original; but, as in the *Manuel des Pechiez*, many lines occur which defy the most ingenious scansion. The language in its state of transition afforded special opportunity for these irregularities; when there was no fixed standard for the sounding of the inflectional -*e* this was apt to be added or omitted at the will of the scribe. The three manuscripts in which the poem has survived, the Harleian, dated about 1360, and the Bodleian and Dulwich, about 1400, show many discrepancies.

The dialect of *Handlyng Synne* is east midland, of a northern type, containing more Scandinavian forms than are found in the language of Chaucer. The number of romance words is much greater than in the Gloucester *Chronicle*, which may be explained partly by locality and partly by the fact that such forms are always more numerous in translations from the French than in original English compositions.

Mannyng's other work, the *Chronicle of England*, is of

less general importance than *Handlyng Synne;* though of
greater metrical interest.   It consists of two parts, the first
extending from the arrival of the legendary Brut in Britain
to the English invasion, the second from the English invasion
to the end of Edward I's reign.   The first part, in octosyllabic
couplets, is a close and fairly successful translation from
Wace's version of Geoffrey of Monmouth's *Historia Regum
Britanniae;* the second, in rimed alexandrines, is taken from
an Anglo-Norman poem by Peter of Langtoft.

Langtoft's alexandrines, which are arranged in sets riming
on one sound, seem to have puzzled Mannyng, and his attempt
to reproduce them in the fourteen-syllabled line of the Gloucester *Chronicle* is not altogether successful.   Sometimes the line
is an alexandrine, but at others, and this is most significant, it is decasyllabic; moreover, though Mannyng tries to
emulate the continuous rime of his original, he generally
succeeds in achieving only couplet rime.   Thus we see dimly
foreshadowed the heroic couplet which Chaucer brought to
perfection.[1]

When, at the request of Dan Robert of Malton, Mannyng
set about his chronicle, it was, probably, with the intention
of following Langtoft throughout; but, on further consideration,
he judged that, since the first part of Langtoft's chronicle
was merely an abridgment of Wace, it was better to go straight
to the original.   So, after an introduction which contains
the autobiographical details already given, and an account of
the genealogy of Brut, he gives a somewhat monotonous and
commonplace version of Wace's poem.   Sometimes, he omits or
abridges; sometimes, he adds a line or two from Langtoft,
or the explanation of a word unfamiliar to his audience, or
pauses to notice contemptuously some unfounded tradition
current among the unlearned.   Once, he digresses to wonder,
with Geoffrey of Monmouth, that Gildas and Bede should
have omitted all mention of king Arthur, who was greater
than any man they wrote of save the saints.   In all other
lands, he says, men have written concerning him, and in
France more is known of the British hero than in the lands that
gave him birth.   But Mannyng's characteristic doubt of
Welsh trustworthiness leads him to question the story of

[1] Sainstbury, *History of English Prosody,* i, 113.

Arthur's immortality. "If he now live," he says contemptuously, "his life is long."

All through his version Mannyng, as might be expected,
shows a more religious spirit than Wace; this is especially
exemplified in the passages in which he points out that the
misfortunes of the Britons were a judgment on them for their
sins, and in the long insertion, borrowed from Langtoft and
Geoffrey of Monmouth, of Cadwalader's prayer; and, as he
nears the end of the first portion of his chronicle, he draws
freely on Bede, telling at great length the story of St. Gregory
and the English boy slaves and the mission of St. Augustine.

The second half of the chronicle is much more interesting
than the first, partly because Mannyng adheres less slavishly
to his original. Wright, in his edition of Langtoft's chronicle,
has accused Mannyng of having frequently misunderstood
the French of his predecessor; but, though instances of mis-
translation do occur, they are not very frequent. The version
is most literal in the earlier part; later, when Mannyng
begins to introduce internal rimes into his verse, the difficulties
of metre prevent him from maintaining the verbal accuracy at
which he aimed.

But, notwithstanding the greater freedom with which
Mannyng treats this part of the chronicle, his gift as a narrator
is much less apparent here than in *Handlyng Synne*. Occasionally, it is visible, as when, for the sake of liveliness, he turns
Langtoft's preterites into the present tense, and shows a preference for direct over indirect quotation. But such interest as is
due to him and not to Langtoft is derived chiefly from his
allusions to circumstances and events not reported by the
latter and derived from local tradition. Thus, he marvels
greatly that none of the historians with whom he is acquainted
makes mention of the famous story of Havelok the Dane and
Aethelwold's daughter Goldburgh, although there still lay
in Lincoln castle the stone which Havelok cast further than
any other champion, and the town of Grimsby yet stood to
witness the truth of the history.

For the reign of Edward I, Mannyng's additions are of
very considerable importance, and, as the authorities for these
can be traced only in a few instances, it is a reasonable conclusion to suppose that he wrote from personal knowledge.

He relates more fully than Langtoft the incidents of the attempt on Edward's life in Palestine, the death of Llywelyn and the treachery of the provost of Bruges who undertook to deliver the English king into the hands of the enemy. It is, however, in connection with Scottish affairs that his additions are most noteworthy. Although he regards the Scots with the peculiar bitterness of the northern English, he follows the fortunes of Bruce, with whom, as we have seen, he had been brought into personal contact, with especial interest.

The fragments of ballads celebrating the victories of the English over the Scots given by Langtoft occur also in Mannyng's version, and, in some cases, in a fuller, and what seems to be a more primitive, form. They are full of barbaric exultation over the fallen foe, and form a curious link between the battle songs in the Old English *Chronicle* and the patriotic poems of Laurence Minot.

One other work has been assigned to Robert Mannyng. This is the *Medytacyuns of þe soper of oure lorde Jhesu. And also of hys passyun. And eke of þe peynes of hys swete modyr, Mayden Marye. þe whyche made yn latyn Bonaventure Cardynall.* In the two manuscripts in which *Handlyng Synne* has survived in a complete form (Bodleian 415 and Harleian 1701), it is followed by a translation of the above work, but this alone is not sufficient evidence as to the authorship. The language, however, is east midland, and the freedom with which the original is treated, together with the literary skill indicated in some of the additions and interpolations, may, perhaps, justify the ascription of this work to Robert Mannyng; but the point is uncertain.

Of Mannyng's influence on succeeding authors it is impossible to speak definitely. The fact that only three manuscripts of his great work survive points to no very extensive circulation, and the resemblance of certain passages in *Handlyng Synne* to lines in the *Vision of Piers Plowman* and the *Canterbury Tales* may very well be due to the general opinion of the day on the subjects of which they treat. It has been noticed that the framework of *Handlyng Synne* is not unlike that of Gower's *Confessio Amantis;* but the custom of pointing the lesson of a dissertation by an illustrative narrative is common to didactic writers of all periods, and Gower's adoption of a method popular among approved moralists must have been intended to add zest to the delight of his audience in stories which were of a distinctly secular character

The literary activity of the south-east of England during this time was less remarkable than that of the west and north; nevertheless, three writers of some importance, William of Shoreham, Dan Michel of Northgate and Adam Davy, call for mention here. Of these writers two were clerics; the third held the position of "marshall" in Stratford-at-Bow.

William of Shoreham's works are contained in a single manuscript (Add. MS. 17,376) now in the British Museum; and, curiously enough, though the seven poems treat of the favourite themes of the medieval homilist, they take the form of lyrical measures. The first deals with the seven sacraments; the second is a translation of the well-known Latin *Psalms* printed in the *Lay Folk's Mass Book*, of which there are other metrical versions in Middle English; the third is a commentary on the ten commandments; and the fourth a dissertation on the seven deadly sins. Then comes a lyric on the joys of the Virgin, and, after that, a hymn to Mary, indicated, by the colophon, to be a translation from Robert Grosseteste. Last of all, is a long poem on the evidences of Christianity, the mystery of the Trinity, the Creation, the war in heaven and the temptation of Adam and Eve. Here the manuscript breaks off, but, from internal evidence, it is clear that the poet intended also to treat of the redemption.

Though he is handicapped by the form of verse chosen, the author shows a good deal of artistic feeling in his treatment of these well-worn themes. His favourite stanzas consist of seven or six lines, the former riming *abcbded*, the latter *aabccb;* but he uses, also, alternately riming lines of varying length and the quatrain *abab*. His poems are characterised by the tender melancholy which pervades much English religious verse; he dwells on the transitoriness of earthly life, the waning strength of man and the means by which he may obtain eternal life and he pleads with his readers for their repentance and reformation.

From a reference in the colophon to Simon, archbishop of Canterbury, we may conclude that the present manuscript dates from the beginning of the reign of Edward III. From other colophons we learn that the poems were composed by William of Shoreham, vicar of Chart, near Leeds, in Kent.

The other important Kentish production of this time was the *Ayenbite of Inwyt* (the "again-biting" of the inner wit, the remorse of conscience), the value of which, however, is distinctly philological rather than literary. Our information as to its author is derived from his preface in the unique manuscript in the British Museum, which states that it was made with his own hand by Dan Michel, of Northgate in Kent, and belonged to the library of St. Austin at Canterbury, and from a note at the end of the treatise, which adds that it was written in English for the sake of ignorant men, to guard them against sin, and that it was finished on the vigil of the holy apostles, Simon and Jude, by a brother of the cloister of St. Austin of Canterbury, in the year 1340.

The *Ayenbite of Inwyt* was not, however, an original work. It was a translation of a very popular French treatise, the *Somme des Vices et des Vertus* (known also as *Li Livres roiaux des Vices et des Vertus*, and *Somme le Roi*), compiled, in 1279, by frère Lorens, a Dominican, at the request of Philip the Bold, son and successor of Louis IX. This, in its turn, was borrowed from other writers, and was composed of various homilies, on the ten commandments, the creed, the seven deadly sins, the knowledge of good and evil, the seven petitions of the Paternoster, the seven gifts of the Holy Ghost, the seven cardinal virtues and confession, many of which exist in manuscripts anterior to the time of frère Lorens.

The treatment of these subjects, especially in the section on the seven deadly sins, is allegorical. The sins are first compared with the seven heads of the beast which St. John saw in the Apocalypse; then, by a change of metaphor, pride becomes the root of all the rest, and each of them is represented as bringing forth various boughs. Thus, the boughs of pride are untruth, despite, presumption, ambition, idle bliss, hypocrisy and wicked dread; while from untruth spring three twigs, foulhood, foolishness and apostasy. This elaborate classification into divisions and sub-divisions is characteristic of the whole work, and becomes not a little tiresome; on the other hand, the very frequent recourse to metaphor which accompanies it serves to drive the lesson home. Idle bliss is the great wind that throweth down the great towers, and the high steeples, and the great beeches in the woods, by which are signified men in high places; the boaster is the cuckoo who singeth always of himself.

Sometimes these comparisons are drawn from the natural history of the day, the bestiaries, or, as Dan Michel calls them, the "bokes of kende." Thus, flatterers are like to nickers (sea-fairies), which have the bodies of women and the tails of fishes, and sing so sweetly that they make the sailors fall asleep, and afterwards swallow them; or like the adder called "serayn," which runs more quickly than a horse, and whose venom is so deadly that no medicine can cure its sting. Other illustrations are borrowed from Seneca, from Aesop, Boëthius, St. Augustine, St. Gregory, St. Bernard, St. Jerome and St. Anselm.

Unfortunately, Dan Michel was a very incompetent translator. He often quite fails to grasp the sense of his original, and his version is frequently unintelligible without recourse to the French work. It is noticeable, however, that it improves as it proceeds, as if he taught himself the language by his work upon it. The same MS. contains Kentish versions of the Paternoster, the creed and the famous sermon entitled *Sawles Warde*, which is abridged from an original at least one hundred years older. It is a highly allegorical treatment of *Matthew*, xxiv, 43, derived from Hugo of St. Victor's *De Anima*, and describes how the house of Reason is guarded by Sleight, Strength and Righteousness, and how they receive Dread, the messenger of Death, and Love of Life Everlasting, who is sent from heaven.

Certain resemblances between the *Ayenbite of Inwyt* and *The Parson's Tale* have led to the supposition that Chaucer was acquainted with either the English or the French version. It has recently been proved, however, that these resemblances are confined to the section on the seven deadly sins, and even these are not concerned with the structure of the argument, but consist rather of scattered passages. And, although the immediate source of *The Parson's Tale* is still unknown, it has been shown that its phraseology and general argument are very similar to those of a Latin tract written by Raymund of Pennaforte, general of the Dominicans in 1238, and that the

digression on the seven deadly sins is an adaptation of the
Summa seu Tractatus de Viciis, composed before 1261 by
William Peraldus, another Dominican friar.

Another interesting production of the south-eastern counties
is a poem of a hundred and sixty-eight octosyllabic lines,
riming in couplets, known as the *Dreams* of Adam Davy, which
appears to date from the beginning of the reign of Edward
II.   The author, who, as he himself informs us, lived near London, and was well known far and wide, tells how, within the
space of twelve months, beginning on a Wednesday in August,
and ending on a Thursday in September of the following year,
he dreamed five dreams, concerning Edward the king, prince
of Wales.   In the first dream he thought he saw the king
standing armed and crowned before the shrine of St. Edward.
As he stood there, two knights set upon him and belaboured
him with their swords, but without effect.   When they were
gone, four bands of divers coloured light streamed out of each
of the king's ears.

The second vision took place on a Tuesday before the
feast of All Hallows, and, on that night, the poet dreamed
that he saw Edward clad in a grey mantle, riding on an ass to
Rome, there to be chosen emperor.   He rode as a pilgrim,
without hose or shoes, and his legs were covered with blood.
This theme is continued in the third vision, on St. Lucy's day,
when the seer thought that he was in Rome, and saw the pope
in his mitre and Edward with his crown, in token that he
should be emperor of Christendom.

In the fourth vision, on Christmas night, the poet imagined
that he was in a chapel of the Virgin Mary and that Christ,
unloosing His hands from the cross, begged permission from
His Mother to convey Edward on a pilgrimage against the
foes of Christendom; and Christ's Mother gave Him leave,
because Edward had served her day and night.

Then came an interval in the dreams, but, one Wednesday
in Lent, the poet heard a voice which bade him make known
his visions to the king; and the injunction was repeated after
the last vision, in which he saw an angel lead Edward, clad
in a robe red as the juice of a mulberry, to the high altar at
Canterbury.

The exact purpose of these verses is very difficult to

determine. The manuscript in which they are preserved (Laud MS. 622) appears to belong to the end of the fourteenth century; but the allusion to "Sir Edward the king, prince of Wales" is applicable only to Edward II. Perhaps they were designed to check the king in the course of frivolity and misrule which ended in his deposition; but the tone is very loyal, and the references to him are extremely complimentary. The poems are, in fact, intentionally obscure, a characteristic which they share with other prophecies of the same class, notably those attributed to Merlin and Thomas of Erceldoune. The same manuscript contains poems on the *Life of St. Alexius*, the *Battle of Jerusalem*, the *Fifteen Signs before Domesday*, *Scripture Histories* and the *Lamentation of Souls*, which show many resemblances to the *Dreams*, and may also be by Adam Davy; if so, he must have been a man of education, since some of them seem to be derived directly from Latin originals

The most important national poems of the first half of the fourteenth century are the war songs of Laurence Minot, preserved in MS. Cotton Galba ix in the British Museum. The author twice mentions his name; from internal evidence it is probable that the poems are contemporary with the events they describe; and, as the last of them deals with the taking of Guisnes, in 1352, it is supposed that he must have died about this time. Diligent research has failed to discover anything further about him, but Minot was the name of a well-known family connected with the counties of York and Norfolk. The language of the poems is, in its main characteristics, northern, though with an admixture of midland forms; and, in three of them, the poet shows detailed acquaintance with the affairs of Yorkshire. Thus, the expedition of Edward Baliol against Scotland, to which reference is made in the first poem, set sail from that county; in the ninth poem the archbishop of York receives special mention; and, in the account of the taking of Guisnes, Minot adopts the version which ascribes the exploit to the daring of a Yorkshire archer, John of Doncaster.

The events which form the subject of these poems all fall between the years 1333 and 1352. The first two celebrate the victory of Halidon Hill, which, in the poet's opinion, is an ample recompense for the disgrace at Bannockburn; the

third tells how Edward III went to join his allies in Flanders,
and how the French attacked Southampton and took an
English warship, the *Christopher;* the fourth relates the king's
first invasion of France, and Philip's refusal to meet him in
battle; the fifth celebrates the victory at Sluys, mentioning
by name the most valiant knights who took part in it; the
sixth is concerned with the abortive siege of Tournay in the
same year; and the seventh tells of the campaign of 1347 and
of the battle of Crecy. Then come two poems on the siege
of Calais and the battle of Neville's Cross. These are followed
by an account of a skirmish between some English ships and
some Spanish merchantmen; and the eleventh and last poem
relates the stratagem by which the town of Guisnes was surprised and taken.

The poetical value of these songs has been somewhat un-
duly depreciated by almost every critic who has hitherto
treated of them. Their qualities are certainly not of a highly
imaginative order, and they contain scarcely one simile or
metaphor; but the verse is vigorous and energetic and goes
with a swing, as martial poetry should. The author was an
adept in wielding a variety of lyrical measures, and in five
poems uses the long alliterative lines which occur in such
poems as *William of Palerne* and *Piers Plowman* in rimed
stanzas of varying length. The other six are all written in
short iambic lines of three or four accents, variously grouped
together by end-rime. Alliteration is a very prominent
feature throughout, and is often continued in two successive
lines, while the last words of one stanza are constantly
repeated in the first line of the next, a frequent device in
contemporary verse. The constant recourse to alliteration
detracts, somewhat, from the freshness of the verse, since it
leads the author to borrow from the romance writers well-
worn tags, which must have been as conventional in their
way as the hackneyed pastoral terms against which Wordsworth revolted. Such are "cares colde," "cantly and kene,"
"proper and prest," "pride in prese," "prowd in pall"; with
many others of a similar nature.

In spite of the highly artificial structure of the verse,
however, the language itself is simple, even rugged, and the
poems dealing with the Scottish wars bear a strong resem-

blance to the rude snatches of folk-song which have already
been mentioned in connection with Mannyng's translation
of Langtoft's chronicle. There is the same savage exultation
in the discomfiture of the Scots, the same scornful references
to their "rivelings" (impromptu shoes made of raw hide)
and the little bags in which they were wont to carry their
scanty provisions of oatmeal. And the very simplicity of the
narrative conveys, perhaps better than a more elaborate
description, the horrors of medieval warfare; in reading these
poems we see the flames spread desolation over the country,
while hordes of pillagers and rough riders are driven in scattered bands to their own land; or we behold the dead men
"staring at the stars" or lying gaping "between Crecy and
Abbeville." Nor is the pomp of military array forgotten;
we see the glitter of pennons and plate armour, the shining
rows of shields and spears, the arrows falling thick as snow,
the red hats of the cardinals who consult together how they
may beguile the king, the ships heaving on the flood, ready
for battle, while the trumpets blow, and the crews dance in
the moonlight, regardless of the waning moon that foretells
disaster on the morrow. Strange merchantmen, transformed,
for the time, into war vessels, loom in the Channel, hiding
in their holds great wealth of gold and silver, of scarlet and
green; but in vain do these pirates come hither with trumpets
and tabors, they are already doomed to feed the fishes. There
is no thought of mercy for a fallen foe; only in one place does
any sense of compassion seem to affect the poet. When he
tells how the burgesses of Calais came to demand mercy from
Edward, he puts into the mouth of their leader a pitiful description of their plight. Horses, coneys, cats and dogs are
all consumed; the need of the petitioners is easily visible in
their appearance; and they that should have helped them are
fled away. But Minot says nothing about the intercession
of queen Philippa, related by Froissart.

Minot seems to have been a professional gleeman, who
earned his living by following the camp and entertaining
soldiers with the recitation of their own heroic deeds. It is
possible, however, that his skill in versification may have led
to his promotion to the post of minstrel to the king, and that
he held some recognised office about the court. His poems,

unlike those of Barbour, which were composed long after the occasions they commemorated, were, probably, struck off to celebrate the events as they arose, and in one of them, that on the siege of Tournay, his exultation seems to have been somewhat premature.   While Barbour's *Bruce* is a long, sustained narrative, composed in the same metre throughout, the verse of Minot is essentially lyric in character, and, as has been seen, ranges over a large variety of measures.

Minot's patriotism is everywhere apparent.   His contempt for the "wild Scots and the tame" (the Highland and Lowland Scots) is undisguised, and he has equally small respect for the lily-flowers of France.   When the English meet with misfortune, he always finds plenty of excuses for them. Thus, in the fight at Southampton, the galleymen were so many in number that the English grew tired, but, "since the time that God was born and a hundred years before, there were never any men better in fight than the English, while they had the strength."   His admiration and loyalty for the king are without measure.   The most is made of Edward's personal bravery at Sluys, his courteous thanks to his soldiers and the esteem shown him by foreign dignitaries, while the poet continually insists on the righteous claim of his sovereign to the throne of France.   And, though his poems are sometimes quite unhistorical in matters of fact, they are important in that they evidently reflect the growing feeling of solidarity in the nation, and the patriotic enthusiasm which made possible the victories of Sluys and Crecy.

CHAPTER XVII

Later Transition English

II

SECULAR LYRICS; TALES; SOCIAL SATIRE

FROM the middle of the thirteenth century to the days of *Piers Plowman*, writers of English were still polishing the tools used in the preceding century. We have seen their predecessors at work in monasteries on saints' lives and religious verse; chroniclers have come under consideration; and the flourishing of romance, both home-grown and imported, has been noted. It remains to discuss the evidence which is gradually accumulating that neither court nor cloister were to exercise a monopoly in the production and patronage of English letters: there was also "the world outside." Certain of the romances—*Havelok* notably—bear traces, in their extant forms, of having been prepared for ruder audiences than those which listened, as did the ladies and gentlemen of plague-stricken Florence towards the close of this period, to tales of chivalry and courtly love and idle dalliance.

A famous collection of Middle English lyrics [1] shows signs that there were writers who could take a keen pleasure in "notes suete of nyhtegales," in "wymmen" like "Alysoun" and in the "northerne wynd." There are still poems addressed to "Jhesu, mi suete lemman," full of that curious combination of sensuousness and mysticism which is so notable a feature of much of the religious verse of these centuries; but more purely worldly *motifs* were beginning to be preserved; tales which were simply amusing and cared little for a moral ending were being translated; and indications appear that the free criticism of its rulers, which has always been a characteristic of the

[1] Harl. MS. 2253, Brit. Mus.

English race, was beginning to find expression, or, at any rate, preservation, in the vernacular.

To the early years of the period under consideration belongs one of the most beautiful of Middle English lyrics:

> Sumer is i-cumen in,
> Lhude sing cuccu.[1]

Its popularity is attested by the existence of the music to which it was sung in the first half of the thirteenth century. If summer had not yet "come in," spring, at any rate, was well on the way when verses like these became possible. A sense of rime, of music, of sweetness, had arrived; the lines were settling down into moulds of equal length, and were beginning to trip easily off the tongue to an expected close. And, instead of the poet feeling that his spirit was most in harmony with the darker aspects of nature, as was the case with most of the Old English writers whose works have been preserved, the poet of the Middle English secular lyric, in common with the poet of *The Owl and the Nightingale*, feels "the spring-running" and cannot refrain from entering into the spirit of it with a gladsome heart:

> Groweth sed and bloweth med,
> And springth the wde nu.[2]
> Sing cuccu!
> Awe bleteth after lomb,
> Lhouth after calve cu:
> Bulluc sterteth, bucke verteth,[3]
> Murie sing cuccu!

The same note is struck, only more often, in the Harleian lyrics above referred to, which are dated, approximately, 1310, and were collected, apparently, by a clerk of Leominster. The slim volume in which these lyrics were printed sixty-five years ago, by Thomas Wright,[4] contains poems familiar, perhaps, to most students of English poetry and familiar, certainly, to all students of English prosody. The measures of the *trouvères* and *troubadours* had become acclimatised in England

---

[1] Harl. MS. 978.   [2] Now.   [3] Runs to the greenwood.
[4] *Specimens of Lyric Poetry composed in England in the Reign of Edward I*, Percy Society, 1842. Some had been printed before by Warton and Ritson.

—Henry III had married a lady of Provence—so far as the
genius of the language and the nature of the islanders permitted; and the attempt to revive the principle of alliteration
as a main feature, instead of, what it has ever been and still
is, an unessential ornament, of English verse was strong in
the land. And first among these spring poems, not so much
in respect of its testimony to the work of perfecting that
was in progress in the matter of metre, as in its sense of the
open air, and of the supremacy of "humanity," is the well-
known Alison lyric beginning

> Bytuene Mershe & Averil
>   When spray biginneth to springe,
> The lutel foul hath hire wyl
>   On hyre lud [1] to synge;
> Iche libbe[2] in love-longinge
> For semlokest of alle thynge,
> He may me blisse bringe,
>   Icham in hire baundoun.[3]
> An hendy hap ichabbe yhent,[4]
> Ichot from hevene it is me sent,
> From alle wymmen mi love is lent [5]
>   & lyht on Alysoun.

There is a world of difference between these lines and the
ideal of convent-life set forth in *Hali Meidenhad.*[6] By natural
steps, the erotic mysticism that produced the poems associated
with the Virgin cult passed into the recognition, not merely
that there were "sun, moon and stars," "and likewise a wind
on the heath," but also that there existed earthly beings of
whom

> Some be browne, and some be whit...
> And some of theym be chiry ripe.[7]

In another of the Harleian poems, "the wind on the heath"
inspires a refrain:

> Blou, northerne wynd,
> Send thou me my suetyng.
> Blou, northerne wynd, blou, blou, blou!

---

[1] In her own language.   [2] Live.   [3] Power.
[4] Good fortune has come to me.   [5] Turned away.   [6] See *ante*, p. 254.
[7] *A Song on Woman*, MS. Lambeth 306, 135, printed by Wright and Halliwell, *Reliquiae Antiquae*, 1, 248.

which, by its very irregularity of form, shows the flexible strength that was to be an integral feature of the English lyric.   Yet another poem has lines:

> I would I were a thrustle cock,
> A bountyng[1] or a laverok,
>   Sweet bride.
> Between her kirtle and her smock
> I would me hide:

which form a link in the long chain that binds Catullus to the Elizabethan and Jacobean lyrists.   And the lines beginning

> Lenten ys come with love to toune,
> With blosmen & with briddes roune[2]

are full of that passionate sense of "the wild joys of living" which led "alle clerkys in joye and eke in merthe" to sing

> Right lovesome thu art in May thu wyde wyde erthe.

The *Proverbs of Hendyng*, "Marcolves sone," are to be found in the MS. that contains the above lyrics and may, therefore, be mentioned here.   They appear to have been collected from older material in their present form before the close of the thirteenth century; and they recall the wisdom literature to which reference has already been made in dealing with Old English proverbs[3] and with the poems attributed to Alfred.   These proverbs are obvious summaries of the shrewd wisdom of the common folk, which is as old as the hills, and not confined to any one race or country:

> Tel thou never thy fo that thy fot aketh,
>   Quoth Hendyng . . .
> Dere is botht the hony that is licked of the thorne;

and they enshrine many phrases that are still common property:

> Brend child fur dredeth,
>   Quoth Hendyng;

but their main interest for us lies in the form of the stanzas which precede the proverb, and which consist of six lines rimed *aabaab;* here it is evident that the nebulous outlines

---

[1] Blackbird.

[2] Song. *Cf. The Thrush and the Nightingale*, Digby MS. 86, Bodl., printed in *Reliquiae Antiquae*, I, 241, "Somer is comen with love to toune," etc.

[3] Cf. *A Father's Instruction, ante,* p. 46.

of earlier attempts have taken shape and form out of the
void, and become the ballad stanza; the unrimed shorter lines
are now linked by end-rime, and the reciter from memory
is aided thereby.

The literature of the Middle Ages was of a much more
"universal," or cosmopolitan, character than that of later
times—it will be remembered that "the book" in which Paolo
and Francesca "read that day no more" was the book of
Lancelot and not a tale of Rimini—and one of the reasons
for this width of range was that letters were in the hands of
a few, whose education had been of a "universal," rather than
a national, type. English literature, in the vernacular, had
to compete for many a long year not only with Latin, which,
even so late as the days of Erasmus, was thought to have a
fair chance of becoming the sole language of letters,[1] but also,
though in a rapidly lessening degree, with Norman-French, the
language of all who pretended to a culture above that of the
common folks. And it is to Latin, therefore, that we have
often to turn for evidence of the thoughts that were beginning
to find expression, not only among monastic chroniclers and
historians, but also among social satirists and writers of political verse. At first the amusement of those only who had
a knowledge of letters, the writing of Goliardic verses and
political satires in Latin, became models for the imitation of
minstrels and writers who set themselves to please a wider
circle, and who made themselves the mouthpieces of those
who felt and suffered but could not express.

Some hint of what the people had liked to hear in the way
of tales is preserved for us in *The Deeds of Hereward*,[2] a son
of Lady Godiva, and an offspring of the native soil, the recital of whose horse-play in the court of the king and of whose
deeds on his speedy mare Swallow would appeal to all who liked
the tale of Havelok, the strapping Grimsby fisher lad, scullery
boy and king's son. But the secular tale and satirical poem of
the thirteenth and fourteenth century appealed to a different

---

[1] Cf. also, its long use in legal documents: "To substitute English for Latin
as the language in which the King's writs and patents and charters shall be
expressed, and the doings of the law-courts shall be preserved, requires a
statute of George II's day." Maitland, in Traill's *Social England*, vol. I.

[2] Preserved in a Latin version only.

audience and are of direct historical value. In Latin and in English, the tyranny and vice and luxury of the times are strongly condemned, the conduct of simoniacal priest and sensual friar is held up to ridicule; and, in that way, the ground was prepared for the seed to be sown later by the Lollards. Monasticism, which had risen to an extraordinary height during the regin of Stephen and borne excellent fruit in the educational labours of men like Gilbert of Sempringham, began to decline in the early years of the thirteenth century. Then came the friars; and their work among the people, especially in relieving physical suffering, was characterised by a self-sacrificing zeal which showed that they were true sons of Assisi; but there were some among those who succeeded them whose light lives and dark deeds are faithfully reflected in the songs and satires of Middle English; and there were others, in higher stations, equally false to their trust, who form the subject of the political verse coming into vogue in the vernacular. Even though it be borne in mind that the mutual antagonism between regulars and seculars, and between members of different orders, may be responsible for some of the scandals satirised, and that there was always a lighter side to the picture—against bishop Golias and his clan there were, surely, people like Richard Rolle of Hampole—yet sufficient evidence remains, apart from the testimony of Matthew Paris, of the steadily growing unpopularity of monks and friars, and the equally steady growth of the revolt of the people against clerical influence.

Social satire of the nature indicated is seen in Middle English in the few examples of the *fabliau* still extant. The short amusing tale in verse appealed greatly to the Frenchman of the thirteenth century; and, though the few that have survived in English show strong signs of their foreign origin, their popularity proved that they were not only accepted as pleasing to "the ears of the groundlings" but as reflecting, with somewhat malicious, and wholly satiric, glee, the current manners of monk and merchant and miller, friar and boy. *The Land of Cokaygne* tells of a land of gluttony and idleness, a kitchen-land, not exactly where it was "always afternoon," but where the monk could obtain some of the delights of a Mohammedan paradise. The very walls of the monastery

are built "al of pasteiis," "of fleis, of fisse and riche met,"
with pinnacles of "fat podinges";

> The gees irostid on the spitte
> Flee; to that abbai, god hit wot,
> And gredith,[1] gees al hote, al hot;

and entrance to this land could only be gained by wading

> Seve ʒere in swineis dritte . . .
> Al anon up to the chynne.

The Land of Cokaygne has relatives in many lands; it lacks
the deep seriousness of the Wyclifian songs that came later,
and the light satirical way in which the subject is treated
would seem to imply that a French model had been used,
but its colouring is local and its purpose is evident.

Dame Siriz, an oriental tale showing traces of the doctrine
of the transmigration of souls, was put into English after
many wanderings through other languages, about the middle
of the thirteenth century, and is excellently told in a metre
varying between octosyllabic couplets and the six-lined verse
of the *Sir Thopas* type. Other renderings of the same story
are contained in *Gesta Romanorum* (28), *Disciplina Clericalis*
(XI) and similar collections of tales; and the imperfect poem
in the form of a dialogue between *Clericus* and *Puella*, printed
by Wright and Halliwell[2] may be compared with it. A tale
of this kind was certain of popularity, whether recited by
wandering minstrel or committed to writing for the pleasure
of all lovers of comedy. To the "common form" of an absent
and betrayed husband, is added the Indian device of the
"biche" with weeping eyes (induced by mustard and pepper),
who has been thus transformed from human shape because
of a refusal to listen to the amorous solicitations of a "clerc."
The device is used by the pander, Dame Siriz, who, for twenty
shillings, promises another "clerc" to persuade the merchant's
wife to yield to his desires.

There is, unfortunately, very little of the famous satirical
beast epic *Reynard the Fox* that can be claimed for England.
Some of the animals were known to Odo of Cheriton, the
fabulist, who makes use of stories of Reynard to point the

---

[1] Cry.　　　　　　　　　　　　　　　[2] *Reliquiae Antiquae*, I, 145.

moral of his sermons; and a short *fabliau* of about the same period as those above mentioned is extant; but this is about all.   In *The Fox and the Wolf* is cleverly related in bold and firm couplets the familiar story of the well and the device of Renauard for getting himself out of it at the expense of the wolf Sigrim.   The teller of the story in Middle English is learned in his craft, and the poem is an admirable example of comic satire, perhaps the best of its kind left to us before the days of Chaucer.   Not only are the two characters well conceived, but they are made the vehicle, as in the romance of the Fleming Willem, of light satire on the life of the times. Before admitting the wolf to the paradise in the bucket at the bottom of the well, the fox takes upon himself the duties of a confessor, and the wolf, to gain absolution, asks forgiveness, not only for the ordinary sins of his life, but, after a little pressing, even repents him of the resentment shown when the confessor made free with the penitent's wife.   Few things show more clearly the failings and vices current in the Middle Ages than do the various stories of the deeds of Reynard in his ecclesiastical disguises; stories that were carved in stone and wood and shown in painted glass, as well as recited and written.   His smug cowled face looks out from pulpits and leers at us from under *miserere* seats.

The literary needs of those who were familiar with the " romances of prys" in which deeds of chivalry were enshrined, and who, with the author of *Sir Thopas*, could enjoy parodies of them, were met by such salutary tales as *The Turnament of Totenham*.   A countryside wedding, preceded by the mysteries of a medieval tournament, is described by Gilbert Pilkington, or by the author whose work he transcribes, in language that would be well understood and keenly appreciated by those of lower rank than "knight and lady free."   It is an admirable burlesque; rustic laddies contend not only for Tibbe the daughter of Rondill the refe, but for other prizes thrown in by the father:

> He shalle have my gray mare [on which Tibbe "was sett"],
>   And my spottyd sowe:

and, therefore, Hawkyn and Dawkyn and Tomkyn and other noble youths "ffro Hissiltoun to Haknay," "leid on stifly,"

"til theyre hors swett," with much "clenkyng of cart sadils"
and many "brokyn hedis," and

> Woo was Hawkyn, woo was Herry,
> Woo was Tomkyn, woo was Terry

when they sat down to the marriage feast of the winner. The
Tale of Thopas exercises its useful office with a rapier; if *The
Turnament of Totenham* performs its duty with a cudgel, the
result, so far as the victim is concerned, is none the less effective.

The middle of the fourteenth century gave us *The Tale of
Gamelyn* which is dealt with elsewhere as a metrical romance
and in connection with the works of Chaucer. It forms an
admirable link between the courtly romance and the poetry
of the outlaws of the greenwood. A younger brother, de-
spoiled of his share in the inheritance, is ill-clothed and given
poor food by his eldest brother, handed over to understrap-
pers to be thrashed and otherwise maltreated. But, after the
fashion of Havelok, Gamelyn proves himself adept at the staff
and strong in the arm; and, after a fair supply of adventures,
with much success and after further tribulation, he becomes
head of a forest band of young outlaws; furthermore, after
justice has been done to his unnatural brother, be becomes
king's officer in the woodland. It is a "loveless" tale of the
earlier Stevenson kind; no courtly dame has part or parcel
therein; nevertheless, in the form in which we now have it,
The Tale of Gamelyn is quite excellent, is, in fact, typically
English in its sense of free life and open air.

Of the two collections of stories referred to above, one,
the most famous of its kind, and the source-book for many
later English writers, the *Gesta Romanorum*, probably took
shape in England, in its Latin form, in the period under discussion. Early preachers and homilists were only too willing
to seize hold of stories from every quarter in order to "point
the moral," and their collections have served many ends
different from the purpose designed. If the "moral" attached to each tale, and dragged in, often, on the most flimsy
excuse, be ignored, the tales of the *Gesta Romanorum* become
readable, for they are often excellently, even though baldly,
told. Other Latin collections of cognate kind, the work of
English compilers, have been referred to in a preceding chap-

ter,[1] and all are of importance in the light they throw on the manners of the time. One, the *Summa Praedicantium* of John de Bromyarde, a Dominican friar, scholar of Oxford and antagonist of Wyclif, devotes a thousand pages to subjects likely to be acceptable to congregations, and deserves more attention than has hitherto been paid it. In the legendaries and poems compiled and written by the monks for homiletic purposes, there are many germs of the tale-telling faculty, and much folk-lore. Things charming and grotesque are inextricably mixed. In the legends of the *Childhood of Jesus*, for instance, there is a delightful account of the reverence paid by the animal creation and by inanimate nature to the Infant during the journey to Egypt; and then the poem is marred by the addition of crude miraculous deeds recorded as afterwards wrought by Him. Many of our tales have originally come from the east; but, in spite of the proverb, they have gathered much moss in rolling westward, and flints from the same quarry that have travelled a fairly direct course look strangely different from others that have zig-zagged hither.

Of Middle English political verses, the earliest preserved are, probably, those on the battle of Lewes, which was fought in 1264. The battle was celebrated by a follower of the fortunes of Simon de Montfort, in a poem which is of considerable philological and metrical importance. The number of French words it contains reveals the process of amalgamation that was going on between the two languages, and lets us into the workshop where the new speech was being fashioned. The interest of the poem is also considerable from the evidence it furnishes that the free-spoken Englishman was beginning to make the vernacular the vehicle of satire against his superiors in the realm of politics, following the example of the writers of the Latin satirical poems then current. The educated part of the race was beginning to show signs of the insular prejudice against foreigners which is not even absent from it to-day—though it could loyally support "foreigners" when they espoused the national cause—and it was, more happily, showing signs of the political genius which has ever

[1] See Chapter x, Map, Neckam, etc.

been a quality of our people. Metrically, these political lyrics in the vernacular are of importance because of the forms of verse experimented in and naturalised. The minstrel who sang or recited political ballads had to appeal to more critical audiences than had the composer of sacred lyrics; he had to endeavour to import into a vernacular in transition something of the easy flow of comic Latin verse. *The Song against the King of Almaigne*,[1] above referred to, is in mono-rimed four-lined stanzas, followed by a "bob," or shorter fifth line, "maugre Wyndesore," "to helpe Wyndesore," etc., and a constant, mocking, two-lined refrain, with a kind of internal rime:

> Richard, thah thou be ever trichard,[2]
> trichen shalt thou never more.

The recurrence of lines consisting of perfect anapæsts,[3] and showing but little tendency towards alliteration, indicates the direction in which popular rimes were looking.

In the civil struggles of the barons' wars, and in the years that followed, the poetry of the people rose to the surface. The Robin Hood ballads, to which we shall recur in a later volume, and a few rude verses here and there, give voice, not only to the free, open life of the outlaw in the greenwood, but, also, to the cry of the down-trodden at the callous luxury of the rich. The real condition of the poor is but rarely reflected in the literature of a nation; the unfree in feudal times were voiceless, and the labouring free of later times have been but little better. Patient beyond belief, the children of the soil do not, as a rule, make literature of their wrongs: we can only learn what is at work by conscious or unconscious revelations in other writings. The ploughman in the eleventh century dialogue of Ælfric had said with truth, "I work hard. . . . Be it never so stark winter I dare not linger at home for awe of my lord. . . . I have a boy driving the oxen with a goad-iron, who is hoarse with cold and shouting. . . . Mighty hard work it is, for I am not free."[4] The "bitter cry"

---

[1] Richard of Cornwall, King of the Romans, brother of Henry III.
[2] Treacherous.
[3] Sitteth alle stille & herkneth to me . . .
Sire Simond de Mountfort hath swore bi ys chyn, etc.
[4] York Powell's translation in *Social England*, i.

of the oppressed people was echoed in the Old English *Chronicle* of the sad days of Stephen and, ignored by court historians and writers of romance, centuries had to elapse before it could find adequate expression in the alliterative lines of *Piers Plowman*, and in the preaching of the "mad priest of Kent" —one of the earliest among Englishmen, whose words are known to us, to declare for the common and inalienable rights of man. It is a far cry from the speech of the land slave to John Ball, Jack Straw, and Wat Tyler, and the intervening years show but fragments of the literature of revolt, but the rude rimes sent across the country by John Ball should no more be forgotten in a history of English literature than the rude beginnings of its prosody, for they contain the beginnings of the literature of political controversy, the first recognisable steps on the road of political and religious liberty that was later to be trodden by Milton and Shelley and Cobbett. In the *Song of the Husbandman*, one of the notable poems of the alliterative revival, which may be dated towards the close of the thirteenth century, in octaves and quatrains rimed alternately on two rimes with linked ending and beginning lines—a complicated measure handled with great skill—the tiller of the soil complains that he is robbed and picked "ful clene"; that, because of the green wax, he is hunted "ase hound doth the hare." And the insolence of the grooms and stable boys, the lackeys and servants, of the great towards the peasantry is told in the rude, coarse lines of *A Song against the Retinues of the Great People*, preserved in the same MS.[1]

> The luthernesse[2] of the ladde,
> The prude[3] of the page,

are the subject of as keen invective as are the deeds of the consistory courts,[4] where the peasants are treated as dogs.

When Edward I died, the writer of an elegy on his death expressed the pious hope that "Edward of Carnarvon" might

> ner be worse man
> Then is fader, ne lasse of myht
> To holden is pore-men to ryht
> & understonde good consail.

It remained an unrealised hope; and the condition of things

[1] Harl. 2253, ed. Wright.   [2] Malicious ill-temper.   [3] Conceit.
[4] *Political Songs of England*, 1839.

in the times of Edward II is reflected in the fugitive literature
of his reign.   The curiously constructed lines in Anglo-Norman
and English *On the King's Breaking his Confirmation of Magna
Charta*, preserved in the Auchinleck MS., Edinburgh, and
the *Song on the Times*, in lines made up of Latin, English and
Anglo-Norman phrases, tell the same tale of ruin and corruption.   Before the end of the reign, Bannockburn had been
fought and won, fought and lost; Scottish girls could sing of
the mourning of their southern sisters for "lemmans loste";
and, in place of an elegy on the death of a king who "ber the
prys" "of Christendome," [1] we have a poem in the Auchinleck
MS. on *The Evil Times of Edward II*, which, in some 470 lines
pitilessly describes the misery of the state and the evil of the
church.   It is a sermon on the old text, "Ye cannot serve
God and Mammon," "no man may wel serve tweie lordes to
queme," and every line bites in, as with the acid of an etcher,
some fresh detail of current manners.   As soon as the young
priest can afford it, he has a concubine; if those in high places
protest, "he may wid a litel silver stoppen his mouth"; the
doctor is the doctor of the comedies of Molière, a pompous
charlatan, ready enough to take silver for his advice, "thouh
he wite no more than a gos wheither" the patient "wole live
or die"; "the knights of old" no longer go forth on brave, if
Quixotic, quests: they are "liouns in halle, and hares in the
field," and any beardless boy can be dubbed of their company;
everywhere are the poor of the land oppressed

> Ac if the king hit wiste, I trowe he wolde be wroth,
> Hou the pore beth i-piled, and hu the silver goth;
> Hit is so deskatered bothe hider and thidere,
> That halvendel shal ben stole ar hit come togidere,
>   and acounted;
> An if a pore man speke a word, he shal be foule
>   afrounted.

Before the fourteenth century had come to a close, the
ravages of the Black Death had brought about radical changes
in the relations of labourers to the soil and had left indelible
impressions on life and letters.   The presence of a disease that,
at its height, meant the death of one out of every two people
in London and, in the eastern counties, of two out of every

---

[1] *Elegy on Edward I*, before cited.

three, led to a relaxation of the current laws of life and to the Peasants' Revolt in 1381. The outbreak of lawlessness consequent upon the dislocation of life in town and country, and the labour troubles that followed, sent outlaws to the greenwood and helped to build up the legends of Robin Hood. Murmurs of discontent grew in volume, and protests against papal authority acquired fresh strength by the existence of the Great Schism. The Lollards began their attacks on social abuses and sought to reform the church at the same time. The people "spoke," and, though the "cause" was not "finished" for many centuries to come, yet the end of many of the political and religious ideals of the Middle Ages was in sight. Wyclif, and those associated with him, had begun their work, the poems that go by the name of *Piers Plowman* had been written and the "commons," in the fullest sense of the word, were beginning their long struggle for political freedom.

CHAPTER XVIII

The Prosody of Old and Middle English

OF Old English poetry, anterior to the twelfth century and, perhaps, in a few cases of that century itself, it has been calculated that we have nearly thirty thousand lines. But all save a very few reduce themselves, in point of prosody, to an elastic but tolerably isonomous form, closely resembling that which is found in the poetry of other early Teutonic and Scandinavian languages. This form may be specified, either as a pretty long line rigidly divided into two halves, or as a couplet of mostly short lines rhythmically connected together by a system of alliteration and stress. Normally, there should be four stressed syllables in the line, or two in each of the half couplets; and at least three of these syllables should be alliterated, beginning with the same consonant or any vowel, as in this line (29) of *The Wanderer:*

· Wenian mid wynnum. Wat se þe cunnað.

Around or between the pillar or anchor stresses, unstressed syllables are grouped in a manner which has sometimes been regarded as almost entirely licentious, and sometimes reduced, as by Sievers, to more or less definite laws or types. Probably, as usual, the truth lies between the two extremes.

To any one, however, who, without previous knowledge of the matter, turns over a fair number of pages of Old English verse, a singular phenomenon will present itself. For many of these pages the line-lengths, though not rigidly equated, will present a coast-line not very much more irregular than that of a page of modern blank verse. And then, suddenly, he will come to pages or passages where the lines seem to telescope themselves out to double their former length. The mere statistical process of enumeration, and of subsequent digestion into classes of more or less resembling type, finds no difficulty in this, and merely regards it as an instance of "stretched" or "swollen" verses, with three or four accents in each half instead of two. Curiosity of a different kind may, perhaps, pine for a little explanation of a more real nature—may wish to know whether this lengthening was parallel, say, to Tennyson's at the close of *The Lotos Eaters*—a definitely concerted thing—or whether it was a mere haphazard licence. But there are no means of satisfying this curiosity except by conjecture. Further, our means of deciding whether, as is usually said, the stressed syllables were bound to be "long" beforehand or not, are very scanty. It seems admitted that more than one short syllable may do the duty of one long; and this is of the highest importance. What, however, is certain is that, in spite of this great variation of length, and in spite of considerable differences, not merely in syllabic volume, between the members of the "stretched" and unstretched groups respectively, there is a certain community of rhythmical tone, sometimes full, sometimes muffled, which not only distinguishes the whole body of this ancient poetry but is distinguishable, with some alteration, in the later revived alliterative verse of Middle English up to the beginning of the sixteenth century. In order to detect and check this, the student should take the *Corpus Poeticum* of Old English and read pages of different poems steadily, letting his voice accommodate itself to the rhythm which will certainly emerge if he has any ear. Different ears will, perhaps, standardise this rhythm differently, and it certainly admits of very wide variation and substitution. The simplest and most normal formula—not necessarily the one which mere statistics will show to be commonest as such, but that which, in itself, or in slight variations from it, predominates—appears to the present writer to be

$$\left.\begin{array}{l}\text{tum-ti-ti}\\\text{ti-tum-ti}\end{array}\right\}\ \text{tum-ti} \mid \text{tum-ti tum-ti.}$$

These are almost the lowest terms of a fully resonant line. They are sometimes further truncated; they are often enlarged by the addition of unstressed syllables; but they are never far off except in the obvious and admitted "magnums."

Long or short, these lines, in all but an infinitesimal proportion of the total, are arranged in mere consecution. A kind of paragraph arrangement—which is, in fact, a necessity —may be often noticed; but there are, save in one famous exception, no "stanzas." This exception is the extremely interesting and, to all appearance, extremely early poem *Deor*. Here, things which are undoubtedly like stanzas (though the number of lines in them is variable) are formed by a refrain:

þaes ofereode, þisses swa mæȝ.[1]

With some rashness, it has been assumed that this semi-lyrical arrangement was the earlier, and that it broke down into the continuous form. It may be so; but, in Old English, at any rate, we have no evidence to show it.

Further, in the main range of this poetry, though not to such an exclusive extent, rime is absent. Attempts have been made to discover it in some of the mainly rimeless poems of later dates; but the instances adduced are probably accidental. In fact, the majority of them, alleged chiefly by German critics, are not properly rimes at all, and are often mere similarities of inflection. The real exceptions are (1) the famous piece in the *Exeter Book* called, significantly, *The Riming Poem*, which exhibits a system, probably imitated from the Norse, of internal, and sometimes frequently repeated, consonance at the ends of lines and half-lines; and (2) a few fragments, especially the inset in the *Chronicle* about the imprisonment and death of the "guiltless aetheling" Alfred. They are exceptions which eminently prove the rule. A quest for assonance had also been made, and a few instances of something like it have been pointed out. But they are very few. Assonance, in fact, has never held any important place in English prosody; and, where it exists in unsophisticated times and instances, it is always, most probably, the result either of inattention or of an attempt to rime. On the whole, the body of Old English verse, as we have it, is one of the most homogeneous to be found in any literature. Alliteration, accent and strict separation of lines or half-lines for its positive laws; rimelessness for its negative: these nearly sum up its commandments, and its result is dominated by an irregular

[1] See *ante*, p. 40.

quasi-trochaic rhythm which will retreat, but always comes
back again.

When, after the lapse of some two centuries, which furnish only scraps of verse, we meet, at, or before, the end of
the twelfth century, with a fresh crop of English poetry, the
results of prosodic scrutiny are strikingly different. Instead
of the just summarised regularity—not in the least cast-iron,
but playing freely round two or three recognised principles,
which are never absolutely deserted, and attempting nothing
beyond their range—we find what may, at first, look like
chaos; what has sometimes been taken for the same dispensation a little obsolescent and broken down, but, when
examined fully and fairly, is seen to be a true period of transition. The old order finds itself in face of a new, which does
not by any means merely replace it or destroy it; but, after
an inevitable stage of confusion, blends with it and produces
something different from either, something destined to be
permanent as far as we can yet see. In all the pieces usually
dated a little before or a little after 1200—the fragments of
St. Godric, *Paternoster*, *The Moral Ode* and others, as well as
the two long compositions of Layamon and Orm—this process
and its results are observable. The new agency is the syllabic prosody (accentual, also, in general character, but
strictly syllabic) of French and of contemporary Latin, with
its almost invariable accompaniment of rime, and its tendency,
invariable also in French, though by no means so in Latin, to
iambic rhythm. It must be sufficient here to examine the
working out of this clash in the two long poems just referred
to, the *Ormulum* and the *Brut*, with slighter remarks on the
others. In both poems it is possible to trace the older principle of a rimeless line of more or less length, divided sharply
in the middle, or a rimeless couplet of two halves, in which,
though not invariably, there is a certain tendency to shorten
the second. But the two writers have been affected by the
opposite and newer system in ways curiously different, but
quite intelligible as results of the clash. Orm has unflinchingly kept to the old principle of rimelessness; but he has as
unflinchingly adopted the new principles of uniformity in
syllabic volume and of regular iambic metrical beat. His

lines are invariably of fifteen syllables, or his couplets of
eight and seven.   That he achieves—as any example, however
selected, must show—nothing but the most exasperating
and wooden monotony, does not matter to him, and it ought
not to matter to us.   He has sacrificed everything to regularity in number and cadence, and he has achieved this.

Layamon's result, if not more actually important, is much
more complicated, much more interesting, with much more
future in it; but, for these very reasons, it is much less easy to
summarise.   In fact, to summarise it in uncontroversial terms
is very nearly impossible.   At first sight, if we can suppose
an eye familiar with Old English poetry and not familiar at
all with Middle English, it may seem to present no great
difference from the former; and there are still some who think
that it does not present any that is vital.   But, when it is
examined a little more carefully, differences the most vital, if
as yet sometimes not more than embryonically vital, emerge.
Regarded as alliterative verse of the old pattern, it can only
be called very bad verse—verse which turns the already
abundant liberties of the original into mere chaotic licence,
for the most part, and which very seldom conforms at all
successfully.   But, in addition to this, it succumbs, constantly
though irregularly, to the temptation which, except in late
and few instances, the old verse had rigidly resisted, and which
Orm was resisting absolutely—the temptation of rime.   And
this rime seems to be forcing on it a new regularisation, that
of equal-halved distichs rimed together in the exact fashion
of the French octosyllabic couplet.

When we turn to the other and smaller poems of the
period we find this process of "slowly quickening into other
forms" even more importantly and interestingly exhibited.
The *Paternoster* is wholly in more or less regular rimed couplets
of the kind just noted.   In *The Moral Ode*, the fifteen-syllabled
line of Orm, which, by the frequency of feminine endings,
already promises the reduction to fourteen, comes even nearer
to the ballad metre of eight and six, and exhibits a still more
valuable characteristic in its tendency towards maintaining
the old syllabic freedom and substitution of trisyllabic feet for
the strict dissyllables of *Ormulum*.   Further, this heritage of Old
English manifests itself in the octosyllabic couplet; and, in the

version of *Genesis and Exodus*, which is assigned to about the middle of the thirteenth century, anticipates exactly the *Christabel* metre which Coleridge thought he invented more than five hundred years later. And, before very long, though at dates impossible to indicate with precision, owing to the uncertainty of the chronology of the documents, other approximations of the old staple line or couplet to the metres of French and Latin (especially the *rime couée* or combination of two eights and a six doubled) make their appearance. These transformations, however, as the liberty of their forms shows, and as may be specially studied with greatest ease in the various adaptations of the octosyllabic couplet, are neither mere aimless haphazard experiments, nor mere slavish following of French and Latin forms previously existing and held up as patterns. They may be much more reasonably regarded as attempts to adjust these latter to the old couplet with its middle division, and its liberty of equality or inequality of syllabic length in the halves; though, in all cases, the special rhythm of the older line or stave has become faint in the ear, and the new metrical swing prevails. An equal division of the halves gives a distich which, for some time, hesitates between eight and six syllables, the latter having the additional assistance of the French alexandrine as pattern. But it proves less suitable for English verse than the longer form, and it is dropped or very rarely used. An unequal division —from the first most popular—into eight and seven or eight and six, gives the long line of Robert of Gloucester—sometimes called, for convenience, a "fourteener" or, by Warton and others, but most improperly, a "long alexandrine." This, when itself "disclosed" in "golden couplets," becomes at once the famous "common" or ballad measure, the most distinctly popular metre for seven hundred years past, and, at certain times, one yielding the most exquisite harmony possible, though very easily degraded and reduced to sing-song. In the course, moreover, of the give and take of this commerce between material and mould, the beginnings of the great decasyllabic, five-foot, or five-stress line emerge with a frequency which has, for the most part, been inadequately noted; as well as, more rarely, the alexandrine itself. In fact, it furnishes the poet, by luck or design, with every possible line from four, or even fewer, syllables to fourteen; while his examples in Latin and French in turn furnish almost endless suggestions of stanza-combination.

In one all-important particular, however, the foreign influence exercised—by French altogether and, by Latin, in the greatest part by far of its recent and accentual verse writing—in the direction of strict syllabic uniformity, is not, indeed, universally, but to a very large extent, and stubbornly, resisted. The rimelessness of Old English might be given up with pleasure; its curious non-metrical, or hardly more than half-metrical, cadences might be willing'y exchanged for more definite harmony; the chains of its forced alliteration might be attenuated to an agreeable carcanet worn now and then for ornament; and its extreme length-licence might be curtailed and regularised. But, in one point which had made for this latter, English refused to surrender; and that was the admission of trisyllabic feet, as some phrase it, or, as some prefer to describe the process, the admission of extra unstressed syllables. The question was, indeed, not settled; *as* a question it, no doubt, never arose; and, when such problems came to be considered, there was a dangerous tendency from late in the sixteenth century till later in the eighteenth to answer them in the wrong way. But practice was irreconcilable. Of the octosyllabic couplet there were, almost from the first, two distinct forms, the strict and the elastic; in nearly all other metres the licence is practically assumed. By 1300, or a little later, say 1325—to admit the latest possible dates for the Harleian lyrics and the bulk of the early romances—all the constitutive principles of modern English prosody are in operation, and are turning out work, rougher or smoother, but unmistakable.

One curious postscript has to be made to these few general remarks. During the period just referred to—from Layamon, that is to say, to the appearance of *William of Palerne* and other things, at a time probably nearer to the middle of the fourteenth century than to its beginning—attempts at the old alliterative metre are absolutely wanting. It is not unusual to meet with assumptions that, though wanting, they must have existed, at any rate in popular literature; and to these assumptions, as to all such, no reasonable answer can be made, except that it may have been so. So far, however, no trace of any such verse in the period referred to has been discovered; nor any reference to such; nor any evidence, direct or indirect, that it existed. About the end of the period it reappears: sometimes simple of itself, with a cadence altered, indeed, but not out of all likeness, after the fashion that was to produce its capital example in *The Vision of Piers Plowman;* sometimes in a very remarkable blend with rime, and with metrical and stanza arrangement, after the fashion of which the most notable instances, in less and more regular kind, are *Gawayne and the Grene Knight* and *Pearl.* But this revival or reappearance has no effect on the main current of English verse; which continues to be distinctly metrical, to be, in effect universally, rimed and to use alliteration only for a separable and casual ornament, not as a constituent and property.

CHAPTER XIX

Changes in the Language to the Days of Chaucer

1. CONTINUITY OF THE ENGLISH LANGUAGE

THE three Germanic peoples—the Jutes from Jutland, the Angles from Schleswig and the Saxons from Holstein—who, in the fifth and sixth centuries, made themselves masters of the greater part of south Britain, spoke dialects so nearly allied that they can have had no great difficulty in understanding each other's speech. It does not appear, however, that, in their original seats, they had any general name for their common race or their common language. The sense of their unity, with the consequent need for a general designation for themselves, would, naturally, be the product of the time when they found themselves settled among a population speaking an alien and unintelligible tongue. In fact, it was probably not by themselves, but by other nations, that the Jutes, Angles and Saxons of Britain were first regarded as forming an ethnic whole; just as in earlier times the larger kindred of which they were part had received the name of Germans from the Celts. The Britons applied to all the Germanic invaders of their country the name of Saxons, because, in the days of Roman rule, that nation had been the most conspicuous among those who ravaged the coasts of Britain; and, as is well known, the Celtic-speaking inhabitants of the British islands still continue to call the English people and its language "Saxon." On the Continent, the Germanic conquerors of Britain seem, for a long time, to have been called indiscriminately sometimes Saxons, after the Celtic practice, and sometimes Angles, the latter being the name

424

of the people which had the largest extent of territory. At the end of the sixth century, pope Gregory I uses only the name *Angli*. This is a somewhat remarkable fact, because the missionaries sent by Gregory laboured in the Jutish kingdom of Kent, which, at that time, was paramount over all the country south of the Humber. Possibly, the explanation of Gregory's choice of this name may be found in the famous story according to which his zeal for the conversion of the pagans of Britain was first awakened by his admiration of the beauty of the boy slaves from the Anglian kingdom of Deira. On the other hand, about A.D. 660, pope Vitalian, writing to an Angle king, Oswiu of Northumbria, addresses him as *rex Saxonum*.

The Roman missionaries naturally followed Gregory's practice; and it was probably from the official language of the church that the Jutes and Saxons learned to regard themselves as part of the "Angle kindred" (Angolcynn, in Latin *gens Anglorum*). The political ascendency of the Angle kingdoms, which began in the seventh century, and continued until the time of the Danish invasions, doubtless contributed to ensure the adoption of this general name. In the early years of the eighth century, Bede sometimes speaks of *Angli sive Saxones*, thus treating the two appellations as equivalent. But, with this sole exception, his name for the whole people is always *Angli* or *gens Anglorum*, and he calls their language *sermo Anglicus*, even when the special reference is to the dialect in which the Kentish laws were written. When he does speak of *lingua Saxonica*, the context, in every instance, shows that he means the language of the East or West Saxons. It is true that Bede was an Angle by birth, and this fact might seem to detract from the significance of his use of the name. But, a century and a half later, the West Saxon king Alfred, whose works are written in his native dialect, never uses any other name for his own language but Englisc—the language of the Angles. It is in the great king's writings that we find the earliest vernacular examples of the name which our language has ever since continued to bear.

In a certain sense it may be said that this name, as applied to the language of the south of England, became more and more strictly appropriate as time went on. For the history of southern English, or of the language of English literature, is, to a considerable extent, concerned with the spread of Anglian forms of words and the disappearance of forms that were specifically Saxon. Moreover, several of the most important of the processes of change that transformed the English of Alfred into the English of Chaucer—the loss of inflections and grammatical gender, and the adoption of Danish words——began in the Anglian regions of the north, and gradually extended themselves southward. Leaving out of account the changes that were due to French influences, we might almost sum up the history of the language during five centuries in the formula that it became more and more "English" and less and less "Saxon."

It will be convenient at this point to give some account of the history of the nomenclature of the various stages in the development of the English language. When, in the sixteenth century, the remains of vernacular literature earlier than the Norman conquest began to attract the attention of scholars, Englishmen naturally found it inconvenient to apply the name of "English" to what to them was, practically, a foreign language, requiring not less study to understand than the Flemish of their own day. It became customary, therefore, to speak of this language as "Saxon." As the few pre-Conquest texts then known were written in the south, this designation may be said to have been accurately descriptive. It was so, however, merely by accident, for those who employed it were accustomed to use the term "Saxons" as a general name for the Germanic inhabitants of England before the Norman conquest. The popular view was that the "English" people and the "English" language came into being as the result of the fusion of "Saxons" and Normans. Traces of this misuse of names, indeed, are to be found in various forms of expression that are still current. Although the double misnomer of "the Saxon heptarchy" no longer appears in our school histories modern writers continue to speak of "the Saxon elements in the English vocabulary," and to misapply the epithet "Saxon" to the architecture of the parts of the country inhabited by the Angles.

The term "Saxon," besides being historically incorrect as a designation for the whole early Germanic population of Britain, was inconveniently ambiguous, because it survived as the proper appellation of a portion of the inhabitants of Germany. In the last years of the reign of Elizabeth, Camden revived the use of the old name *Anglosaxones*, and, probably for the first time, used *lingua Anglosaxonica* for the language of England before the Norman conquest. He explains that *Anglosaxones* means the Saxons of England, in contradistinction to those of the Continent; and, in his English *Remains*, he accordingly renders it by "English Saxons."   Throughout the seventeenth century, and even later, "English Saxon" continued to be the name ordinarily applied by philologists to the language of king Alfred, but, in the eighteenth century, this gave place to "Anglo-Saxon."

Camden's explanation of the compound name was, there can be little doubt, historically correct. In its early use, it was applied to distinguish those Saxons who were considered part of the "Angolcynn," and whose language was called "English," from the "Old Saxons," who remained in Germany; and the structure of the native form *Angulseaxe* shows that the first element was intended as a descriptive prefix. It was, however, natural that the compound should be interpreted as meaning "Angle and Saxon," and, apparently, it was taken in this sense already at the end of the seventeenth century by George Hickes, who also applied the analogous name "Dano-Saxon" to the Old Northumbrian dialect, under the mistaken notion that its peculiar features were the result of Scandinavian admixture. As thus misunderstood, the term "Anglo-Saxon" was accepted as supplying the need for a general name applicable to the Anglian and Saxon dialects in their fully inflected stage. In this comprehensive sense it continues to be extensively used. The proposal of some scholars to restrict its application, on grounds of historical propriety to the Saxon dialect failed to gain acceptance, because what was wanted was an inclusive name for the early language of England, as the object of a well-defined branch of linguistic study. When professorships of "Anglo-Saxon" had been founded at Oxford and Cambridge, it was hardly possible to narrow the meaning of the name to a part of the subject which the professors were appointed to teach.

As a popular designation, the name "Anglo-Saxon" has

the merits of definiteness and intelligibility, which may possibly long preserve it in use. It has, however, the great disadvantage of concealing the important fact that the history of our language from the earliest days to the present time has been one of continuous development. When this fact became evident through the attention bestowed by scholars on the language of the thirteenth century, the inconvenience of the traditional nomenclature could not escape recognition. The language of this period was too different from the Anglo-Saxon of the grammars to be conveniently called by the same name, while, on the other hand, it could hardly be called English so long as "English" was understood to mean a language which the unlearned reader could at once perceive to be substantially identical with his own. An attempt was made to meet the difficulty by the invention of the compound "Semi-Saxon," to denote the transitional stage between "Anglo-Saxon" and "English," but this name was so obviously infelicitous that its introduction helped to procure acceptance for a nomenclature which recognised that the language of Caedmon was no less "English" than that of Chaucer. The great German philologist Jacob Grimm had introduced the practice of dividing the history of a language into three periods, designated by the prefixes "Old," "Middle" and "New" or "Modern"; and, in the latter half of the nineteenth century, many scholars in England adopted "Old English" as the name for that stage of the language which had, till then, been known as Anglo-Saxon. The change found much opposition, on the not wholly unreasonable ground that "Old English" was popularly applied to any form of English that was characterised by abundance of obsolete words and by antiquated spelling, so that the novel use could not but lead to frequent misunderstanding. The advantages of the new nomenclature for purposes of historical treatment are, however, so considerable that it has now come into general use, although a few philologists, both in England and Germany, still decline to adopt it.

The main reason for restoring to the language of Caedmon and Alfred its historical name of "English," is to emphasise the truth that there was no substitution of one language for another in England after the Norman conquest, but only a modification of the original language by gradual changes in pronunciation and grammar, by the accession of new words and the obsolescence of old ones.   The change of nomenclature will be a mere useless pedantry if we allow ourselves to imagine that there was any definite date at which people ceased to speak "Old English" and began to speak "Middle English," or even that there ever was a time when the English of the older generation and that of the younger generation differed widely from each other.   Nevertheless, owing partly to the fact that the twelfth century was an age of exceptionally rapid linguistic change, and partly to other causes hereafter to be explained, it is quite true that, while the literary remains of the first half of the century exhibit a form of the language not strikingly different from that of preceding centuries, those of the latter half present such an amount of novelty in spelling and grammatical features as to make the most superficial observation sufficient to show that a new period has begun.   The date of A.D. 1150, as the approximate point of demarcation between the Old and Middle periods of English, is, therefore, less arbitrary than chronological boundaries in the history of a language usually are; though, if we possessed full information respecting the *spoken* English of the twelfth century, we should have to be content with a much less precise determination.   While the Middle English period has thus a definite beginning, it has no definite ending.   It is, however, convenient to regard it as terminating about A.D. 1500, because the end of the fifteenth century coincides pretty closely with the victory of the printing-press over the *scriptorium*; and many of the distinctive features of literary Modern English would never have been developed if printing had not been invented.

2. Changes in Grammar

The most striking characteristic of Old English, as compared with later stages of the language, is that it retained without essential change the inflectional system which it possessed at the beginning of its history.   So far as regards the verbs, this system was very imperfect in comparison with that of Greek, or even of Latin.   There was no inflected passive, the need of which was supplied by the use of auxiliaries;

and there were only two inflected tenses: the present, which
often had to serve for a future, and the past. The use of
auxiliaries for forming compound tenses was comparatively
rare. The three persons of the plural had only one form,
which, prehistorically, had been that of the third person;
and, in the past tense, the first and third person singular were
alike. On the other hand, the system of declension was nearly
as elaborate as in any of the languages of the Indogermanic
family. Substantives had four cases: nominative, accusative,
genitive and dative. The adjective had two sets of inflections
for gender, number and case—the one used when the substantive was "definite" (as when preceded by the article or some
equivalent), and the other when it was "indefinite." So far
as this description goes, it might appear that the Old English
machinery for expressing the grammatical relations of substantives, adjectives and pronouns was as adequate for its purpose
as even that of Greek. But, owing to the effect of prehistoric
changes of pronunciation, which had assimilated many ter-
minations that were originally distinct, the Old English
declension of these parts of speech was, in fact, full of inconvenient ambiguities. This will be evident if we place side
by side the paradigms of the word *guma*, a man, in Gothic
(which, in this instance, agrees very nearly with primitive
Germanic) and in Old English.

		Gothic.	Old English.
Sing. Nom.		guma	guma
	Accus.	guman	guman
	Gen.	gumins	guman
	Dative	gumin	guman
Plur. Nom.		gumans	guman
	Accus.	gumans	guman
	Gen.	gumanē	gumena
	Dative	gumam	gumum

The Gothic declension of this noun, it will be seen, has only
one weak point, namely, that the accusative plural had assumed
the form of the nominative. But, in Old English, the one form
guman had five different functions. There were in Old English
many other declensions of nouns besides that of which the
word *guma* is an example; and all of them were, more or less,
faulty. The accusative had nearly always the same form as

the nominative. In some nouns the genitive singular, and in others the nominative plural, did not differ from the nominative singular.

These observations apply to the West Saxon or southern dialect of Old English, in which most of the extant literature is written. But, while the West Saxon system of noun-inflection was thus seriously defective, that of the Northumbrian dialect was far worse, because, in that dialect, the final -*n* had come to be regularly dropped in nearly all grammatical endings; and, further, the unaccented final vowels were pronounced obscurely, so that we often find them confused in our texts. It was quite an exceptional thing for the case and number of a substantive to be unambiguously indicated by its form. The ambiguities were, to some extent, obviated by the inflection of the accompanying article or adjective; but the declension even of these parts of speech, though better preserved than that of the substantive, had, itself, suffered from wear and tear, so that there were only a few of the endings that had not a multiplicity of functions.

The imperfection of the Old English system of inflections must sometimes have caused practical inconvenience, and some of the changes which it underwent were due to instinctive efforts to remedy its defects. These changes naturally began where the evil was greatest, in the northern dialect. It used to be believed—and the notion is not altogether extinct—that the almost universal substitution of -*es* for the many Old English endings of the genitive singular and the nominative and accusative plural was a result of the Norman conquest. But, in fact, the beginning of this alteration in the language can be traced to a far earlier time. In the Northumbrian writings of the tenth century we find that, very often, when the traditional ending of a noun failed to indicate properly its case and number, the required clearness was gained by assimilating its declension to that of those nouns which made their genitives in -*es* and their plurals in -*as*. As -*es* was the only ending of nouns that never marked anything but a genitive singular, and -*as* the only ending that never marked anything but a nominative or accusative plural, the improvement in lucidity was very considerable. We lack definite evidence as to the rapidity with which these two endings came, in the northern dialect, to be applied to nearly all substantives, but the process probably occupied no very long time. The change of declension synchronised with a tendency, which prevailed in all dialects, to obscure the pronunciation of the vowels in all unstressed final syllables, so that -as became -es. The practice of forming genitives and plurals, as a general rule, with this ending spread from the northern to the midland dialect; perhaps this dialect may, in part, have developed it independently. In the *Peterborough Chronicle* (about 1154), and in the north midland *Ormulum* (about 1200), we find it fully established. The English of educated Londoners had, in the fourteenth century, lost most of its original southern peculiarities, and had become essentially a midland dialect. Hence, the writings of Chaucer show, as a general rule, only the -es plurals and the -es genitives; the "irregular plurals," as we may now call them, being hardly more numerous than in modern standard English. Words adopted from French often retained their original plurals in -s. The dative case disappeared from midland English in the twelfth century, so that Chaucer's declension of substantives is as simple as that of our own day.

In purely southern dialects, the history of the noun-inflections was quite different. The case-endings of Old English —West Saxon and Kentish—were to a great extent retained, with the alterations that resulted from the general reduction of their vowels to an obscure *e*. One consequence of this "levelling" of vowels was that there was a large number of nouns of which the nominative singular ended in *e*- and the nominative plural in -*en*, as *name*, *namen*, *tunge* (tongue), *tungen* (in Old English *nama*, *naman*, *tunge*, *tungan*); and, as the -*n* was, in these words, felt as a formative of the plural, it was dropped in the oblique cases of the singular. Hence, in these words all the cases of the singular ended in -*e*, and the nominative and accusative plural in -*en*. To the extensive declensions thus arising all nouns ending in -*e* came to be assimilated, including feminine nouns in which this ending had been extended from the oblique cases to the nominative singular, such as *honde* hand (Old English *hond*, dative *honda*), *sunne* sin (Old English *synn*, dative *synne*). We observe here the same instinctive struggle against the ambiguities induced by the progress of phonetic change that we have seen in the noun-declension of the northern and midland dialects, although the remedial devices adopted were different. In the period with which we are here concerned, southern English did not greatly extend the *-es* genitives beyond their orig'nal range, while *-es*, as a plural ending, was nearly confined to those nouns that had *-as* in Old English, and to neuters (like *word*) in which the singular and plural nominatives had had the same form. The Old Eng'ish termination *-um*, which marked the dative plural in all declensions, survived as *-en*. The genitive plural had two forms, *-e* and *-ene* (Old English *-a*, *-ena*); the latter as the more distinct, encroached on the domain of the former, so that "king of kings" was *kingene king* instead of *kinge king* (Old English *cyninga cyning*).

The history of pronominal forms, like that of the declension of nouns, exhibits certain changes serving to relieve the want of distinctness in the traditional system. These changes began in the Anglian districts, and did not, for the most part, reach the Saxon region till after Chaucer's time. The forms of the Old English pronouns of the third person, in all dialects, were, in several instances, curiously near to being alike in pronunciation. The masculine nominative *hē* was not very different from the feminine nominative and accusative *hēo* (also *hīe*, *hī*), and this closely resembled the plural nominative and accusative *hīe* or *hī*. The dative singular masculine and neuter was *him*, and the dative plural was *heom*. The genitive and dative singular of the feminine pronoun was *hire*, and the genitive plural was *heora*. The one form *his* served for the genitive both of the masculine *hē* and of the neuter *hit*. (The forms here cited are West Saxon, the divergences of the other dialects being unimportant.) As the pronouns were most commonly unemphatic, such differences as those between *him* and *heom*, *hire* and *heora*, would, usually, be slighter in speech than they appear in writing, and with the general weakening of unstressed vowels that took place in Middle English they were simply obliterated. In southern Middle English the resulting ambiguities remained unremedied; but in the north and a great part of the midlands, they were got rid of by the process (very rare in the history of languages) of adopting pronouns from a foreign tongue. In many parts of these regions the Danes and Northmen formed the majority, or a powerful minority, of the population, and it is from their language that we obtain the words now written *they*, *their*, *them* and, perhaps, also *she*, though its precise origin is not clear. *She* (written *scæ*) occurs in the *Peterborough Chronicle* about 1154. It does not appear in the *Ormulum* (about 1200), which retains the native pronoun in the form ȝho; the somewhat later east midland *Genesis and Exodus* has both words *ghe or ge* and *sge* or *sche*. After 1300, *scho* is universal in the northern dialect and *sche* in east midland; but *ho* was common in west midland down to the end of the century, and still remains in the local speech of many districts. The *Ormulum* has always *they* (written þeȝȝ), but retains *heore*, *hemm* beside the newer *their*, *them* (written þeȝȝre, þeȝȝm); in the fourteenth century *they*, *their*, *them* are found fully established in all northern and east midland writings, while, in the west, *hy* for "they" continued in use. Early in the twelfth century, the accusative form of all pronouns, except the neuter *hit*, had been replaced by the dative. Chaucer uses *she* and *they*; but his *her* serves both for "her" (accusative, genitive and dative) and for "their," and he has always *hem* for "them." In the south, the curious form *hise* or *is* was used for "them." With regard to the other pronouns it will suffice to mention that the form *ich* (with *ch* pronounced as in "rich") was general in the south, while elsewhere the Old English *ic* became *I* early in the thirteenth century.

The Old English inflections of adjectives and article, and, with them, the grammatical genders of nouns, disappeared almostly entirely early in Middle English. The Kentish dialect of the fourteenth century, indeed, was exceptionally archaic in these points; in the *Ayenbite* (written 1340) we find for instance, the accusative masculine form of the adjective and article in "*ane gratne* dyeuel" (a great devil) and "*thane* dyath," for which Chaucer would have written "a *gret* deuel" and "*the* deeth." In other districts of the south, also, considerable traces of grammatical gender and adjective inflection are found quite late. But the north midland English of the *Ormulum* is, in these respects, nearly identical with that of Chaucer. The article is regularly *the* undeclined; gender is determined purely by sex; and the adjective (with rare exceptions) has no other inflectional endings than the final *-e* used when the adjective precedes a definite or a plural noun.   In the north, where final unstressed vowels had been silent, the adjective and article were uninflected, and grammatical gender had ceased to exist, before the fourteenth century.

Among the most easily recognisable characteristics of Middle English dialects are certain differences in the conjugation of the verb.   In Old English, the third person singular, and all the persons of the plural, of the present indicative ended in -*th*, with a difference in the preceding vowel: thus, *lufian* to love, *lǽran* to teach, give (in West Saxon) *hē lufath, hē lǽreth*, and *wē lufiath, wē lǽrath*.   In the northern dialect, this -*th* had, in the tenth century, already begun to give way to -*s*; and northern writings of about 1300 show -*es* both in the third singular and in the plural as the universal ending.   The midland dialect, from 1200 onwards, had in the plural -*en*, perhaps taken over from the present subjunctive or the past indicative; this ending, often reduced to -*e*, remains in the language of Chaucer.   The third singular ended in -*eth* in midland English (so also in Chaucer); but the northern -*s*, which has now been adopted almost everywhere, even in rustic speech, is found in many midland writings of the fourteenth century, especially in those of the west.   The southern dialect preserved the West Saxon forms with little change: we find *he luveth, we luvieth* in the fourteenth century.   The plural indicative present of the verb *to be* had several quite unconnected forms in Old English· *sindon* and *bēoth* in all dialects, *earon, aron* in Northumbrian and Mercian.   In the thirteenth century, *sinden* occurs in the north midland *Ormulum* and some southern writings.   In the fourteenth century, northern writings have *are* (monosyllabic), midland varies between *aren* or *are* and *been, ben*, while the southern form is *beoth* or *buth*.

The Northumbrian dialect had, in the tenth century, already reduced the -*an* of the infinitive to -*a*, and, in the northern English of the fourteenth century, the infinitive and the first person singular present were destitute of endings (the final -*e*, though often written, being shown by the metre to be silent).   In other dialects, the infinitive ended in -*en*, for which -*e* occurs with increasing frequency from the thirteenth century onwards.   Chaucer and Gower have both forms; their metre requires the final -*e* to be sounded in this as in most of the other instances, but it is probable that, in ordinary speech, it was generally silent before A.D 1400.

The forms of the present participle, which, in Old English, ended in -*ende*, afford a well-marked criterion of dialect in Middle English. The northern dialect had *falland*, the southern *fallinde*; in the midland dialect, *fallande* or *fallende* gradually gave place to *fallinge*, which is the form used by Chaucer.

It is impossible in this chapter to pursue the history of early English inflections in all its details, but, before leaving the subject of the development of the grammar, we must say a few words on the question how far the rapid simplification of the declension and conjugation in the twelfth and succeeding centuries was an effect of the Norman conquest. The view once universally held, and still entertained by many persons, that the establishment of Norman rule was the main cause by which this change was brought about, is now abandoned by all scholars. We have seen that, in the north of England, the movement towards a simpler grammatical system had made no small progress a hundred years before duke William landed; and the causes to which this movement was due were such as could not fail to be increasingly effective. The intimate mixture of Danish and native populations in the north and over a great part of the midlands must, no doubt, have had a powerful influence in reinforcing the tendencies to change that already existed. So far as these districts are concerned, it is not too much to say that the history of English grammar would have been very nearly what it actually was if the Conquest had never taken place. It is peculiarly worthy of note that the southern dialect, which we would expect to be most affected by the French influence, and which, with regard to vocabulary, certainly was so, was, of all dialects of Middle English, the most conservative in its grammar. And there is good reason to believe that, even in the south, the *spoken* language had travelled a considerable distance towards the Middle English stage before the fateful date A.D. 1066. Only twenty years after the Conquest, the Norman scribes of Domesday Book, writing phonetically and without influence from English tradition, spell local and personal names in a way which shows that the oral language had undergone certain changes that do not regularly manifest themselves in native writings until

much later.   And some of the charters of the time of Edward
the Confessor, which exhibit modernisms that are commonly
attributed to the scribes of the late MSS. in which they are
preserved, are, probably, less altered from their original form
than is generally imagined.   This remark applies especially
to informal documents not proceeding from professional
scriveners, such, for instance, as the interesting letter of the
monk Edwin about 1057, printed in Kemble's *Codex Diploma-
ticus*, No. 922.

What the Norman conquest really did was to tear away the
veil that literary conservatism had thrown over the changes of
the spoken tongue.   The ambition of Englishmen to acquire
the language of the ruling class, and the influx of foreign monks
into the religious houses that were the sources of literary instruction, soon brought about the cessation of all systematic
training in the use of English.   The upper and middle classes
became bilingual; and, though English might still be the
language which they preferred to speak, they learned at school
to read and write nothing but French, or French and Latin.
When those who had been educated under the new conditions
tried to write English, the literary conventions of the past
generation had no hold upon them; they could write no otherwise than as they spoke.   This is the true explanation of the
apparently rapid change in the grammar of English about the
middle of the twelfth century.

It would, however, be a mistake to say that the new conditions produced by the Conquest were wholly without influence
on the inflectional structure of the spoken language.   Under
the Norman kings and their successors, England was politically
and administratively united as it had never been before;
intercourse between the different parts of the country became
less difficult; and the greater freedom of intercommunication
assisted the southward diffusion of those grammatical simpli-
fications that had been developed in the northern dialect.
The use of the French language among large classes of the
population, which has left such profound traces in the English
vocabulary, must have tended to accelerate the movement
towards disuse of inflectional endings; though this influence
must remain rather a matter of abstract probability than of
demonstrable fact, because we have no means of distinguishing

its effects from those of other causes that were operating in the same direction. Perhaps the use of the preposition *of* instead of the genitive inflection, and the polite substitution of the plural for the singular in pronouns of the second person, were due to imitation of French modes of expression; but, in other respects, hardly any specific influence of French upon English grammar can be shown to have existed.

In the main, therefore, the differences between the grammar of Old English and that of the English of Chaucer's day must be ascribed to internal agencies, helped to a certain extent by the influence of the language of the Scandinavian settlers. The French influence introduced by the Norman conquest had only a comparitively small effect.

3. PRONUNCIATION AND SPELLING

The runic alphabet that had been used by the heathen English was, soon after their conversion, superseded (for most purposes) by the Latin alphabet of 22 letters, to which afterwards were added the three characters ƿ (*w*, called *wynn*), þ (*th*, called *thorn*), which belonged to the runic alphabet, and ð, differentiated from *d* by the addition of a cross-bar. The last-mentioned character was used indifferently with þ, the two sounds of our modern *th* (in *thick* and in *this*) not being graphically distinguished. The *u* or *v*, and the *i*, were, in ordinary Old English spelling, used only as vowels, the Latin practice of using them as consonants not being followed. On the early coins, the sound expressed in modern French by *u* and in German by *ü* was rendered by writing a V with an I inside it. This compound character in MSS. became *ŷ*, and this was identified with the Roman *y*. Instead of *qu*, the combination *cƿ* was used in Old English; *k* occurs in some MSS., but was commonly replaced by *c*; *z* was used, though very : el- dom, with its contemporary Latin value of *ts*.

It is not necessary to give in this place any account of the changes in orthography during the Old English period. About A.D. 1000, the vowels were probably sounded nearly as in modern Italian, except that *æ* stood for a sound in- termediate between those of *a* and *e* (*i.e.* the modern southern sound of *a* in *pat*), and that *y*, as already remarked, was like the French *u*. The long vowels, which had the same sounds as the corresponding short vowels prolonged, were, at an early period, denoted by doubling, and, later, by a mark (about equally resembling an acute and a circumflex accent) over the letter; but this was often omitted. The consonants had, for the most part, the same sounds as in modern English, but some exceptions must be mentioned. Several consonant letters had more than one sound, and, in the case of most of these, modern English retains the Old English pronunciation, though not always the same written symbol. Thus, in *fan* fan, *æfen* even, *sǣd* seed, *rīsan* rise (sounded "rize"), *þynne* thin, *brōþor* brother, *caru* care, *cealc* chalk, *scēap* sheep, *scōl* school, *gōd* good, *gēar* year, *þing* thing, *sengan* to singe, *docga* dog, *ecg* edge, the Old English sounds of *f, s, þ, c, sc, g, ng* and *cg* were exactly, or nearly, those of the letters occupying the same place in the modern forms of these words. In the middle or at the end of a word, *g* was sounded differently according to the nature of the neighbouring vowels: in *dæg* day it was pronounced like *y* in "year," but in the plural *dagas* days it had a sound that might be written *gh*, differing from the *ch* in *loch* just as *g* differs from *k*. The letter *h*, when initial, was pronounced as at present; but, in other positions, it was pronounced like the German *ch* (either guttural as in *ach* or palatal as in *ich*, according to the sounds which it followed). It will be seen that, with few exceptions, our ancestors of the eleventh century pronounced the consonantal part of their words much as we do, even when they wrote it with different letters.

The striking change in the written language of England during the twelfth century was, to a considerable extent, a matter of mere spelling. As was pointed out in the preceding section, soon after the Norman conquest children ceased to be regularly taught to read and write English, and were taught to read and write French instead. When, therefore, the mass of the new generation tried to write English, they had no orthographical traditions to guide them, and had to spell the words phonetically according to French rules. They used *ch* instead of the old *c*, when it was pronounced as in *cirice* church. The sound of the Old English *sc* in *sceamu* shame, which did not exist at that time in French, was rendered by *ss, ssh, sch*, or *sh*. The French *qu* took the place of *cþ*.

The *f* between vowels (pronounced *v*) was replaced by *u* or *v* (these being still, as long afterwards, treated as forms of one and the same letter, used indifferently for vowel and consonant). The Old English symbol *æ* was dropped, its place being taken by *a* or *e*. The sound of the Old English *y*, in the dialects where it survived, was expressed by *u*; and that of the Old English long *u* was written *ou*, as in French.

Of course these changes did not take place all at once. It is not to be supposed that no one ever read an Old English MS., and there was, for a long time, some mixture of the traditional spelling with the new one. Some few English sounds admitted of no tolerable representation in the French alphabet; and for the expression of these the native characters were retained in use. The letters þ, ð and ƿ were used, though often blunderingly, even by scribes who, in other respects, were thoroughly French in their spelling; though often we find their sounds awkwardly rendered by *t*, *th*, *ht*, or *d*, and *u*. And in the twelfth century, though the continental variety of the Roman alphabet was generally used for writing English, it was found convenient to retain the native form ȝ of the letter *g* for those two of its sounds that the French *g* lacked, namely, those of *gh* and *y* (as in *year*). A new letter was thus added to the alphabet, and, though it came to be written ȝ, exactly like the contemporary form of *z*, it preserved its name "yok" until the fourteenth century. It may be remarked in passing that the ambiguity of pronunciation of this letter has misled modern writers into calling the author of the *Brut* "Layamon" instead of "Laghamon"; the incorrect form, however, has become too well known to be displaced. In addition to the two original values of the "yok," it very early obtained a third use, being employed (without indicating any change of pronunciation) instead of the Old English *h* in certain positions, as in *kniȝt*, *ibroȝt*, *rouȝ*, for which the older spelling was *cniht*, *gebroht*, *ruh*. But, in the fourteenth century, many writers substituted *y* or *i* for ȝ, when pronounced as in ȝeer (year), and *gh* in all other cases. In the thirteenth century, the letters þ and ð went out of use, the former being replaced by the northern French *w*. The letter þ was retained; but, although it was still called "thorn" in the fourteenth century, it seems in Chaucer's time to have been regarded as a mere compendium for *th*, which generally took its place except initially. It may be noted that Thomas Usk, in the acrostic sentence of his *Testament of Love* (1387) spells þin (thine) with the four letters THIN. The adoption of a number of French words like *ioie* (joy), in which *i* was pronounced like the modern English *j*, introduced the consonantal use of this letter into English orthography.

The Old English initial combination *hl* survived (written *lh*) in some dialects down to the fourteenth century; but *hr* was very early reduced to *r*. For the Old English *hw*, Middle English writers substituted *wh*, though the *h* was, at first, often omitted in this combination, as in other positions, by scribes of French education. The northern spelling *qua*, *quilk* for *wha*, *whilk* (who, which) arose from a dialectal pronunciation of *qu* as *wh*, which still survives locally in a few words.

From the twelfth century onwards, the letter *y*, when used as a vowel, was treated as a mere alternative form of *i*.

The *Ormulum* is written in a peculiar phonetic spelling devised by the author himself. This is based, to a considerable extent, on native tradition, though the handwriting is of the continental type. There are, however, some of the new features. Orm uses *ch* and *sh* as we do now, and retains the Old English form of *g* for the two sounds which the French *g* had not. A device peculiar to himself is the appropriation of different shapes of the letter *g* to the two sounds in *god* (good) and *egge* (edge). But the most noteworthy characteristic of his orthography is the method of indicating the quantity of the vowels. The shortness of a vowel, in a syllable ending with a consonant, is shown by doubling the following consonant, as in *Crisstenndom*. When the short vowel ended a syllable in the middle of a word, Orm marked it as in *tākenn*, and very often (though not always) indicated a long vowel by one, two, or even three "acute accents" over the letter. This elaborate and cumbrous system found no imitators, but, as preserved in the author's autograph MS., it is one of the most important aids that we possess for ascertaining the English pronunciation of the time.

The changes in spelling that we have thus far noticed are merely changes in the manner of *representing* sound. There

were others that were the result of altered pronunciation. It
very often happens that very considerable changes take place
in the sounds of a language without affecting the spelling, even
when (as was apparently, the case in Middle English) there is no
general prejudice against deviations from traditional correctness of orthography. Pronunciation, as a general rule, is not
altered deliberately, but unconsciously. In the utterance
of what is intended and believed to be one and the same
vowel or consonant sound, each generation may vary to an
almost imperceptible extent from that which preceded it; and,
if these slight changes are all in the same direction, the difference
may, in the end, become indefinitely great. The normal
result in such cases is that the letter comes to have a new
phonetic value, and the spelling is not effected. The reason
why there are exceptions to this normal course of things in
Middle English was partly that sometimes two originally
distinct sounds so developed as to become identical, and partly
that the orthography of French supplied a kind of external
standard.

The history of the changes in English pronunciation down
to the time of Chaucer is far too intricate to be treated here
with any approach to completeness; but a few of its salient
points may be briefly indicated.

The first remark to be made is that the course of development of several of the Old English sounds was quite different
in different parts of the country. When we compare the modern English pronunciation of *home*, *stone*, with the Scotch and
northern *hame*, *stane*, we see the last term of a divergent development (which began very early) of the Old English long *a*
(pronounced as *a* in father). While the northern dialect
progressively altered the sound in one direction, the midland
and southern dialects progressively altered it in the opposite
direction. We cannot precisely tell how far the change in
the northern pronunciation had proceeded in the fourteenth century, because the spelling was not affected. But,
in other dialects, as we know from various kinds of evidence, the sound was that of the "open $\bar{o}$" as in *lord*, and it
was expressed in writing by *o* or *oo*. The words "goad"
(Old English *gād*) and "good" (Old English *gōd*) are both
written *good* in Chaucer's spelling, but they were not pro-

nounced alike; if the sounds had been confused they would not have been separated again in later pronunciation; and Chaucer never rimes a word that has the "open *o*" with one containing the "close *o*." The latter retained its old pronunciation (that of the French *o* in *rose*), perhaps a little modified in the direction of its modern equivalent, the *oo* in *cool*.

The long *e*, like the long *o*, had an "open" and a "close" pronunciation, which Chaucer also keeps apart in his rimes. The open *ē* comes from the Old English (Anglian) *ǣ*, *ēa*, and the close *ē* from Old English *ē*, *ēo*. A word like *chepe* to buy (from Old English *cēapian*) which had the open *ē*, could not correctly rime with a word like *kepe* to keep (from *cēpan*) which had the close *ē*. In northern dialects, the distinction was so slight that poets freely allowed the two sounds to rime with one another.

In all the dialects of Middle English, the short vowels *ă*, *ĕ*, *ŏ*, when ending an accented syllable, were lengthened, *ĕ* and *ŏ* becoming open *ē* and open *ō*. In Chaucer's pronunciation, *mete* meat (Old English *mĕte*) was an exact rime to *grete*, the plural of the adjective great (Old English *grēate*), but not to *grete* to greet (Old English *grētan*); *þrote* throat (Old English *þrotu*) rimed with *hote* to command (Old English *hātan*), but not with *bōte* benefit (Old English *bōt*).

The Old English *y* (pronounced *ü*) kept its original sound in the south-west, and, perhaps, in parts of the west midland, being written *u* when short, and *ui* or *uy* when long; in Kent, it had become *e* before the Conquest; elsewhere, it was sounded exactly like *i*, and written, like that sound, indifferently *i* or *y*. The words "fire" "sin," "knit," have, accordingly, in the different localities the three types of form *fuir*, *ver*, *fiir; sunne*, *zenne*, *sinne; knutte*, *knette*, *knitte*. Chaucer, whose London English was mainly east midland, uses occasionally a Kentish form like *knette*.

With regard to the pronunciation of consonants, there is little that needs to be said, as, for the most part, the Old English sounds not only continued unchanged down to the end of the fourteenth century, but remain so to the present day. The pronunciation of initial *f* and *s* as *v* and *z* ("vather came vrom Zummerzet"), which sounds so strange to visitors to the south-western counties, was, in the fourteenth century, current all over the south; in fact, the Kentish *Ayenbite of Inwyt* of 1340, exhibits this pronunciation in the orthography with greater regularity than any other extant book. The *gh* sound of the letter ȝ gradually changed into that of *w*, and this change was represented in the spelling. In the earlier of the two MSS. of the poetical chronicle called the *Brut*, written at the beginning of the thirteenth century, the author's name appears as "Laȝamon," but, in the later MS., written before 1300, it is turned into "Laweman." On the other hand, in 1340, the Kentish *Ayenbite* has still forms like *zorȝe* (sorrow) instead of Chaucer's *sorwe*.

4. CHANGES IN VOCABULARY

If the Norman conquest had little influence on the development of English grammar, its effects on the vocabulary of the language were profound. It introduced, as we have already observed, an age in which all educated Englishmen spoke French in addition to their native tongue, and, for the most part, wrote nothing but French and Latin. French became the language of law and government, of war and of all that pertained to the life of the wealthier classes. Of the vernacular literature from the Conquest to the middle of the fourteenth century, by far the greater part consisted of translations from French and Latin. It is true that, down to the end of the thirteenth century, nearly all that was written in English was intended for readers who were comparatively unlearned; but even these readers could be reasonably supposed to have some degree of acquaintance with the fashionable language, for, as a rule, the man who absolutely knew nothing but English probably could not read at all. And when, once more, it became customary to write in English for highly educated people, authors could venture, without any fear of not being understood, to borrow freely from the literary, as well as from the popular, vocabulary of the French language.

Under these circumstances, it is not wonderful that the English language received a large and rapidly increasing accession of French words. A few, indeed, seem to have come in even before the Norman conquest: *catchpoll* (*kæcepol*) occurs in a glossary of the early eleventh century, and *proud* (Old English *prūt*, Old Norse *prūðr*), if it be really French, must have been adopted much earlier. In the *Peterborough Chronicle* written about 1154, the French words amount to nearly a score. Their character is significant. They include *emperice* empress, *cuntesse* countess (of Anjou), *curt* court (king Henry II "held mycel curt" at London in 1154), *dubbian* to dub a knight, *prison, privilege, rente, tenserie* (the name of an impost). We are told that king Henry II "dide god *iustice* and makede *pais* (peace)." It is noteworthy, as indicative of foreign influence in the monasteries that we find such words as *miracle* and *procession*, and that *carited* (charity) appears as the technical name at the abbey of Peterborough for a banquet given to the poor.

About a hundred words of French origin may be collected from the southern and south midland homilies of the twelfth century, although these works are, to a great extent only slightly modernised transcripts of older originals. Most of these new words, as might be expected, relate to matters of religion or of ecclesiastical observance; but a few, such as *poor, poverty, riches, honour, robbery*, must have been already in popular use. The north midland *Ormulum*, written about 1200, is almost entirely free from French words. The author intended his work to be recited to illiterate people, and, therefore, strove to use plain language. But his employment of such a word as *gyn*, ingenuity (a shortened form of the French *engin*) shows that, even in his neighbourhood, the vernacular of the humbler classes had not escaped the contagion of French influence.

At the beginning of the thirteenth century, Layamon uses nearly a hundred French words many of which, it is interesting to note, are not identical with those occurring in the corresponding passages of his original. In the later text of the *Brut*, written about 1275, the reviser has not unfrequently substituted words of French etymology for the native words used by Layamon himself.

The southern version of the *Ancren Riwle*, which is nearly contemporary with Layamon's *Brut*, is much more exotic in vocabulary, more than four hundred French words having been enumerated as occurring in it. It appears, however, from certain passages in this work, that the women for whose instruction it was primarily written were conversant not only with French, but also with Latin. We may, therefore, presume that the author has allowed himself greater freedom in introducing literary French words than he would have done if he had been addressing readers of merely ordinary culture. Still, it is probable that a very considerable number of the words that appear in this book for the first time had already come to be commonly used among educated English people. The occurrence of compounds of French verbs and adjectives with native prefixes, as *bi-spused* (espoused), *mis-ipaied* (dissatisfied), *unstable*, is some evidence that the writer was in these instances making use of words that were already recognised as English.

In the writings of the end of the thirteenth century and the first half of the fourteenth, the proportion of Romanic words is so great that we may correctly say that the literary English of the period was a mixed language. The interesting group of poems, perhaps all by one author, consisting of *Alisaunder, Arthur and Merlin* and *Cœur de Lion*, contain many long passages in which nearly every important verb, noun, and adjective is French. Nor is this mixed vocabulary at all peculiar to works written in the south of England. In *Cursor Mundi*, and even in the prose of Richard Rolle, which are in the northern dialect, there is, on the average, at least one French word in every two lines. The alliterative poetry of the west midland and northern dialects from about 1350 onwards has an extraordinary abundance of words of French origin, many of which are common to several of the poets of this school, and do not occur elsewhere. The notion prevalent among writers of the seventeenth and eighteenth centuries that Chaucer corrupted the English language by the copious introduction of French words, was curiously wide of the mark. In reality, his language is certainly less marked by Gallicisms than that of most of the other poets of his time, and even than that of some poets of the early years of the fourteenth century. It cannot be absolutely proved that he ever, even in his translations, made use of any foreign word that had not already gained a recognised place in the English vocabulary.

The English literature of the eleventh century is almost wholly written in the southern dialect, which was comparatively little exposed to Scandinavian influence. We find in it therefore, only a very small number of Norse or Danish words, such as *fēlaga* a business partner, "fellow"; *lagu* law; *hūscarl* "house-carl," member of the king's household; *hūsbonda* master of a house, "husband"; *hūsting* assembly of the "house-carls"; *ūtlaga* outlaw.   But when, in the thirteenth century, the language spoken in the north and the north midlands again began to appear in a written form, the strongly Scandinavian character of its vocabulary becomes apparent.   The diction of the *Ormulum*, whose author bore a Scandinavian name, is full of Danish words, many of which are not otherwise found in English literature, though some of these are preserved in modern rustic dialects.   In *Cursor Mundi*, in *Genesis and Exodus*, in *Havelok*, in the writings of Robert Mannyng of Brunne in Lincolnshire, and in the west midland alliterative poetry, the large Scandinavian element must, even if other peculiarities of dialect had been absent, have been quite sufficient to render these works very difficult reading for natives of the south of England.   In several instances, native words that were in extremely common use were superseded by Danish synonyms: *call* took place of *cīgan* (another Old English word of the same meaning, *cleopian*, remained as *clepe*), *niman* was displaced by *take* and *weorpan* by *cast*.

The freedom with which words could be adopted from French to express complex and abstract notions had a marked effect in checking the augmentation of the English vocabulary by means of composition.   The new compounds that arose in Middle English down to the end of the fourteenth century are extremely few.   Individual writers occasionally ventured on experiments in this direction, especially in translations of Latin formations like Dan Michel's *ayenbite* ("again-biting") for remorse; or Wyclif's *hamersmyter* for the *malleator* of the *Vulgate*, and *soul-havers* for *animantia*; but their coinages seldom found general acceptance.   The prefixes *be-*, *for-* and *with-* (in the sense of "against"), were, however, used to form many new verbs.   The old derivative suffixes, for the most part, continued in use.   New abstract nouns were formed from adjectives and substantives by the addition of the endings *-ness*, *-hode* and *-hede* (the modern *-hood*, *-head*) and *-ship*; new adjectives in *-sum*, *-ful*, *-lich* (*-ly*); and new agent-nouns in *-ere*. The ending *-ing* was more and more frequently added to verbs to form nouns of action, and, before the end of the fourteenth century, the derivatives so formed had come to be used as mere gerunds. The suffix *-liche* (*-ly*) became a regular means of forming adverbs. As the Old English endings *-en* and *-icge*, used to form nouns denoting persons of the female sex, had become obsolete, the French *-esse* was adopted, and added to native words, as in *goddesse*, *fiendesse* and *sleeresse* (a female slayer). In the southern dialect of the thirteenth century, there appears a curious abundance of feminine agent-nouns formed from verbs by adding the suffix *-ild*, of which there are one or two examples in Old English, though, singularly enough, they have been found only in Northumbrian. Instances of this formation from the *Ancren Riwle* are *beggild* a woman given to begging, *cheapild* a female bargainer, *gruc-child* a female grumbler, *mathelild* a female chatterer, *totild* a woman fond of peeping; other words of this formation which do not imply any disparagement are *fostrild* a nurse, and *motild* a female advocate. Besides the feminines in *-esse*, the fourteenth century shows a few examples of the practice, which afterwards became so common, of appending Romanic suffixes to native words. Hampole has *trowable* for credible, Wyclif *everlastingtee* (after *eternitee*), and Chaucer *slo-gardrie* and *slogardie* ("sluggardry"), and *eggement* instigation (from the verb "to egg").

Several of the new words that came into very general use in or before the fourteenth century are of unknown or doubtful origin. Such are the verb *kill*, which appears first in Layamon under the form *cullen;* and the substantive *smell* (whence the verb), which superseded the Old English *stenc* (stench), originally applicable no less to a delightful odour than to an unpleasant one. Some of the new words, as *left* (hand), which took the place of the Old English *wynstre*, and *qued* bad, have cognates in Low German, but are not likely to have been adopted from the continent; they more probably descend from non-literary Old English dialects. *Boy* and *girl* (the latter originally applied to a young person of either sex), *lad* and *lass*, are still of uncertain origin, though conjectures more or less plausible have been offered.

Not less remarkable than the abundance of new words added to the English vocabulary in the early Middle English period is the multitude of Old English words that went out of use. Anyone who will take the trouble to go through a few pages of an Old English dictionary, noting all the words that cannot be found in any writer later than about the year 1250, will probably be surprised at their enormous number. Perhaps the most convenient way of illustrating the magnitude of the loss which the language sustained before the middle of the thirteenth century will be to take a piece of Old English prose, and to indicate those words occurring in it that became obsolete before the date mentioned. The following passage is the beginning of Aelfric's homily on St. Cuthbert, written about A.D. 1000. Of the words printed in italics, one or two occur in the *Ormulum* and other works of the beginning of the thirteenth century, but the majority disappeared much earlier.

Cuthbertus, se hālga biscop, scīnende on manegum geearnungum and hāligum *geþincþum*, on heofenan rīce mid þam ælmihtigum *Scyppende* on ēcere blisse *rīxiende*, *wuldraþ*.

Bēda, se *snotera* Engla þēoda *lāreow*, þises hālgan līf *endebyrdlīce* mid wunderfullum herungum, ægþer *ge* æfter *ānfealdre gereccednysse ge* æfter *lēoþlicere gyddunge*, āwrāt. Ūs sǣde sōþlīce Bēda þæt se *ēadiga* Cūthberhtus, þā þā he wæs *eahtawintre* cild, arn, swā swā him his *nytenlice* yld *tihte*, plegende mid his *efenealdum;* ac se ælmihtiga God wolde stȳran þære *nytennysse* his gecorenan Cūthberhtus þurh *mynegunge gelimplices lāreowes*, and āsende him tō ān *þrywintre* cild, þæt his *dyslican* plegan mid *stæþþigum* wordum wīslīce *þrēade*.

Cuthbert, the holy bishop, shining in many merits and holy honours, is in glory, reigning in the kingdom of heaven with the Almighty Creator.

Beda, the wise teacher of the English peoples, wrote this holy man's life in order with wonderful praises, both according to simple narration and according to poetic song. Beda has truly told us that the blessed Cuthbert, when he was a child of eight, ran, as his ignorant age impelled him, playing with children of his own age; but Almighty God willed to guide the ignorance of his chosen Cuthbert by the admonition of a fitting teacher, and sent to him a child three years old, who rebuked his foolish play wisely with serious words.

In the first thirty lines of Aelfric's homily on St. Gregory, there occur the following words, none of which survived beyond the middle of the thirteenth century: *andweard* present, *gedeorf* labour, *gecnyrdnyss* study, *gesǣliglīce* blessedly, *bīgeng* worship, *ætbregdan* to turn away, *gebīgan* to subdue, *drohtnung* manner of life, *swutellīce* plainly, *wer* man, *gereccan* to relate, *ēawfæst* pious, *ācenned* born, *æþelboren* nobly born, *mǣgþ* kindred, *wita* senator, *geglengan* to adorn, *swēgan* to sound, be called, *wacol* watchful, *bebod* command, *herigendlīce* laudably, *geswutelian* to manifest.

It is common to regard the obsolescence of Old English words after the Conquest as a mere consequence of the introduction of new words from French. The alien words, it is supposed, drove their native synonyms out of use. It is not to be denied that this was, to a considerable extent, the case. On the whole, however, it would probably be more true to say that the adoption of foreign words was rendered necessary because the native words expressing the same meanings had ceased to be current. When the literary use of English had for one or two generations been almost entirely discontinued, it was inevitable that the words that belonged purely to the literary language should be forgotten. And a cultivated literary dialect always retains in use a multitude of words that were once colloquial, but which even educated persons would consider too bookish to be employed in familiar speech. There were also, no doubt, in the language of English writers from Alfred onwards, very many compounds and derivatives which, though intelligible enough to all readers, were mere artificial formations that never had any oral currency at all. When the scholars of England ceased to write or read English, the literary tradition was broken; the only English generally understood was the colloquial speech, which itself may very likely have lost not a few words in the hundred years after Aelfric's time.

It might, perhaps, have been expected that the special vocabulary of Old English poetry would have survived to a greater extent than we find it actually to have done. We should not, indeed, expect to find much of it in that large portion of Middle English poetry which was written in foreign metres and in imitation of foreign models. But, about the year 1350, there arose a school of poets who, though they were men of learning and drew their material from French and Latin sources, had learned their art from the unliterary minstrels who had inherited the tradition of the ancient Germanic alliterative line. These poets have an extraordinarily abundant store of characteristic words, which are not found in prose literature or in the contemporary poetry of a different school. It might naturally be supposed that this distinctive vocabulary would consist largely of the words that had been peculiar to poetic diction in Old English times. But, in fact, nearly all the words marked in Sweet's *Anglo-Saxon Dictionary* with the sign (†) as poetical are wanting in Middle English. The fourteenth century alliterative poets use some of the ancient epic synonyms for "man" or "warrior": *bern, renk, wye* and *freke*, representing the Old English *beorn, rinc, wiga* and *freca*. A few words that in Old English were part of the ordinary language, such as *mælan* (Middle English *mele*), to speak, are among the characteristic archaisms of the later alliterative poets. The adjective *æþele*, noble, became, in the form *athil*, one of the many synonyms for "man," and often appears as *hathel*, probably through confusion with the Old English *hæleþ*, a man. The word *burde*, a lady, which is familiar to modern readers from its survival in late ballad poetry, seems to be the feminine of the Old English adjective *byrde*, high-born, of which only one instance is known, and that in prose. Several of the poetic words of the west midland school are of Scandinavian origin, as *trine* and *cair* (Old Norse *keyra*, to drive), which are both used for "to go." The very common word *tulk*, a man, represents, with curious transformation of meaning, the Old Norse *tulkr*, an interpreter. It is possible that some of these words, which are not found in modern dialects, were never colloquial English at all, but were adopted by the poets of the Scandinavian parts of England from the language of the ruling class.

The disappearance of the greater part of the old poetical vocabulary is probably due to its having been, in later Old English times, preserved only in the literary poetry which obtained its diction from the imitation of written models. To this poetry the alliterative poets of the fourteenth century owed nothing; the many archaisms which they retained were those that had been handed down in the unwritten popular poetry on which their metrical art was based.

5. ENGLISH DIALECTS IN THE FOURTEENTH CENTURY

Writers on the history of the English language have been accustomed to quote, as if it related to the condition of things in the year 1385, the following passage from Trevisa: "All the language of the Northumbrians, and specially at York, is so sharp, slitting and froting, and unshape, that we southern men may that language unnethe [hardly] understand." This sentence, however, is not Trevisa's own, but translates a quotation by Higden from William of Malmesbury's *Gesta of Pontificum*, written before 1125. The fact that Higden and Trevisa reproduce Malmesbury's words without comment, can hardly be said to prove anything. Still, although Trevisa's adoption of Malmesbury's statement is not, considered by itself, very good evidence as to the amount of dialectal divergence existing in his own time, it appears likely that, on the whole, the difference between the speech of the north and that of the south had rather increased than diminished between the twelfth and the fourteenth century. It is true that the decay of the old inflexions had removed some of the dialectal distinctions of the earlier period, and that greater freedom of intercommunication between different parts of the country had not been without effect in producing some mixture of forms. But, on the other hand, the development of pronunciation had been divergent, and the gains and losses of the vocabulary had been, to a great extent, different in the different regions.

It must be remembered that, throughout the fourteenth century strongly marked differences of dialect were not, as now, confined to the less educated classes; nor is there any clear evidence that any writer attempted to use for literary purposes any other dialect than that which he habitually spoke. It is true that Wyclif was a man of northern birth, and that the language of his writings is distinctly of the midland type. But this is only what might have been expected in the case of a distinguished Oxford teacher, whose life, probably from early boyhood, had been spent at the university. Men of the highest culture continued to write in each of the three or four principal varieties of English. The dialects may have been somewhat less unlike in their written than in their spoken form, because the spelling was too much under the influence of tradition to represent accurately the divergent development of the original sounds. But, in spite of the nearness of Canterbury to London, it is probable that Chaucer would not have found it quite easy to read the *Ayenbite of Inwyt*, which was written about the time when he was born; nor would he have felt much more at home with the writings of his contemporaries among the

west midland alliterative poets or those of northern poets like
Laurence Minot. At any rate, a modern reader who has
learned to understand Chaucer without great difficulty commonly finds himself very much at a loss when first introduced
to the *Ayenbite*, the *Morte Arthure*, or *Sir Gawayne*. Northern
prose, indeed, is to us somewhat easier, because, owing to the
loss of inflexions, its language is, in some respects, more modern than even that of Chaucer.

An outline of the distinctive features of Middle English
dialects has already been given in the sections of this chapter
treating of grammar and pronunciation. The following comparative list of forms of words may assist the reader to obtain a
general notion of the extent and nature of the diversities of the
written language of different parts of the country in the
fourteenth century.

	Kentish	*South-Western*	*E. Midland*	*W. Midland*	*Northern*
Fire	veer	vuir, fuir	fiir	fuir	fier
Sin	zenne	sunne	sinne	sinne	sin
I shall say	Ich ssel zigge	Ich schal sigge	I shal seyn	I shal saie	I sal sai
She says	hy zeyth	heo seyth	she seyth	ho saith	scho sais
They say	hy ziggeth	hy siggeth	they seyn	hy, thai sayn	thai sai
Living	liviynde	liviinde	livinge	living	livand
Her name	hare nome	hor nome	her name	hur name	her nam
Their names	hare nomen	hure nomen	hir names	hur namus	thair names

The English of Scotland, so far as we know, was hardly used
for literary purposes until the last quarter of the fourteenth
century, when Barbour wrote his *Bruce*. It is doubtful whether
the other works ascribed to Barbour are not of later date, and
the *Bruce* itself has come down to us in manuscripts written a
hundred years after the author's time. The specific features
distinguishing the Scottish dialect from northern English across
the border will, therefore, be more conveniently reserved for
treatment in a later chapter.

It must not be supposed that the forms above tabulated
were the only forms current in the districts to which they are
assigned, or that none of them were used outside the regions
to which they typically belong. Local varieties of speech
within each dialect area were doubtless many, and the orthography was unfixed and only imperfectly phonetic. Literary
works were copied by scribes who belonged to other parts of
the country than those in which the works were composed;
and, consequently, the texts as we have them represent a mixture of the grammar, pronunciation and vocabulary of different

dialects. Vernacular writers, especially poets, often added to their means of expression by adopting words and forms from dialects other than their own. Hence, although in the last years of the fourteenth century the establishment of a common literary language was still in the future, and the varieties even of the written speech continued to be strongly marked, there are few writings of the period that can be regarded as unmixed representatives of any single dialect.

The tendencies that ultimately resulted in the formation of a uniform written language began to act before the fourteenth century closed. In London, the seat of legislative and administrative activity, the influx of educated persons from all parts of the kingdom led to the displacement of the original southern dialect by the dialect of the east midlands, which, in virtue of its intermediate character, was more intelligible both to southern and northern men than northern English to a southerner or southern English to a northerner. The fact that both the university towns were linguistically within the east midland area had, no doubt, also its effect in bringing about the prevalence of this type of English among the educated classes of the capital. The works of Chaucer, which, in the next age, were read and imitated not only in the southern kingdom but even in Scotland, carried far and wide the knowledge of the forms of London English; and the not very dissimilar English of Oxford was, in like manner, spread abroad through the enormous popularity of the writings of Wyclif and his associates. Even in the lifetime of these two great writers, it had already become inevitable that the future common English of literature should be English essentially of the east midland type.

CHAPTER XX

The Anglo-French Law Language

THE profound effects of the Norman conquest on the vocabulary of the English language have already been considered. It remains to notice a special cause which had its own peculiar influence on the language, namely, the long retention of French in the courts of law. The words thus naturalised have become a part of the current speech of Englishmen, and have passed into the language in which English books have been written. This long familiarity with the structure and vocabulary of another tongue had its effect on literary style, just as the long familiarity with Latin had in the case of the monastic writers.

The effect on the vocabulary is certain and considerable, though it is impossible to draw any definite line and decide which words are due to the use of the French language in the courts, and which to its more general use outside the courts. Again, it would require special investigation in the case of individual words to determine when they ceased to be known only to lawyers and became familiar (frequently with a changed significance) to laymen.

It is to the Year Books that we must turn to see what the language of the courts actually was in the Middle Ages. These books form a series (not unbroken) of summaries of cases decided from the reign of Edward I to that of Henry VIII, while there is a note book of even earlier cases, of the reign of Henry III.[1] Maitland has shown good reason for concluding that this note book was used by Bracton in writing his great treatise.

Some portions of these Year Books have been edited in recent years [2] but, for the present purpose, the most important

---

[1] *Bracton's Note Book*, ed. F. W. Maitland.

[2] Cf. the *Rolls Series*, edited by Horwood and Pike, and the *Selden Society Series*, edited by Maitland, vols. I, II, III.

edition is that of the Year Books of Edward II edited by Maitland for the Selden Society. To volume 1 of this series Maitland prefixed a most valuable *Introduction*, from which the following pages [1] are extracts, reprinted by permission of the council of the Selden Society:

We know "law French" in its last days, in the age that lies between the Restoration and the Revolution, as a debased jargon. Lawyers still wrote it; lawyers still pronounced or pretended to pronounce it. Not only was it the language in which the moots were holden at the Inns of Court until those ancient exercises ceased, but it might sometimes be heard in the courts of law, more especially if some belated real action made its way thither. The pleadings, which had been put into Latin for the record, were also put into French in order that they might be "mumbled" by a serjeant to the judges, who, however, were not bound to listen to his mumblings, since they could see what was written in "the paper books." [2]   What is more, there still were men living who thought about law in this queer slang—for a slang it had become. Roger North has told us that such was the case of his brother Francis. If the Lord Keeper was writing hurriedly or only for himself, he wrote in French. "Really," said Roger, "the Law is scarcely expressible properly in English." A legal proposition couched in the vulgar language looked to his eyes "very uncouth." So young gentlemen were adjured to despise translations and read Littleton's *Tenures* in the original. [3]

Roger North was no pedant; but he was a Tory, and not only was the admission of English to the sacred plea rolls one of those exploits of the sour faction that had been undone by a joyous monarchy, but there was a not unreasonable belief current in royalist circles that the old French law books enshrined many a goodly prerogative, and that the specious learning of the parliamentarians might be encountered by deeper and honester research. Nevertheless, that is a remarkable sentence coming from one who lived on until 1734: "Really the Law is scarcely expressible properly in English."

Had it been written some centuries earlier it would have been very true, and its truth would have evaporated very slowly. The Act of 1362, which tried to substitute *la lange du paiis* for *la lange francais, qest trope desconue* as the oral language of the courts, is

---

[1] Pp. 456–460.

[2] Roger North, *Lives of the Norths*, 1826, 1, 30.

[3] *Lives of the Norths*, 1, 33; Roger North, *A Discourse on the Study of the Laws*, 1824, p. 13.

an important historical landmark.[1] But we know that it was
tardily obeyed, and indeed it attempted the impossible. How
tardy the obedience was we cannot precisely tell, for the history
of this matter is involved with the insufficiently explored history of
written pleadings. Apparently French remained the language of
" pleadings " properly so called, while English became the language
of that "argument" which was slowly differentiated from out of the
mixed process of arguing and pleading which is represented to us
by the Year Books. Fortescue's words about this matter are well
known.[2] In 1549 Archbishop Cranmer, contending with the rebels
of Devonshire over the propriety of using English speech in the
services of the Church, said, "I have heard suitors murmur at the
bar because their attornies pleaded their causes in the French
tongue which they understood not."[3] In Henry VIII's day, when
the advocates of a reception of Roman law could denounce "thys
barbarouse tong and Old French, wiiych now seruyth to no purpose
else," moderate reformers of the Inns of Court were urging as the
true remedy that students should be taught to plead in good French:
the sort of French, we may suppose, that John Palsgrave, *natyf de
Londres et gradué de Paris*, was teaching.[4] No doubt they felt with
Roger North that "really the Law is scarcely expressible properly
in English."

The law was not expressible properly in English until the *lange
du paiis* had appropriated to itself scores of French words; we may
go near to saying that it had to borrow a word corresponding to
almost every legal concept that had as yet been fashioned. Time
was when the Englishman who in his English talk used such a word
as "ancestor" or "heir," such a word as "descend," "revert," or "remain," must have felt that he was levying an enforced loan. For
a while the charge of speaking a barbarous jargon would fall rather
upon those who were making countless English words by the simple
method of stealing than upon those whose French, though it might
be of a colonial type, had taken next to nothing from the vulgar
tongue. Very gradually the relation between the two languages
was reversed. An Act of Parliament could do little to hasten the
process; more might be done by patriotic schoolmasters.

---

[1] Edw. III. stat. 1, c. 15 (Commissioners' edition). Observe *francais*, not
francaise. Having written *trop*, the scribe puts a tittle over the *p*, which
seems to show that he meant *trope*. The word *tittle* is useful. Thereby we
mean "a small line drawn over an abridged word, to supply letters wanting"
(Cotgrave). It is the Spanish *tilde*, which we see, *e. g.* in *doña*.

[2] *Fortescue de Laudibus*, c. 48.

[3] Cranmer, *Remains* (Parker Soc.), p. 170.

[4] Maitland, *English Law and the Renaissance*, pp. 43, 72.

When the history of English law is contrasted with the history of its next of kin, the existence of law French is too often forgotten. It is forgotten that during the later middle age English lawyers enjoyed the inestimable advantage of being able to make a technical language. And a highly technical language they made. To take one example, let us think for a moment of "an heir in tail rebutted from his formedon by a lineal warranty with descended assets." Precise ideas are here expressed in precise terms, every one of which is French: the geometer or the chemist could hardly wish for terms that are more exact or less liable to have their edges worn away by the vulgar. Good came of this and evil. Let us dwell for a moment on an important consequence. We have known it put by a foreigner as a paradox that in the critical sixteenth century the national system of jurisprudence which showed the stoutest nationalism was a system that was hardly expressible in the national language. But is there a paradox here? English law was tough and impervious to foreign influence because it was highly technical, and it was highly technical because English lawyers had been able to make a vocabulary, to define their concepts, to think sharply as the man of science thinks. It would not be a popular doctrine that the Englishry of English law was secured by *la lange francais qest trope desconue;* but does it not seem likely that if English law had been more homely, more *volksthümlich*, Romanism would have swept the board in England as it swept the board in Germany? . . .

Now, as regards vocabulary, there is a striking contrast between the earliest and the latest Year Books. A single case of Henry VIII's day shows us "deer, hound, otters, foxes, fowl, tame, thrush, keeper, hunting." We see that already the reporter was short of French words which would denote common objects of the country and gentlemanly sport. What is yet more remarkable, he admits "owner."[1] But in Edward II's day the educated Englishman was far more likely to introduce French words into his English than English words into his French. The English lawyer's French vocabulary was pure and sufficiently copious. It is fairly certain that by this time his "cradle speech" was English; but he had not been taught English, and he had been taught French, the language of good society. Even as a little boy he had been taught his *moun et ma, toun et ta, soun et sa.*[2] Of our reporters we may be far more certain that they could rapidly write French of a sort than that they had ever written an English sentence. John of Cornwall and Richard Penkrich had yet to labour in the grammar schools.

---

[1] Y. B. 12 Hen. VIII, f. 3 (Trin. pl. 3); Pollock, *First Book of Jurisprudence,* 281.

[2] See the treatise of Walter of Biblesworth in Wright, *Vocabularies,* 1. 144.

Let us look for a moment at some of the words which "lay in the mouths" of our serjeants and judges: words descriptive of logical and argumentative processes: words that in course of time would be heard far outside the courts of law. We see "to allege, to aver, to assert, to affirm, to avow, to suppose, to surmise (*surmettre*), to certify, to maintain, to doubt, to deny, to except (*excepcioner*), to demur, to determine, to reply, to traverse, to join issue, to try, to examine, to prove." We see "a debate, a reason, a premiss, a conclusion, a distinction, an affirmative, a negative, a maxim, a suggestion." We see "repugnant, contrariant, discordant." We see "impertinent" and "inconvenient" in their good old senses. We even see "sophistry." Our French-speaking, French-thinking lawyers were the main agents in the distribution of all this verbal and intellectual wealth. While as yet there was little science and no popular science, the lawyer mediated between the abstract Latin logic of the schoolmen and the concrete needs and homely talk of gross, unschooled mankind. Law was the point where life and logic met.

And the lawyer was liberally exercising his right to make terms of art, and yet, if we mistake not, he did this in a manner sufficiently sanctioned by the genius of the language. Old French allowed a free conversion of infinitives into substantives. Some of the commonest nouns in the modern language have been infinitives: *dîner*, *déjeuner*, *souper*, *pouvoir*, *devoir*, *plaisir;* and in the list whence we take these examples we see *un manoir* and *un plaidoyer*. English legal language contains many words that were thus made—"a voucher, an ouster, a disclaimer, an inter-pleader, a demurrer, a cesser, an estover, a merger, a remitter, a render, a tender, an attainder, a joinder, a rejoinder"—though in some cases the process has been obscured. . . . Were we still "to pray oyer of a bond," we should use a debased infinitive, and perhaps it is well that nowadays we seldom hear of "a possibility of reverter" lest a pedant might say that *revertir* were better. Even the Latin roll felt this French influence: "his voucher" is *vocare suum,* and *recuperare suum* is "his recovery."

But the most interesting specimen in our legal vocabulary of a French infinitive is "remainder." In Edward II's day name and thing were coming to the forefront of legal practice. The name was in the making. When he was distinguishing the three writs of formedon (or better of *forme de doun*) it was common for the lawyer to slip into Latin and to say *en le descendere, en le reverti, en le remanere*. But the French infinitives also were being used, and *le remeindre* (the "to remain", the "to stay out" instead of the reversion or coming back) was soon to be a well-known substantive. It was not confused with a *remenaunt*, a remnant, a part which remains when part is gone. What remained, what stayed out instead of coming back, was the land.[1] In French translations of such deeds as create remainders it is about as common to see the Latin *remanere* rendered by *demorer* as to see an employment of *remeindre*, and it is little more than an accident that we do not call a remainder a demurrer and a demurrer a remainder. In both cases there is a "to abide"; in the one the land abides for the remainder-man (*celui a qi le remeindre se tailla*); in the other case the pleaders express their intention of dwelling upon what they have said, of abiding by what they have pleaded, and they abide the judgment of the court. When a cause "stands over," as we say, our ancestors would say in Latin that it remains, and in French that it demurs (*loquela remanet: la parole demoert*): "the parol demurs," the case is "made a *remanet*." The differentiation and specification of "remain" and "demur," "remainder" and "demurrer," is an instance of good technical work. . .

We might dwell at some length on the healthy processes which were determining the sense of words. There is, for example, *tailler* (to cut or carve), which can be used of the action of one who shapes or, as we say, "limits" a gift in some special manner, but more especially if the result of his cutting and carving is a "tailed fee." There is *assez* (enough) with a strange destiny before it, since it is to engender a singular "asset." We might endeavour to explain how, under the influence of the deponent verbs *sequi* and *prosequi* which appear upon the Latin roll, the phrase *il fut nounsuivy* (he was nonsuited) is a nearer equivalent for *il ne suivit pas* than for *il ne fut pas suivi*. Of our lawyers as word-makers, phrase-makers, thought-makers, much might be said.

[1] Pollock and Maitland, *Hist. Eng. Law*, ii, 21; Challis, *Law of Real Property*, 2nd ed., p. 69.

APPENDIX TO CHAPTER VII

THE OLD ENGLISH SUNG, OR BALLAD, METRE

[It has been thought desirable to print in this place the following account of Old English metre as adjusted on the stress-system to ballads.]

The chief characteristic of the old popular metre, which suddenly assumes such prominence in later Old English literature, is that in each half-line, instead of the two beats of the rhetorical metre, we have four beats, two of which are chief beats with full-stress, while the other two are half-stress. Between every two of the four beats there is, generally, an unstressed sinking. Elision of the sinking may take place in any position, and is usual before a final half-stress.

The Old English sung, or ballad, metre is, fundamentally, a four-beat rhythm which must end in a stress. It differs from the ordinary four-foot ballad verse in this, that a far greater difference is postulated between the force of the four stresses. In any natural English four-beat doggerel, granted it be not of expert composition, we come upon the distinction of full-stresses (′) and minor stresses, here called half-stresses (ˋ); *e.g.*

<blockquote>The kíng was ìn the coúnting-hòuse.</blockquote>

In Old English verse, these stresses and half-stresses could not be arranged as one liked: the line had to be balanced.

Fully balanced lines can be divided thus:

A.   (× ×) ⌐ (× ×) ⌐ (×) × ⌐(×) ⌐.

Modern English forms:

<blockquote>The kíng was ìn the coúnting-hòuse.</blockquote>

<blockquote>The queén was ìn the párlour.</blockquote>

Old English examples:

<blockquote>and þa eárme mèn hit beceórodòn</blockquote>

<blockquote>his ríce mèn hit maéndon.</blockquote>

B. $(\times \times) \triangleq \times (\times) \triangleq (\times \times) \triangleq \times (\times) \triangleq.$

Examples in modern English are rare.   Cf. the inner-rimed line:

> Jack and Jill went up the hill.

Old English example:

> ne wearð dreorlicre daed.

C. $(\times | \times) \triangleq \times (\times) \triangleq \triangleq (\times) \triangleq.$

Examples in modern English nursery songs are extremely rare, because of the modern dislike to two chief stresses coming together.

Old English example:

> þaet he aelþeodige.

AC. $(\times | \times) \triangleq \times (\times) \triangleq \times (\times) \triangleq (\times) \triangleq.$

Examples in modern English nursery songs are extremely numerous:

> and in my lady's chamber,
>
> sing a song of sixpence.

Old English examples:

> He wearð wide geond þeodland
>
> and wurden underþeodde.

D.   Imperfectly balanced form: $\triangleq (\times \times) \triangleq (\times) \triangleq (\times) \triangleq.$
This form always tends to become

> $\triangleq (\times \times) \triangleq \times \triangleq (\times) \triangleq$ or $\triangleq (\times) \times \triangleq (\times) \triangleq (\times) \triangleq.$

Modern English:

> four and twenty blackbirds

tends to become

> four and twenty blackbirds.

Old English:

> and utlaendisce.

E.   Perfectly balanced form: $\triangleq (\times \times) \triangleq \times (\times) \triangleq (\times) \times \triangleq.$
Modern English (with inner rime):

> Jack fell down and broke his crown.

Old English:

> se cyng waes swa swiðe stearc.

The Old English ballad verse, in contradistinction to its modern representative, was quantitative in all four stresses.

That is to say, a stress had to fall either on one long syllable or two short ones. According to Lachmann's original theory, which he applied to some High German ballads, but which must be applied to all Old English ballads, the stress then fell gradually throughout the length of the two syllables, e.g.

and

Ac Godwine hine þa gelette,

Godes wiþer saecan | Godes lage braecon.

This is most clearly seen in B and E, where two shorts so used pair absolutely with final stress and half-stress, e.g.

Eac he saette be þam haran

þaet hi mosten freo faran,

and

he swa swiðe lufode þa hea deor

swilce he waere heora faeder.

But, at the end of the line, the quality of a syllable constituting a half-stress was indifferent, the pause lending its support; a half-stress could not at that place be divided into two short syllables (since the second would perforce have to fall too low), but only a full-stress. Cf. the example referred to above:

his rice men hit maendon.

It seems, then, that final feet (with indifference as to the quantity of the half-stress) could be carried over into the middle of a half-line before either a real or artificial inner pause or a change of musical melody

wide | and side || þa hwile þe | he leofode,

Eac he saette be þam haran.

a. The normal (inner) foot has a maximum of two unstressed syllables and one stressed long (or two short) syllable(s).

β. Every foot is subject to complete elision of unstressed syllables—but complete elision in a whole half-line is extremely rare.

γ. Between a full-stress and a half-stress complete elision is frequent and more than one syllable unusual, *e.g.*

> and Gód him geuðe (no sinking)

> þa hwíle þe he leofode (one syllable).

Modern English example:

> when ín cáme a bláckbird.

On the other hand, after a half-stress before a full-stress, complete elision is, practically, never found. In the overwhelming majority of cases (*c.* 98 or 99%) one sinking syllable occurs, though two are found very frequently. The number of exceptions is negligible:

> ac Gódwine hine þa gelette (two syllables)

> ne wearð dreorlicre daed (one syllable).[1]

The first foot was composed of the sinking, called the anacrusis or *auftakt*, and the first stress. In the earliest form of the strophe it would seem to have been the rule that the anacrusis of the first line of the couplet should be one syllable longer than that of the second and should never exceed two syllables; the dissyllabic anacrusis was, apparently, used to mark the beginning of a new passage.

In the poem of 959, out of some 24 couplets, 13 have the anacrusis of the first line longer than that of the second; in 8 the anacruses are equal (or both lacking), in only three cases is there a monosyllabic anacrusis in the second line and none in the first, *e.g.*

> { On his dagum hit godode georne
> { And God him geuðe,

> { þaet he wunode in sibbe
> { þa hwíle þe | he leofode.

The fourth, or final, foot differs from the others in the following characteristic:

No final sinking (⌣ ×) was allowed, *i.e.* feminine rime did not exist in our sense, both such syllables being stressed.

---

[1] For a further discussion of this subject, the reader may be referred to a paper by the present writer, read before the London Philological Society. 7 June, 1907.

Hence the line could only end in a stress whether full or half in strength.

In the falling types A, AC, C, D, the last foot usually consists of a single stressed syllable.

$$\begin{cases} \text{he saette mycel deorfriδ} \\ \text{and he laegde laga þaerwiδ} \end{cases}$$

A. and God him geuδe.

C. syδδan Dene comon.

AC. gif hi woldon libban.

D. his maeges Eadwardes.

Cf. the modern English nursery rimes:

The maid was in the garden

Took him by the left leg

as chanted by mothers to their children with the heavy final half-stress.

With the ending ᴗ ᴗ ᴗ.

(It must be noted that in Old English ballad verse a single long syllable is fairly often divided into ᴗ – or ᴗ – as well as into ᴗ ᴗ. This may be due to the artificial stress on the second member, e.g. A. swiδost þara cyninga.)

A. þa hwile þe, he leofode

AC. Her com Eadward aeþeling

C. and he þar wunode.

Much less frequently the ending – × – is found in A, AC, C, e.g.

A. Aelfere ealdorman

AC. wala, þaet waes hreowlic siδ

C. þaet he aelþeodiʒe.

From this last two are derived the final feet of such nursery rime rhythms as

"was n't that a dainty dish."

In the rising types B and E the usual form is one unstressed syllable and a final full-stress, which may be divided into two syllables. The ending with a dissyllabic sinking before the final stress is rarely met with in B and E.

B. and his geferan he todraf

E. Se cyng waes swa swiðe stearc.

With anapaestic ending

E. ac se uplica wrecend hatað his gemynd.

We have several examples of the verse form ⏑ × ⏑ ⏑ ⏑ ⏑:

on þaere earman byr(i)g

to þan leofan Gode.

We have, further, a number of clear instances of three-beat short verses, perhaps originally meant for strophic use, in conjunction with four-beat verses, *e.g.*

cinges geseon

þaet gedon wearð.

It is a question whether every one of those so-called four-beat verses without any sinkings (even between half-stress and subsequent full-stress) is not to be reckoned here as three-beat.

Side by side with the introduction of this metre into literary use, there are also to be found instances of rime and assonance.

The use of rime and assonance tends to destroy the old system of linked half-lines, but in two different directions. First, in proportion as rime and assonance grew in power, alliteration, which had originally been the connecting link between the two half-lines, diminished in importance, until eventually it was used mainly *within* each half-line as an adornment. Different alliterating letters occurred in each half-line, and rime or assonance succeeded as a bond.

Hence, the half-lines became independent and the four-beat couplet resulted. Secondly, rime or assonance was further used to link the full long lines into couplets. These long lines were then felt to be too long, and a simple means of avoiding such undue length was to use either a weak four-beat half-line or, more usually, a three-beat half-line together with a full four-beat half-line (of six to eight syllables) to make up the whole. A new line with a variable caesura, either after the 3rd or the 4th beat, was thus constructed. Examples are found in the poem in the *Chronicle* under 1057, *e.g.*

> Her com Eádward Aéþeling | to Englalóndè

and

> Eádmund cíng | írensíd waes geclýpod.

But it must not be forgotten that both strophic forms are usually found in these Old English poems without the need of either rime, assonance or alliteration. The strophic system seems to have been originally, perhaps, purely rhythmic, and rime, assonance and alliteration merely its adornments.

Lastly, this sung verse is found in other Germanic languages as well as in Old English. The most notable instance of its employment elsewhere is in the famous paraphrase poem of Otfried, who expressly repudiates the solemn rhetorical metre, which must have smacked to him of the worship of the heathen gods. This metre could not have been of Otfried's own composition, since it was not only the metre of the *Nibelungenlied* but the basic metre of other German ballad poems, and is identical with the poems in the *Chronicle*. The following examples of Frisian metric forms seem to show that these also were based on the same old Germanic metrical scheme, originally the common property of all the Teutonic peoples. It is remarkable that the Old Frisian forms (which do not, of course, correspond to the Old English, but to the Middle English stage of the development of this metre) show all the specific Middle English developments. These are:—(1) in consequence of the lengthening of short vowels in open syllables expansions like ◡ ×, originally the equivalent of ◡, become equal to ◡ ×; (2) the use of alliteration as an adornment within the half-line and rime to link the two half-lines together; (3) the apparent loss of the final half-stress in Old Frisian is only found in lines not of Frisian popular origin:

A.   with hórne and with hlúdè.

B.   wel was hím ande sine héi.

AC.   Hi welde tha stérka Frésàn

(riming with "únder sínne tègetha tián").

C.   da dat bréef réed was

(riming with "hoe froe dat manich Fresa was").

D.?   Tha thi Kening Kerl thit understod
riming with

E.   Tornig was him hir umbe sin mod.

It is probable that all D forms $\angle \times \angle \times \angle \times \angle$ had at this epoch become $\angle \times \angle \times \angle \times \angle$ as most likely in the example above. The same tendency is found in Otfried, in Middle High German and Middle English.

The Frisian and the English were the nearest akin, and we have in both languages a common ballad metre. Perhaps the clearly popular character of this metre explains the absence of erotic songs and popular ballads from Old English literature. Vulgar ballads of all description were in this metre originally, and what epic classical matter was drawn from them was transformed (not always without leaving traces) into the rhetorical courtly metre. In England, the popular metre remained deposed in favour of its younger sister, the rhetorical metre, longer than elsewhere, and its sphere must have been exclusively the vulgar.

J. S. W.